MASTERING TRADEMARK AND UNFAIR COMPETITION LAW

CAROLINA ACADEMIC PRESS MASTERING SERIES

RUSSELL WEAVER, SERIES EDITOR

For other titles, please go to caplaw.com.

Mastering Administrative Law, Second Edition
Linda D. Jellum

Mastering Adoption Law and Policy
Cynthia Hawkins DeBose

Mastering Alternative Dispute Resolution
Kelly M. Feeley, James A. Sheehan

Mastering Appellate Advocacy and Process, Second Edition
Donna C. Looper, George W. Kuney

Mastering Art Law, Second Edition
Herbert Lazerow

Mastering Bankruptcy
George W. Kuney

Mastering Civil Procedure, Third Edition
David Charles Hricik

Mastering Constitutional Law, Second Edition
John C. Knechtle, Christopher J. Roederer

Mastering Contract Law
Irma S. Russell, Barbara K. Bucholtz

Mastering Corporate Tax, Second Edition
Gail Levin Richmond, Reginald Mombrun, Felicia Branch

Mastering Corporations and Other Business Entities, Second Edition
Lee Harris

Mastering Criminal Law, Second Edition
Ellen S. Podgor, Peter J. Henning, Neil P. Cohen

Mastering Criminal Procedure, Volume 1: The Investigative Stage, Third Edition
Peter J. Henning, Cynthia E. Jones, Ellen S. Podgor,
Karen McDonald Henning, Sanjay K. Chhablani

Mastering Criminal Procedure, Volume 2: The Adjudicatory Stage, Third Edition
Peter J. Henning, Cynthia E. Jones, Ellen S. Podgor,
Karen McDonald Henning, Sanjay K. Chhablani

Mastering Elder Law, Second Edition
Ralph C. Brashier

Mastering Employment Discrimination Law, Second Edition
Paul M. Secunda, Jeffrey M. Hirsch, Joseph A. Seiner

Mastering Environmental Law
Joel A. Mintz, Tracy D. Hester

Mastering Evidence
Ronald W. Eades

Mastering Family Law
Janet Leach Richards

Mastering First Amendment Law
John C. Knechtle

Mastering Income Tax, Second Edition
Gail Levin Richmond, Christopher M. Pietruszkiewicz

Mastering Intellectual Property
George W. Kuney, Donna C. Looper

Mastering International Sales Law
Herbert Lazerow

Mastering Interviewing and Counseling
Kelly M. Feeley, Rebecca C. Morgan

Mastering Labor Law
Paul M. Secunda, Anne Marie Lofaso, Joseph E. Slater, Jeffrey M. Hirsch

Mastering Legal Analysis and Communication
David T. Ritchie

Mastering Legal Analysis and Drafting, Second Edition
George W. Kuney, Donna C. Looper

Mastering Legislation, Regulation, and Statutory Interpretation, Third Edition
Linda D. Jellum

Mastering Native American Law, Third Edition
Angelique Wambdi EagleWoman, Stacy L. Leeds

Mastering Negotiable Instruments (UCC Articles 3 and 4) and Other Payment Systems, Second Edition
Michael D. Floyd

Mastering Negotiation
Michael R. Fowler

Mastering Partnership Taxation
Stuart Lazar

Mastering Products Liability
Ronald W. Eades

Mastering Professional Responsibility, Second Edition
Grace M. Giesel

Mastering Property Law, Revised Printing
Darryl C. Wilson, Cynthia Hawkins DeBose

Mastering Sales
Colin P. Marks, Jeremy Kidd

Mastering Secured Transactions: UCC Article 9, Third Edition
Grace M. Giesel

Mastering Tort Law, Third Edition
Russell L. Weaver, Edward C. Martin, Andrew R. Klein, Paul J. Zwier, II, John H. Bauman

Mastering Trademark and Unfair Competition Law, Second Edition
Lars S. Smith, Llewellyn Joseph Gibbons

Mastering Trusts and Estates
Gail Levin Richmond, Don Castleman

MASTERING TRADEMARK AND UNFAIR COMPETITION LAW

SECOND EDITION

Lars S. Smith

SAMUEL J. STALLINGS PROFESSOR OF LAW
UNIVERSITY OF LOUISVILLE
LOUIS D. BRANDEIS SCHOOL OF LAW

Llewellyn Joseph Gibbons

DISTINGUISHED UNIVERSITY PROFESSOR
UNIVERSITY OF TOLEDO COLLEGE OF LAW

CAROLINA ACADEMIC PRESS
Durham, North Carolina

LIBRARY OF CONGRESS CATALOGING-IN-PUBLICATION DATA

Names: Smith, Lars S., author. | Gibbons, Llewellyn Joseph, author.
Title: Mastering trademark and unfair competition law / Lars S. Smith & Llewellyn Joseph Gibbons.
Description: Second edition. | Durham, North Carolina : Carolina Academic Press, 2024. | Series: Mastering series | Includes bibliographical references and index.
Identifiers: LCCN 2024011060 | ISBN 9781531028985 (paperback) | ISBN 9781531028992 (ebook)
Subjects: LCSH: Trademarks—Law and legislation—United States. | Trademark infringement—United States. | Trademarks (International law) | Internet domain names—Law and legislation—United States. | Competition, Unfair—United States.
Classification: LCC KF3180 .S65 2013 | DDC 346.7304/88—dc23
LC record available at https://lccn.loc.gov/2024011060

Carolina Academic Press
700 Kent Street
Durham, North Carolina 27701
(919) 489-7486
www.cap-press.com

Printed in the United States of America

Dedicated to—

My wife of 37 years, Barbara, and our two wonderful daughters, Lindsey and Alison. Thanks also to my colleagues at the Brandeis School of Law for many years of encouragement and support, and my many students from around the globe who inspired my teaching and research.

(lss)

My favorite sister, usually-best friend, and often worst critic, Joan, and my favorite niece without any qualifications, Christina.

&

It may take a village to raise a child, but it takes good friends and mentors to survive law school, enter the profession, and become a law professor. I would like to thank Ann B., Ann L., Barbara, Bruce and Nancy, Chandler, Charles and Olga, Elizabeth and Andrew, and Terri, who left us much too soon.

(ljg)

A special thank you to Professor Susan Richey, who inspired in the authors life-long passions for trademarks, as well as Zhang Nan, Wang Xiaoli and Zhang Aiguo, whose ongoing questions motivated some of the revisions, increased our appreciation of international and cross border trademark issues, and helped us to appreciate their importance to future US-educated trademark lawyers.

(lss & ljg)

Finally, a special shout out to Barbara L. Nielsen, who courageously slogged through the manuscripts for both editions of Mastering Trademark Law and whose invaluable editorial advice improved the book.

(lss & ljg)

CONTENTS

Table of Cases xxi
Series' Editor Foreword xxv
About the Authors xxvii
Preface to the Second Edition xxix

Chapter 1 · Introduction to Trademark Law **3**
- Roadmap 3
- Checkpoints 7

Chapter 2 · Historical Development of Trademark Law **9**
- Roadmap 9
- A. Ancient Use of Marks 9
- B. Development of the Common Law of Trademarks 10
- C. Federal Legislation 11
- Checkpoints 11

Chapter 3 · What Is a Mark? **13**
- Roadmap 13
- A. Definition 14
- B. Trademarks as Source Identifiers 15
  - 1. Single Source 16
  - 2. Trademark versus Brand 16
    - a. Brand 16
    - b. Trade Names 17
- C. Types of Marks 17
  - 1. Trademarks 17
  - 2. Service Marks 18
  - 3. Collective Marks 19
  - 4. Certification Marks 19
- D. Inherent versus Acquired Distinctiveness 20
  - 1. Spectrum of Distinctiveness 20
    - a. Consumer Perception 21

b. Evidentiary Effect of Distinctiveness 21
2. Inherently Distinctive Marks 21
a. Fanciful Marks 22
b. Arbitrary Marks 22
c. Suggestive Marks 22
E. Descriptive Marks and Acquired Distinctiveness/Secondary Meaning 24
1. Descriptive Marks Defined 24
2. Acquired Distinctiveness/Secondary Meaning 25
3. Generic Terms 27
4. De Facto Secondary Meaning 27
5. Composite Marks 28
Checkpoints 29

Chapter 4 · Protecting Goodwill **31**
Roadmap 31
A. Maintaining a Mark 31
B. Loss of Rights 33
1. Abandonment through Nonuse 33
a. Time and Use 34
b. Intent 34
c. Proof 36
2. Abandonment through Conduct 36
a. Genericism 37
b. Naked Licensing 39
c. Quality Control Provisions 40
d. Assignment-in-Gross 41
3. Changing the Appearance of the Mark or Nature of Goods Sold 41
4. Maintaining Registration 42
C. Residual Goodwill 43
Checkpoints 43

Chapter 5 · Trade Dress **45**
Roadmap 45
A. Distinctiveness of Trade Dress 46
B. Trade Dress and Functionality 47
1. Utilitarian Functionality 49
2. The *Morton-Norwich* Factors for Determining Utilitarian Functionality 50

3. Aesthetic Functionality 53
C. Trade Dress and Patent Law 54
D. Functionality as Ongoing Concern 55
Checkpoints 56

Chapter 6 · Geographical Indications and Other Quasi Marks 57
Roadmap 57
A. Geographical Indications 57
B. Statutorily Protected Words and Phrases 58
Checkpoints 59

Chapter 7 · Ownership and Development of Rights in a Mark 61
Roadmap 61
A. Ownership 62
B. Obtaining Trademark Rights 63
1. Rights through Use 63
2. Use in the Ordinary Course of Business 64
a. Commerce Regulated by Congress 65
b. Foreign Marks 66
3. Use of Marks on Goods 68
4. Use of Marks with Respect to Services 69
C. When Do Common Law Trademark Rights Arise? 69
1. Mark Distinctiveness 69
a. Inherently Distinctive Marks 70
b. Marks Requiring Proof of Secondary Meaning 70
2. Limited Sales 71
3. Pre-Sales Activity 72
4. Relation of Federal Registration to When Common Law Rights Arise 73
a. Registration and Mark Distinctiveness 74
b. Registration, Token Use, and Limited Sales 74
c. Registration, Analogous Use, and Pre-Sales Activity 75
D. Extent of Common Law Rights 76
1. Scope of Goods and Services Covered 76
2. Geographical Limits on Protection under the Common Law 76
E. Priority 77
1. Priority under the Common Law 77
a. Inherently Distinctive Marks 78
b. Marks Requiring Proof of Secondary Meaning 78

c. Geographically Remote Use 79
2. Priority Based on Registration 80
a. Preexisting Common Law Rights 80
b. Constructive Notice 80
c. Constructive Use 80
d. Intent-to-Use Applications and Constructive Use 82
e. Priority between Pending Applications 83
f. *Dawn Donut* Rule 83
g. Prior User Rights against a Registered Mark 83
h. Limited Area Defense 84
Checkpoints 85

Chapter 8 · Trademark Registration 87
Roadmap 87
A. State versus Federal Registration 88
B. The Federal System of Registration 88
1. Principal Register 89
2. Supplemental Register 89
C. Trademark Registration Prosecution Process 90
1. Trademark Screening 91
2. Bases for Filing 92
a. Section 1(a) Use-Based Application 92
b. Section 1(b) Intent-to-Use Application 93
c. Combined § 1(a) and § 1(b) Applications 93
d. Foreign Applicants 93
3. Section 44(d) 94
4. Section 44(e) 94
5. Section 66(a) 95
6. Filing the Application 95
7. Process of Examination 96
8. Letters of Protest 98
9. Opposition to Registration 99
D. Limits on Registration 100
1. Section 2(a): Immoral or Scandalous Matter; Deceptive Matter; Matter Which May Disparage, Falsely Suggest a Connection, or Bring into Contempt or Disrepute 100
a. Unconstitutional Limitations on Registration under Section 2(a)—Marks Which May

Disparage, or Bring into Contempt or Disrepute, and Marks Which Are Immoral or Scandalous 101
b. Section 2(a): Deceptive Matter versus Section 2(e)(1): Merely Deceptively Misdescriptive Marks 102
c. Section 2(a): Matter Which Falsely Suggests a Connection 103
2. Section 2(b): Flags, Coat of Arms, or Other Official Insignia 104
3. Section 2(c): Living Individuals and Deceased Presidents 105
4. Section 2(d): Marks Likely to Cause Confusion 106
5. Section 2(e): Descriptive, Misdescriptive, Geographical, and Functional Marks 107
a. Descriptive Designations 108
b. Deceptively Misdescriptive Designations 108
c. Primarily Geographically Descriptive Designations 109
d. Primarily Geographically Deceptively Misdescriptive Designations 110
e. Surnames 110
f. Functional Designs 110
6. Section 2(f): Acquired Distinctiveness and Refusals Based on Dilution 111
E. Post-Registration Matters 112
1. Incontestability 112
2. Defenses to Incontestability 113
3. Cancellation 114
4. Expungement and Reexamination of Registrations 114
F. The Madrid Protocol 117
Checkpoints 117

Chapter 9 · Traditional Trademark Infringement 119
Roadmap 119
A. Elements of Trademark Infringement 120
B. Traditional Likelihood-of-Consumer-Confusion Test 122
1. Relevant Consumer 122
2. Consumer's Presumed Standard of Care 123
C. Likelihood-of-Consumer-Confusion Factors 124
1. Strength of the Mark 125

a. Conceptual Strength of the Trademark 126
b. Commercial Strength of the Trademark 127
2. Proximity of the Goods 127
3. Similarity of the Marks 128
a. Appearance (Sight) 130
b. Sound 131
c. Meaning 131
4. Evidence of Actual Confusion 132
5. Marketing Channels Used 133
6. Type of Goods and the Degree of Care Likely to Be Exercised by the Purchaser 133
7. Defendant's Intent in Selecting the Mark 134
8. Likelihood of Expansion of the Product Lines 134
9. Other Relevant Factors 134
D. Passing Off, Reverse Passing Off, Post-Sale Confusion, Reverse Confusion, and Initial-Interest Confusion 135
1. Passing Off 135
2. Reverse Passing Off 135
3. Post-Sale Confusion 136
4. Reverse Confusion 137
a. Application of Likelihood-of-Confusion Factors 138
i. Strength of the Mark 138
ii. Similarity of the Marks 139
iii. Marketing Channels 139
iv. Actual Confusion 140
v. Consumer's Degree of Care 140
vi. Defendant's Intent 141
vii. Likelihood of Expansion 141
b. Defenses in a Reverse-Confusion Case 142
c. Remedies in a Reverse-Confusion Case 143
5. Initial-Interest Confusion 143
E. Third-Party Liability or "Indirect Infringement" 144
1. Contributory Infringement 145
2. Vicarious Infringement 146
F. Respondeat Superior and Employees 146
G. Likelihood-of-Confusion Test and the First Amendment 147
Checkpoints 147

Chapter 10 · Trademark Infringement by Dilution 149
Roadmap 149
A. Infringement by Trademark Dilution 149
1. State Law Evolution 150
2. Federal Dilution Law 151
a. The FTDA 151
b. *Moseley* and the Trademark Dilution Revision Act (TDRA) 152
B. TDRA: Elements of a Trademark-Infringement-by-Dilution Case 153
1. Famous Trademarks 153
2. Dilution by Blurring 155
3. Dilution by Tarnishment 156
4. Federal Registration Bars State Dilution Actions 157
Checkpoints 157

Chapter 11 · False or Deceptive Commercial Advertising 159
Roadmap 159
A. False or Deceptive Commercial Advertising 160
B. Standing 160
C. The Elements of a § 43(a)(1)(B) Claim 160
1. First Element: False or Misleading Speech 161
a. Explicitly or Literally False Statements 161
b. Implicitly False Statements 161
c. Statements Based on Tests 162
2. Second Element: Commercial Speech 162
a. Whether the Communication Is an Advertisement 163
b. Whether the Communication Refers to a Specific Product or Service 163
c. Whether the Speaker Had an Economic Motive for the Speech 163
3. Third Element: Materiality 164
4. Fourth Element: Damages 164
D. Remedies 165
1. Actual Damages 165
2. Defendant's Profits 165
3. Corrective Advertising 165
4. Compensation for Loss of Goodwill 166

5. Enhanced Damages 166
6. Attorney Fees 166
E. Defenses 167
Checkpoints 167

Chapter 12 · Defenses to Infringement 169
Roadmap 169
A. Senior-User and Intermediate Junior-User Defenses 170
1. Senior User 170
2. Section 33(b)(5): Limited-Area Exception 171
3. Remote Intermediate Junior-User Defense—The "*Tea Rose-Rectanus*" Doctrine 172
B. Fair Use 173
1. Statutory Fair Use 173
2. Nominative Fair Use 174
C. Parody and Other First Amendment Defenses 177
1. Trademark Parody 177
2. Artistic or Other Creative Expressive Uses of a Mark 181
a. Traditional Likelihood of Consumer Confusion 182
b. Adequate Alternative Avenues 182
c. No Artistic Relevance (*Rogers v. Grimaldi*) 183
D. Dilution 185
E. Genericism/Merely Descriptive 186
F. Functionality 189
G. Statute of Limitations and Equitable Defenses 190
1. Statute of Limitations 190
2. Acquiescence or Laches 191
3. Unclean Hands 192
4. Antitrust/Trademark Misuse 193
5. Bad Faith and Sham Litigation 193
Checkpoints 194

Chapter 13 · Trademark Remedies 197
Roadmap 197
A. Injunctions 198
1. Likelihood of Success on the Merits 199
2. Irreparable Harm 199
3. Balance of the Hardships 200
4. Public Interest 200
5. Other Factors 201

6. Permanent Injunctions Compared to Preliminary Injunctions 201
B. Damages 201
1. Defendant's Profits 202
2. Plaintiff's Actual Damages 203
a. Lost Profits by Plaintiff 203
b. Reasonable Royalty 203
c. Corrective Advertising 203
3. Treble Damages 204
4. Punitive Damages under State Law 205
5. Attorney Fees 205
6. Rebuttable Presumption of Willfulness for False Domain Name Registration 206
C. Statutory Damages 206
D. Barring Importation into the United States 207
Checkpoints 207

Chapter 14 · Domain Names and Trademark Law **209**
Roadmap 209
A. History 210
B. Federal Trademark Dilution Act (FTDA) Cases 211
C. Anticybersquatting Consumer Protection Act (ACPA) 215
D. Uniform Domain Name Resolution Policy (UDRP) 217
Checkpoints 222

Chapter 15 · Trademarks and the Internet **223**
Roadmap 223
A. Domain Name Used as Email Address 224
B. Search Engine Liability 225
1. Meta Tags and Wallpaper 225
a. Meta Tags 226
b. Wallpaper 228
2. Keyword Advertising, Banner Advertising, or Sponsored Advertising 229
a. Keyword Advertising 230
i. *1-800 Contacts, Inc. v. WhenU.Com, Inc.* 230
ii. *Rescuecom Corp. v. Google, Inc.* 231
b. Banner Advertising or Sponsored Advertising 233
i. Banner Advertising 234
ii. Sponsored Advertising 235

C. Website Liability for Third-Party Trademark Infringement 239
1. Search Engines 239
2. Auction Sites 240
D. Linking 243
E. Phishing 245
F. Trademarks in Virtual Worlds and Games 245
Checkpoints 247

Chapter 16 · Introduction to International Trademark Law 249
Roadmap 249
A. U.S. Trademark Law and Its Relationship to U.S. Treaty Law 250
B. Background of International Trademark Law 251
1. Paris Convention for the Protection of Industrial Property 251
2. Madrid System for the International Registration of Marks 252
3. Nice Agreement on International Classification and Services 254
4. ARIPO, OAPI, Andean Pact, MERCOSUR, NAFTA, Pan-American Convention, and the European Community Trademark 255
5. Agreement on Trade-Related Aspects of Intellectual Property Rights (TRIPS Agreement) 255
C. Internationally Recognized Trademark Subject Matter 256
1. Trademarks 257
2. Geographical Indications 257
a. Paris Convention for the Protection of Industrial Property of 1883 259
b. Lisbon Agreement for the Protection of Appellations of Origin and Their International Registration of 1958 259
c. TRIPS Agreement's Geographical Indication Provisions 260
D. Registration, Use, and Priority 261
1. Registration 261
2. Use and Priority Date 262
3. Well-Known Marks 262
E. Ownership and Trademark Rights 263
F. Minimum Levels of Process for the Enforcement of Trademark Rights 264

G. Remedies 264
1. Equitable Remedies 264
2. Damages 265
3. Other Remedies 265
4. Border-Control Measures 266
5. De Minimis Imports 266
H. Criminal Penalties 266
I. Reach of Lanham Act to Foreign Activity 267
Checkpoints 268

Mastering Trademark and Unfair Competition Law Master Checklist **271**
Roadmap 271

Appendix 1 · Trademark Application and Post-Registration Process Timelines **275**
Roadmap 275

Appendix 2 · Procedural Issues before the PTO and on Appeal **315**
Roadmap 315
A. Examination Process at PTO 316
B. Trademark Trial and Appeal Board (TTAB) 317
C. Director of the PTO 318
D. Judicial Appeals 318
1. United States Court of Appeals for the Federal Circuit 319
2. United States District Court 320
E. Appeals Process 322

Appendix 3 · Trademark Searching **323**
Roadmap 323
A. Introduction 323
B. Trademark Searching 324
1. Importance of Trademark Searches 324
2. The Process of Trademark Searching 324
3. Digital Dimensions of Trademark Searches 325
4. Strategic Considerations 325
5. Legal and Business Implications 325
C. Searching Trademarks Using Traditional Methods 326
1. Accessing the USPTO Database 326
2. Utilizing the WIPO Global Brand Database 326
3. Best Practices for Traditional Searches 327

4. Strategic Use of Traditional Search Methods 327
D. Searching for Domain Names and Integration with Trademark Registries 328
1. Importance of Domain Name Searches 328
2. How to Conduct Domain Name Searches 328
3. Best Practices for Domain Name Searches 329
4. Integrating Domain Name Searches with Trademark Strategy 329
E. Searching Social Media Sites for Trademark Protection 329
1. Importance of Social Media Searches 330
2. How to Conduct Social Media Searches 330
3. Strategic Considerations in Social Media Searches 330
4. Best Practices for Social Media Searches 331
5. Challenges in Social Media Searches 331
F. International Considerations and Translation Issues in Trademark Registration 331
1. Understanding Linguistic Challenges 332
2. Legal Implications of Translation 332
3. Strategic Recommendations for International Trademark Registration 333
G. Essential Elements of a Trademark Opinion Letter 333
1. Introduction and Purpose 334
2. Description of the Search Process 334
3. Analysis of Search Results 334
4. Legal Opinion and Risk Assessment 335
5. Recommendations and Strategic Advice 335
6. Conclusion 336
7. Considerations for Drafting 336

Index 337

TABLE OF CASES

1-800-Contacts, Inc. v. FTC, 194
1-800 Contacts, Inc. v. WhenU. Com, Inc., 230–233
ADCO Indus.-Techs, L.P., In re, 104
Abercrombie & Fitch Co. v. Hunting World, Inc., 20
Abercrombie & Fitch Stores, Inc. v. American Eagle Outfitters, Inc., 126
Abitron Austria GmbH v. Hetronic International, Inc., 267–268
Allard Enterprises, Inc. v. Advanced Programming Resources, Inc., 71
America Online, Inc. v. IMS, 224
AMF, Inc. v. Sleekcraft Boats, 124
Bayer Co. v. United Drug Co, 38–39
Becton, Dickinson & Co., In re, 48
Belmora LLC v. Bayer Consumer Care AG, 263
Big O Tire Dealers, Inc. v. Goodyear Tire & Rubber Co, 137, 143, 204
Blue Bell Inc. v. Farah Manufacturing Company, Inc., 63, 65
Board of Regents, University of Texas v. KST Elec, 153
Boston Prof. Hockey Ass'n., Inc. v. Dallas Cap & Emblem Mfg., Inc., 214
Brookfield Communications, Inc. v. West Coast Entertainment Corp, 227
Budge Mfg. Co. Inc., In re, 103
Buti v. Perosa, 66
Central Hudson Gas & Elec. Corp. v. Pub. Serv. Comm'n, 162
Century 21 Real Estate Corp. v. Lendingtree, Inc., 175
Champion Spark Plug. Co. v. Sanders, 202
Chance v. Pac-Tel Teletrac Inc., 73, 75
Clark & Freeman Corp. v. Heartland Co. Ltd, 41, 42
Dastar Corp. v. Twentieth Century Fox Film Corp, 136
Daubert v. Merrell Dow Pharmaceuticals, Inc., 162
Dawn Donut Co. v. Hart's Food Stores, Inc., 83
Door Sys., Inc. v. Pro-Line Door Sys., Inc., 193
Dreamwerks Prod. Group, Inc. v. SKG Studio, 131
DSPT International, Inc. v. Nahum, 217
eBay, Inc. v. MercExchange, LLC, 199

Eastern Railroad Presidents Conf. v. Noerr Motor Freight, Inc., 193–194
Eco Manufacturing LLC v. Honeywell International Inc., 48
E. I. du Pont de Nemours & Co, In re, 106
Emergency One, Inc. v. American FireEagle, Ltd., 34
E.S.S. Entertainment 2000, Inc. v. Rock Star Videos, Inc., 245–247
Ewert v. eBay, Inc., 241
Experience Hendrix, L.L.C. v. Hendrixlicensing.com, Ltd, 130–131, 133
Experience Hendrix, LLC v. Electric Hendrix, LLC, 133
Fennell v. Butler, 201
Ferrari S.p.A. Esercizio Fabbriche Automobili e Corse v. McBurnie, 43
Fleetwood Co. v. Hazel Bishop, Inc., 320
Geoffrey, Inc. v. Toys 'R Us, Inc., 156–157
Government Employees Ins. Co. v. Google, Inc., 233, 235
Grupo Gigante SA De CV v. Dallo & Co., Inc., 67, 263
GTE Corp. v. Williams, 172
Hanover Star Milling Co. v. Metcalf ("Tea Rose"), 76, 79, 172
Hard Rock Cafe Licensing Corp. v. Concession Services, Inc., 145
Iancu v. Brunetti, 100, 101
Intermatic Inc. v. Toeppen, 213
Interactive Products Corp. v. a2z Mobile Office Solutions, Inc., 243
International Bancorp, LLC v. Societe des Bains de Mer et du Cercle des Etrangers a Monaco, 66
Inwood Laboratories, Inc. v. Ives Laboratories, Inc., 48–50, 145, 241
ITC Ltd. v. Punchgini, Inc., 67, 263
Jack Daniel's Properties, Inc. v. VIP Prod. LLC, 119, 147, 177–179, 181, 184, 185
J.G. Wentworth, S.S.C. Ltd. Partnership v. Settlement Funding, LLC, 227, 236
Johnson & Johnson, In re, 71
Jones Day v. Blockshopper, LLC, 244
Jordache Enterprises, Inc. v. Hogg Wyld, Ltd, 178–179
Kellogg Co. v. National Biscuit Co., 25, 27
Knight-McConnell v. Cummins, 243
KP Permanent Make-Up, Inc. v. Lasting Impression I, Inc., 174
Lamparellow v. Falwell, 216
Lands' End, Inc. v. Manbeck, 68
LaQuinta Corp. v. Heartland Corp, 204
Lexmark International, Inc. v. Static Control Components, Inc., 263
Lockheed Martin Corp. v. Network Solutions, Inc., 241
Louis Vuitton Malletier S.A. v. Haute Diggity Dog, LLC, 147, 155, 179, 180, 186
Marketquest Group, Inc. v. BIC Corp., 141

Matal v. Tam, 100, 101
Mattel, Inc. v. MCA Records, Inc., 184
Mobil Oil Corp. v. Pegasus Petroleum Corp, 144
Morton-Norwich Products, Inc., In re, 50, 110
Moseley v. V Secret Catalogue, Inc., 11, 152
National Conference of Bar Examiners v. Multistate Legal Studies, Inc., 187
National Data Corp., In re, 130
Nationwide Payment Solutions, LLC v. Plunkett, 199
Nautilus Group, Inc. v. Savvier, Inc., 128
New Kids on the Block v. News America Publishing, Inc., 173, 175
Noerr-Pennington doctrine, Eastern Railroad Presidents Conf. v. Noerr Motor Freight, Inc., 193
Palm Bay Imports, Inc. v. Veuve Clicquot Ponsardin Maison Fondee En 1772, 130
Panavision Int'l, L.P. v. Toeppen, 213, 214
Park 'N Fly, Inc. v. Dollar Park & Fly, Inc., 113
Parks v. LaFace Records, 182, 183, 184
Pebble Beach Co. v. Tour 18 I, Ltd, 176
People for the Ethical Treatment of Animals v. Doughney, 178, 217
People's United Bank v. Peoplesbank, 199
Playboy Enterprises, Inc. v. Netscape Communications Corp, 227, 234
Playboy Enterprises, Inc. v. Welles, 227, 229
Procter & Gamble Co. v. Amway Corp, 163
Proctor & Gamble Co. v. Johnson & Johnson Inc., 65
Qualitex Co. v. Jacobson Products Co, 14, 46, 47, 49, 54
Rescuecom Corp. v. Google, Inc., 230, 231–233
Ritchie v. Simpson, 99
Rodeo Collection, Ltd. v. West Seventh, 125
Rogers v. Grimaldi, 178, 181, 183, 184, 246
Romag Fasteners, Inc. v. Fossil Group, Inc., 202
Rosetta Stone Ltd. v. Google, Inc., 233, 236–237, 239–240
Sandforth's Case 10
San Francisco Arts and Athletics v. United States Olympic Committee, 59
Silverman v. CBS, 35–36
Site-Pro-I, Inc. v. Better Metal, LLC, 227
Social Technologies LLC v. Apple Inc., 75
Southern v. How, 10
Spraying Systems Co. v. Delavan, Inc., 320
Sporty's Farm L.L.C. v. Sportsman's Market, Inc., 216
Starbucks Corp. v. Wolfe's Borough Coffee, Inc., 154
Steele v. Bulova Watch Co., 267

Sweetarts v. Sunline, Inc., 77
T.A.B. Systems v. PacTel Teletrac, 75
Ticketmaster Corp. v. Tickets.com, Inc., 243
Tiffany (NJ) Inc. v. eBay Inc., 145, 237–238, 241
Times Mirror Magazines, Inc. v. Las Vegas Sports News, L.L.C., 212
Toyota Motor Sales v. Tabari, 133
Trade-Mark Cases, 11
TrafFix Devices, Inc. v. Marketing Displays, Inc., 48–52, 55, 111
Twin Peaks Prods., Inc. v. Publishing Int'l, Ltd., 183
Two Pesos, Inc. v. Taco Cabana, Inc., 46, 47
United Drug Co. v. Theodore Rectanus Co., 15, 79, 172
United Mine Workers v. Pennington, 193
Vidal v. Elster, 105
Wal-Mart Stores, Inc. v. Samara Brothers, Inc., 20, 46, 47
Washington Post Co. v. TotalNews, Inc., 244
Wreal, LLC v. Amazon.com, 138–142
Yahoo! Inc. v. XYZ Companies, 245
Zatarains, Inc. v. Oak Grove Smokehouse, Inc., 174

SERIES EDITOR'S FOREWORD

The Carolina Academic Press Mastering Series is designed to provide you with a tool that will enable you to easily and efficiently "master" the substance and content of law school courses. Throughout the series, the focus is on quality writing that makes legal concepts understandable. As a result, the series is designed to be easy to read and is not unduly cluttered with footnotes or cites to secondary sources.

In order to facilitate student mastery of topics, the Mastering Series includes a number of pedagogical features designed to improve learning and retention. At the beginning of each chapter, you will find a "Roadmap" that tells you about the chapter and provides you with a sense of the material that you will cover. "Checkpoints" at the end of each chapter encourage you to stop and review the key concepts, reiterating what you have learned. Throughout the book, key terms are explained and emphasized. Finally, a "Master Checklist" at the end of each book reinforces what you have learned and helps you identify any areas that need review or further study.

We hope that you will enjoy studying with, and learning from, the Mastering Series.

Russell L. Weaver
PROFESSOR OF LAW &
DISTINGUISHED UNIVERSITY SCHOLAR
UNIVERSITY OF LOUISVILLE,
LOUIS D. BRANDEIS SCHOOL OF LAW

ABOUT THE AUTHORS

Lars S. Smith has been a faculty member at the University of Louisville Brandeis School of Law since 2000, where he holds the Samuel J. Stallings Chair in Law. He currently serves as the Associate Dean for Experiential Education, and has served as Interim Dean and Associate Dean for Academic Affairs. He received his JD from New England Law Boston, and his LL.M. from Franklin Pierce Law Center.

Professor Smith teaches in the areas of intellectual property, business and commercial law. His courses include Business Planning, Contracts, Intellectual Property Survey, Law and Economics, Property, Secured Transactions, and Trademark Law. Professor Smith has also served as the faculty advisor to the Brandies School of Law's Entrepreneurship Law Clinic. Professor Smith's scholarship focuses on issues related to intellectual property, commercial law and technology.

Professor Smith has received several awards for his research and teaching. Smith's article Trade Distinctiveness: Solving Scalia's Tertium Quid Trade Dress Conundrum, was selected as one of the leading intellectual property articles by the Intellectual Property Law Review in 2006. In 2011, Professor Smith received a Fulbright Scholarship Award to teach at Zhongnan University of Economics and Law in Wuhan, China, and in 2012 Professor Smith received the University of Louisville Distinguished Faculty Award in Teaching.

Professor Llewellyn Joseph Gibbons, a member of the Toledo Law faculty since 1998, holds a JD from Northeastern University School of Law and an LLM from Temple University School of Law. Gibbons teaches various courses, including Antitrust, Copyright, Cyberlaw, E-commerce, IP Licensing & Management, and Trademark law. His research spans online dispute resolution, technology transfer, and e-commerce, with a focus on licensing and contracting.

Gibbons coordinates Toledo Law's IP certificate program and various joint degree programs. In 2017, he was honored as a Distinguished University Professor, the highest faculty accolade at the University of Toledo. An elected member of the American Law Institute and a Fellow of the American Bar Foundation, Gibbons is also a prolific author and sought-after speaker internationally. Federal and state courts have cited Gibbons' scholarship. He was a head tutor for the WIPO Academy Distance Learning Program in IP Management and a Fulbright Scholar. He also held the prestigious Wenlan Scholar Chair of Law at Zhongnan University of Economics and Law in Wuhan, China.

PREFACE TO THE SECOND EDITION

Trademark law remains one of the most dynamic areas of legal practice. Modern businesses are increasingly aware of the significant value that a strong trademark can bring to their brand and the importance of ensuring effective trademark protection. Consumers now perceive trademarks not only as indicators of source, origin, or sponsorship but also as essential elements of their social identity. This second edition reflects the ongoing developments in trademark law and our commitment to providing an up-to-date and practical resource for our readers.

In this second edition, we continue to cover the fundamentals of state and federal trademark law and practice, while expanding our discussion of the Madrid System and other key aspects of international trademark law. We also incorporate analysis of major trademark cases between 2012 and 2024, including *Vidal v. Elster*, *Matal v. Tam*, *Iancu v. Brunetti*, *Booking.com B.V. v. United States Patent and Trademark Office*, and *Jack Daniel's Properties, Inc. v. VIP Products LLC*, and which have significantly influenced the landscape of trademark law.

The second edition also attempts to be more useful to new trademark practitioners as well as attorneys who rarely handle trademark matters. Our goal is to provide a comprehensive overview that will be valuable to both law students and practitioners who are new to trademark law as well as practical appendixes.

We are grateful for the continued support of the University of Louisville, Brandeis School of Law, the University of Toledo College of Law, and our colleagues. We extend our special thanks to Barbara Nielsen for her invaluable editorial suggestions, willingness to review draft chapters on very short notice, and close collaboration over many months, editing the text and assisting in the preparation of roadmaps and checklists. We would also like to thank Elizabeth Lai Featherman for her support and comments regarding changes that would make Mastering Trademark Law most useful to new practitioners and paralegals.

MASTERING TRADEMARK AND UNFAIR COMPETITION LAW

CHAPTER 1

Introduction to Trademark Law

ROADMAP

- Value and role of trademarks
- Use of trademarks
- Sources of law and persuasive authority
- Trademark terminology

Trademarks can be some of the most valuable assets owned by businesses. In 2022, Interbrand, a brand consultant firm, published its latest survey of the Best Global Brands. Interbrand estimated the value of the top trademarks in the world. Heading the list was Apple, valued by Interbrand at nearly $482 billion, followed by Microsoft and Amazon, valued at around $278 billion and $274 billion, respectively. Even the 100th-ranked brand, Sephora, was valued at over $5 billion. These valuations are almost an order of magnitude higher than in the previous edition of this book, where we reported that the most valuable brand at the time, Coca-Cola, was valued by Interbrand at $72 billion, followed by IBM and Microsoft, valued at around $70 billion and $59 billion, respectively.

How can something as ephemeral as a brand or trademark achieve such great value? The key is to understand the purpose behind the use of trademarks. At its most basic, the role of a trademark is to help a merchant distinguish the source of its goods from those of its competitors. Merchants inform consumers that certain products and services sold under a particular mark come from the same producer. Consumers then rely on these trademarks to assist them in deciding on which products and services to buy.

From that basic understanding, the unique economic and noneconomic value of trademarks has expanded over time. For many consumers, a trademark no longer merely acts as a source identifier that serves as a symbol of quality; rather, it also signals social status, even individual or group identity. This cachet adds dramatically to the value of certain luxury brands, expanding their scope of protection. These newer trademark uses will also be discussed in this book as part of trademark infringement by dilution.

Consumers often do not have much information about the companies supplying the goods. Nevertheless, they come to know these companies' brands intimately, often imbuing them with great significance. For example, consumers often have strong feelings about their preferred brand of soft drink. When the Coca-Cola Company changed the formula for its COCA-COLA brand soft drink, it did so based on research that consumers preferred the taste of the new drink. However, when NEW COKE was introduced, consumers revolted, forcing the company to return to the original formula. The trademark had taken on a meaning to loyal COCA-COLA soft drink consumers that went beyond mere product distinction.[1] These consumers developed an emotional attachment to the brand to the point that any noticeable change in the product was a breach of a sacred trust the consumers had in the uniqueness of the product. That attachment, also known as goodwill, is now valued at over $57 billion (but down significantly from its high point of $82 billion in 2014).

This book examines the law governing the use of trademarks to market goods and services. In it, we trace the history of the development of trademark law from its beginnings in the law of unfair competition to modern developments such as domain name disputes. We focus on how a business develops use into a trademark and protects those rights against infringers trying to appropriate the goodwill of the trademark holder. An important dynamic in trademark law is the interplay between the development of trademark law under the common law and statutory protection of trademarks under the federal Lanham Trademark Act. We also examine the process of registering trademarks with the United States Patent and Trademark Office (variously referred to as either "PTO" or "USPTO" throughout this book).

In this era of global markets, trademarks are often the focus of cross-border disputes between international businesses and national governments. We examine the effect of international treaties that protect trademarks and some-

1. What consumers did not know or appreciate is that Coca-Cola had been quietly and subtly tweaking the formula for many years without notifying the public.

times conflict with the U.S. domestic trademark laws. In particular, competing rules governing the regulation of famous and well-known marks can put global companies in a bind. For example, the online auction site eBay must navigate seemingly inconsistent liability standards in the United States and Europe for the sale of counterfeit products via its site. Starbucks battled local merchants that had set up coffee shops in China using similar signage and trademarks long before it could open its first franchise in the mainland of the People's Republic of China.

This book will refer to two primary sources of trademark law. First is the Lanham Act, 15 U.S.C. §§ 1051–1141n. The Lanham Act represents the federal legislation governing the law of trademarks. Courts and commentators typically refer to the sections of the Lanham Act included in the initial legislation before it became part of the United States Code (for example, Lanham Act § 1, instead of 15 U.S.C. § 1051). We will use the same convention, as this is how casebook authors commonly cite the Lanham Act.

Second is the common law of trademarks, mainly developed by the federal courts. Judicial decisions play a particularly significant role in the law of trademarks. Trademark legislation, including the Lanham Act, provides only the basic framework upon which trademark law is built. The decisions of federal judges and the Trademark Trial and Appeal Board (TTAB) and the PTO's regulations complete the body of federal trademark law.

In addition to primary sources, the book will also refer to several secondary sources. The first is the American Law Institute's Restatement (Third) of Unfair Competition (1995). Although the Restatement was written to summarize the development of state case law in the area of unfair competition law, including trademarks, many courts and commentators accept that state and federal trademark law are generally consistent both in purpose and application. It is, therefore, common for a federal court deciding a case under the Lanham Act to cite to this source. We will cite to the "Restatement" and the accompanying section, such as Restatement § 18.[2]

The PTO has prepared a comprehensive manual to assist its trademark-examining attorneys in evaluating applications to register a trademark with the PTO. This manual is called the *Trademark Manual of Examining Procedure*, which is shortened to TMEP. The TMEP represents the PTO's interpretation of the statutes, regulations, and judicial opinions that collectively constitute

2. Occasionally, students may see citations to the Restatement of Torts in older cases. The sections on trademarks were removed from the Restatement of Torts and placed in the Restatement of Unfair Competition in 1995.

"trademark law"; however, while courts, including the U.S. Supreme Court, have cited the TMEP, it still remains merely a highly persuasive authority. When citing this source, this book will cite to the "TMEP" and accompanying section, such as TMEP § 1201. The TMEP, because it reflects the PTO's understanding and interpretation of statutory and case law, is revised frequently, so users should be sure that they are looking at the most recent version or, in the case of historical reference, the TMEP for the relevant period.

Finally, there are many authoritative secondary resources on trademark law. One academic treatise stands out in this area of the law: J. Thomas McCarthy, *McCarthy on Trademarks and Unfair Competition.* Courts and commentators often cite Professor McCarthy's treatise for its authoritative summary of the state of trademark law. Anyone doing serious research into the law of trademarks is well advised to refer to McCarthy. Sometimes, we will refer to this authoritative resource. When citing this source, we will simply cite "McCarthy" and the accompanying section, such as McCarthy § 1.01. Another is Siegrun D. Kane, *Kane on Trademark Law: A Practitioner's Guide*, the treatise most used by trademark practitioners. Many students find Kane particularly useful because of its conciseness and practitioner-driven focus.

Trademarks have long been recognized as playing an essential role in global trade, and so a number of foreign sources on trademark law also exist. The Paris Convention, the first major international treaty requiring specific minimum standards of trademark protection by its signatories, was adopted in the late 19th century. Since then, most nations have expanded their treaty obligations for trademark protection. The Paris Convention has been revised to adapt to changes in circumstances, but trademark law also plays an important role in the Agreement on Trade-Related Aspects of Intellectual Property, a supplement to the General Agreement on Tariffs and Trade (referred to as GATT TRIPS, or TRIPS). The World Trade Organization (WTO) treaty further refines member nations' trademark law obligations.

The terms "trademark owner" and "trademark holder" are used interchangeably in the case law and trademark literature. While these terms may be treated as synonymous for most purposes, there is one caveat: The PTO's preferred usage is "trademark holder" when referring to the possessor of a foreign trademark registration. This book will use the term "trademark owner" since it is the preferred usage of the PTO in the TMEP and in the Restatement, in popular casebooks, and by many leading trademark scholars.

A quick note on the updates to the second edition. We have made numerous changes to the book, some necessitated by changes made by Congress to the Lanham Act, others based on the interpretation of trademark law by courts. Congress amended the Lanham Act to address a perceived misapplication of the law by courts regarding certain remedies provided under the Lanham Act. At the same time, the Supreme Court declared parts of the Lanham Act as enacted by Congress over a half century ago to be unconstitutional under current First Amendment jurisprudence. Interesting times indeed! On this latter point, the Supreme Court has actively reviewed several trademark cases since the last edition, including cases analyzing the interplay between expressive speech and trademark law.

CHECKPOINTS

- Trademarks are valuable assets to most businesses.
- Trademark use has evolved with new business models.
- Companies doing business in a global marketplace are exposed to conflicting obligations regarding trademark use and protection.
- The Lanham (Trademark) Act is the principle federal statutory law governing trademarks used in interstate commerce.
- The Restatement (Third) of Unfair Competition is a useful source regarding state common law trademark law.
- Two treatises on trademark law which are well known and frequently used and cited by courts are *McCarthy on Trademarks and Unfair Competition* and *Kane on Trademarks: A Practitioner's Guide.*
- The *Trademark Manual of Examining Procedure* (TMEP) is published by the PTO and states the PTO's interpretation of existing trademark law and regulations.
- The TMEP instructs the trademark-examining attorney on the PTO's policies regarding compliance with existing law.
- Courts often rely on the TMEP as legal authority, but it is not law; rather, it is merely highly persuasive authority.

CHAPTER 2

Historical Development of Trademark Law

ROADMAP

- Trademark uses in history
- Early trademark law
- Federal legislation
- The Trademark Dilution Revision Act

This chapter will present an overview of the history of trademark law, from its ancient to its English origins as a common law tort through to its evolution to current modern trademark law in the United States: Lanham Trademark Act, the Federal Trademark Dilution Act, and the Trademark Dilution Revision Act of 2006.

A. Ancient Use of Marks

The use of individualized designations to identify the origin of products goes back thousands of years. For example, cattle brands and quarry marks are examples of markings used to signify ownership or source. Identifying marks were often put on ancient pottery and were well-known in the Roman Empire. With the growth of trade and the development of trade guilds, designations of source proliferated, often to allow consumers to trace back the origin of goods to the worker who produced the goods. Common examples include the use of marks on weapons and textiles as well as guild marks.

B. Development of the Common Law of Trademarks

While using such identifying designations can be traced back to ancient times, the development of trademark law as it is currently understood has more recent roots. Commentators trace some of the earliest trademark cases to 16th-century England. In particular, *Sandforth's Case*, decided in 1584, has been identified as the earliest case of trademark infringement. K.M. Stolte, *How Early Did Anglo-American Trademark Law Begin? An Answer to Schechter's Conundrum*, 8 FORDHAM IP, MEDIA & ENT. L.J. 505 (1998). A clothier brought the case based upon a competitor's use of an identical mark on inferior goods. The holding (but not the name) of this case was referred to in the 17th-century case *Southern v. How.* It was this later case which came to be cited as the origin of the common law protection for trademarks in the 19th- and early 20th-century U.S. trademark cases.

By the early 1800s, courts in England and state courts in the United States had begun to recognize a separate tort of "passing off," or "palming off," based upon the tort of deceit. Since this tort required proof of intent to deceive, it failed to provide broad protection for trademarks. In addition, since tort law is a legal cause of action, an equitable remedy such as an injunction was rarely granted under this theory.

Toward the late 19th century, state courts moved away from the common law concept of deceit as the underpinning of trademark law and started to emphasize preventing the likelihood of consumer confusion as the basis for protecting trademarks. In addition, courts also recognized a property interest in trademarks as the embodiment of a business's goodwill, thus allowing for injunctions and other equitable remedies in trademark suits.

C. Federal Legislation

The U.S. Congress enacted the first federal legislation regarding trademarks in the 1870s. In passing this legislation, Congress relied on its powers granted in Article I, Section 8, cl. 8, commonly referred to as the patent and copyright clause. The U.S. Supreme Court struck down this legislation in the *Trade-Mark Cases*, 100 U.S. 82 (1879), holding that trademarks were not related to invention or discovery (patent or work of authorship) as required under Art. 8, cl. 8 of the U.S. Constitution. Congress later passed new trademark legislation in 1881 and 1905, relying on its powers under the Commerce Clause instead. Accordingly, federal protection of trademarks is limited to those marks used in interstate, foreign, or any other commerce that Congress may lawfully regulate. Federal trademark legislation was substantially rewritten in 1946 with the passage of the Lanham Act. Over time, courts have used the Lanham Act's robust language to protect trade dress, combinations of colors, single colors, sounds, and scents as trademarks.

Historically, the focus of federal trademark law was on consumer protection. This changed in 1995 when Congress enacted the Federal Trademark Dilution Act (FTDA). The FTDA protected famous marks from uses that dilute their distinctiveness, even absent a likelihood of consumer confusion. In response to a U.S. Supreme Court case, *Moseley v. V Secret Catalogue, Inc.*, 537 U.S. 418 (2003), requiring that an owner of a famous trademark had to show *actual* dilution rather than a *likelihood* of dilution, Congress then enacted the Trademark Dilution Revision Act of 2006 (TDRA). The TDRA legislatively overruled *Moseley*. Owners of famous trademarks are now required to demonstrate only a *likelihood* of trademark dilution to obtain an injunction. The TDRA also contained several technical amendments, including a formal recognition of two types of dilution (blurring and tarnishment), a new clarifying definition of "famous mark," and provisions for the defense of fair use of a famous mark.

CHECKPOINTS

- Trademarks were first used in the ancient world and Roman Empire by tradespeople who wanted to identify their products.
- During trademark law's infancy in the United States, courts recognized a tort-based cause of action that required intent to deceive.

Over time, courts came to recognize a property-based cause of action in trademark disputes, thus allowing for injunctions and other equitable remedies.

- Currently, the federal statutory law governing trademarks is based in the Constitution's Commerce Clause.
- Congress enacted the Trademark Dilution Revision Act in 2006, requiring famous mark owners to show only a likelihood of dilution and recognizing both blurring and tarnishment as causes of action for dilution.

CHAPTER 3

What Is a Mark?

ROADMAP

- Definition
- Marks as source identifiers
- Types of marks
- Trademarks
- Service marks
- Collective marks
- Certification marks
- Inherent versus acquired distinctiveness
- The spectrum of distinctiveness
- Inherently distinctive marks
- Secondary meaning
- Generic terms
- Composite marks

This chapter will define the term "trademark," identify the essential characteristics of a trademark as a source identifier, discuss the differences between types of marks, and review the minimum legal requirements for a designation to serve as a trademark that is capable of enabling consumers to distinguish the goods or services originating from a merchant (source) from those originating from a competitor merchant.

A. Definition

Lanham Act § 45 defines a trademark as follows:

> The term "trademark" includes any word, name, symbol, or device, or any combination thereof used by a person, to identify and distinguish his or her goods ... from those manufactured or sold by others and to indicate the source of the goods, even if that source is unknown.

Key to this definition is that a designation serves as a trademark when it

- identifies the source of the goods sold under the designation, and
- distinguishes the source of those goods from that of other manufacturers.

If the designation fails to accomplish either of these functions, then it cannot be protected as a trademark.

The definition of a trademark raises two concerns for merchants. The first is whether the chosen designation can function as a mark. This concern focuses on whether the mark is distinctive enough for consumers to perceive the designation as functioning as a source identifier. The second is whether the merchant has, in fact, correctly used the designation in a manner appropriate to create trademark rights. These concerns focus on whether the merchant has created a connection in the minds of consumers between the designation and the source of the goods sold under that designation so that the designation indicates a source.

Before discussing the technical distinctions between the different types of trademarks, it is crucial to see how broad this definition is. Although trademark law historically only provided full trademark protection to what were referred to as "technical trademarks," consisting only of words and logos, the law has evolved to include almost any type of source identifier as having the potential to be a trademark. The U.S. Supreme Court stated in *Qualitex Co. v. Jacobson Products Co.*, 514 U.S. 159 (1995), that under the definition in Lanham Act § 45, any designation that can carry meaning might serve as a trademark. Relying on this understanding of the breadth of the definition of a trademark, the Court in *Qualitex* held that a single color alone could function as a trademark. NBC has a registered trademark in three particular musical tones, and a company has even registered a floral scent reminiscent of plumeria blossoms for a brand of yarn. More recently, companies have attempted to register tactile marks, where the source identifier is the feel of the product, or taste marks, often with little success so far.

B. Trademarks as Source Identifiers

Trademark law only protects designations that are used to identify source. Selecting a word mark, choosing a new and distinctive logo, or creating a unique design for a product does not by itself create trademark rights. As stated by the Supreme Court,

> There is no such thing as property in a trade-mark except as a right appurtenant to an established business or trade in connection with which the mark is employed. The law of trade-marks is but a part of the broader law of unfair competition; the right to a particular mark grows out of its use, not its mere adoption; its function is simply to designate the goods as the product of a particular trader and to protect his good will against the sale of another's product as his; and it is not the subject of property except in connection with an existing business.

United Drug Co. v. Theodore Rectanus Co., 248 U.S. 90, 97 (1918).

Although nearly a century old, this explanation of what constitutes a trademark still holds true today, even though trademark law as a doctrine has grown considerably since the case was decided. One area where the protection for a trademark has expanded beyond the Supreme Court's understanding of a trademark in 1918 is the federal registration of trademarks under the 1946 Lanham (Trademark) Act and its amendments. Today, it is possible to apply to register a mark based on a bona fide intent to use the mark in the future, even before the applicant has actually used the mark. Filing such an application grants constructive use rights nationally as of the date of application. Even so, that priority date hinges on obtaining a registration, which can only be issued after bona fide use of the mark in interstate commerce. Thus, the central idea that rights in a mark derive from use is still valid. Registration of trademarks is dealt with in greater detail later in Chapter 8.

1. Single Source

The trademark must identify a single source of goods or services to consumers. It is basic trademark law that a designation functions as a trademark when it indicates to consumers that a single party controls the nature and quality of the goods and services sold under the mark. Said another way, "The owner of a mark is the party who controls the nature and quality of the goods sold or services rendered under the mark." TMEP § 1201.01.

The source of the goods or services can be anonymous. Consumers do not have to know who produces the goods or services, only that a single source controls the quality of the goods or services.

Issues concerning source arise when the goods and services provided are not sold directly by the mark's owner but rather by licensees or related parties. Licensing will be discussed in greater detail later in Chapter 4, but for this section, what is essential is that a single entity ultimately controls the quality and nature of the goods. If the licensor exerts such control, the designation functions as a trademark.

2. Trademark versus Brand

The term "trademark" is the more formal legal term for what consumers and marketers commonly refer to as "brand." These terms are often used interchangeably, although there can be subtle but important distinctions. Marketing professionals sometimes use "brand" in a broader sense, to describe the overall image and public perception of a company and its goods and services. Brand, as understood in this sense, is different from a trademark. Trademarks must be used to distinguish the source of particular goods and services, not to describe the company itself or its business method. While it is possible for the design of a place of business to function as a trademark (see the discussion of trade dress in Chapter 5), this use of the term "brand" in a marketing sense is usually broader than mere trademark.

a. Brand

Brand may sometimes refer to a particular line of goods sold by a company, such as the KIRKLAND brand of home products sold by the Costco Wholesale Corporation. In fact, the law treats both KIRKLAND and COSTCO as used here as trademarks because they are used to indicate the sources of products. Trademark case law categorizes the term COSTCO as a house mark designating a broad group of products sold by the Costco Wholesale

Corporation. KIRKLAND is the designation of a more limited line of goods sold by Costco under its own brand. Other examples include HONDA CIVIC for automobiles and APPLE MACBOOK for portable laptop computers.

b. Trade Names

Another area of confusion is with trade names. A trade name is a designation chosen by a company to identify the business to consumers, usually as distinct from the company's legal name in its articles of incorporation. This use may also be referred to as a "DBA," short for "doing business as." For example, P&G is the trade name for The Procter & Gamble Company. Technically, a trade name is not a trademark because, when used in this sense, it does not designate the source of goods or services but rather identifies the entire business and its operations. Often, however, a company's trade name also functions as one of its trademarks. Thus, IBM is the trade name of International Business Machines Corp. and the key trademark used on its products and services. The key distinction is whether the company has used the designation to indicate the source of goods and services sold or just the company itself as a business entity.

C. Types of Marks

Designations indicating source can be divided into four major categories of marks: trademarks, service marks, collective marks, and certification marks. This section will discuss the different types of marks.

1. Trademarks

The term "trademark" has two meanings: First, it is the general name of the area of the law governing the use of designations to identify the source of goods. Second, the term "trademark" also refers to a specific type of mark. When the term "trademark" is used in its more limited sense, it is meant as a designation to identify the source of a tangible good. Thus, whenever a designation identifies the source of a physical product, it is a trademark.

Proper use of a trademark is as a label attached to the product or displayed on a product's packaging. The key here is that the mark must be associated with the product in such a way so as to create an association between the trademark and the product. This can vary depending on the type of product. Many trademarks are permanently affixed to goods. Examples include the apple symbol on the lid of an Apple MACBOOK, the mark NIKE and the "swoosh" symbol sewn onto a shirt or hat, or the prancing horse symbol on the grille of a Ford MUSTANG automobile.

Many products do not lend themselves to having the mark affixed to the physical goods themselves, or they may be sold in packaging. Packaging is the material the manufacturer uses to wrap or protect the goods, which the consumer discards once the consumer begins to use the product. Appropriate use of a trademark on packaging is for the mark to be printed on it so that the consumer sees the mark at the point of purchase. Examples include the label on a COCA-COLA brand soft drink bottle or TIDE laundry detergent container, or the wrapper around a SNICKERS candy bar.

The key to either use is consumer association. As long as consumers make a goods-source association between the mark, manufacturer, and product, then the trademark is appropriate.

2. Service Marks

A service mark is, as its name suggests, a mark that is used to identify the source of services, as opposed to goods. While this definition is clearly circular, providing a simple definition of a service mark is difficult. The PTO defines "service" for purposes of registering a service mark as follows:

> (1) a service must be a real activity;
>
> (2) which must be performed to the order of, or for the benefit of, someone other than the applicant; and
>
> (3) the activity performed must be qualitatively different from anything necessarily done in connection with the sale of the applicant's goods or the performance of another service.

TMEP § 1301.01(a).

For example, KROGER is a service mark for grocery store services, and H&R BLOCK is a service mark for tax preparation services. In both cases, the service provided is an actual activity for the benefit of their consumers, and not merely as part of the marketing efforts of those businesses. In contrast, the automobile manufacturer Ford Motor Company cannot claim FORD as a service mark for its advertising department or for selling FORD automobiles since there is nothing qualitatively different about Ford Motor Company's marketing of the cars it manufactures. However, it can claim FORD as a service mark for promoting the services of its independent dealers because the dealers are not part of Ford Motor Company, and selling advertising services for independent dealers is a different business than manufacturing cars.

Appropriate use of a designation as a service mark requires that the merchant creates an association between the service provided and the mark, so that potential purchasers of the services perceive the mark's use to indicate the source of the services. Valid use of a service mark includes displaying the mark in advertising for the services, such as on brochures, print, internet or television advertising, or even on employee uniforms. Use of the designation on letterhead or business cards can be problematic if the consumer makes no association between the services provided and the designation attempting to serve as the service mark.

3. Collective Marks

Collective marks are designations used to indicate membership in a collective organization, such as PHI BETA KAPPA (identifying the membership in the national honor society of Phi Beta Kappa), or INTERNATIONAL BROTHERHOOD OF ELECTRICAL WORKERS (indicating membership in a labor union of electrical workers). Thus, collective marks do not function to indicate a single source of a product as does a traditional trademark. Instead, collective marks indicate that the person using the mark is affiliated with a single group. No one member of the group owns the mark; instead, the collective organization itself owns the collective mark. The key is that anyone using the collective mark is related by being associated with the same collective organization.

4. Certification Marks

Certification marks also do not indicate a single source of goods or services but rather that the goods or services provided under the mark meet a standard or quality set by a single standard-setting organization. In this way, consumers can know that goods sold by different merchants meet a minimum standard. For example, AAA APPROVED AUTO REPAIR is a certification mark for automobile repair shops that meet the American Automobile Association's "standards as to quality of customer service, facility appearance, staff qualifications and training, community reputation, scope of service and repairs, and insurance." Another example is FAIR TRADE CERTIFIED, a certification mark of Fair Trade USA, a non-profit corporation that ensures that farmers and farm workers are paid a fair price for the goods sold under the mark.

Certification marks differ from collective marks in that the user of a certification mark is not related to other users of the mark, whereas users of a collective mark are members of the same group. The owner of a certification mark must permit any business that meets the certification standard to use the certification mark on the appropriate goods or services. Trade associations are often the owners of certification marks. For example, WI-FI is a certification mark owned by the Wi-Fi Alliance. This organization promotes the adoption of networking interoperability standards and the growth of wireless networking. Geographical indications are related to certification marks and are discussed in Chapter 6.

D. Inherent versus Acquired Distinctiveness

To function as a trademark, a designation must be able to distinguish the source of goods or services sold. The designation cannot function as a mark if it is not distinctive. Thus, whether a designation is distinctive is essential to the determination of whether it is protectable as a mark and its strength as a mark.

1. Spectrum of Distinctiveness

The Second Circuit Court of Appeals set out the generally accepted test for determining a mark's distinctiveness in the case *Abercrombie & Fitch Co. v. Hunting World, Inc.*, 461 F.3d 1040 (1972). According to *Abercrombie*, a mark's distinctiveness is evaluated on a spectrum running from inherently distinctive, to merely descriptive, and finally to generic and unable to serve as a mark for some class of goods. The *Abercrombie* spectrum is most relevant when discussing word marks, since it encourages a court to analyze the meaning of the mark as it is understood in the societal, linguistic, and commercial context in which the mark is used. Even so, some courts have applied it to other forms of marks, with varying degrees of success. *See, e.g., Wal-Mart Stores, Inc. v. Samara Bros., Inc.*, 529 U.S. 205 (2000).

a. Consumer Perception

Where a designation falls in the *Abercrombie* spectrum is determined by consumers' understanding of the terms in the claimed mark. In deciding how to categorize a mark, courts consider how the relevant consumers will perceive the mark in the marketplace context. The marketplace is the commercial context in which consumers interact with the mark and all other relevant uses of the mark by either members of the public or by competitors. The relevant group is generally made up of the potential product or service purchasers. Some courts have broadly defined this to include investors or others with an actual or potential economic interest in the mark. It is the mark's meaning to these groups that matters.

b. Evidentiary Effect of Distinctiveness

One of the most critical aspects of determining the distinctiveness of a mark is evidentiary. If a mark is categorized as being inherently distinctive, then a court will presume that consumers understand that the designation is functioning as a trademark from the date of its first use in commerce. By comparison, a mark that is merely descriptive requires proof that consumers have come to understand that the designation is functioning as a mark. Only at this point in time can the merchant claim its first use in commerce as a use that grants trademark rights. In addition, inherently distinctive marks are often considered strong marks and granted greater protection by courts when determining whether trademark infringement has occurred. Both of these concerns will be discussed in greater detail.

2. Inherently Distinctive Marks

As noted, marks that are categorized as inherently distinctive are protected from their first use in commerce to identify and distinguish the source of goods. The owner of the mark does not need to prove that consumers perceive the designation as functioning as a mark, and use of the mark anywhere establishes common law rights in that jurisdiction (assuming that the use is in good faith and not infringing). Procedurally, this means that the mark owner may assert rights in the mark from its very first use, giving the mark owner the earliest possible common law priority date. As a result, a trademark owner will claim that its mark is inherently distinctive to gain an advantage in trademark litigation.

Inherently distinctive marks are divided into three subcategories of marks: fanciful, arbitrary, and suggestive. Although each is treated as inherently distinctive and thus entitled to the earliest possible priority date, proving that a designation is inherently distinctive is easiest with a fanciful or arbitrary mark, as opposed to a suggestive mark.

a. Fanciful Marks

A fanciful trademark is a term that is invented by the merchant to be used as a trademark. It does not exist in the English lexicon and is not a word in a foreign language that can be translated into English. Since the term is invented, it is considered by courts to be a strong trademark when evaluating whether the mark has been infringed. Some of the most well-known marks are fanciful terms, such as MACBOOK for laptop computers, XEROX for photocopiers, or EXXON for gasoline and diesel fuels. Because there is no reason to use a fanciful mark except to refer to the mark holder's goods or services, courts give fanciful marks broad protection.

b. Arbitrary Marks

An arbitrary mark is a word that exists in the English language but is used in a way that is incongruous with its dictionary meaning. Because it is used to indicate the source of goods and services unrelated to its meaning, courts presume that consumers will readily understand that the term, as used, is functioning as a trademark. As with fanciful marks, arbitrary marks are considered strong marks and are generally given broader protection than other forms of marks. Examples of arbitrary marks include APPLE for computers, AMAZON for online retail sales, and DELTA by different businesses for airline services and plumbing fixtures. These marks are arbitrary because there is no logical connection between the meaning of the marks as understood by consumers and the goods or services that are associated with the marks.

c. Suggestive Marks

Suggestive marks suggest some link between the mark and the product or service but do not describe it. Often, they emphasize some feature or benefit of the goods or services without giving too much information. This subtle distinction is important because if the mark is too descriptive, it will not be protected as inherently distinctive. The PTO describes the distinction as follows: "Suggestive marks are those which require imagination, thought or perception to reach a conclusion as to the nature of the goods or services.

Thus, a suggestive term differs from a descriptive term, which immediately tells something about the goods or services." TMEP § 1209.01(a).

From a marketing perspective, suggestive marks can be very effective tools to help sell the product since they help remind the consumer of the product. Often, marketing specialists prefer trademarks that help sell the product, and it can be a challenge for an attorney working with a marketing department to find a compromise between a mark that merely describes the product and thus is very weak and one that is suggestive but not descriptive.

The primary test relied on by courts to determine if the mark is suggestive or descriptive is the imagination test. Courts consider whether the mark requires imagination, thought, or perception to connect the mark and the product. In applying this test, courts often consider whether the mark requires the consumer to make several mental leaps to understand the connection between the mark and the goods.

The key is whether the mark directly describes some aspect of the product or merely implies some connection that requires imagination, thought, and perception to conclude the nature of goods or services. For example, the mark GUNG-HO, an expression generally understood to mean "enthusiastic and eager," was held to require some imagination to conjure up a line of military action figures and was therefore a suggestive trademark. By comparison, if the mark directly conveys some feature or function of the product, it is not suggestive, for example, DELICIOUS food.

Courts have also considered other tests for suggestiveness. One consideration is whether the mark incorporates terms that competitors need to use to describe their products. If so, this is evidence that the mark is merely descriptive and not suggestive. Other tests that may be relevant in analyzing whether the term merely describes the product or service include the use of the designation in dictionary definitions and trade publications. Registration and use by other parties of similar marks on similar products may also be helpful in determining whether the designation is suggestive.

Line-drawing between suggestive marks and descriptive terms can be difficult. Some examples of suggestive marks include Brown-In-Bag for a bag that holds meat that does not need to be removed during cooking, CITIBANK for an urban bank, and MOVIEBUFF for a searchable database containing entertainment industry-related information. Conversely, designations deemed merely descriptive include THE SPORTS AUTHORITY for a sporting goods chain of stores, FOOD FAIR for supermarket services, and RICH 'N CHIPS for chocolate chip cookies.

E. Descriptive Marks and Acquired Distinctiveness/Secondary Meaning

Courts accept that consumers perceive that certain types of designations inherently function as trademarks. However, often, merchants choose designations that are very descriptive of the goods sold under the mark. They do so because they wish their designations to highlight some aspect of the good or service, such as its function. Since these designations incorporate terms that are commonly used when describing goods or services, trademark rights cannot attach automatically from the first use in commerce. If a trademark cannot be categorized as inherently distinctive, courts will require that the merchant establish that the designation functions as a mark. The merchant can do so by establishing that the mark has acquired the requisite distinctiveness so that consumers now understand that the designation is indicating source, not describing product features.

1. Descriptive Marks Defined

As the term suggests, descriptive marks incorporate elements that immediately describe some function or feature of the product. Said differently, if a designation merely describes the product's characteristics, functions, qualities, ingredients, properties, or uses, then that designation is merely descriptive and is not protectable as a trademark without acquired secondary meaning.

The designation does not have to describe all the features or functions of the goods or services to be descriptive; including just one may be enough. For example, the mark AUTO SHOPPER is merely descriptive of a newspaper periodical that advertises new and used automobiles, even if trucks and motorcycles, or boats, are also advertised in the periodical.

Determining whether a mark is merely descriptive must be done in relation to the goods or services sold under the mark, and not in the abstract. In addition, the designation must be evaluated in its entirety. Even if the mark contains descriptive terms, it may nevertheless be suggestive when considered together with the other parts of the mark.

Descriptive marks pose two related problems in trademark law. First, a consumer's first reaction to such terms is to perceive them as merely conveying information about some benefit the consumer will obtain from the product. Consumers are not relying on such descriptive terms to indicate the source of the goods, at least not initially. Second, descriptive marks incorporate terms that competitors will likely need to use to describe their products. If trademark law allowed one merchant to appropriate common terms of the industry as trademarks and then prohibited competitors from using them when advertising their products, this would put the competitors at a significant non-reputational competitive disadvantage in selling their products.

2. Acquired Distinctiveness/Secondary Meaning

While consumer perceptions and competitor needs are a concern, courts accept that over time, a merchant may be able to create sufficient consumer understanding to develop trademark rights in a descriptive designation. This means that consumers now perceive that the designation indicates the source when used on or in relation to the goods or services, rather than merely describing a characteristic of the goods or services. When this happens, the mark is said to have developed "acquired distinctiveness" (as compared to inherent distinctiveness). As stated by the U.S. Supreme Court, it must be shown that "the primary significance of the term in the minds of the consuming public is not the product but the producer." *Kellogg Co. v. Nat'l Biscuit Co.*, 305 U.S. 111, 118 (1938).

Somewhat unhelpfully, courts have also described this process as the designation's having developed "secondary meaning." Secondary meaning does not connote a lesser meaning, but an additional meaning developed later. In other words, consumers no longer perceive the primary, descriptive meaning of terms in the designation when used in relation to the goods but instead now perceive the designation's secondary meaning, that of source, to be the designation's principal meaning when used on the goods. Thus, when courts say that a descriptive designation has developed secondary meaning, they hold that the designation is protected as a mark.

When and how a descriptive designation develops acquired distinctiveness or secondary meaning is an evidentiary question. Since a descriptive designation is not protected as a trademark unless it indicates the source, the merchant must prove that potential purchasers of the goods or services have come to perceive that the designation now indicates the source.

In order to prove that a descriptive designation has developed secondary meaning, the merchant must establish several facts in each instance:

1. The relevant potential consumers of the product
2. The meaning of the designation to that group of consumers
3. That an appreciable number of consumers perceive that the descriptive designation is indicating the source of the product

Determining the class of relevant consumers is essential because it is the perception of potential consumers of the product that is relevant, not the general public, unless, of course, the product is consumed by the public at large. When determining whether a designation is descriptive, the court should consider the designation as it relates to the goods or services sold under the designation and the context in which it is used, not in the abstract.

Proof of secondary meaning is a question of fact. The merchant claiming that a descriptive designation has developed secondary meaning will have the burden of proving that the designation has become distinctive of the goods. The amount of proof necessary to show that the merchant has developed secondary meaning in the designation will vary depending on how descriptive the designation is. The more descriptive the designation, the greater the amount of evidence necessary to convince a court or the PTO that the merchant claiming the mark has established acquired distinctiveness (secondary meaning).

The merchant may meet its burden of proof through two types of evidence: direct and circumstantial evidence. Direct evidence of secondary meaning comes from consumers. This can sometimes include testimony of consumers (including affidavits), but the merchant will usually introduce consumer surveys. Circumstantial evidence of acquired distinctiveness includes facts that indirectly demonstrate that consumers have come to understand that the designation now indicates the source of the goods sold under that designation. These facts support the inference that the merchant has been successful in educating consumers that the designation indicates the single source of the products. Indirect evidence of secondary meaning includes facts such as the length of time of exclusive use of the designation on the merchant's products; the amount of sales of goods under the designation; and the amount of effort in advertising the product under the designation, which would include the amount of money and extent of advertising as well as news stories (or other free publicity).

3. Generic Terms

Descriptive terms are at the outer limits of designations that can be protected as trademarks. At some point, however, the designation is so highly descriptive that no amount of effort by the merchant can create trademark rights. Such designations are categorized as generic terms on the spectrum of distinctiveness.

A generic term is one that is in essence the product's name, which consumers understand is the common or class name for the goods or services. No merchant is allowed to claim exclusive rights in such terms. However, how does one distinguish between generic terms and descriptive marks? As with the difference between suggestive marks and descriptive terms, the consumer's perception is the touchstone. The meaning consumers ascribe to the words as they experience them in the marketplace determines their legal status under trademark law as generic or descriptive terms.

For purposes of trademark registration, the PTO has set out a two-part test to determine whether a term is generic: First, determine the class of goods or services at issue. Second, determine whether the relevant consuming public understands that the term primarily refers to that class of goods or services. The PTO has stated that the "test turns upon the primary significance that the term would have to the relevant [consuming] public." TMEP § 1209.01(c)(i).

4. De Facto Secondary Meaning

Sometimes, under certain market conditions, consumers come to identify the source of a particular product with a single manufacturer under a functionally generic term. This is known as "de facto secondary meaning." Because generic terms can never serve as trademarks, no amount of de facto secondary meaning can create trademark rights in a generic term.

The classic example is when the manufacturer of the goods holds a patent that prevents competitors from selling the product. Because no one else is selling the goods, consumers associate the source of the product exclusively with the patent holder. This happened in the classic case, *Kellogg Co. v. National Biscuit Co.*, 305 U.S. 111 (1938). National Biscuit was the sole producer of shredded wheat cereal for many years because of its patents. Unfortunately, it sold the product under the name "shredded wheat," which the Court held was the generic term for the product. Despite evidence that National Biscuit had spent much money advertising its product and trying to develop goodwill in the term, resulting in many consumers' coming to identify National Biscuit as the sole source of shredded wheat cereal, the Court held that, after the patents expired, Kellogg was not prevented from using the generic term for its own brand of shredded wheat cereal.

5. Composite Marks

A composite mark is a trademark that consists of various elements, such as a design with words. It may also consist of a word mark that has several different terms.

Whether a mark is made up of various constituent parts is mostly irrelevant, if all of the parts are inherently distinctive. However, a composite mark often combines different component parts that are not each separately distinctive. For example, a composite word mark may consist of various terms that are descriptive of the goods. The question then becomes whether a designation consisting of such non-distinctive parts is protectable as a trademark. There are several considerations in evaluating composite designations to determine if they are protectable as trademarks.

The first is that a court should consider a composite designation as a whole, and not dissect it into smaller parts. This is called the anti-dissection rule. It is generally understood that consumers perceive marks in their entirety, and not each component part separately. This perception is described as the commercial impression of the mark to consumers. Once the court has determined the commercial impression of the mark, the court should analyze the mark in its entirety. Some parts of the mark are more distinctive or memorable than others to the consumer, and the court may give appropriate weight to these factors. This analytic approach is consistent with the rule that how consumers perceive a designation determines whether it functions as a trademark.

The second consideration, notwithstanding the anti-dissection rule, is whether the mark has component parts that are more prominent than others; consequently, it is appropriate for a court to consider whether any portion of the mark is dominant. If the dominant part is descriptive, then that dominant part may affect the entire commercial impression of the mark.

The final consideration is whether the mark may be inherently distinctive in its entirety even if it consists of various elements that are each descriptive of the goods or services sold under the mark. Thus, marks like SUGAR & SPICE for baked goods and SNO-RAKE for a snow removal hand tool were both held non-descriptive of their respective products.

CHECKPOINTS

- Trademark law only protects designations that are used to identify source.
- Trademarks indicate the source of goods to consumers and that a single party controls the nature and quality of the goods and services sold under the mark.
- There are four main types of marks: trademarks, service marks, collective marks, and certification marks.
- In order to be protectable, a mark must be distinctive and distinguish the goods in question from those of other manufacturers. A mark's distinctiveness is evaluated on a spectrum running from inherently distinctive marks, through those that are merely descriptive, and finally to generic terms.
- There are three types of inherently distinctive marks: fanciful, arbitrary, and suggestive.
- Marks that are descriptive of the nature and quality of the goods may be protected only if they have sufficient use in commerce to create "secondary meaning" or "acquired distinctiveness"—an association in the mind of the consumer between the mark and the goods.
- Generic terms (those that very closely describe the goods) may never be protected as trademarks.
- Marks are to be considered in their entirety and thus may contain descriptive and fanciful terms or images and still achieve protection. This is known as the anti-dissection rule.

CHAPTER 4

Protecting Goodwill

ROADMAP

- Maintaining a mark
- Loss of rights
- Abandonment through nonuse
- Proof of abandonment
- Abandonment through conduct
- Genericism
- Naked licensing
- Quality control provisions
- Assignment in gross
- Changing the nature of the mark or the goods sold
- Maintaining registration
- Residual goodwill

A. Maintaining a Mark

A mark represents the goodwill that a merchant has established in the trade for goods and services sold under the mark. The strength of goodwill is based upon the extent to which consumers have made a goods-source association, that is, the degree to which consumers understand that the mark signifies the merchant as the single source for goods sold under the trademark. This goodwill represents the property interest that a merchant has in its mark. When consumers no longer make the goods-source association concerning a trademark, the merchant has lost any goodwill it owned in the mark, and the mark ceases to function as a trademark.

To preserve rights in its mark, a mark owner must protect the goodwill that it has established in the mark and not allow that goodwill to dissipate. The key to preserving trademark goodwill is the mark owner's ensuring that the mark continues to signify to consumers that goods and services provided under the mark come from a single source. To the extent the mark owner permits others to use the mark, the mark owner must ensure that all the goods sold under the mark are of consistent quality.

This requires the owner of the mark to take specific actions and to avoid others. For example, a mark owner should police the use of its mark by licensees and ensure that consumers understand that the merchant is the sole source of products sold under the trademark. Many mark owners also take steps to educate the public about how to properly use their mark to avoid the mark's becoming generic, something that is discussed in Section B.2 of this chapter.

One issue is whether a mark owner must sue every party that infringes its mark or risk losing its rights to the mark. Occasionally, courts have suggested as much. Usually, this occurs when the mark owner fails to enforce its rights for a significant period of time and then later attempts to assert its rights in the mark. Some courts have stated that such a failure to stop infringement results in a loss of rights in the mark. However, numerous other courts have stated that there is no duty to sue infringers to maintain rights in the mark.

The better view is that one of two consequences may result from a failure to enforce trademark rights. First, the mark may no longer signify the merchant as the source of goods or services sold under the mark. This result would likely only occur if the merchant has ceased to use the mark or if the infringers are so numerous and their use is so pervasive that the mark is approaching genericism; essentially, the mark can no longer serve as a source identifier. If the merchant cannot establish any goodwill associated with the mark, the merchant no longer owns any enforceable trademark rights.

Second, even if the merchant maintains some goodwill in the mark, it may be prohibited from asserting its rights in the mark against a particular defendant based upon excessive delay in enforcing its rights. This issue is addressed further in Chapter 12.

B. Loss of Rights

In trademark terminology, a merchant does not own the mark "in gross," that is, in the designation as such, but rather only to the extent of the goodwill the merchant has developed. Should the mark owner fail to adequately protect its goodwill in the mark, the mark owner is subject to losing its exclusive right to use the mark on the goods and services for which it had previously established such goodwill. The loss of rights can be against the entire world, called abandonment, or against specific parties. In the latter case, with respect to the loss of rights against specific parties, the ability to sue infringers may be limited based on certain equitable defenses, such as laches (discussed in Chapter 12).

Section 45 of the Lanham Act establishes two bases upon which a court may find a mark abandoned:

1. When use has been discontinued with no intent to resume use, or
2. Through the course of conduct of the mark owner

The difference between the first and second types is intentional versus unintentional abandonment. *See* McCarthy §§ 17:1–22. Technically, abandonment only really occurs with the first category, intentional nonuse. With the second category of abandonment, the mark owner is not intentionally giving up rights but acts in a way inconsistent with maintaining goodwill in the mark. Thus, to avoid consumer confusion, the parties' relative rights must be adjusted according to consumer understanding of the meaning of the mark.

1. Abandonment through Nonuse

Abandonment of a mark through nonuse occurs "[w]hen its use has been discontinued with intent not to resume such use." Lanham Act § 45. Thus, there are two elements to this form of abandonment under the Lanham Act: (1) nonuse and (2) intent not to resume such use.

These elements raise several issues. First, how long must the mark owner cease use? Second, what does "intent not to resume" mean? Finally, what level of proof is necessary to establish abandonment?

a. Time and Use

Regarding the first issue, there is no stated minimum time to establish abandonment. However, the statute does create a presumption of abandonment: "Nonuse for 3 consecutive years shall be prima facie evidence of abandonment." Lanham Act §45. However, it is merely a legal presumption of abandonment, shifting the burden of proof to the mark owner. Before the three-year limitation, the party asserting abandonment (usually the defendant) has the burden of proving that the mark owner did not intend to resume use after discontinuing use.

However, once three consecutive years have passed, the burden shifts to the mark owner, and the mark is deemed abandoned unless the mark owner can establish that it did intend to resume the use of the mark.

What constitutes adequate use to avoid the presumption of abandonment is more than mere token use. For example, in *Emergency One, Inc. v. American FireEagle, Ltd.*, 228 F.3d 531 (4th Cir. 2000), the court held that the presumption of abandonment applied where the company had not manufactured any new fire trucks under the AMERICAN EAGLE brand for over three years, starting in 1992. The court held such nonuse constituted abandonment, despite the fact that fire trucks can be useful for over 20 years, that the company had sold several reconditioned AMERICAN EAGLE fire trucks in 1993 and 1994, and that the company sold merchandise bearing the brand name. The court held that promotional and incidental use of a mark was insufficient to overcome the Lanham Act's requirement that the use not be merely to reserve rights in the mark.

b. Intent

Regarding the second issue, the statute clarifies that it is the mark owner's intent to resume use of the mark that matters, not the owner's intent to abandon it. The distinction focuses on the use of the mark and not on efforts to preserve trademark rights. If all a mark owner had to establish was that it did not intend to abandon the mark, then it is unlikely that any mark would ever be found to be abandoned. This would allow a mark owner to warehouse unused marks long after any goodwill associated with the mark had dissipated. The statute reinforces the requirement that the mark owner intends to resume use by defining the relevant level of use as a "bona fide use of such mark made in the ordinary course of trade, and not made merely to reserve a right in a mark." Lanham Act §45. Thus, a mere token use of the mark will not prevent abandonment.

Courts have held that the mark owner must have some plans to resume commercial use of the mark. The accepted standard is that a mark is deemed abandoned once use has been discontinued with an intent not to resume use within the reasonably foreseeable future. The question is, what amount of time in the future is too long to have plans to resume commercial use of the mark?

In the *Emergency One* case discussed above, the court held that the nature of a product can affect the analysis of what constitutes the "reasonably foreseeable future," a period of time that can vary by industry and the particular facts of the case. In this case, the court held that because firetrucks last a long time, "it might be reasonable for a fire truck manufacturer to spend five or six years considering the reintroduction of a brand, even though the same passage of time would be unreasonable for a maker of a more ephemeral product, say potato chips." *Id.* at 537.

The issue of what constitutes the reasonably foreseeable future was considered in detail in *Silverman v. CBS*, 870 F.2d 40 (1989). CBS owned the trademarks in the show *Amos and Andy* (including the characters). The show, originally broadcast on radio starting in 1928, was turned into a TV program that ran from 1951 to 1953 and continued for over a decade thereafter in syndication. In 1966, CBS stopped all broadcasting and licensing of the show, so that at the time of the lawsuit, the program had not been broadcast for 21 years. CBS had taken the program off the air because of complaints from civil rights groups regarding its portrayal of African Americans. Stephen Silverman wanted to produce a Broadway show about the characters, but CBS refused to grant a license to him to use the marks. Silverman then argued that CBS had abandoned the trademarks. CBS countered that it had the intent to resume the use of the marks at some indefinite period of time in the future when it was publicly acceptable to air the show again, and thus it had not abandoned the marks. To demonstrate its intent to resume use of the marks, CBS offered proof that it had renewed the copyrights, challenged infringing uses, and permitted the limited use of the characters in documentaries and educational programs.

The Second Circuit Court of Appeals held that CBS had abandoned the marks. The court determined that the statute required the mark owner to intend to resume use within the reasonably foreseeable future. The court held that the statute required concrete plans to resume use, not just the hope to use the mark again should market conditions change. The court stated that even after prolonged nonuse and without concrete plans to resume use, a company could almost always assert truthfully that at some point, should conditions change, it would resume use of its mark. Moreover, CBS's activities—the challenging of infringing uses and the sporadic licensing for essentially non-commercial uses of the *Amos and Andy* marks—were not bona fide uses in commerce and so not sufficient use to forestall abandonment.

Under the Lanham Act, CBS's motive for the nonuse of the *Amos and Andy* marks was irrelevant. CBS voluntarily stopped using the marks for over 20 years, and it did not demonstrate any intent to resume their use within the foreseeable future. Thus, CBS failed to rebut the presumption of abandonment. The court stated that a proprietor who temporarily suspends use of a mark can rebut the presumption of abandonment by showing reasonable grounds for the suspension and specific plans to resume use of the mark in the reasonably foreseeable future when the conditions permit the merchant to resume its use. However, a proprietor may not protect a mark if it discontinues using it for more than 20 years and has no present plans to use or permit its use in the reasonably foreseeable future. A bare assertion of possible future use is not enough. The trademark owner should have developed or be developing concrete plans to resume the use of the mark.

c. *Proof*

As to the final issue of the burden of proof, because abandonment results in a forfeiture of a valuable property right, most courts require that proof of abandonment as a defense in an infringement suit be made based upon clear and convincing evidence. Clear and convincing evidence has a high probability that it is accurate or is substantially more likely than not to be true. The Federal Circuit Court of Appeals has a different burden of proof in an opposition or cancellation proceeding before the TTAB. The Federal Circuit has held that abandonment may be proven by a preponderance of the evidence. A preponderance of the evidence is the lowest burden of proof in a civil trial. The preponderance of the evidence means that something is merely more likely than not to be true. Therefore, as a matter of strategy, it will often be more effective to challenge the trademark registration than to seek a declaratory judgment or to assert abandonment as a defense in a trademark infringement action.

2. Abandonment through Conduct

The second form of abandonment set out in the Lanham Act occurs "[w]hen any course of conduct of the owner, including acts of omission as well as commission, causes the mark to become the generic name for the goods or services on or in connection with which it is used or otherwise to lose its significance as a mark." Lanham Act § 45.

This category of abandonment occurs through the unintentional acts of the trademark owner. According to the statute, these "unintentional acts" may consist of either failing to act or affirmatively acting in a manner that causes the mark to become generic or otherwise to lose its significance as a mark.

This language provides for two distinct methods of how a mark may be abandoned: first, by the mark becoming a generic term for the goods or services sold under the mark; and second, when the mark "otherwise [loses] its significance as a mark." The first method of loss of rights, the mark's becoming a generic term, is based on the combination of the conduct (or lack thereof) of the mark owner and consumer's perception of the mark.

The second method generally involves transfer problems with licensing the mark or assigning ownership of the mark. Both forms of transfer require the mark owner to pay attention to certain formalities, and if those formalities are not adequately followed, this failure can result in the abandonment of the mark.

a. Genericism

Genericism is often raised as a defense to trademark infringement and so is addressed in greater detail in Chapter 12. This section will briefly discuss the efforts a mark owner may undertake to protect its mark from becoming generic. When a mark has become generic, typically, the mark owner failed to educate consumers adequately about the proper use of the term as a mark. The risk of genericism is most significant with new, unique products, and so the mark owner must take special care to educate consumers about the proper usage of the mark. The key is that the mark owner must ensure that the designation does not lose its significance as a trademark, that is, as a source identifier.

In the history of trademark law, there are numerous examples of successful products whose marks became the product's very name. These include aspirin, cellophane, dry ice, escalator, trampoline, and zipper. There are many more. The key in each case was that consumers co-opted the trademark as the generic name for the product. Once that happened, the mark became generic, and the merchant lost its mark.

Since it is the consuming public's understanding of a term that dictates whether it is generic, a mark owner often must take steps to avoid having the public use its mark as a generic description for its product. Many casebooks include examples of advertisements by the Xerox Corporation educating consumers about the proper use of the trademark XEROX. For example, such advertising often exhorts consumers to say "make a photocopy," not "make a xerox," or "can you copy this for me," not "can you xerox this for me." Numerous well-known trademarks today run the risk of becoming generic terms for their goods or services, such as KLEENEX, or GOOGLE.

While it is difficult for a mark owner to prevent consumers from changing how they use language, if the mark owner allows competitors to use the term uncontrolled, this may result in the loss of rights through genericism, too. The term "Pilates" for a form of exercise was held generic on this basis. In such a situation, the mark owner can try to sue the competitor to prevent them from using the term in this fashion. However, once the meaning has changed, even competitors will be allowed to use the former trademarked designation as a generic word for the product.

In *Bayer Co. v. United Drug Co.*, 272 F. 505 (S.D.N.Y. 1921), for example, Bayer had a patent on the analgesic compound acetylsalicylic acid (ASA), sold under the trademark ASPIRIN. The patent was issued in 1900 and expired in 1917. When the drug was first sold, it was dispensed under prescription, often in powder form in packets that often only listed the packaging as containing "aspirin." By 1904, various manufacturing chemists who purchased the drug from Bayer started making tablets and selling them to consumers in containers describing the tablets as "aspirin" on their labels without the chemical name. Thus, during the exclusivity of the patent, consumers never learned the chemical name and came to believe that the drug was called "aspirin."

When the compound came off patent, competitors began manufacturing the drug themselves and selling it prepackaged directly to consumers as aspirin. When Bayer sued for trademark infringement, the court held that "aspirin" had become the generic term for the analgesic. This meant pharmacists and tablet makers could sell the compound to consumers under this name, even if Bayer had not manufactured it. Judge Learned Hand noted that this was Bayer's fault for allowing the manufacturing chemists and tablet makers to market the product in a manner that did not reinforce Bayer's trademark rights. "Nothing would have been easier than to insist that the tablet makers should market the drug in small tin boxes bearing the plaintiff's name, or to take over the sale just as it did later. Instead, they allowed the manufacturing chemists to build up this part of the demand without regard to the trademark. Having made that bed, they must be content to lie in it." *Id.* at 512.

Bayer did not lose entirely. The court held that since pharmacists and manufacturing chemists were trained to understand chemical names in the wholesale market, they, as consumers, understood that the generic term for the compound was acetylsalicylic acid. As a result, suppliers were prohibited from using the term "aspirin" as a generic term in commercial sales to professionals. This meant that Bayer's competitors were free to market their retail version of the acetylsalicylic acid to the general public as "aspirin" but could only market their wholesale version as "acetylsalicylic acid" to pharmacists and manufacturing chemists. Consequently, a mark may become generic to some but not all potential consumers or in some markets. The mark owner retains trademark rights in those markets where the mark has not become generic.

b. Naked Licensing

Normally, a trademark identifies a single source of goods sold under the mark, and the source is the actual manufacturer. However, mark owners often choose to build their brands (and extend their trademark rights) by having third parties manufacture and sell goods under the mark, whether in addition to the mark owner's own use or based entirely on new uses by third parties. When a mark owner allows third parties to use its mark, it does so by licensing the mark. Under a license agreement, the licensee is permitted to use the mark on the goods and services in the geographic territory or market specified in the license to enhance the sale of the licensee's products. However, the goodwill in the mark developed by the licensee inures exclusively to the benefit of the mark owner. Thus, economically, the licensee takes advantage of the existing goodwill in the mark to enhance sales of its products, and the licensor/mark owner receives royalty payments and the enhanced goodwill created by the licensee's use.

The risk here is that the licensee's use may be uncontrolled, causing consumers to no longer believe that the mark indicates that a single party is responsible for the quality of the goods sold. When the licensor does not exercise quality control over the goods (or services) produced under the licensee, this is called a "naked license." The problem with a naked license is that it deceives the public regarding the "genuineness" of the goods or services and legally constitutes abandonment of the mark by the mark owner.

To avoid this, courts require that the mark owner be responsible for controlling the quality of goods sold (or services provided) by the licensee. Where the licensor engages in uncontrolled licensing, this conduct will cause the mark "to lose its significance as a mark," as stated in subsection 2 of the Lanham Act § 45 definition of abandonment.

c. Quality Control Provisions

The degree of quality control that is required to avoid a naked license has posed problems for courts. Because licenses are contractual agreements, the first issue is whether the agreement must address the obligations of the licensor to control quality and the licensee to maintain quality. Courts have generally held that the issue is one of actual control, irrespective of any contractual powers of control. A license agreement that includes a provision for quality control is evidence that the licensor is maintaining quality. However, even if no such provision is explicit, the licensor can still meet this requirement if it has in fact ensured quality.

Of course, if the license agreement includes stringent quality provisions, and the licensor fails to enforce them, this will weigh against a court's finding that the mark owner met its duty to maintain quality.

Courts have stated that the absence of quality control will result in a loss of trademark rights, regardless of the actual quality of goods sold. This is because the issue is whether the licensor is controlling the quality of the goods sold under the mark, not the actual quality of the licensee's goods.

Whether the licensor is exercising sufficient control over quality to avoid a forfeiture of its trademark rights is an issue of fact to be addressed in light of all the circumstances of the case. The court will consider such factors as the nature of the licensed product and the amount and level of inspections. What is adequate for one type of product, such as a low-cost promotional good, may not be adequate for another, such as a sophisticated medical device. Ultimately, the understanding of the product's reasonable consumers will decide whether the mark owner is exercising actual quality control over the licensee's products (or services).

Courts are reluctant to find a forfeiture of trademark rights. Courts have found that under some conditions, the licensor may reasonably rely on the licensee's efforts, such as when the licensor has a longstanding relationship with the licensee to maintain quality control. Some courts have held that even a complete absence of exercise of quality control may not result in a loss of rights if the licensor can reasonably rely on the reputation and expertise of the licensee. Such cases usually involve former business associates, employees, or family members as licensees, where it would be reasonable for the licensor/mark owner to assume that the licensee would continue to maintain a certain level of quality.

d. Assignment-in-Gross

A trademark has no independent significance apart from the goodwill it symbolizes. Stated differently, the mark owner does not own the mark "in gross" but rather only as it relates to the trade in goods or services actually sold under the mark. Therefore, to transfer the mark, the owner of the mark also must transfer the goodwill that the mark represents. For registered marks, this rule is made explicit in Lanham Act § 10(a)(1), which states that a "registered mark ... shall be assignable with the goodwill of the business in which the mark is used, or with that part of the goodwill of the business connected with the use of and symbolized by the mark."

If a trademark owner attempts to sell a trademark divorced from its associated goodwill, this is an assignment-in-gross and constitutes an abandonment of the mark. The anti-assignment-in-gross rule aims to prevent consumer deception by assuring the continuity of the goodwill symbolized by the mark.

If the purchaser of the mark attempts to use the mark on unrelated goods, then the new owner of the mark may not trace its rights in the mark back to when the assignor began using the mark (priority date). For example, in *Clark & Freeman Corp. v. Heartland Co. Ltd.*, 811 F. Supp. 137 (S.D.N.Y. 1993), Clark & Freeman Corp. attempted to acquire rights in the mark HEARTLAND from Sears, Roebuck & Co., to establish an earlier priority date. Sears, the assignor, used the mark HEARTLAND on women's boots, but Clark & Freeman only used the mark on men's shoes and boots. The court held that because the markets for women's boots and men's boots and shoes were distinct, Clark & Freeman could not rely on Sears's priority date. In effect, the mark HEARTLAND for women's shoes had been abandoned because Clark & Freeman did not continue the goodwill that Sears had developed in the women's shoe market.

Practitioners must look at the market to determine whether goodwill has been effectively transferred. Courts often say that the assignee must step into the assignor's shoes for the assignment to be valid. (Pun intended.)

3. Changing the Appearance of the Mark or Nature of Goods Sold

When a mark owner changes the appearance of a mark or the type of goods or services sold under the mark, the mark owner would like to trace its goodwill back to its rights to the original or first use in commerce. However, if there is a significant enough change, the owner may lose rights in the original mark (unless the owner continues to use the mark), and if the owner stops using the original mark, then the mark owner will only be able to claim rights in the new mark from the date when that new use first began.

Whether the mark owner can use the priority date of the original mark depends on whether the new version of the mark creates the same commercial impression in the minds of consumers as the original version of the mark. If the mark does create the same commercial impression, then the owner may trace its goodwill in the reconfigured mark to when it started using the original mark. However, if the new mark creates a new commercial impression with consumers, then the mark owner's rights in the new mark only begin with the first commercial use of the new mark. If the owner no longer uses the original version of the mark, a court may also find that the original mark was abandoned. The mark owner may wish to take affirmative steps to maintain its use of the original mark, using it, for example, on a line of nostalgia or commemorative products associated with the holiday season or using the mark in connection with anniversaries or special occasions, in order to avoid abandonment and to maintain trademark rights.

Similarly, if the mark owner changes the nature of the goods sold, the question will be whether the new goods are sufficiently related to the original goods that consumers will believe come from the same source. As long as this goods-source link is maintained, the mark owner can trace the goodwill back to when it started selling the original goods. This will be true even if the merchant stops selling the original goods, so long as consumers believe that the source of the new goods is the same. There is no bright-line test as to whether the new goods are sufficiently related to the goods formerly sold under the mark to tack-back to the original priority date. For example, in *Clark & Freeman Corp.*, a reasonable merchant (or consumer) might have viewed the market as "shoes" rather than distinguishing the market for men's shoes from those of women's pixie boots, as the court did. A good rule of thumb is to consider whether a reasonable consumer would assume that the new goods were produced by the same source as the old goods.

4. Maintaining Registration

Trademark registrations are valid for 10 years from the date of registration and must be renewed in the year before or within six months after the 10-year anniversary of the registration date. Lanham Act § 6. An extra fee is charged if renewal occurs within the latter six-month grace period. If no renewal is filed within this period, the registration is deemed abandoned.

Failure to renew a registration does not result in loss of common law rights. That is, while the various benefits of registration are lost due to the abandonment of a federal registration, this has no bearing on the common law rights the mark owner has developed based on the use of the mark in commerce.

C. Residual Goodwill

There are circumstances where even though the mark owner has ceased the use of a mark, with no intent to resume its use, the owner may still be able to claim rights in the mark. This can occur when consumers continue to make a goods-source association between the disused mark and the merchant. The mark owner may still protect this lingering goodwill. Such persisting goodwill rebuts the presumption of abandonment arising from the statutory period of nonuse. In one well-known case, *Ferrari S.p.A. Esercizio Fabbriche Automobilie Corse v. McBurnie,* 11 U.S.P.Q.2d 1843 (S.D. Cal. 1989), Ferrari had ceased selling sports cars under the trademark DAYTONA SPYDER for 13 years. Despite such an extended period of nonuse, the court held that the mark was not abandoned, even though Ferrari did not intend to resume use of the mark, because consumers still associated the mark with Ferrari. The dissipation of goodwill was prevented, in part, by Ferrari's continuing sale of parts and the public's use of such a long-lasting product.

CHECKPOINTS

- A mark represents the goodwill that a merchant has established in the trade for goods and services sold under the mark, and goodwill represents the property interest that a merchant has in its mark. The strength of goodwill is based upon the extent to which consumers have made a goods-source association with respect to a trademark.
- When consumers no longer make the goods-source association, the merchant has lost any goodwill it owned in the mark, and the mark ceases to function as a trademark.
- Some courts have imposed a duty on mark owners to sue infringers or risk losing their trademark rights; other courts have rejected such a duty. However, a mark owner's failure to sue infringers risks the

mark's becoming generic or infringers being able to assert equitable defenses such as acquiescence or laches.

- Section 45 of the Lanham Act establishes two bases upon which a court may hold a mark abandoned: when use has been discontinued with no intent to resume use or through the course of conduct of the mark owner.
- There is no stated minimum time to establish abandonment. However, the statute does create a presumption of abandonment after three consecutive years of nonuse.
- To abandon a mark, the owner merely has to intend not to resume its use in the reasonably foreseeable future. Proof of intent to abandon is not required.
- Most courts require that proof of abandonment be made based upon clear and convincing evidence, although the Federal Circuit Court of Appeals only requires a preponderance of the evidence in proceedings before the TTAB.
- Abandonment may also occur if the mark owner's conduct (including the owner's failure to act) causes the mark to become the generic name for the goods or services or otherwise to lose its significance as a mark.
- A trademark license permits a licensee to use a merchant's mark on goods and services in a specified geographic territory or market. The goodwill developed by the licensee inures exclusively to the benefit of the merchant licensor. Courts require that the mark owner be responsible for controlling the quality of goods sold (or services provided) by the licensee.
- A naked license is when the licensor fails to exercise quality control over the goods/services sold by the licensee. This deceives the public as to the genuineness of the goods/services and legally constitutes abandonment of the mark.
- If a trademark owner attempts to sell a trademark divorced from its associated goodwill, this is referred to as an assignment-in-gross and constitutes an abandonment of the mark. The purpose of the anti-assignment-in-gross rule is to prevent consumer deception by assuring the continuity of the goodwill symbolized by the mark.

CHAPTER 5

Trade Dress

ROADMAP

- Definition of trade dress
- Distinctiveness of trade dress
- Trade dress and functionality
- Trade dress and patent law

Trade dress is a specialized type of trademark that includes both the product's design and the packaging that contains the product. Generally, consumers can readily distinguish the product from the packaging that contains the product. However, sometimes, the product may be sold in such a manner that it is unclear whether something is the packaging of the product (product packaging) or the product itself (product design). This chapter will discuss the trademark issues in product packaging and product design and limitations on which features may be protected as a trademark.

Trade dress may also cover certain physical aspects of marketing of services, such as the design, layout, and ambiance of a restaurant. Because of the nature of trade dress, which is embodied in the physical design of the product or service or its packaging, determining if the design can indicate source creates unique concerns. Specifically, in evaluating whether design or packaging is protectable as a trademark, courts must consider issues relating to distinctiveness, the overlap with patent law, and functionality. Since functionality is a defense against trade dress infringement, it is dealt with specifically in Chapter 12.

A. Distinctiveness of Trade Dress

As with a word or logo mark, the product or packaging design must be sufficiently distinctive to indicate the source of the goods or services. The question that has challenged courts is whether trade dress can be protected as an inherently distinctive mark or whether it always requires proof of secondary meaning. Before 1981, courts always required the owner of trade dress to prove that the trade dress had acquired secondary meaning through its commercial use. In 1981, many federal appellate courts started to treat trade dress similarly to other marks and held that trade dress could be inherently distinctive without requiring proof of secondary meaning (acquired distinctiveness).

The issue came before the Supreme Court in *Two Pesos, Inc. v. Taco Cabana, Inc.*, 505 U.S. 763 (1992). In that case, the Court had to determine if trade dress, which consisted of the design of a Mexican restaurant, required proof of secondary meaning even if it was held to be inherently distinctive. The Court ruled that there was no statutory reason under the Lanham Act to treat trade dress differently from other trademarks and so ruled that inherently distinctive trade dress requires no further proof of distinctiveness.

This holding confused trademark practitioners because some lower courts interpreted it to mean that all forms of trade dress could be inherently distinctive. This led to complex definitional problems for courts trying to determine whether a product's design or packaging could be inherently distinctive.

The Supreme Court clarified its *Two Pesos* holding in *Qualitex Co. v. Jacobson Products Co.*, 514 U.S. 159 (1995). In *Qualitex*, the mark at issue was the green-gold color of commercial cleaning press pads. The Court ruled that, although a single color could indicate a product's source, a single color alone was not sufficiently unique to be protected without proof of secondary meaning. Yet *Qualitex* left it unclear whether this rule applied only to a single-color trade dress or whether other types of trade dress marks were so limited.

Five years later, the Supreme Court again addressed this issue. In *Wal-Mart Stores, Inc. v. Samara Brothers, Inc.*, 529 U.S. 205 (2000), Wal-Mart had copied various designs from a line of children's clothing produced by Samara Brothers without the manufacturer's permission, including seersucker material with appliqués. Samara Brothers argued that the designs of its children's clothing were inherently distinctive trade dress, so no proof of secondary meaning was required.

The Supreme Court disagreed, holding that a product's design is like a descriptive term and always requires proof of secondary meaning. The Court explained that it did not hold in *Two Pesos* that all forms of trade dress could be inherently distinctive. The Court reasoned that a consumer's first perception of a product's design was that it was chosen to make the product look or function better, not to indicate the source. In this regard, product design is similar to descriptive terms, which also always require proof of secondary meaning to function as trademarks. The Court distinguished a product's packaging, which it held could be understood by consumers to function to identify the product's source. Here, the Court compared the squat, orange bottle for TIDE brand laundry detergent, which it held was chosen to distinguish the product on store shelves, to the design of a penguin-shaped cocktail shaker, which the Court held was primarily designed to "render the product itself more useful or more appealing." The Court reasoned that consumers would first perceive the design of a penguin-shaped cocktail shaker as an attractive product and not as indicating the source of the product of a particular merchant.

However, the *Wal-Mart* decision did not resolve the issue for all trade dress, as the Court itself discussed. For example, it was unclear where this left the trade dress involved in *Two Pesos* (i.e., the design and décor of a restaurant), which the Court had previously accepted as inherently distinctive. Not certain how to categorize this form of trade dress, the Court stated that such trade dress was more akin to product packaging, or *tertium quid*, Latin for "a third thing." It further stated that in a case where it is unclear whether the claimed trade dress is either product packaging or product design, any doubt should be resolved by finding that the trade dress is akin to product design and requires proof of secondary meaning. Relying on the *tertium quid* idea, later courts have held that interior décor may not fit into the product design category and that such décor can be inherently distinctive.

B. Trade Dress and Functionality

Trade dress cannot be protected as a trademark if it is functional. The Supreme Court noted the need for the functionality doctrine in *Qualitex*:

> The functionality doctrine prevents trademark law, which seeks to promote competition by protecting a firm's reputation, from instead inhibiting legitimate competition by allowing a producer to control a useful product feature.

514 U.S. 159, 164–65.

The following are three examples of trademarks or trade dress that courts found functional. In *TrafFix Devices, Inc. v. Marketing Displays, Inc.*, 532

U.S. 23, 33 (2001), the Supreme Court found that a dual-spring design on road signs was functional and not protected as trade dress. The Court stated, "Where the design is functional under the *Inwood* formulation, there is no need to proceed further to consider if there is a competitive necessity for the feature." In *Eco Manufacturing LLC v. Honeywell International Inc.*, 357 F.3d 649, 654 (7th Cir. 2004), the Seventh Circuit found that the trade dress for a round thermostat was functional and not protected. The court reasoned that "the round design is not an arbitrary flourish in the configuration of Eco's thermostat; it is essential to the operation of the device." And in *In re Becton, Dickinson & Co.*, 675 F.3d 1368 (Fed. Cir. 2012), the Federal Circuit affirmed the TTAB's ruling that the color yellow on medical syringe barrels was functional and could not be trademarked. The court agreed with the TTAB that yellow conveyed important safety information to medical personnel.

Lanham Act § 43(a)(3) puts the burden of proving the non-functionality of unregistered trade dress on the party asserting trademark protection for the unregistered trade dress. If the trade dress is registered, then the burden of proving functionality shifts to the alleged infringer to prove that the trade dress is functional. This burden shifting is similar to proof of descriptiveness and genericness. Functionality can also be raised at any time as a defense to infringement of a registered mark, even if that registration is incontestable, Lanham Act § 33(b)(8), and is a statutory ground for cancelling a registration at any time, Lanham Act § 14(3). Since this defense can be raised at any time, functionality is similar to a claim that the mark is (or has become) generic.

The twofold purpose of trademark law under the traditional likelihood of consumer confusion test is to encourage honest merchants to invest in creating high-quality products and to prevent the likelihood of consumer confusion. Sometimes, especially in the context of trade dress, granting a trademark on the trade dress or design of a product may convey a significant non-reputational competitive advantage to the trademark owner by protecting some useful feature of the product. The functionality doctrine in trademark is designed to limit trademark protection to the signaling function of the trademark and to assure that trademarks do not inadvertently become perpetual backdoor patents. If a trademark owner desires to protect some useful feature of his or her product, then the trademark owner should seek patent protection. Patent law, rather than trademark law, protects the utilitarian aspects of a product. Patent applications are carefully examined to determine if the claimed invention is new, useful, or non-obvious to one of ordinary skill in the art and whether the patent application adequately discloses the claimed invention.

After a lengthy, detailed examination, the PTO may grant a patent protecting the claimed invention for a term of up to 20 years.

The Lanham Act does not protect the functional features of a trademark or trade dress since it is a "well-established rule that trade dress protection may not be claimed for product features that are functional." *TrafFix Devices*, 532 U.S. at 29 (citing *Qualitex*, 514 U.S. at 164–65). The underlying theory of the trademark functionality doctrine is that there is a fundamental right to copy a competitor's products or designs except to the extent that the competitor has been granted an exclusive right for a limited period of time under copyright or patent law to prevent copying. In several cases, the Supreme Court has said that trademark law should be strictly interpreted to prevent it from becoming a potential perpetual form of quasi-patent or quasi-copyright protection. In *Qualitex*, the Supreme Court firmly established that trademark law only protects the signaling function of the trademark to indicate the source, origin, sponsorship, or affiliation, serving as the physical embodiment of the goodwill of the trademark owner.

Trademark functionality may be characterized as either utilitarian functionality or aesthetic functionality. Utilitarian functionality usually refers to trademark characteristics that affect a product's cost or tangible quality. For example, if it is cheaper to produce a product in a specific color or shape, then the product's trade dress characteristics are utilitarian. Aesthetic functionality focuses on the characteristics of the trademark or trade dress. These characteristics convey a significant competitive advantage that cannot be duplicated through alternative trademarks. For example, protecting a trademark in the colors orange and black for Halloween products would convey a significant non-reputational advantage to a single competitor. Such a trademark should be denied as aesthetically functional.

1. Utilitarian Functionality

The Supreme Court set out the standard for utilitarian functionality in *Inwood Laboratories, Inc. v. Ives Laboratories, Inc.*, 456 U.S. 844, 850 n.10 (1982): "In general terms, a product feature is functional if it is essential to the use or purpose of the article or if it affects the cost or quality of the article." If a product feature satisfies this test because the feature is essential to the use or purpose of the article, or because it affects the cost or quality of the article, then that feature is functional and thus can never be protected under trademark law as trade dress. *TrafFix Devices, Inc. v. Marketing Displays, Inc.*, 532 U.S. 23

(2001). In *TrafFix Devices*, the Court rejected using a competitive necessity test when evaluating whether trade dress was functional. Instead, it emphasized that the engineering-based definition described in *Inwood*, which focuses on the benefit of the feature to the use of the product, is the proper test. If the feature is directed to and essential to the use or purpose of the product, a competitor can copy that feature, even if alternative designs are possible. This is so even if consumers have come to associate the functional design elements with a single manufacturer.

2. The *Morton-Norwich* Factors for Determining Utilitarian Functionality

Whether trade dress is functional is a question of fact. The court will usually first consider evidence regarding the utilitarian aspects or nature of the trademark or trade dress. In *In re Morton-Norwich Products, Inc.*, 671 F.2d 1332 (C.C.P.A. 1982), the Court of Customs and Patent Appeals (the predecessor court to the Federal Circuit Court of Appeals) laid out a four-factor test for determining the functionality of trade dress. Although not adopted directly by the Supreme Court in the *TrafFix Devices* case discussed above, these four factors are still often relied on to evaluate evidence to determine the functionality of trade dress.

The *Morton-Norwich* factors that bear on the issue of functionality are

- the existence of a utility patent that discloses or claims the utilitarian advantage of the trademark or trade dress sought to be registered as a trademark;
- advertising by the trademark or trade dress owner featuring the design's utilitarian advantages;
- the lack of functionally equivalent alternate designs; and
- the comparative simplicity or cost savings resulting from the article's manufacturing method.

In re Morton-Norwich Products, Inc., 671 F.2d at 1340–41.

The *Morton-Norwich* test requires that the court weigh each factor in the context of the unique factual circumstances relating to the trademark or trade dress in the relevant marketplace and give each factor the appropriate weight under the circumstances. No one factor is dispositive. However, the courts usually will give great weight to whether the trademark or trade dress features are disclosed or claimed in a utility patent.

The first factor is whether an expired utility patent covers the claimed trademark or trade dress. (Design patents are rarely cited in the context of a functionality defense. Unlike a utility patent that protects a useful invention, a design patent merely protects a product's ornamental, aesthetically pleasing, non-utilitarian aspects. Design patents and trademarks can exist harmoniously in the marketplace.) A trademark infringement claim will not usually be filed during the patent's life because the competitor copying the trademark or trade dress covered by an unexpired utility patent is more likely to be sued for patent infringement. However, once the utility patent has expired, the owner of the now-expired utility patent may desire to use trademark law to gain or maintain a competitive advantage in the marketplace. For example, even if the court has evidence of a utility patent and the trade dress falls squarely within the claims of the utility patent, that is merely "strong evidence that the features therein claimed are functional." *TrafFix Devices*, 532 U.S. at 30. Because there is a statutory presumption that if a patent is issued, the claimed invention is new, useful, and non-obvious, "the previous patent adds great weight to the statutory presumption that features are deemed functional until proved otherwise by the party seeking trade dress protection." *Id.* In the case of a trademark or trade dress that is covered within the claims of a patent, "one who seeks to establish trade dress protection must carry the heavy burden of showing that the feature is not functional, for instance, by showing that it is merely an ornamental, incidental, or arbitrary aspect of the device." *Id.* The courts are unclear as to what weight a patent or a denied patent application should receive in weighing a defense that a trademark is functional. At the very least, the statements made in the patent application and during patent prosecution are evidence of which features the applicant believes to be useful. Yet, a mere application or a denied application does not receive a statutory presumption of functionality. Perhaps the best rule is to treat an application similar to advertising by the trademark owner.

The second factor is advertising by the trademark or trade dress owner. Here, the court must be careful to distinguish between mere non-factual statements, such as puffery, and factual statements that the trademark owner asserts to the public, claiming that this product has some new or superior characteristic that gives the product a non-reputational advantage among consumers. For example, if a merchant advertises that the product is now available in an easy-hold, no-spill bottle, the merchant may have conceded that these are functional features of the trade dress.

The third factor is the lack of functionally equivalent designs. This factor has become more problematic in post-*TrafFix Devices* litigation. Under *TrafFix Devices*, once a trademark or trade dress is found to be functional, the court does not have to analyze the availability of alternative designs. The possibility of alternative designs does not permit trademark law to protect the functional features of a trademark or trade dress. However, courts may look to the possibility of alternative designs to determine whether the product feature is functional in the first place. This seems to require some circular reasoning. If the court has determined that a feature is functional, it may not consider the possibility of alternative designs. If a court has not yet determined whether a feature is functional, perhaps in close cases, the court may consider possible alterative designs in determining the functionality.

The fourth factor is the cost savings or ease of manufacture. If a feature is easier or cheaper to produce, then the feature is functional. The trademark or trade dress permits the trademark owner to compete in the marketplace more efficiently and at potentially lower prices, or at the same price with increased profits. Again, this is a factor of functionality under *TrafFix Devices*. After weighing each of the *Morton-Norwich* factors individually, the court determines whether the challenged feature of the trade dress is functional in the context of the specific product and market. For example, the color orange is functional for hunting vests, but not for cleaning products.

Because the Supreme Court has not used the terms "de facto functional" and "de jure functional" in the most recent line of cases addressing trademark functionality, and because this distinction is not found in the Lanham Act, the PTO does not use this terminology. Instead, the PTO merely rejects an application on the grounds of functionality. However, the Supreme Court has not formally rejected this distinction, and many circuit courts of appeal continue to recognize a distinction between them. The utilitarian trademark functionality doctrine can be conceptualized as either those features that are "de facto functional" and may be entitled to trademark protection or those features that are "de jure functional" and which are not entitled to trademark protection. If a trademarked trade dress is "de facto functional," the design of a product's trade dress has some function, for example, all bottle designs may serve as containers for a product. De facto functional marks provide no significant non-reputational competitive advantages in the marketplace. A de facto functional trade dress or product design can be registered or used as a common law trademark.

In contrast, if a claimed trademark trade dress is "de jure functional," then it means that the design of the trade dress functions better than competing designs. For example, a de jure functional bottle design may be easier to hold, cheaper to fill, cheaper to produce, or able to store a greater quantity of product in a smaller volume of space. These advantages may be unique to the specific bottle design. De jure functionality does convey non-reputational competitive advantages in the marketplace. Consumers may desire the de jure functional trade dress not because of the reputation of the producer (goodwill) but rather because of the innate nature of the functional trade dress, e.g., a parent may choose to purchase a de jure functional trade dress bottle because the bottle is more manageable for a child to hold, not because of the reputation of the beverage bottle producer. De jure trade dress features, *if at all protectable*, must be protected under patent law with a utility patent.

3. Aesthetic Functionality

The doctrine of aesthetic functionality is criticized by scholars and some courts as unwieldy, unnecessary, and difficult to apply. There is no bright-line rule used by courts to distinguish between those desirable design elements that the trademark owner may protect under trademark law and those design elements that grant the trademark owner an unprotected unfair competitive advantage in the marketplace. The Restatement (Third) of Unfair Competition states that a "manufacturer thus does not forfeit trademark rights simply because prospective purchasers find the design aesthetically pleasing. A design is functional because of its aesthetic value only if it confers a significant benefit that cannot practically be duplicated by the use of alternative designs." *Id.* § 17 cmt. c. Determining aesthetic functionality requires that the court use objective evidence of a lack of adequate alternative designs. Often this is a difficult task. Consider this example: A trademark owner revives interest in Art Deco tableware and claims a trademark for a formal silver tea set in an Art Deco trade dress. Art Deco is a style of design that was popular from the 1920s until about World War II. Competitors may need to produce competing tableware products in the Art Deco style, not because competitors wish to free-ride on the goodwill of a competitor but rather because there is a market for Art Deco-styled products. In cases of aesthetic functionality, consumers are attracted not to a particular producer of the product but rather to the design of the product itself. Other period design styles such as Rococo, Gothic, Georgian, Victorian, or Postmodern will not suffice to meet the consumer demand for aesthetically complimentary Art Deco table settings. In this case, permitting one competitor to have a protected trade dress in an Art Deco silver tea set would prohibit competitors from offering similarly designed tea sets and related goods, in essence giving one competitor a potentially perpetual backdoor design patent on Art Deco tableware and related products.

C. Trade Dress and Patent Law

Although trademark functionality and patent law are discussed earlier in this chapter, this section will explicitly pull the various threads of discussion together. Trade dress and patents can overlap where the design features claimed to operate as a source identifier are also embodied in a product or invention. This overlap can be problematic, potentially extending the duration of protection beyond the scope provided under patent law. The Supreme Court addressed this concern as follows:

> It is the province of patent law, not trademark law, to encourage invention by granting inventors a monopoly over new product designs or functions for a limited time … after which competitors are free to use the innovation. If a product's functional features could be used as trademarks, however, a monopoly over such features could be obtained without regard to whether they qualify as patents and could be extended forever (because trademarks may be renewed in perpetuity).

Qualitex Co. v. Jacobson Products Co., Inc., 514 U.S. 159, 164–65 (1995).

An inventor can obtain a utility patent for a product (or feature of a product) if it is useful, new, and non-obvious. If that feature is also visible to customers, it may be that such a patented feature can be marketed as an identifier of source, that is, as trade dress.

The essential elements of a patent are the claims. In the patent claims, the inventor sets out his or her property interest in the invention. The patent claims are analogous to the metes and bounds in a deed describing real property. The question then is, what is the effect on trade dress protection of a product feature described in the claims of a patent? The Supreme Court stated in *TrafFix Devices* that "[a] utility patent is strong evidence that the features therein claimed are functional." 532 U.S. 23 at 29. Thus, if the product design features that the business argues are trade dress are disclosed in the patent claims, the business will have to overcome the strong evidentiary presumption that the features are functional and, therefore, not protectable. However, this presumption does not apply to a mere recitation of trade dress in the patent's specifications, abstract, or drawings. Such statements may not be sufficient standing alone to provoke this presumption of functionality. There is no such evidentiary presumption in the case of a design patent because a design patent merely protects the ornamental, non-functional (useful) aspects of a product.

How a business might overcome this strong presumption is not entirely clear. The Supreme Court has stated that if "arbitrary, incidental, or ornamental" features were included in the patent claims, these might be protectable as trade dress. However, features that are merely ornamental or arbitrary would likely not meet the patent requirement that the feature be useful and thus would not be in the claims. Based on this, the effect of the restriction in patent law against the inclusion of nonuseful elements in patent claims is likely to result in the "strong presumption" against trade dress, serving as a near-complete bar to protection for trade dress included in the claims of a patent.

D. Functionality as Ongoing Concern

Functionality is a doctrine that may be raised at any point in the life of a trademark or trade dress. Whether a trademark or trade dress is functional may change as markets, laws, and technology change. For example, say a solar cell power manufacturer has a trademark on a purple and green color combination. One day, 20 years from now, science determines that purple and green in combination have thermal properties that make solar cells more efficient and desirable to consumers for non-reputational reasons, or that regulations could require using purple and green for safety reasons. If this were to happen, a defendant would then be free to raise the issue of trademark functionality before the courts.

CHECKPOINTS

- The design of a product, or its packaging, is referred to as trade dress, and it may be eligible for protection as a trademark if it is capable of serving as an identifier of the source of the product.
- There is no basis in the Lanham Act to treat trade dress differently from other types of trademarks.
- Trade dress may be either inherently distinctive or require proof of acquired distinctiveness (secondary meaning), depending on the type of trade dress.
- Product packaging may be inherently distinctive.
- Product design trade dress and trade dress consisting of a single color of a product both require proof of acquired distinctiveness (secondary meaning) in all cases.
- Trade dress that is neither product packaging nor product design, such as the design of a restaurant, is *tertium quid* (translation: "a third thing" [or] "neither this nor that") and can be inherently distinctive. However, any doubt should be resolved in favor of finding such trade dress to be akin to product packaging, thus requiring proof of acquired distinctiveness (secondary meaning).
- If the features claimed as a product's trade dress are functional, such features can never be protected as a trademark.
- Trade dress is functional when its features are essential to the use or purpose of the product or affect the cost or quality of the product.
- When the features of a product claimed to be trade dress are also contained in the claims of a utility patent, this is strong evidence that those features are functional.

CHAPTER 6

Geographical Indications and Other Quasi Marks

ROADMAP

- Geographical indications
- Quasi marks

Designations serve mark-like functions but are not necessarily protected as marks under the Lanham Act or state law. This chapter will discuss "geographical indications," which are analogous to certification marks, and designations, such as "Olympic," which are protected under trademark law and enjoy special rights under other statutes.

A. Geographical Indications

While U.S. trademark law historically required that a mark indicate a single manufacturing source for goods, a sui generis body of law developed internationally around using specific designations to indicate that goods sold under the designation come from a single geographic region. Such a designation is a "geographical indication of origin," or GI. Another name for GI is "appellation of origin." The basis for the protection of GIs is the understanding that goods produced in the same region, according to set production methods, embody a unique quality derived from that geographic region. Examples include wine, cheeses, and other agricultural products. Protection for GIs is required by

Article 22(1) of the World Trade Organization's (WTO) 1995 Agreement on Trade Related Aspects of Intellectual Property Rights (TRIPS).

Use of a GI does not require that the same manufacturer produce the goods but rather that every manufacturer selling goods under the GI produce its goods according to the rules set by a standard-setting organization. For example, the mark PROSCIUTTO DI PARMA is a GI covering a type of ham produced in the region of Italy described as follows:

> Territory of the Province of Parma, located at a distance of not less than five kilometres South of the Via Emilia, reaching a height of no more than 900 metres, limiting to the East with the Enza river and to the West with the Stirone stream.

The United States does not have a registration system for GIs as such, instead protecting GIs through trademark law: as trademarks, collective marks, or certification marks. For example, VINO NOBILE DI MONTEPULCIANO is a registered certification mark with the PTO. The registration is owned by Consorzio del Vino Nobile di Montepulciano, which certifies that wines sold under this mark come from the specific geographic region of Italy called Montepulciano. Many of the United States' trading partners, particularly European countries, dispute that protecting GIs under the traditional trademark law complies with the United States' treaty obligations and have been pressing the United States to adopt laws granting protection for GIs according to the European model.

B. Statutorily Protected Words and Phrases

Some words or phrases have statutorily created trademark-like rights. Federal law protects the marks of specific statutorily designated organizations. Some examples include the NATIONAL SOCIETY OF THE DAUGHTERS OF THE AMERICAN REVOLUTION, BOY SCOUTS, GIRL SCOUTS, LITTLE LEAGUE, and THE AMERICAN NATIONAL THEATER AND ACADEMY. The unauthorized use of other statutory marks is a criminal offense, for example, "Red Cross," "Geneva Cross," and emblem of Greek red cross; 4-H CLUB; SMOKEY BEAR; and WOODSY OWL and the slogan GIVE A HOOT, DON'T POLLUTE. Other words or symbols have designated statutory uses that preclude their trademark use: the Copyright Act designates the letter "C" in a circle (©), the word "Copyright," and the abbreviation "Copr." to identify a claim that a literary or artistic work is protected under copyright law; the use of the letter "P" in a circle (℗) to indicate phonorecords of sound recordings; and the use of the words "mask work," the symbol *M* and the letter "M" in a circle (Ⓜ) to designate mask works. The Trademark Act designates the letter "R" in a circle (®) to indicate that the mark is registered for the relevant goods or services. These symbols or legal terms may not be registered as trademarks.

Protection for such quasi-trademarks can be quite broad. For example, the term "Olympic" and other Olympic Games symbols are protected under 36 U.S.C. § 220506. This statute provides the U.S. Olympic Committee (USOC) with the exclusive right to use such symbols without regard to the nature of the goods or services for which they might be used. The USOC is very aggressive in litigating to protect the OLYMPIC designations and has been quite successful. For example, in a case upholding an injunction against the use of the mark "Gay Olympics," the Supreme Court held that Congress was within its powers to grant the USOC exclusive rights in the term OLYMPIC that were broader than protection available to ordinary trademarks under the Lanham Act. The Court further held there was no First Amendment conflict with providing such broad protection. *San Francisco Arts & Athletics v. USOC*, 483 U.S. 522 (1987).

CHECKPOINTS

- Geographical indications are designations that identify the geographic region where a product comes from and that the product has some unique qualities because of its geographic source.
- The United States has no unique system for protecting geographical indications but rather protects such designations under traditional principles of trademark law.
- Most geographical indications may be eligible for protection as certification marks in the United States.
- Other forms of designations are protected by special federal statutes, such as the designation BOY SCOUTS OF AMERICA.
- Such special statutory designations may have broader protection than trademarks protected under the Lanham Act.

CHAPTER 7

Ownership and Development of Rights in a Mark

ROADMAP

- Ownership of a trademark
- Obtaining rights in a mark
- The rise of common law trademark rights
- The extent of common law trademark rights
- Priority of rights between mark users

This chapter focuses on the basic rules for turning a word, name, symbol, or device into a trademark. As mentioned earlier, U.S. trademark law developed out of the common law of unfair competition. However, in more recent times, it has become the province of statutory law as well as treaties. Even so, trademark law retains a strong common law tradition, particularly with the rules governing how a merchant obtains protection for its trademarks.

A. Ownership

The traditional view is that the owner of a mark for particular goods or services is the person who first establishes rights in the mark. This system is based upon the standard property law maxim "first in time, first in right." To obtain rights in a mark, a merchant must create an association in the minds of consumers between the mark and goods or services sold under the mark. The value of this association is often referred to as "goodwill."

This simple idea, however, is complicated by several considerations. First is the issue of what the merchant must do to be the first to establish the use of the designation as a trademark. The rules regarding what conduct by a merchant constitutes "use" to establish trademark rights differ between common law marks and registered marks.

The next issue is the scope of the merchant's rights in the mark. A merchant is said only to own exclusive rights in a mark to the extent that the merchant actually has developed goodwill in the mark. This goodwill is generally limited to the types of goods and services that are sold under the mark. Even a federal registration is only granted based upon showing actual use of the mark in interstate commerce for specific goods and services. Because of treaty obligations, the one exception to this rule is for foreign registered marks, which may be registered in the United States without proof of actual use in the United States.

The geographical extent of trademark rights is a particular issue with marks protected solely under the common law. Trademarks are territorial by nature, based upon the goodwill developed with consumers. This means that two (or more) parties may own the same common law mark for the same goods in the United States, so long as they operate in geographically distinct markets. The geographical scope of protection is expanded by federal registration, which normally protects the mark in the entire United States through the legal fiction of constructive use. Even here, however, a federal registration may be limited geographically where a merchant in good faith and without knowledge began using its mark before the registrant filed its application.

B. Obtaining Trademark Rights

1. Rights through Use

The basic common law rule is simple: a business develops trademark rights from actual use of the mark in commerce. According to the Restatement, "a designation has been used as a trademark ... when the designation is displayed or otherwise made known to prospective purchasers in the ordinary course of business in a manner that associates the designation with the goods, services, or business of the user...." Restatement § 18.

Under this definition, the touchstone for developing common law trademark rights is the consumer. The merchant claiming trademark rights in a designation must demonstrate that its use of the designation to indicate the source of goods or services was done in such a way that consumers will understand that the designation is being used as a trademark. The key is what consumers perceive. If consumers do not perceive the use to be as a trademark, then no trademark rights will accrue to the merchant.

Trademark law does not protect designations based on their creativity or innovation. It only protects the association (goodwill) between a designation and merchant as the source of goods sold under the designation. The effect of this rule is that no amount of internal planning or discussion regarding the designation will create trademark rights. Intent to create trademark rights is not an element of proving common law rights in a mark: what is required is actual bona fide use in commerce that results in an association between the mark and the source of the goods.

Even if the manufacturer has placed the mark on labels attached to the goods, this alone will not create rights. Again, the key is that the manufacturer must use the marks on the goods so that consumers are made aware of the mark as a source identifier.

The classic case making this point is *Blue Bell, Inc. v. Farah Manufacturing Co.*, 508 F.2d 1260 (5th Cir. 1975). In that case, two clothing manufacturers were attempting to establish ownership of the mark TIME OUT for clothing. Neither party was aware of the other's activities (thus negating bad faith), so the ownership of the mark came down to priority of use. The main issue was whether shipment by Farah to its regional managers was sufficient to create trademark rights in the designation. The court held that it was not, stating, "Secret, undisclosed internal shipments are generally inadequate to support the denomination 'use.'" Therefore, shipments of goods to distributors and internal distribution of the goods within the organization, even if those distributions are described as "sales," are insufficient to create rights. However, if the products are sold to outside or non-affiliated distributors, these sales may constitute bona fide commerce use to create trademark rights.

Use solely by consumers of abbreviations and nicknames is one exception to the rule requiring the merchant to use its designation as a trademark. Occasionally, consumers will refer to a trademark in a fashion not officially adopted by the merchant, such as when they shorten the mark. Most courts accept that if the merchant can establish that the nickname or abbreviation is equivalent to the official mark in the minds of consumers, then the merchant will likely be able to protect such consumer use. Samples of marks that began as nicknames or abbreviations include BIG BLUE for IBM and COKE for COCA-COLA.

2. Use in the Ordinary Course of Business

To obtain rights, the merchant must use its mark in the ordinary course of its business. According to the Restatement, "[t]he requirement that the use be in the ordinary course of business is intended to distinguish bona fide commercial use from uses made merely to reserve rights in the designation." Restatement § 18 cmt. c. Thus, under the common law, only those merchants that have adopted a mark for purposes of actual trade can claim rights in the mark.

What amounts to a bona fide commercial use will depend upon the nature of the merchant's business. No set minimum number of uses, or extent of use, must be proven to show bona fide commercial use. The critical question is what is the nature of the typical use of a mark in the merchant's type of business. If the claimed use is supported by evidence that it is a type of use that may occur in the course of the merchant's business, then that is sufficient to create rights. For example, limited seasonal use, use as part of test marketing, or infrequent use associated with selling luxury goods can all be bona fide commercial uses. Even a single use can be enough to establish rights in a trademark, so long as such use is evidence of an intent by the merchant to begin commercial exploitation of the mark in the ordinary course of business.

The ordinary course of business excludes uses that are merely to reserve rights. This means that a merchant may not claim as bona fide use any use that is merely done to establish priority under trademark law. For example, when the merchant attaches the designation to goods already being sold under a different mark to establish a first use date (priority date), this is not a bona fide use.

Factors to be considered in determining whether the mark was used include

1. The amount of use
2. The nature or quality of the transaction
3. The typical use within a particular industry

An example of a public use that is insufficient to amount to an adequate use in commerce is where the merchant has affixed labels containing the new designation to goods that already have existing marks affixed. Since the sole intent is to create rights in the mark but not to establish a trade in the goods under the mark, no trademark rights will accrue from the use. This occurred in the *Blue Bell Inc. v. Farah Manufacturing Co.* case cited above. Another leading case is *Procter & Gamble Co. v. Johnson & Johnson, Inc.*, 485 F. Supp. 1185 (S.D.N.Y. 1979). In that case, Proctor & Gamble (P&G) attempted to warehouse trademarks for possible future use. P&G created a "minor brands" program to establish and maintain ownership over trademarks not assigned to any existing or foreseeable commercially available product. Under the minor brands program, P&G relabeled other branded products (or goods purchased from another manufacturer) with a trademark in the minor brands program so that the goods could then be shipped and sold in interstate commerce. The relabeled goods were sold uniformly for a nominal amount ($2 per case), regardless of the product size, cost, or quality. These relabeled goods were not listed in P&G's catalogs, price lists, or other published materials. The court rejected P&G's minor brands program as token use, not a bona fide use in commerce.

a. Commerce Regulated by Congress

The basic rule requiring use applies to trademarks protected under both federal and state law. However, because Congress can only regulate commerce as permitted by the Constitution, common law rights in trademarks protected under the Lanham Act are limited to uses of marks that occur in interstate commerce or in commerce with foreign nations under Article I, Section 8, Clause 3, of the Constitution. Consistent with this constitutional limitation, Congress has broadly defined "commerce" in the Lanham Act as "all commerce which may lawfully be regulated by Congress." Lanham Act § 45.

Since the Supreme Court has held that Congress can regulate all economic activities that substantially affect interstate commerce, a power that the Court has interpreted quite broadly, there are few limits on the ability of Congress to regulate trademark law. In fact, few uses of trademarks are truly intrastate only and do not affect interstate commerce. As a result, in almost all cases where state common law would protect a trademark, federal law will also do so. For example, operating a single restaurant serving out-of-state customers has been considered a sufficient use of a mark in commerce under the Lanham Act.

Lanham Act § 45 defines "use in commerce" as "the bona fide use of a mark in the ordinary course of trade, and not made merely to reserve a right in a mark." The "bona fide use" requirement was added with the 1988 amendments to the Lanham Act and made the Lanham Act consistent with the common law requirement that use must occur in the "ordinary course of business," as stated in the Restatement. Together, these two definitions mean that the protection for unregistered trademarks under Lanham Act § 43(a) extends to all bona fide uses of a common law trademark in the ordinary course of trade to the full extent of Congress's Commerce Clause powers. Section 32(1) provides roughly equivalent protection to registered trademarks.

b. Foreign Marks

Because the United States follows the territorial view of trademark rights, courts have consistently held that use of a mark outside of the United States cannot create common law rights in the United States. This is supported by the view of the Lanham Act that use of a mark that occurs entirely in foreign commerce, that is, commerce that occurs entirely outside the borders of the United States and does not affect U.S. commerce, is not a sufficient "use in commerce," as provided for in the Lanham Act. This is true even if the owner of the foreign mark advertises in the United States. *See, e.g., Buti v. Perosa, S.R.L.*, 139 F.3d 98 (2d Cir. 1998) (advertising in United States for Italian restaurant held not to constitute use of the mark in commerce within the meaning of the Lanham Act). Of course, if the advertising results in U.S. consumers' engaging in foreign commerce, that is, commerce between U.S. citizens and foreign citizens, then such activities would amount to use in commerce which Congress can regulate, and thus, would be a use in commerce. *See, e.g., International Bancorp, LLC v. Société des Bains de Mer et du Cercle des Étrangers à Monaco*, 329 F.3d 359 (4th Cir. 2003) (CASINO DE MONTE CARLO mark used in commerce because U.S. citizens purchased casino services sold by foreign casino operator, which amounted to trade with a foreign nation that Congress could regulate under the Commerce Clause).

The use in commerce limitation can cause problems with foreign marks that are well-known internationally. Under the TRIPS Agreement, discussed further in Chapter 16, the United States is obligated to protect well-known foreign trademarks even if they have not been used in the United States. While some courts have held that there is some limited protection for well-known foreign marks under the Lanham Act, *see, e.g., Grupo Gigante SA De CV v. Dallo & Co., Inc.*, 391 F.3d 1088 (9th Cir. 2004) (well-known Mexican trademark held infringed in United States, despite owner's never having used the mark in the United States), not all federal courts universally accept that view. *See, e.g., ITC Ltd. v. Punchgini, Inc.*, 482 F.3d 135, 160 (2d Cir. 2007) (internationally well-known Indian trademark not protectable in United States, where marks abandoned in the United States). This disagreement between the circuit courts exists despite the United States' treaty obligations under Article 6*bis* of the Paris Convention to protect well-known marks. This is because the Paris Convention is not self-executing; it requires domestic enabling law to effectuate the United States' international obligations.

However, well-known foreign trademarks may be protected under state common law. The U.S. Court of Appeals for the Second Circuit certified two questions of state law to New York's highest court. *ITC Ltd. v. Punchgini, Inc.*, 518 F.3d 159, 160 (C.A.2, 2008). As to the first question, whether "New York common law permit[s] the owner of a famous mark or trade dress to assert property rights therein by virtue of the owner's prior use of the mark or dress in a foreign country," the New York State Court of Appeals answered that New York State common law does not recognize a doctrine of well-known marks, but "when a business, through renown in New York, possesses goodwill constituting property or commercial advantage in this state, that goodwill is protected from misappropriation under New York unfair competition law. This is so whether the business is domestic or foreign." *ITC Ltd. v. Punchgini, Inc.*, 880 N.E.2d 852, 859 (N.Y. 2007), State common law protection may be sufficient to satisfy the United States' international obligation to protect foreign unregistered well-known marks that are not used in the United States. Of course, the scope and limits of each state's common law protection of foreign marks is a matter for the courts of that state so relying on state common law protection may create a patchwork of inconsistent protections for foreign trademark owners.

3. Use of Marks on Goods

Proof of use of a mark in commerce for goods is generally straightforward. The merchant must affix the mark on a label or the packaging for the goods and then sell the product to consumers. The Lanham Act § 45 states it more formally:

> [A] mark shall be deemed to be in use in commerce—
>
> (1) on goods when—
>
> (A) it is placed in any manner on the goods or their containers or the displays associated therewith or on the tags or labels affixed thereto, or if the nature of the goods makes such placement impracticable, then on documents associated with the goods or their sale, and
>
> (B) the goods are sold or transported in commerce.

This association of the designation with the product creates trademark rights. Thus, Apple, Inc., developed trademark rights in its apple logo by affixing it to computers and then selling those computers to the public.

The traditional affixation rule, which required the mark to be physically attached to the goods to establish rights in the mark, has given way to the realities of the modern marketplace. Today, the critical test is whether the merchant has established a link between the mark and the merchant as the source of the goods. Affixation is still the primary method of demonstrating this, but use in advertising and marketing may suffice. For example, using a trademark on a menu, in sales solicitations, or on delivery vans has been held to be sufficient. *See* Restatement § 18 cmt. d. Use of a trademark for goods in a mail-order catalog has also been held to be a sufficient use to create rights in the mark. *See, e.g., Lands' End, Inc. v. Manbeck*, 797 F. Supp. 511 (E.D. Va. 1992) (use of mark next to picture of merchandise in catalog held to be a display associated with the goods). A merchant may assert even pre-sales advertising and marketing when it wishes to establish rights to the mark before actual sales have occurred. The Restatement states that "pre-sales activity can qualify as a trademark use if the use is calculated to produce the required association between the mark and the user's goods and is done in the user's ordinary course of business." Restatement § 18 cmt. d.

4. Use of Marks with Respect to Services

With services, the association process with the mark is more attenuated because the mark cannot be affixed to the service. Instead, what is required is that the merchant displays the designation in some form of advertising for the service, such as on brochures, business cards, employee uniforms, other forms of advertising, or in locations likely to create a consumer association between the mark and the service.

Lanham Act § 45 defines use of a mark for services as follows:

> [A] mark shall be deemed to be in use in commerce—
>
> ...
>
> (2) on services when it is used or displayed in the sale or advertising of services and the services are rendered in commerce ....

The typical methods for a merchant to establish rights in a service mark are to use the mark to render the services or advertise the service. For example, Target Brands, Inc., developed rights for the TARGET service mark by advertising the company's retail department store services in print advertisements in newspapers, in online advertising, and on the signs for the stores.

C. When Do Common Law Trademark Rights Arise?

Since common law rights in a mark come from use in commerce, a critical question is, when do those rights attach? To determine when common law trademark rights arise, courts consider three main issues: (1) whether the mark is inherently distinctive or has acquired distinctiveness; (2) how much use of the mark is needed to create rights in the mark; and (3) when pre-sales activity creates priority.

1. Mark Distinctiveness

The first issue is whether the mark is inherently distinctive or requires proof of acquired distinctiveness through the development of secondary meaning. A complete discussion of trademark distinctiveness is covered in Chapter 3.

a. Inherently Distinctive Marks

One of the benefits of using an inherently distinctive mark is that rights to the mark arise from the first bona fide use in the ordinary course of trade. As soon as a merchant affixes a label to a product with an inherently distinctive mark on it and sells that product to consumers, the merchant will have created rights in that mark. Thus, inherently distinctive marks are protected from the first bona fide use in commerce, commonly the first sale to consumers of the merchant's goods.

If the merchant sells its products through independent distributors, the first sale to a distributor of goods with a label containing the mark should suffice to establish the first sale.

b. Marks Requiring Proof of Secondary Meaning

By comparison, with non-distinctive marks, such as descriptive terms or product design trade dress, a merchant does not establish rights in the designation until the designation has acquired distinctiveness (secondary meaning). Consumers do not perceive non-distinctive designations to function as source identifiers when they first encounter them in the marketplace. It is only after the merchant has used the mark for a sufficient amount of time for the mark to develop secondary meaning with consumers that the merchant can claim trademark rights in the designation. Thus, it is unlikely that the first sale of a good to consumers under a descriptive designation will create trademark rights immediately; it is only after consumers have become educated through repeated exposure to the designation or through advertising demonstrating that the descriptive term is now being used to indicate source that trademark rights will attach.

A merchant seeking to prove such acquired distinctiveness under the common law would do so by submitting evidence that consumers have come to perceive the designation to function as a trademark. The merchant could introduce two types of evidence of secondary meaning: direct and indirect.

Direct evidence of secondary meaning is evidence of actual consumer perceptions of the designation. The typical form of such direct evidence is through consumer surveys. When properly constructed, such surveys should show that the consumers now perceive the previously non-distinctive term to primarily indicate the source of products when that mark is used in connection with such products. Although surveys are not required, some courts consider them the best evidence of secondary meaning.

Direct testimony of consumers is also possible; even so, the testimony of a few consumers is unlikely to establish that the consuming public perceives the mark's secondary meaning. Surveys, by comparison, can canvas statistically significant numbers of consumers.

Indirect or circumstantial evidence of secondary meaning includes evidence of the use of the designation as a trademark for some time sufficient to develop trademark rights in the designation. Relevant evidence would include the length of time that the designation has been used, the exclusivity of use, the amount of sales, and the amount and manner of advertising of the goods sold under the designation (including the amount spent on such advertising or free publicity, including news stories).

As noted, while a well-constructed survey is considered strong evidence of secondary meaning, strong circumstantial evidence of secondary meaning can be enough to establish trademark rights in the designation. A discussion of consumer surveys is found in Chapter 9. A good source of circumstantial evidence is "look for" advertising. If the merchant has engaged in advertising exhorting the consumer to "look for" the designation when shopping for the product, this demonstrates the merchant's efforts to create secondary meaning. For example, trade dress described as "colored parallel dashes arranged in parallel rows extending across the entire surface of the goods so as to resemble a cross-hatch or herringbone configuration" was held to have developed secondary meaning in part because of the company's advertising which stated that consumers should "look for the cross hatch trademark." *In re Johnson & Johnson*, 186 U.S.P.Q. 559, 560 (T.T.A.B. 1975).

2. Limited Sales

The second issue courts consider is the extent to which the merchant must achieve a certain level of success in the marketplace with the goods for the first use to count legally as a bona fide use in commerce. Courts have stated that sporadic, casual, or nominal use of a designation will not create trademark rights. To the extent that such use is done merely to reserve rights in the mark (sometimes referred to as trademark warehousing), no common law rights in the mark will accrue.

How much use then is necessary to create trademark rights? The courts still need to articulate a bright-line rule. The Sixth Circuit stated in *Allard Enterprises, Inc. v. Advanced Programming Resources, Inc.*, 146 F.3d 350 (6th Cir. 1998), that rights "may be established even if the first uses are not extensive and do not result in deep market penetration or widespread recognition." Other courts have emphasized that the use must be public and more than de minimis.

Trademark law does not consider the merchant's success as a merchant but rather whether the merchant is honestly using the mark to indicate source and to compete in the marketplace. This is especially true for high-value unique goods such as works of art, specially designed goods, or custom-made goods. The merchant must show a continuous effort to use the mark to identify goods. Thus, even a single use in trade may establish trademark rights if followed by continuous commercial utilization. The determination is done on a case-by-case basis and is fact-specific to the mark, the goods, and the use.

So, what if the merchant claims trademark rights based on a single sale? A single sale of a good can be problematic; it may appear to be an attempt to reserve rights in the mark, which is not a bona fide use. However, because courts have never required much market success to create rights, a single sale may itself be sufficient to create trademark rights, for example, expensive specialized machinery.

What if the designation is also non-distinctive, such as a descriptive term or product design trade dress? In that case, limited sales will likely be insufficient to establish acquired distinctiveness (secondary meaning), and so the designation may not yet be protectable as a mark.

3. Pre-Sales Activity

Sometimes, pre-sales activity can create rights in a mark, even before the first sale. The issue typically arises in disputes between parties claiming rights in the same mark for similar goods or services where each party's claimed first use is close in time.

There is no single test that all courts have adopted. The Second Circuit describes the analysis as one relying on the equities of the case. The Ninth Circuit has described the analysis as one focusing on the totality of the circumstances. Typically, no single event establishes priority, but rather, a series of undertakings over time to bring a good to market does. The common theme linking the various Circuit tests is that the undertakings are sufficiently public and directed to consumers to create some recognition of the trademark among members of the relevant consuming public.

In explaining the totality of circumstances relevant to determining priority in a dispute over a service mark, the Ninth Circuit listed the following factors to consider:

- the genuineness and commercial character of the activity;
- the determination of whether the mark was sufficiently public to identify or distinguish the marked service in an appropriate segment of the public mind as that of the holder of the mark;
- the scope of the non-sales activity relative to what would be a commercially reasonable attempt to market the service;
- the degree of ongoing activity of the holder to conduct the business using the mark;
- the amount of business transacted; and
- other similar factors which might distinguish whether a service has actually been "rendered in commerce."

Chance v. Pac-Tel Teletrac Inc., 242 F.3d 1151 (9th Cir. 2001) (holding that plaintiff's "mailing of the 35,000 postcards, which generated 128 responses to its 800 number and no sales, cannot be considered a first use under the law" based on the totality-of-the-circumstances test).

4. Relation of Federal Registration to When Common Law Rights Arise

Although federal registration confers important procedural and statutory rights upon the owner of a mark, registration does not create the actual rights in the mark. With the limited exception of a Lanham Act §44(e) application based on foreign registration, a registration can only be issued after the applicant has engaged in a bona fide use of the mark in interstate commerce. This is because under U.S. trademark law, actual use, not registration, creates the underlying exclusive right to a mark. Therefore, a mark owner can only obtain a federal registration for a mark for those goods and services for which the owner can show it has actually used the mark. The entire process of obtaining a registration of a mark with the PTO is covered in Chapter 8.

As a corollary to this rule, a refusal by the PTO to register a mark does not preclude the owner from claiming common law rights in the mark. The PTO's refusal to register a mark merely denies the owner of the mark the various statutory benefits of federal registration.

Nevertheless, registration does alter the nature of common law rights, even if registration is ultimately based on use. One of the areas where the effect of registration makes substantial changes to the common law is with respect to the priority of rights. This is discussed in greater detail below in Section E.

a. Registration and Mark Distinctiveness

The rules governing when a mark is sufficiently distinctive, whether inherently or through acquired distinctiveness (secondary meaning), to obtain a federal registration are identical to the rules governing when a mark is protectable under the common law. The sole difference is that a federal registration can only be obtained for use in interstate commerce.

b. Registration, Token Use, and Limited Sales

Before the 1988 amendments to the Lanham Act, the PTO allowed an applicant to apply for registration based solely on "token use." Token use is a use that a merchant made of a designation merely to apply for federal registration, even if the merchant had no current intent to use the mark on goods to be sold. This was allowed because federal law did not provide a mechanism for securing trademark rights without use. This requirement of actual use in commerce created uncertainty for any merchant that would begin to plan a product's introduction long before it had any sales upon which to secure a registration. Allowing a federal trademark application based on token use prevented a competitor from adopting the mark before the merchant could bring the goods to market. Unfortunately, it also meant that the right to obtain a registration could be based upon a use that would not be sufficient to establish rights under the common law limited use rules.

However, since the 1988 amendments, "token use" may no longer serve as an adequate basis for trademark registration. As a result of the amendment preventing token use from amounting to a protectable use in commerce, a merchant must establish that it is using the mark on goods in the ordinary course of trade. What is considered "ordinary" will vary from industry to industry. For example, in seasonal use, where goods are only sold during a limited time frame during the year, sales during that period may be the ordinary use for that industry and sufficient to create rights in the mark sufficient to support registration. The consequence of this change in the Lanham Act is that the right to obtain a registration based upon a bona fide use in interstate commerce is now aligned with the common law concept of use in the ordinary course of trade.

c. Registration, Analogous Use, and Pre-Sales Activity

Under the 1988 amendments to the Lanham Act, Congress added the intent-to-use basis for a trademark registration, Lanham Act § 1(b), and changed the sufficient-use level to support registration. The purpose of this change was to prohibit token use (a use made solely to reserve rights in the mark) as a basis to support federal registration of a mark. One consequence of this change is that the Lanham Act now requires that the claimed trademark use be a use in the ordinary course of trade.

Even though pre-sales activities cannot be the basis for supporting an application to register a mark, the Trademark Trial and Appeal Board (TTAB) of the PTO does recognize the right to oppose a registration based on analogous use, even if the opposer could not file its own application to register a mark based on that level of use. The opposition must be based upon a use analogous to trademark use. In this situation, the party is not using the mark in a manner consistent with the use in commerce requirements of the Lanham Act; instead, it is engaging in other acts that develop goodwill with the consuming public.

According to the Federal Circuit Court of Appeals, to prove analogous use the mark owner must show

- an intent to appropriate the mark, and
- that the activities that constitute analogous use substantially impacted the purchasing public.

T.A.B. Systems v. PacTel Teletrac, 77 F.3d 1372 (Fed. Cir. 1996) (holding that pre-sales activities such as press releases created public identification of the mark with PacTel, where no evidence of how many of PacTel's potential customers received the press releases).

Thus, the mark owner must establish that it was creating an association in the minds of consumers between the goods and the services that will be provided later and that it will eventually be the source of those goods and services.

In *Social Technologies LLC v. Apple Inc.*, 4 F.4th 811 (9th Cir. 2021), the Ninth Circuit extended the *Chance v. Pac-Tel Teletrac Inc.* totality-of-the-circumstances analysis to determine whether a registrant had done enough to establish that its pre-sales activity met the use-in-commerce requirement when filing a statement-of-use for an application filed on an intent-to-use basis. In the case, the court concluded that under the totality of the circumstances, it was clear that the applicant had "rushed to release its Memoji application solely to reserve its rights in the MEMOJI mark and form the basis of a lawsuit against Apple." *Id.* at 820. The court upheld the cancellation of the mark because the registrant accelerated the development and release of its app to form the basis of a lawsuit against Apple, Inc., for trademark infringement and not for any bona fide business purpose.

D. Extent of Common Law Rights

Because common law rights are based on use in commerce, the nature of such use determines the extent of rights created. There are two particular aspects to defining the extent of rights: the type of goods and services covered by the mark and the geographical extent of these rights.

1. Scope of Goods and Services Covered

Marks symbolize the goodwill developed by the merchant in the mark. This goodwill represents the associations consumers make between the goods or services sold and the merchant as the source of those goods or services. Thus, the actual types of goods and services sold by the merchant under the mark establish the goodwill.

Under the common law, a merchant obtains rights to the extent that it uses the designation "in a manner that associates the designation with the goods, services, or business of the user...." Restatement § 18. Thus, the rights obtained are established and limited by the associations created by the manner of use.

The merchant may be able to establish protection of the mark for goods and services that are not the same as those sold under the mark. Issues related to the infringement of marks used on similar goods or in markets into which the merchant may expand are dealt with in Chapter 9.

2. Geographical Limits on Protection under the Common Law

Common law trademarks are protected only to the geographical extent the merchant has developed rights in the mark. The Supreme Court affirmed this rule in *Hanover Star Milling Co. v. Metcalf*, 240 U.S. 403 (1916), where it held that a trademark cannot extend to a territory where the merchant has not engaged in trade. While this rule clearly includes the territory in which the merchant has used the mark, the rule may also include territory where the merchant has yet to begin sales. This may be referred to as a natural zone of expansion.

To determine whether the mark owner has developed common law rights in a geographical region other than where it primarily sells its goods or services, the issue is whether the mark owner has created sufficient consumer association between the mark and the goods in the region. Some courts describe this as the "market penetration" test. The Eighth Circuit Court of Appeals explained that the relevant factors include the value of sales, the number of customers relative to the region's population, relative and potential growth of sales, and length of time selling in the market. *Sweetarts v. Sunline, Inc.*, 380 F.2d 923 (8th Cir. 1967).

E. Priority

When two parties claim rights to the same mark for the same or similar goods, determining the owner of the mark is usually based upon priority of adoption of the mark (sometimes referred to as priority of appropriation). In a simple dispute, a court will consider the above rules, determine the date on which each of the parties first established rights in the mark based on those rules, and then award ownership of the mark to the party with the earlier first use or priority date. While this is a straightforward determination in many cases, in some situations, determining priority may be a little more involved. In particular, the rules concerning descriptive marks and disputes between owners of common law marks and registered marks are a bit more challenging.

1. Priority under the Common Law

Determining priority based upon common law rights differs between inherently distinctive marks, on the one hand, and non-inherently distinctive marks, such as descriptive marks, surname marks, and product design trade dress, all of which require proof of acquired distinctiveness (secondary meaning), on the other.

a. Inherently Distinctive Marks

Determining priority for inherently distinctive marks is a relatively straightforward process. Since a merchant can establish rights in an inherently distinctive mark through proof of its first sale, the party with priority is the merchant who can prove the earlier date of such sale. Of course, if one party relies on use analogous to trademark use, then such earlier non-trademark use may establish priority. However, this is just an extension of the first-to-use rule.

b. Marks Requiring Proof of Secondary Meaning

Priority for non-inherently distinctive marks, such as descriptive terms, surnames, or product design trade dress, is not so straightforward. Since a merchant cannot establish rights in such a mark until it has developed a secondary meaning for the designation, no prior user rights are established until such date. Therefore, the party can only establish priority by demonstrating the earliest date on which it developed secondary meaning for the designation.

In a dispute between two parties for similar marks, the party wishing to establish priority must prove that it developed a secondary meaning in the mark before the junior user adopted the mark. Thus, the senior user must establish a secondary-meaning date that is earlier than the date on which the junior user began its first use of the mark, not the date on which the junior user established secondary meaning for its use of the mark.

This may be an anomalous result. However, courts will focus on the fact that if the senior user has not developed secondary meaning, it does not own a mark. If the senior user does not own a mark, then it cannot establish a first-use date in the mark that precedes the junior user's first-use date.

This can best be explained through an example. Assume Merchant A adopts and uses a descriptive mark on January 1, 2024. Merchant B adopts and uses the same mark for the same goods in the same geographical region on June 1, 2024. For Merchant A to establish priority of appropriation of the mark, Merchant A must prove that the mark had developed acquired distinctiveness (secondary meaning) before June 1, 2024.

The consequence of the senior user's failure to prove the existence of secondary meaning before the junior user began to use the mark means that there is no infringement. Since there is no infringement, both parties may continue to use the mark.

Proving the priority of developing secondary meaning can be difficult to do where a significant amount of time has passed. This is because the mark owner must prove what consumers understood about the designation at some point in time in the past. However, it is unlikely that the merchant has any direct evidence of what consumers understood then. A survey done at the time of trial is of limited value for what consumers thought years earlier regarding a trademark. Therefore, the senior user will have to rely on circumstantial evidence, such as evidence of long-term usage, effort, expenditure of money advertising the mark, and sales volume to prove the date the mark acquired secondary meaning.

c. Geographically Remote Use

Because rights in common law trademarks are limited to the territory where the merchant has used the mark, the circumstance exists for two parties to adopt the same mark in different parts of the country and to develop trademark rights separately. What should a court do when the parties' territories eventually overlap?

The U.S. Supreme Court established the rule in such circumstances in *Hanover Star Milling Co. v. Metcalf*, 240 U.S. 403 (1916), and *United Drug Co. v. Theodore Rectanus Co.*, 248 U.S. 90 (1918). The Court held that if a junior user begins using the mark in a geographically remote area after the senior user has established rights, then the remote user has priority in the territory where it has used the mark. This is referred to as the good-faith junior-user defense, otherwise known as the *Tea Rose/Rectanus* defense.

To establish the *Tea Rose/Rectanus* defense, the junior user must show the following:

1. That the junior user's use occurred in a remote territory. A territory is remote if local consumers are unaware of the senior user's mark.
2. That the junior user adopted its mark in good faith, without knowledge of the senior user's mark.

This rule, laid down in the early 20th century, still represents the rule under federal common law. Obviously, with the advent of national advertising and the internet, it has become more difficult to show that any territory in the United States is geographically remote. However, many merchants operate only regionally, so it is still possible to assert a *Rectanus* defense.

2. Priority Based on Registration

Obtaining federal registration of a trademark on the Principal Register changes several of the common law rules regarding priority. Federal registration generally grants superior rights to a merchant that registers its mark with the PTO. Nevertheless, there are circumstances where prior common law rights will defeat priority granted by the Lanham Act. This section discusses those issues. Note: issues relating to obtaining and maintaining a registration with the PTO, including terminology, are discussed separately in Chapter 9.

a. Preexisting Common Law Rights

It is possible for a party that is technically the junior user of a mark to apply for and obtain a registration for that mark, even if another party has priority under the common law. Registration of the mark by the junior user does not eliminate the senior user's existing rights in the mark. Lanham Act § 7(c)(1). This is true even if the registered mark becomes incontestable. Lanham Act § 15.

That said, such prior common law rights may be limited after a registration has been granted to the other merchant. The limits placed on the scope of the rights of merchants that have existing, protectable common law trademarks are discussed below.

b. Constructive Notice

Pursuant to Lanham Act § 22, federal trademark registration is constructive notice of the registrant's claim to the mark. This section effectively provides a registrant with national priority in the mark as of the registration date, since anyone beginning use of the mark on the same class of goods after this date cannot claim to have begun use of the mark in good faith. Constructive notice negates the *Rectanus* defense, which requires proof of good faith. Thus, if the junior user began using the mark after the registration date of the registrant's mark, even in a remote geographical location, the registrant will be deemed to have priority.

c. Constructive Use

Before the 1988 amendments to the Lanham Act, Lanham Act § 22 was the section a registrant would rely on to establish national priority. However, when Congress amended the Act in 1988, it added a new constructive use section. Since the 1988 amendments became effective in 1989, the benefit of

Lanham Act § 22 constructive notice has been overshadowed by Lanham Act § 7(c) constructive use rights.

For all applications filed after November 16, 1989, Lanham Act § 7(c) grants the applicant a constructive use date effective as of the date of filing the application, which provides the applicant with a national right of priority as of that date. This constructive use date is contingent upon the ultimate registration of the mark. This means an applicant cannot assert priority based on this constructive use unless and until the registration has issued. Once the registration has issued, this constructive use date becomes the registrant's priority date for most disputes regarding the priority of adoption of the mark.

The effect of the constructive use date is that if a dispute arises between the registrant and a merchant claiming common law rights in a similar mark, and the merchant began using its mark after the date of the registrant's application date, the registrant will have priority. This is true even if the party claiming common law rights began its use in good faith in a particular geographical region before the registrant actually entered the market.

The Lanham Act § 7(c) constructive use date is not effective against anyone who, before the registrant's application date, had already

(1) used its mark,
(2) filed an application to register its mark (including an application based on an intent to use the mark), or
(3) obtained an earlier priority date for its application based on a prior filed foreign application for its mark under Lanham Act § 44(d), so long as that person had not abandoned the mark.

Since the registrant's constructive use date hinges on registration, the applicant's right to stop a junior user's use of the mark may not ripen until after the registration issues. How this plays out in fact depends on the basis for the application. Consider when a merchant files an application to register a mark that is already being used in commerce. In that case, the merchant can still sue the junior user for trademark infringement based on the merchant's existing common law rights. However, if the junior user can establish a *Rectanus* defense because it began using its mark in good faith in a territory geographically remote from the senior user, the senior user must wait until the registration has been issued before it can rely on its constructive use date to establish priority.

d. *Intent-to-Use Applications and Constructive Use*

The one area where the Lanham Act grants substantial rights different from common law rights is with Lanham Act § 1(b) intent-to-use applications. Under the common law, it is only use in commerce that can create protectable rights. A merchant cannot claim rights in a designation until the merchant has begun to use the designation as a mark. Before 1989, an application to register a mark could only be filed based on existing common law rights.

Along with the addition of Lanham Act § 7(c), the 1988 amendments to the Lanham Act also added Lanham Act § 1(b), which now allows a party to apply to register a mark based solely on having a bona fide intent to use the mark (referred to as an "ITU" application). A registration will not be issued for such an application until the applicant has begun to use the mark. However, the applicant is granted a constructive use date effective as of the date the registrant filed its application to register its mark. The creation of the intent-to-use application was established along with the elimination of token use, as discussed above.

Constructive use of a mark based on the date of application is particularly beneficial when the application to register the mark is based upon Lanham Act § 1(b). So long as the mark is ultimately registered, the registrant can assert priority of ownership in the mark nationwide, effective as of the application date.

With an ITU, the applicant does not yet have any common law rights in the mark since the applicant has not used the mark. This means that another merchant can begin to use the mark, creating common law rights in the mark before the applicant has any rights in the mark at all. Thus, in this case, the applicant is the junior user (if it has begun to use the mark at all), and the party using the mark is the senior user.

As a result, the following scenario may arise: Merchant A files an application to register its mark, establishing Merchant A's constructive use date. Afterward, Merchant B begins to use the mark, establishing common law rights in the mark. At this point in time, Merchant B is the party with priority under the common law. Merchant A will not be able to claim priority over Merchant B, since Merchant A's constructive use priority hinges on its being granted a registration. In other words, having a pending ITU application accords the applicant no rights in the mark. Again, at this point, it is still Merchant B, who is using the mark, who has exclusive rights to use it.

However, once Merchant A's application has ripened into a registration, then Merchant A (now the registrant) can assert its constructive use priority based on its date of application. Since Merchant A's constructive use date precedes Merchant B's first use in commerce, the registrant, Merchant A, now, in effect, becomes the senior user, and Merchant B no longer has any rights in the mark.

e. Priority between Pending Applications

If a dispute arises between two pending applications to register the same mark for the same class of goods or services, the PTO will grant registration to the mark with the earlier-filed application. The examiner reviewing the later-filed application will disregard any statements in the application regarding the date the mark was first used in commerce. If the party with the later-filed application believes that it has a superior right to the mark, that party must challenge the earlier-filed application by filing an opposition to it or by seeking to have the registration canceled should a registration be granted to the mark claimed in the earlier-filed application.

f. Dawn Donut *Rule*

Although a merchant obtains nationwide priority in its mark based on obtaining a federal registration, this does not mean that the merchant is automatically entitled to an injunction in every situation merely because it has priority. In *Dawn Donut Co. v. Hart's Food Stores, Inc.*, 267 F.2d 358 (2d Cir. 1959), the court held that to be granted an injunction, a plaintiff must prove a likelihood of confusion. In this case, the defendant adopted and used the same mark as Dawn Donut after Dawn Donut's registration was issued. However, since Dawn Donut did not trade in the area and did not intend to do so in the foreseeable future, the court refused to issue an injunction merely because Dawn Donut had priority. The defendant used the mark in a geographically remote area where consumers were unaware of Dawn Donut's DAWN mark. However, the court stated that Dawn Donut could obtain an injunction against the defendant as soon as it could demonstrate an intent to use the mark in the defendant's territory, since it was likely (almost certain) that such use would confuse consumers. As discussed previously, in the global internet-marketplace era, it is increasingly becoming more difficult to be a remote user, especially if the junior user has a web presence.

g. Prior User Rights against a Registered Mark

As noted above, the Lanham Act § 7(c) constructive use right does not apply to any merchant that used and had not abandoned its mark before the date of a registrant's application. This means that the merchant using its mark before the registrant's application (the prior user) will have protectable common law rights in the mark.

In the case where the prior user is also the senior user, the issue then becomes one of common law priority. Such a senior user can make an argument that it is the party entitled to registration and seek to have the junior user's registration canceled (subject to the five-year limitation stated in Lanham Act § 14(1)).

If the junior user's registration has become incontestable, the prior user will not be able to challenge the registrant's right to use its mark based on priority. This is made clear in Lanham Act § 15. However, according to this section, the prior user will maintain the right to continue to use its mark to the extent that the registrant's use of the mark would be an infringement under common law trademark law. According to the language of Lanham Act § 15, the prior user's territory is frozen as of the registrant's date of registration (not application). The trademark concept of incontestability is covered in greater detail in Chapter 8.

h. Limited Area Defense

A slightly different scenario exists where the prior user began to use its mark before the registrant applied to register but after the registrant began its use. This is referred to as the intermediate junior user. The factual situation would look like this:

Merchant A begins to use the mark.

Merchant B, in good faith, begins its use of the mark.

Merchant A files to register the mark.

Because Merchant A did not file until after Merchant B began to use its mark, Merchant A cannot rely on Lanham Act § 7(c) constructive use to claim priority over Merchant B. Merchant B falls under the Lanham Act § 7(c)(1) exception. In such a situation, Merchant B, the intermediate junior user, may be able to assert a limited area defense under Lanham Act § 33(b)(5). This would allow Merchant B to continue to use the mark in its limited territory even after Merchant A's registration becomes incontestable.

To assert the limited use defense, an intermediate junior user must show

- that it adopted its mark in good faith, that is, without knowledge of the registrant's mark,

- before the registrant's constructive use date (the date on which the registrant filed its application to register its mark);
- that the intermediate junior user has used the mark continuously;
- the extent of the territory in which it was using the mark in at the time; and
- that it used the mark in a remote geographical region.

Assuming the intermediate junior user can establish the above, the intermediate junior user will have the right to continue to use its mark in that territory. However, the intermediate junior user's rights are frozen and cannot be enlarged beyond that territory.

CHECKPOINTS

- Trademark rights are developed by use in commerce—through use or display in the ordinary course of business—to create an association with the business in the consumer's mind. The primary question is whether a consumer will perceive the designation as something done in a way that consumers will understand as a trademark.
- The business must use its mark in the ordinary course of business. Under the Lanham Act, this means use which Congress can regulate.
- To develop rights, the merchant must affix its trademark to goods or display the mark in its advertising for services.
- Inherently distinctive marks establish rights when first used. In contrast, non-inherently distinctive marks, such as descriptive marks or product design trade dress, do not establish rights until a merchant can show that the designation has acquired secondary meaning in the minds of consumers.
- Federal registration does not create rights in a mark but rather merely provides benefits to marks that have already obtained common law rights through use. Marks that are refused registration do not lose common law rights.
- Under the common law, rights exist when the mark is used to associate the designation with the goods, services, or business of the user.

Under the property law maxim "first in time, first in right," common law priority exists in the first merchant to achieve rights by using the mark on the goods in question.

- Superior priority is granted to the user who registers its mark with the PTO first, including effective national notice of the applicant's ownership in the mark, and a constructive use as of the date of the application. An application based on an applicant's intent to use a mark receives the benefit of the constructive use date, but not until registration is granted.
- The benefit of nationwide priority based on constructive use is subject to certain limitations. Under the *Dawn Donut* rule, the registrant is not entitled to an injunction against a junior user in a remote area until the registrant can establish an intent to use the mark in the junior user's area. Further, Lanham Act § 7(c) priority is subject to a senior user's common law rights under § 15, and a junior user's limited use existing as of the date of application under § 33(b)(5).

CHAPTER 8

Trademark Registration

ROADMAP

- State versus federal registration
- The registration process
- Screening the mark
- Lanham Act § 1(a) use
- Lanham Act § 1(b) intent to use
- Lanham Act § 44 foreign applications
- The application process
- Examination
- Limits on registration
- Post-registration matters
- The Madrid Protocol

In addition to relying on common law rights, a business may also register its trademarks. While not required under U.S. law, obtaining a registration is generally recommended. A registered trademark provides both practical advantages, such as providing notice to others of the registrant's claim to the mark, and procedural benefits, including the presumption of validity of the mark. In addition, a business may rely on its domestic registration as a basis on which to register the mark in other countries, based upon several international treaties governing trademark registration. This chapter will discuss the benefits, process, and scope of trademark registrations, including some international registration issues under the Madrid Protocol. See Chapter 16 for further discussion of international trademark issues.

A. State versus Federal Registration

The United States has two systems for registering trademarks: the federal registration system provided for under the Lanham Act and the various state registration systems. While multiple state registration systems may seem cumbersome, the state registration systems provide little, if any, additional benefit to obtaining a federal registration or relying on common law protection. First, a state registration cannot limit federally protected trademark rights. Second, most state statutes do not grant statewide protection, instead limiting protection to the territory where the mark owner can establish priority. As a result, there is little reason to file for state registration application instead of relying on common law trademark rights. Even so, many small businesses do decide to register their marks through the state registration systems. They do so in the states where they operate and receive the minor procedural benefit of establishing a date on which they can assert rights. Because of the severe limitations of state registrations, the rest of this chapter will focus solely on the federal trademark registration system.

B. The Federal System of Registration

The Lanham Act provides for a centralized federal trademark registration system, maintained by the PTO. Although trademarks are protected in the United States without registration based on their bona fide use in commerce, federal registration of trademarks provides significant benefits. Because a registration is only granted if an applicant can establish that it already owns a protectable common law trademark, the scope of rights in registered trademarks has a higher degree of certainty. The registration system also reduces the cost of enforcement by streamlining the process of proving ownership and the scope of protection in litigation. Finally, because the registration system is publicly accessible and searchable, it is a valuable resource for businesses wishing to determine the availability of a mark for specific goods and services.

Two registers are provided for under the Lanham Act: the Principal Register and the Supplemental Register.

1. Principal Register

Most applicants seek registration on the Principal Register because only marks registered on the Principal Register receive all federal registration benefits. The benefits of federal trademark registration on the Principal Register, when compared to common law trademark rights, as outlined by the PTO, include

- public notice of the registrant's claim of ownership of the mark;
- a legal presumption of the registrant's ownership of the mark and the registrant's exclusive right to use the mark nationwide on or in connection with the goods and/or services listed in the registration, effective as of the date the registrant's application was filed;
- the use of the U.S. registration as a basis to obtain registration in foreign countries;
- the ability to file the U.S. registration with the U.S. Customs and Border Protection agency to prevent importation of infringing foreign goods; and
- the right to use the symbol "®" to show that the mark is federally registered.

Of the benefits outlined above, public notice of the registrant's ownership of the mark and the legal presumption of the registrant's exclusive right to use the mark in connection with the goods or services listed in the registration are the most important in domestic trademark litigation. There are further benefits to owning a federal registration on the Principal Register that accrue with time, such as incontestability.

2. Supplemental Register

The Supplemental Register is used for designations that have not yet gained trademark significance but are capable of doing so, such as descriptive marks to which secondary meaning (acquired distinctiveness) has not yet attached. Accordingly, a mark that is clearly eligible for registration on the Principal Register may not be registered on the Supplemental Register.

A registration on the Supplemental Register cannot be directly transferred to the Principal Register. A completely new § 1A application is required for this transition. Additionally, having a trademark on the Supplemental Register does not provide a qualifying foundation for registration on the Principal Register under Lanham Act § 2(f), as outlined in TMEP § 1212.04(d).

Nevertheless, an alternative pathway exists for achieving registration on the Principal Register—specifically, if a trademark owner can demonstrate that the mark has been used substantially exclusively and continuously for at least five years. In the case of continuous use, this usage can serve as an independent basis for registration under Lanham Act § 2(f). Designations that can never achieve trademark status, such as generic terms or those barred under Lanham Act §§ 2(a) through (c), (e)(3), and (e)(5), cannot be registered on the Supplemental Register. Registration on the Supplemental Register is not an admission that the mark had not yet developed acquired distinctiveness, for example, in infringement litigation.

Registration on the Supplemental Register confers few substantive rights beyond those available under the common law. For example, a designation registered on the Supplemental Register cannot achieve incontestable status, cannot bar importation of infringing items into the United States, and does not receive a constructive use date, nor can an applicant file an intent-to-use application to obtain a registration on the Supplemental Register. However, there are a few advantages, including federal jurisdiction for infringement actions; the ability to preclude registration of a substantially similar mark, even on the Principal Register; and the right for the owner to display the registered mark symbol (®) next to the designation.

C. Trademark Registration Prosecution Process

This section will outline the bases for filing an application for trademark registration as well as the process of doing so, including screening the availability of the proposed mark.

1. Trademark Screening

Perhaps one of the most difficult decisions facing a merchant is selecting a mark that does not violate the trademark rights of others; therefore, before a business applies to register its mark with the PTO, it should conduct a search to determine if the mark is available. Such a search is best performed before a business first uses the mark regardless of whether it ever seeks to register the mark. In this way the business can minimize the chance of being sued for trademark infringement. However, an applicant seeking to register a trademark with the PTO is under no obligation to perform a screening search; it is merely a suggested best practice.

A natural starting point for trademark owners aiming to establish an online presence is to investigate the availability of domain names that match or meaningfully incorporate the proposed trademark. To this end, potential registrants should employ the services of domain name registrars like GoDaddy, Network Solutions, or Domain.com (note that the mention of these platforms is not an endorsement but rather indicative of some of the options available). These platforms typically offer various services, including a search function to check the availability of desired domain names.

It is crucial, however, to distinguish between domain names and trademarks at this juncture. While a domain name serves as a mere address on the internet, it does not inherently provide the owner with trademark protections. Thus, once a suitable domain name is identified and secured, the trademark screening process must persist to ensure that the chosen domain name also meets the legal criteria for trademark registration.

The screening process involves searching available databases for uses of similar marks, to determine whether the mark is too similar to another mark such that it might be said to infringe an existing mark. A preliminary PTO database search using the trademark search system (the prior version was called Trademark Electronic Search System—TESS) is a good place to start. This database contains a record of all currently registered trademarks as well as pending applications, applications that the PTO denied, and registrations that are no longer active. The trademark search system was recently upgraded, and now can be used to more easily conduct knockout searches (looking for near identical marks).

Although the PTO's database contains many trademarks, it is not a comprehensive source of all trademarks protected under U.S. law. Many common law trademarks are not registered and are subject to complete protection by their continued bona fide use in commerce. In addition, the common law scope of protection for many registered marks may exceed the scope of their registrations based upon expanded use of the mark beyond that claimed in the registration.

In order to do a complete search that captures registered and common law marks, many businesses rely on professional trademark-search companies, such as Thomson CompuMark or CoreSearch. These companies have access to numerous databases that track trademarks' use in advertising, yellow pages directories, and on the internet. In addition, a search company will also search databases of company names, trade name filings, and domain name registrations. The results of such a trademark screening search may run into hundreds of pages.

A merchant may also screen its proposed mark for foreign use and registration. A foreign applicant is entitled to the priority date of its earlier filed foreign application if it files in the United States within six months of the foreign application. Thus, there is a six-month window where a foreign applicant can have priority. Also, the merchant may wish to consider whether the mark has a scandalous, offensive, or just plain silly meaning in countries where the merchant may intend to do business in the future and other factors that may make the mark's use or registration problematic in other countries.

2. Bases for Filing

The Lanham Act provides several bases upon which an application to register a mark with the PTO may be filed. Because the process varies somewhat between these bases, the PTO and applicants generally refer to applications filed by the section of the Lanham Act providing grounds for the application. We follow that convention in this book.

a. Section 1(a) Use-Based Application

The first basis for applying to register a mark is under Lanham Act § 1(a), where the applicant is claiming a right to a registration based upon an actual bona fide use of the mark in commerce in the United States. When it files the application, the applicant must be selling somewhere in the United States all of the goods and services under the mark for which it is seeking registration. The use of the mark does not have to be extensive; the only limitation is that it must be a bona fide use in commerce. See Appendix 1 for a diagram and more detailed discussion of the application process, including a timeline, under Lanham Act § 1(a).

b. Section 1(b) Intent-to-Use Application

If the applicant has not yet begun to use the mark to sell goods or offer services, the applicant will file a Lanham Act § 1(b) application. Here, the applicant bases its application upon the applicant's bona fide intent to use the mark on the goods and services listed in the application. The applicant need not have used the mark at all and may have done little or no preparation to start selling goods or services under the mark. The key is only that the applicant has a bona fide intention to use the mark in the future in the United States when it files the application. An application under § 1(b) is also often referred to as an "ITU" application. If the applicant begins using its mark before a final decision is made on registrability, the applicant can file an amendment to allege use, which would convert the application into a § 1(a) used-based application. See Appendix 1 for a diagram and more detailed discussion of the application process, including a timeline, under Lanham Act § 1(b).

c. Combined § 1(a) and § 1(b) Applications

An applicant is entitled to file an application that combines both actual use and ITU bases. The advantage of this approach is that the applicant obtains the same filing date for all forms of use of the mark. The downside is that a final registration will not be issued until the applicant has established that it has used the mark on all of the goods or services listed in the application. So, if the merchant has used the mark on books but also desires to register the mark for e-books, the registration will not be issued until the merchant also offers e-books in commerce.

d. Foreign Applicants

A foreign applicant may also apply to register its mark in the United States based upon a foreign application or registration. This right is based upon the United States' accession to various international treaties governing trademarks, such as the Paris Convention and the Madrid Protocol. The applicant is basing its application solely on ownership of a foreign registration or on a foreign application. If the foreign applicant is using the mark in the United States, the foreign applicant would also be entitled to file under Lanham Act § 1(a) should it have common law rights that are different from its foreign registration rights. This may occur because the foreign registration is for one class of goods or services, while the mark is being used on different types of goods or services in the United States.

Note: U.S.-based applicants cannot rely on Lanham Act § 44 to claim priority or file for registration with the PTO based on their foreign applications or registrations. The PTO explains the reasoning as follows: "The United States, by definition, is not a country that has a treaty with the United States. Therefore, the term 'country of origin' in § 44(b) means some country other than the United States, and the term 'person' in § 44(b) means a person who can claim a country of origin other than the United States." TMEP § 1002.05. Therefore, we refer to parties that comply with § 44(b) as foreign applicants in this section.

3. Section 44(d)

A foreign applicant who has filed an application to register its mark in its own country may be entitled to the foreign priority filing date for the application with the PTO. As long as the U.S. application is filed within six months of the original foreign filing, the application will be given a priority date based on the foreign filing date. The major benefit of § 44(d), then, is to grant the applicant a priority date based upon an earlier-filed foreign application. See Appendix 1 for a diagram and more detailed discussion of the process of filing an application, including a timeline, under Lanham Act § 44(d). Section 44(d) is not a basis for mark registration, merely the extension of an early priority date.

4. Section 44(e)

The owner of a foreign trademark registration that has been granted registration in the registrant's country of origin may file to register the same mark for the same goods in the United States. Such application is based solely upon the existence of the foreign registration, not on use in the United States (however, eventually the mark must be used in the United States—see the discussion about maintaining registrations below). The applicant must have a bona fide intent to use the mark in the United States with a § 44(e) application. However, unlike with an ITU application, the PTO will issue a registration before actual use in commerce for a § 44(e) application. Unless the application is combined with a § 44(d) application and thus entitled to an earlier priority date, an application filed under § 44(e) will receive a priority date based on the filing date of the U.S. application and not the priority date of the underlying foreign application or registration. See Appendix 1 for a diagram and more detailed discussion of the application process, including a timeline, under Lanham Act § 44(e).

5. Section 66(a)

Finally, a foreign applicant can file an application with the International Bureau of the World Intellectual Property Organization (WIPO) under the Madrid Protocol and request an extension of an existing home registration or application to the United States. Section F of this chapter will deal with the Madrid Protocol in greater detail. See Appendix 1 for a diagram and more detailed discussion of the application process, including a timeline, under Lanham Act § 66(a).

6. Filing the Application

Although filing a paper application with the PTO is possible (for a higher fee), the PTO now prefers that the application process be done completely online. One of the advantages of an electronic filing is that the applicant receives an email confirmation almost instantly, rather than waiting for the PTO to enter the paper-filed application into the system and for a receipt to arrive in the mail. Also, when filing electronically, the date and time the electronic application is submitted is the filing date as of receipt by the PTO. A single day can be critical in establishing priority, and thus, seniority, in a trademark dispute.

In order to obtain a filing date and thus establish nationwide priority, an application must contain the following five elements:

1. The name of the applicant
2. A name and address for correspondence
3. A clear drawing of the mark
4. A listing of the goods or services
5. The filing fee for at least one class of goods or services

These minimum requirements are the same regardless of whether the application is filed under Lanham Act § 1 or § 44. In order to obtain a registration, the applicant must also supply the following additional information:

6. Date of first use of the mark anywhere

7. Date of first use of the mark in commerce which can be regulated by the U.S. Congress
8. The citizenship of the applicant, or its place of incorporation
9. The address of the applicant
10. One or more bases (1(a), 1(b), etc.)
11. The international class of goods or services, if known
12. If the mark is not in standard characters, a description of the mark
13. If the mark includes non-English wording, an English translation of that wording
14. If the mark includes non-Latin characters, a transliteration of those characters, and either a translation of the transliterated term in English, or a statement that the transliterated term has no meaning in English

Item number 11, the international class of goods or services, refers to a classification system agreed to under the Nice Agreement Concerning the International Classification of Goods and Services for the Purposes of the Registration of Marks. The Nice Agreement divides all goods and services into 35 classifications for goods and 11 for services. In addition to assisting the examination process by grouping like goods and services into the same class, the PTO uses the classification system to determine the fee that is due. The applicant pays a fee for each international class that the goods or services fall into for which the applicant seeks to register. The Nice Agreement is discussed further in Chapter 16.

7. Process of Examination

After its receipt of an application for trademark registration, the PTO gives the application an application number and assigns the application to a trademark-examining attorney, "the examiner." The examiner reviews the application on two bases: first, to determine if the formalities of the application have been met, and second, to determine if there are any substantive grounds for a refusal to register the mark. If there are any reasons to refuse registration of the mark, the examiner will issue an office action detailing the reasons for the refusal. The applicant is always allowed to respond to the initial office action to overcome the examiner's grounds for refusal.

The formalities deal with the sufficiency of the application itself, as detailed above. If any of items 1 to 5 discussed in section 6 above are missing, the application cannot be granted a filing date and will be refused registration. In contrast, the applicant can typically provide additional information in order to overcome a refusal based on items 6 through 14; once the applicant has supplied the missing information or revised the application to meet the examiner's concerns, the application form will be sufficient.

The substantive review involves the examiner's review of whether the mark, as applied to the goods and services listed in the application, is legally permitted registration under Lanham Act § 2. If the examiner concludes that the mark is not registerable, the examiner will detail the grounds for refusal in the office action. The substantive grounds for a refusal are discussed below in section D on limits on registration.

The trademark application process involves an ex parte prosecution, meaning that there is no adverse party to the application. Because of this, the burden is on the examiner to establish a prima facie case that the mark is not registerable. Once the examiner has done this, the burden shifts to the applicant to overcome the grounds for the refusal.

Although not technically an adversarial process, if the examiner has issued a refusal to register the mark on substantive grounds, the examiner has done so based on a legal judgment applying Lanham Act § 2. Thus, responding to an office action is similar to a pleading in an adversarial matter, in that doing so requires the applicant to make sufficient legal and factual arguments to persuade the examiner that the analysis is incorrect. The applicant can assert that the examiner has drawn the wrong legal conclusion based on the law and submit evidence that refutes the examiner's factual conclusions.

For office actions issued in cases with applications filed under §§ 1 and 44, the deadline to file a response to an office action is three months from the date of issuance of the office action by the examiner. An extension of time can be requested for up to an additional three months, with a maximum time to file the response of six months. The time frame is always six months in a case filed under § 66 (i.e., Madrid Protocol applications). 37 C.F.R. § 2.62.

If the examiner approves the registration, the mark is published in accordance with Lanham Act § 12(a) in the Official Gazette of the Patent and Trademark Office. Pursuant to Lanham Act § 13(a), anyone who believes that the registration will harm them can challenge the application by filing an opposition proceeding with the Trademark Trial and Appeal Board (TTAB) within 30 days after the date of publication. Oppositions are discussed in Section 9 of this chapter.

If the examiner issues a final refusal, the applicant is entitled to appeal that refusal to the TTAB. The appeal is adversarial because the applicant is now the petitioner, and the examiner is the respondent. TTAB proceedings are discussed in more detail in Section 9 of this chapter.

Assuming that no one files an opposition, or if the applicant wins the examiner's appeal of a final refusal, the application is approved. If it was filed as a Lanham Act § 1(a) use-based application, the PTO will issue a registration certificate to the applicant. If the application was filed as a Lanham Act § 1(b) ITU application, the application is then approved pending the filing of a statement of use showing that the applicant has begun using the mark in commerce. A statement of use must be filed within six months of the approval of the mark. However, an applicant may request up to five extensions to submit a statement of use. The first extension is granted automatically upon request. The final four extensions may only be granted upon a showing of cause, a low standard. Lanham Act § 1(d)(2). For example, if the applicant is developing the product but has not yet reached the point where manufacturing or distribution can begin, this would be an acceptable ground for an additional six-month extension. However, the total of all extensions can never exceed three years.

It is important to remember that a refusal by the PTO to register a mark does not preclude the owner from actually using the mark. Use, not registration, creates the underlying exclusive right to a mark, and the denial of a registration does not terminate any common law rights the trademark owner may have.

8. Letters of Protest

With the passage of the Trademark Modernization Act of 2020, Congress granted statutory authority for the process by which third parties can submit evidence to the PTO during its review of a pending application. Lanham Act § 1(f). The PTO issued regulations establishing procedures for this process, referred to as "letters of protest." TMEP § 1715. This process is separate from filing an opposition, described in the next section.

The Office of the Deputy Commissioner for Trademark Examination Policy (Deputy Commissioner) reviews letters of protest, not the examining attorney. The Deputy Commissioner determines if the letters of protest comply with the procedures and contain objective evidence that should be entered into the application record and considered by the examining attorney.

In general, letters of protest must contain objective evidence relevant to a ground for refusal of registration of the trademark. The PTO recommends that such letters are filed before the application is published for opposition by third parties. If a letter of protest is filed after the publication date, the evidence submitted must establish a prima facie case for refusal, not merely relevant to refusal. Generally, letters of protest will not be considered by the PTO if filed more than 30 days after publication.

9. Opposition to Registration

As noted, under Lanham Act § 13(a), anyone who believes that the registration of the mark will damage them is entitled to challenge the application by filing an opposition proceeding with the TTAB. Although the opposition period initially lasts for 30 days, a party may ask to have the opposition period extended by 30 days. The period may be further extended, but only based upon showing of good cause and in no event longer than 180 days after publication.

An opposition is an adversarial proceeding, and it results in a truncated trial before the TTAB. The parties to the opposition include the applicant and the party that feels the registration of the mark will damage it, called the opposer. The opposer starts the proceeding by timely filing an opposition stating the grounds for which the opposer believes the registration of the mark will damage the opposer. The applicant then has to file an answer to avoid a default judgment.

The opposer may oppose registration on any grounds for which the registration of the opposed mark will damage the opposer. These grounds include those listed in Lanham Act § 2, but may include other grounds such as the likelihood of consumer confusion with an unregistered mark. In fact, according to Lanham Act § 2(f), a mark can only be refused registration based on dilution by way of an opposition proceeding.

Who may challenge registration through an opposition proceeding has been interpreted quite broadly. In *Ritchie v. Simpson*, 170 F.3d 1092 (Fed. Cir. 1999), the court held that to have standing, an opposer must show that it has a real interest in the case, which the court described as a direct and personal stake in the outcome. Ritchie had opposed O.J. Simpson's application to register the marks O.J. SIMPSON, O.J., and THE JUICE for various goods and services, claiming that the marks were immoral and scandalous. The TTAB had rejected Ritchie's opposition, holding that he did not have standing because the claimed damage was not different from that of the general public. The Federal Circuit reversed the TTAB, holding that the Lanham Act does not require an opposer to show a personal interest in the proceeding different from that of the general public. Ritchie had alleged that he would be damaged by the registration of the marks because the marks disparaged his values as a family man; he further alleged that the marks were scandalous because they would appear to justify physical violence against women. The Federal Circuit stated that on this basis, Ritchie had a real interest and personal stake in the outcome.[1]

D. Limits on Registration

The Lanham Act is structured so that the right to obtain a registration is presumed. This is stated in the preamble to § 2, which states that "[n]o trademark by which the goods of the applicant may be distinguished from the goods of others shall be refused registration on the principal register on account of its nature unless...." Thus, as long as the designation sought to be registered functions as a trademark, the PTO may only refuse registration based on one of the statutorily designated refusals. These are outlined below.

1. Section 2(a): Immoral or Scandalous Matter; Deceptive Matter; Matter Which May Disparage, Falsely Suggest a Connection, or Bring into Contempt or Disrepute

Historically, § 2(a) described a variety of types of marks that were required to be refused registration by the PTO. In two recent decisions, *Matal v. Tam*, 582 U.S. 218 (2017), and *Iancu v. Brunetti*, 139 S. Ct. 2294 (2019), the U.S. Supreme Court held part of the language of § 2(a) to be unconstitutional under the First Amendment to the U.S. Constitution as a content-based regulation of speech. As a result, the PTO is no longer allowed to reject certain marks under § 2(a), and these decisions put the application of other parts of § 2(a) into question. Given that each ground has its own particular rules and issues, each will be treated separately and analyzed under the Supreme Court's recent

1. Richie objected to the registration of the SIMPSON marks on the basis of the Lanham Act's 2(a) prohibition on the registration of disparaging marks. This clause of section 2(a) was later struck down by the US Supreme Court in *Matal v. Tam*. See next section for a discussion of *Tam*.

case law. The PTO has set out how it has interpreted the effect of these two decisions in TMEP § 1203.01.

a. Unconstitutional Limitations on Registration under Section 2(a)—Marks Which May Disparage, or Bring into Contempt or Disrepute, and Marks Which Are Immoral or Scandalous

Lanham Act § 2(a) had prohibited the registration of marks that may "disparage ... or bring ... into contemp[t] or disrepute" any "persons, living or dead." However, applications to register trademarks may no longer be rejected on this basis after the Court's holding in *Matal v. Tam*, 582 U.S. 218 (2017).

Tam had applied to register the mark THE SLANTS for his band. The PTO had rejected the application based on the finding that a substantial composite of people of Asian descent would find the mark to be offensive. In a fractured opinion, the Supreme Court held that this bar against registration was an unconstitutional violation of the First Amendment as viewpoint-based regulation of speech (the Justices agreed on the outcome, but there was no majority opinion on applying the First Amendment to trademarks). A majority agreed that issuing a registration was neither government speech nor an exception to the rule against content-based speech regulation.

Two years after *Tam*, the Supreme Court heard *Iancu v. Brunetti*, 139 S. Ct. 2294 (2019), an appeal based on a refusal to register a trademark because it consisted of immoral or scandalous matter. In that case, Brunetti had attempted to register the mark FUCT for a line of clothing. Because the mark was phonetically indistinguishable from the "past participle form of a well-known profanity," the PTO rejected the mark as scandalous. Expanding on its analysis in *Tam*, the Court held that this basis for refusing a mark's registration was also unconstitutional. Unlike in *Tam*, the majority held that the § 2(a) restriction against registering immoral or scandalous marks was viewpoint-based, allowing the PTO to engage in viewpoint discrimination in violation of the First Amendment.

Thus, in the wake of the *Tam* and *Brunetti* decisions, the PTO may not reject an application to register a mark based on its being disparaging, immoral, or scandalous under § 2(a). The Court was clear that it limited its rejection of these provisions based on its viewpoint-based restrictions of speech. The Court specifically avoided addressing any viewpoint-neutral aspects of § 2(a).

b. Section 2(a): Deceptive Matter versus Section 2(e)(1): Merely Deceptively Misdescriptive Marks

Whether a designation includes a deceptive element will depend on the nature of the goods and consumers' understanding of the designation as it relates to the goods. For example, the trademark APPLE for computers is not deceptive even though computers do not contain any apples. This is because consumers would not understand the term APPLE to convey some information about the product in the context where it is used on computers. Instead, consumers would perceive APPLE to be an arbitrary use of the term and thus an inherently distinctive mark. With designations that include a deceptive element, consumers do understand that the designation is describing, albeit falsely, some characteristic of the product. So, LAMBSKIN for leather goods that do not contain lamb's skin potentially would be deceptive.

Two types of designations will be refused registration based on having deceptive elements. The first type are designations comprising deceptive matter under § 2(a). The second type are marks that are merely deceptively misdescriptive of the goods or services under § 2(e)(1).

The distinction is based on the effect of the deceptiveness on consumers' purchasing decisions. If a consumer believes the deception in a way that causes the consumer to alter their purchasing decisions, then the designation is § 2(a) deceptive; if a designation is deceptive under § 2(a), it can never be registered. In contrast, if the applicant has developed secondary meaning in a deceptively misdescriptive mark under § 2(e)(1), the designation can be registered. As a result, distinguishing between a § 2(a) deceptive designation and a § 2(e)(1) merely deceptively misdescriptive designation can be important for the applicant.

The PTO will determine if a designation is deceptive based on a three-part test:

1. Is the term misdescriptive of the goods' character, quality, function, composition, or use?
2. If so, are prospective purchasers likely to believe that the misdescription actually describes the goods?
3. If so, is the misdescription likely to affect a significant portion of the relevant consumers' decision to purchase?

If the answers to the first two questions are found to be affirmative, then the designation is deceptively misdescriptive of the goods or services sold under the mark and may be rejected under § 2(e)(1). If the examiner determines that the answer to the third question is also affirmative, then the designation is deceptive and will be refused under § 2(a).

In the seminal case *In re Budge Manufacturing Co.*, 857 F.2d 773 (Fed. Cir. 1988), the court conducted a rigorous analysis to determine the registrability of the trademark LOVEE LAMB, intended for car seat covers made from synthetic material mimicking lamb's wool. Applying the legal framework delineated under Lanham Act §§ I(e)(1) and 2(a), the court first established that the term "lamb" was "misdescriptive" of the goods in question, given that the seat covers were not composed of authentic lamb's wool. Subsequently, under the same test, the court found that consumers were apt to be misled by this misdescription, particularly because lamb's wool is a material often employed in manufacturing seat covers. Therefore, the court concluded that the mark was "merely deceptively misdescriptive" under the auspices of Lanham Act § I2(e)(1).

However, the inquiry did not end there. The court proceeded to apply the final prong of the legal test, contemplating whether consumers were likely to believe the misdescription and would likely be influenced by it when making purchasing decisions. The court ruled that the LOVEE LAMB trademark was, in fact, "deceptive" under Lanham Act § 2(a), thereby disqualifying it for registration.

While this limitation could arguably be seen as a viewpoint-based limitation on trademark registration since the truth of the speech is at issue, the TTAB has interpreted the *Brunetti* decision not to apply to the "false suggestion" clause and it would likely hold that the deception clause would likewise be constitutional. This is also in keeping with the Supreme Court's numerous trademark holdings that have generally upheld decisions regarding trademark infringement.

c. Section 2(a): Matter Which Falsely Suggests a Connection

Section 2(a) also bars the registration of a mark that falsely suggests a connection with persons, institutions, beliefs, or national symbols. The term "person" is broad and can include a juristic person, such as a corporation or deceased person (if the person's heirs or successors can assert rights to the person's identity).

The mark in question does not have to incorporate the full legal name: "a nickname or other designation by which the public knows a person may be unregistrable...." TMEP § 1203.03. The key is that the suggested connection is to a real person known by the public.

As stated by the PTO,

> To establish that a proposed mark falsely suggests a connection with a person or an institution, it must be shown that:
>
> (1) the mark is the same as, or a close approximation of, the name or identity previously used by another person or institution;
>
> (2) the mark would be recognized as such, in that it points uniquely and unmistakably to that person or institution;
>
> (3) the person or institution named by the mark is not connected with the activities performed by the applicant under the mark; and
>
> (4) the fame or reputation of the person or institution is such that, when the mark is used with the applicant's goods or services, a connection with the person or institution would be presumed.

TMEP § 1203.03(b)(i). The TTAB has held this section to be a viewpoint-neutral restriction on speech. *In re ADCO Indus.-Techs, L.P.*, 2020 U.S.P.Q.2d 53786 (Trademark Trial & App. Bd. Feb. 11, 2020).

2. Section 2(b): Flags, Coat of Arms, or Other Official Insignia

The PTO will refuse registration of any mark comprising the official flag, coat of arms, or other insignia of the United States, a state or municipality, or a foreign nation, or a simulation of a flag, coat of arms, or other official insignia. Insignia include such symbols as the Great Seal of the United States but would not include national symbols such as the Statue of Liberty or the Eiffel Tower, since those are not official symbols of the government. However, if the mark is merely a stylized version of the official insignia, the mark will be entitled to registration. The test to determine if the mark consists of an impermissible simulation is based upon consumers' general recollection of the symbol, done without careful analysis or side-by-side comparison.

Since this restriction appears to be a viewpoint-neutral limitation on trademark registration (no analysis is needed of the content of the speech), it would likely be seen as viewpoint-neutral by courts and the PTO post-*Tam* and *Brunetti*.

3. Section 2(c): Living Individuals and Deceased Presidents

If the mark consists of or comprises a name, portrait, or signature identifying a particular living individual, then the mark will be refused registration. The only way to overcome such a rejection is to obtain the written consent of the particular living individual. The reference does not have to be to the person's legal name, but rather can be in any manner that identifies the particular person. For example, the PTO refused registration of the mark BO BALL, which was to be printed on a ball made of white leather with red-stitched seams. The TTAB upheld the rejection because the name "Bo" identified Bo Jackson, then a well-known baseball and football star, who had not consented to the use of his nickname.

The TTAB has set out a four-factor test for rejection based on likeness to a living individual:

1. The mark must be the same as, or a close approximation of, the person's name or identity.
2. The mark must be recognized as such.
3. The person in question must not be connected with the goods or services of the applicant.
4. The person must be sufficiently famous that a potential consumer is likely to make a connection with that person.

Similarly, the PTO will reject an application that incorporates the name, portrait, or signature of a deceased President of the United States during the life of his widow, if any, except by the written consent of the widow. Note that § 2(c) does not use gender-neutral language. Since this appears to be a viewpoint-neutral limitation on trademark registration (no analysis is needed of the content of the speech), it is likely that this restriction would be seen as viewpoint-neutral by courts and the PTO post-*Tam* and *Brunetti*.

In *Vidal v. Elster*, 602 U.S. ___, slip op. (2024) the U.S. Supreme Court upheld a rejection by the PTO of an application to register the trademark TRUMP TOO SMALL because it comprised the name of a living individual, Donald Trump, without his consent. The Court noted that the "names clause" of section 2(c) is a content based, albeit viewpoint neutral, regulation of speech. Observing that much of trademark law is content based, the Court held that "trademark rights have always coexisted with the First Amendment, despite the fact that trademark protection necessarily requires content-based distinctions." Slip op. at 6. The Court distinguished the *Tam* and *Brunetti* decisions, which held unconstitutional trademark restrictions that were viewpoint based. The decision appears to be in line with the Court's trademark and First Amendment jurisprudence in the *VIP Products* case from 2023.

4. Section 2(d): Marks Likely to Cause Confusion

Section 2(d) of the Act prohibits the registration of a mark that is likely, when used on or in connection with the applicant's goods, to cause confusion with a mark already registered in the PTO, or a mark previously used in the United States.

The language of § 2(d) tracks very closely to the infringement sections of the Lanham Act, §§ 32(a) and 43(a). Therefore, the analysis for refusing to register a mark is similar to the analysis for determining whether the use of a mark infringes another mark based upon a likelihood of consumer confusion. However, because prosecution of an application is an ex parte process, the PTO limits the scope of the examiner's likelihood-of-confusion analysis.

First, the examiner will only consider currently registered marks and prior pending applications when determining whether the mark seeking to be registered is likely to be confused with another mark. If the owner of an unregistered trademark believes the registration will harm it, it can intervene in the prosecution during the opposition period; otherwise, unregistered marks will not be considered by the PTO.

Second, the examiner will only consider the goods and services listed in the application, and compare them to those goods or services listed in the existing registrations or prior pending applications of other marks, for purposes of determining whether there is a likelihood of confusion. The examiner will not analyze any goods or services not listed, regardless of any actual use in commerce. This is another reason why choosing the correct description of goods and services in a trademark application is important.

Third, the PTO limits the factors that the examiner may consider when conducting the review. The Federal Circuit developed its own multi-factor test for likelihood of confusion in *In re E. I. du Pont de Nemours & Co.*, 476 F.2d 1357 (C.C.P.A. 1973), referred to as the *du Pont* factors (there are 13 separate factors). However, because of the examiner's limited ability to take evidence, the examiner cannot evaluate all 13 factors adequately. This is not to say those other factors are not relevant, but only that they are beyond the level of review that an examiner can undertake in an ex parte proceeding. The other factors may be considered in subsequent proceedings, particularly inter partes proceedings, such as those before the TTAB or district court.

Given these concerns, the PTO has directed examiners to focus on the following six factors:

1. The relatedness of the goods or services
2. The similarity of the marks
3. The similarity of trade channels
4. The conditions under which and buyers to whom sales are made
5. The number and nature of similar marks in use on similar goods
6. The existence of a valid consent agreement between the applicant and the owner of the previously registered mark

When evaluating these factors, the examiner is trying to determine if it is more likely than not that consumers will be likely to confuse the source of the goods listed in the application as coming from the same source as those sold under the senior registration or identified in a prior pending application. Although the examiner will consider all six factors, not every factor may be relevant, given the facts and circumstances of each case. Nor is there a mathematical formula for applying the factors. In some cases, a single factor can outweigh others, such that the mark is denied registration on this basis even though the examiner determined that numerically more factors weighed in favor of the applicant.

Since the likelihood of confusion under the *du Pont* factors is similar to a standard likelihood of confusion in trademark litigation, this section will not go over how the issues should be considered. Chapter 9 contains a full discussion of the trademark infringement factors.

5. Section 2(e): Descriptive, Misdescriptive, Geographical, and Functional Marks

The Lanham Act § 2(e) provides that a mark will be refused registration if it

- is merely descriptive or deceptively misdescriptive of the goods or services;
- is primarily geographically descriptive of the goods or services;

- is primarily geographically deceptively misdescriptive of the goods or services;
- is primarily merely a surname; or
- comprises any matter that, as a whole, is functional.

As discussed in Chapter 3, a designation cannot function as a mark if it is not distinctive. For the same reason, such a designation must also be refused registration. Thus, the essence of these grounds for refusal is that the mark is not distinctive and therefore will not be understood by consumers to function as a trademark.

Sometimes the applicant can overcome this refusal based on a claim of acquired distinctiveness, although this does not apply to all such marks. This is discussed further in subsection b below.

a. Descriptive Designations

The PTO considers a mark to be descriptive if it "describes an ingredient, quality, characteristic, function, feature, purpose, or use of the specified goods or services." TMEP 1209.01(b). The analysis used by the PTO is basically the same one used by courts in determining descriptiveness and is discussed in greater detail in Chapter 3.

In analyzing whether to refuse a registration under § 2(e)(1) for descriptiveness, the examiner must evaluate whether the mark is merely descriptive and not registerable, or whether it is suggestive or arbitrary, and thus inherently distinctive and immediately registerable. TMEP § 1209.02. Once again, the PTO relies on generally the same legal analysis as courts to make this distinction. Arbitrary and suggestive marks are discussed in greater detail in Chapter 3.

b. Deceptively Misdescriptive Designations

As discussed above regarding § 2(a) deceptive marks, the PTO will reject a mark that is merely deceptively misdescriptive of the goods or services. However, unlike deceptive marks, a mark rejected for being deceptively misdescriptive may ultimately be registrable, if the applicant can show that the mark has developed secondary meaning. The reason for this is that the trademark's deceptiveness no longer affects the consumers' purchasing decisions.

The PTO will not reject a trademark merely because it is misdescriptive. It must be deceptively misdescriptive. To be misdescriptive, the mark must immediately falsely convey to the relevant consumer some aspect, ingredient, function, or feature of the good. Next, the examiner must determine that consumers are likely to believe the misdescription. If the misdescription is not plausible in the consumer's minds, then the mark is not deceptively misdescriptive. For example, LIQUID CRAYON was held not deceptively misdescriptive of pens and markers that neither were made up of, nor contained, liquefied crayons.

c. Primarily Geographically Descriptive Designations

A primarily geographically descriptive designation is one that the consumer perceives as merely describing the geographical source of the goods and lacking any secondary meaning, for example, "Florida oranges" for oranges grown in Florida. The PTO considers three factors in determining whether a mark is primarily geographically descriptive.

The first factor is that the mark's primary significance is as a generally known geographical location. The key is that the term's primary significance must be geographical. It is not enough that there is a geographical location with the same name. However, the term does not have to be the location's official name; it can be a term by which the location is commonly known, such as the "Big Apple" for New York City. TMEP § 1210.02.

The second factor is that the goods or services must originate in the place identified in the mark, which includes where the goods are manufactured, produced, or sold. The goods can originate in another location in addition to the place identified in the mark and still meet this requirement. TMEP § 1210.03.

The third factor is that purchasers make an association between the goods and the geographical location, that is, that purchasers are likely to believe that the goods or services originate in the geographical place identified in the mark. If the mark is remote or obscure, the PTO assumes that the consuming public is unlikely to make a goods/place or services/place association. TMEP § 1210.04.

If all three elements are met, then the mark is properly refused registration under § 2(e)(2). Of course, if the applicant has filed to register a certification mark, where the mark certifies that goods come from a specific geographical location or region, then the application should not be refused on this basis. Thus, the mark ROQUEFORT for cheese is a valid certification mark owned by the Community of Roquefort, a municipality in France, which indicates that the cheese has been manufactured from sheep's milk only and has been cured in the natural caves of the community of Roquefort, Department of Aveyron, France.

d. Primarily Geographically Deceptively Misdescriptive Designations

A primarily geographically deceptively misdescriptive designation is a designation that deceives the consumer as to the geographical origin of the goods, for example, "Cuban tobacco" for tobacco grown in Kentucky. There are four elements used to prove that a designation is primarily geographically deceptively misdescriptive.

1. As with a geographically descriptive mark, the primary significance of the mark must be geographic.
2. The goods or services must not originate in the place identified in the mark.
3. Purchasers would be likely to believe that the goods or services originate in the geographical place identified in the mark.
4. The goods/place or services/place association made by a consumer must be material to the consumer's decision to purchase those goods/services.

This is the same test for denying registration for a mark on the basis that it is geographically deceptive under § 2(a).

e. Surnames

The PTO must reject a trademark if it is primarily merely a surname, unless the applicant can establish that it has developed secondary meaning in the mark under § 2(f). The designation must be primarily perceived as a surname to the purchasing public regardless of whether it actually is a surname. However, it is not enough that someone uses the designation as a surname, such as Cotton or King.

f. Functional Designs

As with the common law, where functional designs cannot be protected as trademarks, no mark may be registered if it is functional. Lanham Act § 2(e)(4). Issues concerning functionality are dealt with in greater detail in Chapters 3 and 12. For registration purposes, the challenge for the examiner is establishing that the trade dress is functional. The TMEP states that an examiner should normally analyze one or more of the following four factors established in *In re Morton-Norwich Products, Inc.*, 671 F.2d 1332 (C.C.P.A. 1982):

1. Whether the trade dress is covered by a utility patent that discloses the utilitarian advantages of the design sought to be registered

2. Whether there is any advertising by the applicant that touts the utilitarian advantages of the design
3. Facts pertaining to the availability of alternative designs
4. Facts pertaining to whether the design results from a comparatively simple or inexpensive method of manufacture

TMEP § 1202.02(a)(v).

The TMEP states that it is not necessary to consider every factor in each case. In particular, the Supreme Court subsequently rejected the third factor, availability of alternative designs, as a comprehensive test for functionality in *TrafFix Devices, Inc. v. Marketing Displays, Inc.*, 532 U.S. 23 (2001). The PTO recognizes this holding and states in the TMEP that "[i]t is important that the functionality inquiry focus on the utility of the feature or combination of features claimed as protectable trade dress." TMEP § 1202.02(a)(v).

The TMEP notes that since preserving competition is a stated policy goal of the functionality doctrine, determining if alternative designs are available is still a useful tool for analyzing whether trade dress is functional, even if it is not ultimately determinative of it. Thus, an examiner may inquire about alternative designs. If this evidence suggests that the design is the best, or alternatives are not readily available, the examiner may still reject an application on this basis.

Finally, the U.S. circuit courts have historically distinguished between a product design that is de facto functional (i.e., serves some purpose) and de jure functional (legally incapable of serving as a trademark). The PTO no longer uses this terminology since the Supreme Court has never used it, and the terminology does not appear in the Lanham Act. Nevertheless, you may see it used in older circuit court, district court, and TTAB decisions.

6. Section 2(f): Acquired Distinctiveness and Refusals Based on Dilution

The Lanham Act provides that certain marks refused registration under § 2 may nevertheless be registered under § 2(f) if the applicant can establish that the mark has developed acquired distinctiveness (secondary meaning). However, only a few categories qualify. A mark can never be registered under § 2(f) if it has been rejected under §§ 2(a), (b), (c), (d), (e)(3), or (e)(5). This leaves the possibility that marks rejected as merely descriptive (§ 2(e)(1)), primarily geographically descriptive (§ 2(e)(2)), and primarily merely a surname (§ 2(e)

(4)) are capable of being registered once the examiner is provided proof of secondary meaning.

Proof of secondary meaning can take three basic forms. First, the applicant can establish acquired distinctiveness through the submission of actual evidence. This evidence can comprise affidavits, declarations, depositions, or other appropriate evidence. Second, the applicant can claim distinctiveness through proof of substantially exclusive and continuous use of the designation as a mark in commerce for the five years before the date on which the claim of distinctiveness is made. This will establish a prima facie case for acquired distinctiveness, which the PTO usually accepts, although the examiner may ask for additional evidence of distinctiveness. Finally, an applicant can establish a prima facie case for acquired distinctiveness based on ownership of an existing registration for the same mark for similar goods.

Section 2(f) also provides that a mark may not be refused registration based on dilution by blurring or tarnishment, except through an opposition proceeding under § 13. This means that an examining attorney cannot consider issues of dilution when reviewing an application. This leaves the responsibility of preventing registration of marks that are likely to dilute famous trademarks to the owners of such marks.

E. Post-Registration Matters

See Appendix 1 for a diagram and detailed discussion of the process of maintaining a trademark registration post-grant, including a timeline.

1. Incontestability

After five years of continuous use of a registered mark, the registrant may file an affidavit of such continuous use (a § 15 affidavit) to establish the incontestability of the registration. Having an incontestable registration sounds more impressive than it is. Incontestable registration is only conclusive proof of the following:

1. Validity of the registered mark. This cuts off any challenges on the basis that the mark is merely descriptive.
2. Registration of the mark.

3. The registrant's ownership of the mark. A senior user cannot argue that the registrant is the junior user of the mark, and thus not the owner of the mark, for the goods listed in the registration.
4. The registrant's exclusive right to use the registered mark in commerce.

In *Park 'N Fly, Inc. v. Dollar Park & Fly, Inc.*, 469 U.S. 189 (1985), the U.S. Supreme Court held that the Lanham Act does not distinguish between the defensive assertion of incontestability as a shield against an infringement claim, and the offensive assertion that the registrant's mark is conclusively valid and therefore the registrant does not have to prove distinctiveness for an arguably merely descriptive mark. Once a registration is incontestable, the registration is conclusive proof of the facts listed above for all purposes in trademark litigation.

2. Defenses to Incontestability

Notwithstanding these protections, many defenses to an incontestable registration make the status of incontestable less strong than it sounds. The main defenses, listed in § 33(b), are the following:

1. The registration was obtained fraudulently.
2. The mark has been abandoned.
3. The registered mark is being used in a manner which misrepresents the source of the goods or services on which the mark is used.
4. The use of the name, term, or device charged to be an infringement is being used in a descriptive manner.
5. The junior user adopted and used its mark before the registrant's national priority date (but only for the area where the junior user used its mark continuously prior to such date).
6. The junior user's mark was registered and used prior to the registration of the registrant's mark date (but only for the area where the junior user used its mark continuously prior to such registration or the publication).
7. The mark has been or is being used to violate the antitrust laws of the United States.
8. The mark is functional.
9. Equitable principles, including laches, estoppel, and acquiescence, are applicable.

3. Cancellation

Lanham Act § 14 provides that anyone who is damaged by a registration, including because of dilution, can petition, or file a complaint, to have that registration canceled. A trademark registration may be canceled in two ways: (1) by way of a petition to cancel filed with the PTO under § 14 or (2) by order of a court under § 37.

A petition to cancel a trademark registration results in a truncated trial heard by the TTAB. It is an *inter partes* proceeding between two separate parties, the registrant and a third-party challenger, as opposed to an *ex parte* proceeding between the PTO and the applicant. The party challenging a registration may do so for any reason for which registration may have been denied within five years of the registration's being issued. After five years, the statutory bases upon which a mark may be canceled are limited. A mark may be canceled at any time for the following reasons:

1. The mark has become generic.
2. The mark is functional.
3. The mark has been abandoned.
4. The registration was obtained fraudulently.
5. The registration is barred by § 2(a), 2(b), or 2(c).

Notably absent from these statutory grounds is the claim that the mark is likely to cause confusion with the petitioner's mark. Even if the petitioner can prove actual consumer confusion, the registration cannot be canceled on this basis after five years. In this way, the § 14 five-year-rule effectively acts as a statute of limitations.

Section 37 provides that a registration can also be canceled by order of a court hearing a case under the Lanham Act. This authority includes the ability to cancel a registration, to restore a previously canceled registration, or to "otherwise rectify the register with respect to the registrations of any party to the action."

4. Expungement and Reexamination of Registrations

As part of the Trademark Modernization Act of 2020, Congress added two new procedures to the Lanham Act by which a third party may challenge existing registrations: ex parte expungement (Lanham Act § 16A) and ex parte reexamination (Lanham Act § 16B). These sections create processes by which a third party may ask the PTO to cancel a registration due to nonuse. The benefit of these two new procedures is that they are ex parte procedures pursued by an examiner, unlike cancellation, which is an inter partes process pursued by the petitioner directly.

As stated in § 16A(a), "any person may file a petition to expunge a registration of a mark on the basis that the mark has never been used in commerce on or in connection with some or all of the goods or services recited in the registration." Thus, the expungement procedures aim to remove registrations that have never been used (the procedures do not apply to marks that were used and have gone abandoned). A typical expungement situation is where the applicant has claimed more goods in an international class in its application than it can establish use for. This situation can occur because the PTO only requires the submission of one specimen per class. Each international class covers many types of goods and services, and an applicant can list many goods per class while only submitting a specimen for a single good.

If a third party discovers that the registered mark has never been used for certain (or even all) goods listed in the registration, that party can submit a petition to expunge the disputed goods from the registration (or, if no goods were used, fully cancel the registration). To start the process, § 16A states the party must submit a petition to the PTO. TMEP § 1716.02(b) sets out the full requirements for a complete petition: the critical element for the petition is that the petitioner make a verified statement that they have conducted a reasonable investigation of nonuse, and that the petitioner includes copies of evidence supporting the claim of nonuse. TMEP § 1716.02(c). The PTO evaluates the petition to decide whether to institute expungement proceedings. This decision is not reviewable. TMEP § 1716.02. If the PTO decides to move forward, it assigns the matter to an examiner, who begins an office action process with the registrant directly. The process is similar to examination for registration, except that the sole issue is whether the registrant has ever used the mark in commerce for the goods challenged. See TMEP § 1716.03 for the full procedure.

Because use in commerce is not required for a U.S. registration granted based on a foreign registration or on extensions of protection granted to foreign applicants based solely upon filings under §§ 44(d) or 66(a), expungement may be inappropriate. Therefore, a foreign registrant may respond to an expungement proceeding by claiming excusable nonuse. 15 U.S.C. § 1066(f). In order to overcome the petition for expungement, the registrant must introduce evidence "showing that any nonuse is due to special circumstances that excuse such nonuse." *Id.*; 37 C.F.R. § 2.93(b)(5)(ii). The USPTO has interpreted this to require the same statements and evidence as those required to establish excusable nonuse for a § 8 affidavit. The USPTO has established two requirements for § 8 affidavits to support excusable nonuse, namely:

1. State that the registrant was unable to commence use due to special circumstances beyond the holder's control, and
2. "[R]ecite facts to show that nonuse as to those goods, services, or classes is due to special circumstances that excuse the nonuse and is not due to an intention to abandon the mark."

37 C.F.R. § 2.161(a)(6)(ii).

It should be noted that the nonuse at issue with an expungement is not a justification for cancellation under the new reexamination procedures. 15 U.S.C. § 1066b. As stated by the USPTO, "In the context of an expungement proceeding, requiring a showing that the mark was never used, allowing for an allegation of excusable nonuse, would conflict with the use requirement under section 1 for issuance of the registration." Changes to Implement Provisions of the Trademark Modernization Act of 2020, 86 FR 64300-01 (November 17, 2021).

Cancellation based on expungement can only be brought after the expiration of three years after the date of registration and before the expiration of ten years following the registration date. Lanham Act § 16A(i)(1); *see also* § 14(6).

The new reexamination procedure is so similar to expungement that the PTO has included the requirements for filing a reexamination petition in the same TMEP sections as expungement. The only real difference is that a reexamination procedure requires an allegation that the mark was not used on goods or services listed in the registration before a specified relevant date. In the case of applications filed based on use in commerce under § 1(a), the relevant date is the application's filing date. For applications filed based on an intent to use under § 1(b), "the relevant date is the later of the filing date of an amendment to allege use identifying the goods and/or services listed in the petition, pursuant to section 1(c) of the Act, or the expiration of the deadline for filing a statement of use for the goods and/or services listed in the petition, pursuant to section 1(d), including all approved extensions thereof." 37 C.F.R. § 2.91(a)(2)(ii).

F. The Madrid Protocol

The Madrid Protocol is the trademark registration treaty that the U.S. entered into in 2003. It provides a mechanism for parties to file a single application for multiple countries. To file a trademark application under the Protocol, an applicant files its Madrid Protocol-based application (the international application) with the trademark office of the country where the applicant is located (office of origin). This international application is based upon an existing national application or registration. The applicant's office of origin will then refer the international application to the World Intellectual Property Organization (WIPO), in Geneva, Switzerland. WIPO then sends the application to the trademark office in each country designated in the international application, to be processed as if it were a domestically filed application in each of those countries. The benefit to the applicant is that it only files once and obtains a single filing date for all of the subsequently filed domestic applications. See Appendix 1 for a diagram and more detailed discussion of maintaining a Madrid Protocol trademark registration post-grant, including a timeline. Chapter 16 contains a more detailed explanation of the advantages of filing under the Madrid Protocol.

CHECKPOINTS

- Federal trademark registration is not required, but it is recommended. It provides notice to others, provides procedural benefits, and allows mark owners to rely on their U.S. registration when seeking registration in other countries.
- Marks on the Principal Register receive the full range of benefits of registration, including public notice, legal presumptions of validity and ownership, use as a basis to obtain foreign registration, the ability to use the Customs and Border Patrol to stop infringing goods at the border, and the right to use the ® symbol.
- Trademark registration involves three main steps: the strongly recommended but optional clearance search, the application, and the examination process. The application and any necessary filings during the examination process may be made online. There are several bases for filing: those based on actual bona fide use (§ 1(a)),

the intent to use (§ 1(b)), and foreign applications or registrations (§§ 44(d), 44(e), and 66(a)).

- An application may be rejected if the mark is deceptive; contains the coat of arms or official seal or other insignia of the United States or a state or municipality therein or a foreign nation; creates an association with living individuals or deceased presidents; causes confusion with existing registrations; is a descriptive, geographic, or functional mark; and, finally, has not acquired distinctiveness. However, the Supreme Court has held that an application may not be rejected because it contains matter that is disparaging, or is scandalous or immoral, as unconstitutional content based regulation of speech.
- Owners of registrations that have been used continuously for five years may file an affidavit of continuous use to establish incontestability. An "incontestable" registration may still be canceled if it has become generic, is functional, has been abandoned, if registration was obtained fraudulently, or the registration is barred by §§ 2(a)–(c) of the Lanham Act.
- Under the Madrid Protocol, a party may file a single application to register its mark in several countries based on an application in the country of origin. However, each national trademark office makes an individual determination as to whether the application meets that country's requirements for trademark registration.

CHAPTER 9

Traditional Trademark Infringement

ROADMAP

- The elements of trademark infringement
- The traditional trademark infringement test
- Likelihood of confusion and its factors
- Non-traditional theories of trademark infringement
- Third-party liability
- Respondeat superior

"Confusion as to source is the bête noire of trademark law—the thing that stands directly opposed to the law's twin goals of facilitating consumers' choice and protecting producers' good will." *Jack Daniel's Properties, Inc. v. VIP Prod. LLC*, 143 S. Ct. 1578, 1584 (2023).

This chapter will analyze traditional trademark infringement using the likelihood-of-consumer-confusion test under the Lanham Act. The same standard for determining trademark infringement applies to registered and unregistered trademarks. Traditional trademark infringement requires showing a likelihood of consumer confusion as to source, sponsorship, affiliation, or origin.

There are other forms of trademark infringement, for example, dilution of a famous trademark, which prohibits trademark uses that blur or lessen the capacity of a famous trademark to serve as a single source identifier or that tarnish the image of the mark. The elements of a trademark dilution claim are addressed in Chapter 10.

A. Elements of Trademark Infringement

To prevail on a claim of trademark infringement under the Lanham Act, plaintiff must prove that (1) plaintiff has a protectable ownership interest in the mark, and (2) defendant's use of the mark is likely to cause consumer confusion. If the trademark is federally registered on the Principal Register, the infringement claim may be brought under Lanham Act § 32. Claims for unregistered marks may be brought under Lanham Act § 43(a). Sometimes, litigants will plead both sections, if applicable, to avail themselves of the broadest possible protection.

Sections 32(1) and 43(a)(1) of the Lanham Act serve different but complementary purposes in the context of trademark law. Section 32(1) explicitly addresses the infringement of a registered trademark. Section 32(1) allows the owner of a federally registered trademark to file a civil action against any person who, without consent, uses a replica, counterfeit, copy, or imitation of the registered trademark in a manner that is likely to cause confusion or deceive consumers. To prevail under this section, the plaintiff must show that they have a valid, federally registered trademark and that the defendant's use of the mark is likely to cause confusion. Strategically, one may proceed under § 32(1) when they have a federally registered mark and wish to assert only those rights. Federal registration offers various benefits, such as the presumption of validity and nationwide priority.

Conversely, § 43(a) is generally the choice for parties with unregistered marks or when the legal issue extends beyond mere trademark infringement to other aspects of unfair competition, like false advertising. Section 43(a) provides a broader scope of protection and is often cited for claims of "unfair competition," which includes trademark infringement, false advertising, and false endorsement. Importantly, § 43(a) does not require federal registration of the trademark to bring an action because it covers both registered and unregistered marks. It allows for a civil action against any person who uses a word, term, name, symbol, device, or any combination thereof that is likely to cause confusion or mistake, or deceive as to the origin, sponsorship, or approval of goods or services.

It is an essential element to any trademark infringement claim that the plaintiff owns the trademark registration or has common law trademark rights in the alleged infringed trademark. Rights in a trademark may arise through actual use (common law trademark rights), exclusive license, or through actual use plus constructive national use by federal registration on the PTO's Principal Register. Federal registration creates a rebuttable presumption and is prima facie evidence of the trademark's validity in connection with the goods and services for which it was registered and ownership of the trademark. Lanham Act § 7(c). Note: if the registration has become incontestable under § 15, then the registrant's ownership and right to use the mark on the goods listed in the registration is conclusive. Lanham Act § 15.

Without evidence of federal registration, the plaintiff has the burden of proof to show the putative trademark is valid, the scope of the goods and services covered by the mark, the geographical area in which the mark was used, and the date of first use establishing common law trademark protection. Consequently, the plaintiff may be asked to prove that the trademark has a secondary meaning, the date when the trademark acquired a secondary meaning, and the geographical area in which the plaintiff is entitled to common law trademark rights. This may be a heavy burden to meet, and these issues must be proven before the trial court will undertake the more problematic likelihood-of-consumer-confusion analysis.

In addition to the two elements identified above, Lanham Act §§ 32(1) and 43(a) state that the defendant's use must be "in commerce." Separately, § 45 has a definition of "use in commerce" which limits when a mark has been used for purposes of creating rights in a mark. The question is whether the § 45 definition creates a limitation on what constitutes a likelihood of confusion. McCarthy states that the § 45 language is a "statutory vestige of the old common law 'affixation' requirement'" and should not serve as a limitation on proving likelihood of confusion today. McCarthy notes that most courts agree with this analysis. McCarthy § 25:53. Thus, the general understanding is that the use in commerce language in §§ 32(1) and 43(a) is included as an acknowledgment that the Lanham Act was passed under Congress's Commerce Clause power.

Sometimes it is stated that the defendant must make a "trademark use" of the plaintiff's mark. This requirement is non-statutory; neither § 32 nor § 43(a) includes such a requirement, but merely that the defendant's use be in connection with "the sale, offering for sale, distribution, or advertising of any goods or services," or "with any goods or services" respectively. Professor McCarthy, therefore, contends that this requirement is mistaken. McCarthy § 25:11.50.

Lanham Act § 32 also requires that the defendant's use be without the consent of the registrant. This also should not limit confusion analysis, even if stated as an element of a prima facie case: if the defendant's use is with consent, then there are no grounds for a trademark infringement suit because a trademark license is, in essence, a covenant not to sue for uses consistent with the license terms.

B. Traditional Likelihood-of-Consumer-Confusion Test

Under traditional trademark law, anyone, even a competitor, has a right to use another's trademark if that use does not create a likelihood of consumer confusion. To determine whether a specific use creates a likelihood of consumer confusion, each U.S. circuit court, the PTO, and the individual state courts have established their own multi-factor tests. All of these tests are fundamentally similar. The tests all strive to identify the specific factors influencing how consumers perceive, use, and understand trademarks in the marketplace. The various likelihood-of-consumer-confusion tests differ—one circuit's test may conflate two or more factors, while another circuit's test will tease out the same substantive analysis into multiple individually identified factors. Of course, some federal appellate courts have adopted another circuit's test in toto; however, in those circuits, the common law interpreting the likelihood of consumer confusion may have taken different paths. Finally, some circuits will give some factors greater or lesser weight under some circumstances. Because each circuit has its own test, this is one area of trademark law in which carefully selecting the appropriate forum may provide a significant litigation advantage.

1. Relevant Consumer

The first issue facing the factfinder is determining who is the relevant consumer for the trademark infringement analysis.

The relevant consuming public may not be readily apparent. The answer may be the person to whom the product is marketed, the person who actually purchases the product, and finally the person who decides which product is to be purchased. In the case of assigned law school textbooks, the student is the purchaser of the textbook and the actual consumer or user of the textbook. Still, for trademark purposes, the relevant consumer may be the professor assigning the casebook. This may be more apparent in the case of prescription pharmaceutical products. The patient is the purchaser and consumer in the common term "consumer." However, the patient is likely to need clarification on similarly trademarked prescription products because the patient purchases the pharmaceutical product as the physician prescribes it and the pharmacist dispenses it. In the case of prescription pharmaceuticals, for trademark purposes, the relevant consumer for purposes of the likelihood-of-consumer-confusion test is more likely to be the dispensing pharmacist or the prescribing physician. So courts often consider the individual who is the decision-maker or the market-demand creator to be the relevant consumer under trademark law for the likelihood-of-consumer-confusion analysis.

2. Consumer's Presumed Standard of Care

The second issue to be considered by the factfinder before weighing the likelihood-of-consumer-confusion factors is when to protect consumers. Rarely does the law protect imprudent fools. Trademark law demands that consumers exercise the appropriate degree of care, caution, and power of perception given market choice. Consequently, trademark law only protects the reasonably prudent consumer. No use of a trademark may be so clear that no consumer will ever be likely to be confused. So trademark law requires that an appreciable number of reasonably prudent consumers will likely be confused by the challenged use of the trademark before the confusion rises to an impermissible level. At least one court has held that a showing that 15 percent of prudent consumers are confused is strong evidence of a likelihood of consumer confusion. However, there is no definitive agreement among courts regarding the minimum percentage of consumers that constitute an "appreciable number" of prudent consumers. This, again, is an area in which forum shopping may be helpful.

C. Likelihood-of-Consumer-Confusion Factors

Although each U.S. circuit court and the PTO have established their own multi-factor tests to determine the likelihood of consumer confusion, all of these tests are very similar. The eight-factor test set out by the Ninth Circuit in *AMF, Inc. v. Sleekcraft Boats*, 599 F.2d 341 (9th Cir. 1979), is often used as a model in law school casebooks to explore the likelihood-of-consumer-confusion analysis. According to *Sleekcraft*, a court must weigh all eight factors individually in light of the specific trademark, consumer profile, and market for the trademark goods. No one factor is dispositive, and courts may weigh each factor differently according to the case's specific facts. Furthermore, the *Sleekcraft* factors are nonexclusive; depending on the circumstances of the trademark infringement litigation, the factfinder may consider additional factors as necessary. The eight *Sleekcraft* factors are

1. Strength of the mark
2. Proximity of the goods
3. Similarity of the marks
4. Evidence of actual confusion
5. Marketing channels used
6. Type of goods and the degree of care likely to be exercised by the purchaser
7. Defendant's intent in selecting the mark
8. Likelihood of expansion of the product lines

All circuits require that the trier of fact specifically weigh each factor, but the trier of fact is free to weigh the factors according to the specific facts present in the trademark infringement action and give differing weights to each of the factors, and some tests permit or encourage the factfinder to consider factors not explicitly delineated in the test. Occasionally, a court may go so far as to say that it is apparent that the likelihood of confusion is not possible, and so consideration of the factors is not necessary, but this is uncommon. Generally, the courts will analyze each factor, giving it due weight given the facts of the case. This may include very little or no consideration of a factor if the facts so warrant or a finding that the factor is neutral, that is, not weighing in favor of either party.

While analyzing these factors, the factfinder is supposed to place herself in the consumer's position, under the same real-world circumstances the consumer encounters when interacting with the trademark and the associated product. Rarely is the standard some serene judicial chambers; rather, more often the standard is the noisy hustle and bustle of the marketplace. For example, an alcoholic beverage is sold not only from well-lit, static supermarket shelves but also in smoky, dimly lit, noisy cocktail bars to consumers who may be otherwise impaired in their ability to distinguish among trademarks. The amount of time a reasonable consumer spends making the purchasing decision is also significant. A reasonably prudent consumer may only take a few seconds to decide to make an inexpensive impulse purchase such as chewing gum, but that same consumer may ponder for months or even years the purchase of an automobile or other expensive machine.

1. Strength of the Mark

The purpose of examining the strength of the senior user's trademark is to determine the scope of protection that the court will afford the trademark. The more distinctive or unique the trademark becomes, the greater the zone of protection afforded the trademark. Courts assume that as a trademark grows stronger, consumers are more likely to be confused by the use of the trademark by someone other than the trademark owner, because stronger marks are more likely to be remembered and associated by consumers with the senior trademark holder. The strength of the trademark is measured using two tests: conceptual strength and commercial strength. A court will first determine the trademark's conceptual strength and then the mark's commercial strength. Some courts may describe this process as the "imagination test" and the "needs test." "The 'imagination test' focuses on the amount of imagination required in order for a consumer to associate a given mark with the goods or services it identifies.... The 'needs test' focuses on the extent to which a mark is actually needed by competitors to identify their goods or services." *Rodeo Collection, Ltd. v. West Seventh,* 812 F.2d 1215, 1218 (9th Cir. 1987). So trademarks that require more imagination for the consumer to discern the nature of the product also present no need or a lesser need for competitors to use the trademark to describe their product; therefore, the courts give imaginative trademarks a greater zone of protection against infringement.

a. Conceptual Strength of the Trademark

Conceptual strength refers to a mark's classification under the *Abercrombie* test, which was set out in *Abercrombie & Fitch Stores, Inc. v. American Eagle Outfitters, Inc.*, 280 F.3d 619 (6th Cir. 2002). This test is sometimes described as the "spectrum of distinctiveness," discussed in greater detail in Chapter 3. Using the *Abercrombie* test, trademarks are classified according to a distinctiveness spectrum that runs from weakest to strongest: generic, descriptive, descriptive with secondary meaning, suggestive, and arbitrary or fanciful.

A generic term is used by consumers to refer to the product itself, not a particular brand, and receives no trademark protection.

A descriptive designation describes a characteristic of the good and receives no trademark protection. A descriptive designation that has acquired secondary meaning in the minds of the consuming public can serve as a trademark and receives the most limited trademark protection.

A suggestive mark is a designation that does not describe the product but rather suggests something about the product that requires the consumer to use some imagination to determine the nature of the product. COPPERTONE, the trademark for a brand of suntan lotion, is a good example of a suggestive trademark. Suggestive trademarks are legally presumed at their first use to have acquired secondary meaning and receive a greater zone of trademark protection against trademark infringement.

Finally, an arbitrary or fanciful trademark has no intrinsic connection with the product. An arbitrary trademark is a common English language term with no relationship to the product, and a fanciful trademark is a made-up term used as a trademark. APPLE is an arbitrary trademark used by the consumer electronics company; the fruit "apple" has no intrinsic connection with electronic consumer goods. KODAK is a made-up (fanciful) designation used as a trademark by a photographic products company. A legitimate competitor may desire to use the designation "copper tone" in its ordinary English meaning to describe an attribute of the competitor's product, for example, "use the competitor's suntan oil product and get a nice 'copper tone' tan." However, because there is rarely a legitimate reason to use arbitrary or fanciful terms in a trademark sense except to refer to the actual trademarked brands, arbitrary and fanciful trademarks receive the most significant degree of trademark protection.

b. Commercial Strength of the Trademark

The commercial strength of a trademark may enhance the zone of protection for a conceptually weak trademark, such as a descriptive trademark with secondary meaning, or broaden the zone of protection for already strong marks. The commercial strength of the trademark is based on actual marketplace recognition. Therefore, this determination includes factors analogous to those used to determine whether a mark has a secondary meaning. Courts may consider (1) advertising expenditures, (2) consumer surveys linking the mark to a source, (3) record of sales success, (4) unsolicited media coverage, (5) attempts to plagiarize the trademark, and (6) the length and exclusivity of the plaintiff's use of the mark. All of these factors are evidence of the strength of the trademark in the mind of the consuming public.

The factor often given the most weight is the relative degree of exclusivity of using the trademark for the same or related goods in the relevant marketplace. A court will likely discount the use of the same or similar trademark on unrelated goods in different markets. The court will first look at the relative degree of exclusivity of the senior user's use of the mark on goods in the relevant market. The more exclusive the senior user's use of the trademark, the stronger the trademark; thus, the mark is entitled to a more robust zone of protection. However, if the marketplace is crowded with many similar marks for the same or related goods, then each of those trademarks is weaker vis-à-vis the other competing trademarks. Other courts have given special weight to the amount spent on advertising or the market dominance or success of the trademark owner.

2. Proximity of the Goods

Related goods are more likely than unrelated goods to create a likelihood of consumer confusion because the consuming public is likely to presume a relationship where there is none. The more likely a consumer is to make such an association, the less similarity between the trademarks is required to find a likelihood of consumer confusion. To determine relative degree of "proximity" of goods, courts consider whether the goods are (1) complementary, (2) sold to the same type of purchasers, and (3) similar in use or function. Proximity of the goods is less important if the goods are clearly labeled or if consumers exercise a high degree of care because then consumers are merely faced with consumer choice and product discrimination in the marketplace context.

Complementary goods are goods that are usually used or purchased together. For example, pancake mix and pancake syrup are complementary goods, while guns and butter are not complementary goods. Complementary goods are particularly vulnerable to creating a likelihood of consumer confusion.

Goods are sold to the same type of consumers if consumers for each product would readily buy or substitute the two goods. So, a company that sells doughnut mix wholesale to bakeries does not sell doughnut mix to the same type of purchasers who buy finished baked goods or noncommercial home-use doughnut mix. However, the wholesale doughnut mix company may claim other commercial institutional baked goods producers such as restaurants, cafeterias, or hospitals as the same type of purchaser as bakeries for its doughnut mix product.

Similarity in use or function requires an analysis of the trademarked product. The most straightforward test is whether the two goods in the minds of consumers are substitutable. In determining this, courts will consider the purposes for which consumers purchase the goods, how the goods function, the innate quality of the goods, and the price points at which the goods are sold. For example, in *Nautilus Group, Inc. v. Savvier, Inc.*, 427 F. Supp. 2d 990 (W.D. Wash. 2006), the court examined a $40 BodyFlex exercise device (described as a bungee cord with a molded plastic stick in the middle) and a $1,200 BowFlex exercise device (described as exercise cables and rods that permit training with up to 400 pounds of resistance). While both were exercise devices, they were marketed to different classes of consumers and did not perform the same function. As one prominent commentator observed, "Startling examples of 'exceptions that prove there is no rule' are found in both the apparel and food categories." Kane § 8:1.3. However, when the products present health and safety issues, courts have applied a stricter standard. It is worth reiterating here what has been said previously, that each case will stand or fall on its own facts and the ability of an advocate to persuade a court to weigh the factors in the light most favorable to a client.

3. Similarity of the Marks

The more similar the trademarks are in appearance, sound, and meaning, the more likely it is that a court will find a likelihood of consumer confusion. Note, though, the two trademarks do not need to be alike in all three aspects to be determined to be similar. Similarity to any one of the three—sight, sound, or meaning—is sufficient. However, if the two trademarks are essentially dissimilar overall, then a court is unlikely to find a likelihood of consumer confusion.

The trademarks must be considered in their entirety and as they appear to consumers in the marketplace. Consumers do not have perfect recall of trademarks, nor are trademarks usually presented to the consumer for side-by-side comparison. Therefore, a court should refrain from engaging in a side-by-side comparison of the two marks; instead the court should examine each trademark individually, striving to determine how consumers perceive the trademarks as they appear in the marketplace. Nor should a court dissect the trademarks into individual design elements; instead the court must view the trademarks based on their overall commercial impression. An element-by-element analysis would violate the anti-dissection rule. The anti-dissection rule in trademark law holds that a trademark must be viewed in its entirety, rather than dissected into isolated elements, when determining the likelihood of confusion with another mark.

However, certain elements of a mark may dominate the commercial impression it creates. These "dominant" elements are often given greater weight in a likelihood of consumer-confusion analysis. Factors that may make some aspects of a mark "dominant" in the commercial impression include the following:

- Visual Prominence: Elements that are larger or more visually prominent than other elements, for example, often dominate the commercial impression of the mark.
- Positioning: Elements located at the beginning of the mark or in an otherwise prominent position, for example, are generally considered more significant.
- Uniqueness or Distinctiveness: Unusual or unique elements are more likely to dominate the commercial impression than generic or descriptive elements.
- Distinctiveness: Distinctive fonts, colors, or design elements could fall under this category.
- Commercial Strength: Some words or designs in a mark may have more commercial strength due to consumer recognition or marketing emphasis. These elements may dominate the commercial impression.
- Conceptual Strength: The element that most clearly conveys the theme or main idea of the mark may dominate its commercial impression.

- Memorability: Elements that are easier to remember may dominate the commercial impression because they are likely to be recalled by consumers.

For example, in *Palm Bay Imports, Inc. v. Veuve Clicquot Ponsardin Maison Fondee En 1772*, 396 F.3d 1369 (Fed. Cir. 2005), the court found that the word "VEUVE" dominated the commercial impression of the mark "VEUVE CLICQUOT". Similarly, in *In re National Data Corp.*, 753 F.2d 1056 (Fed. Cir. 1985), the court discussed the anti-dissection rule and the importance of assessing the mark as a whole while still acknowledging that more prominent features are generally accorded greater weight in the likelihood-of-confusion analysis. Thus, while the anti-dissection rule mandates that a mark should be considered in its entirety, some elements may be considered "dominant" due to their visual prominence, positioning, distinctiveness, and other factors. These dominant elements often carry more weight in a likelihood-of-confusion analysis. These elements of the mark are often hotly contested when the factfinder makes a similarity determination.

Similarities between the trademarks are often given greater weight than differences between the two trademarks. But not all similarities are weighed the same. In the case of trademarks that contain generic or descriptive elements and distinctive elements, the court will focus on the distinctive elements of the trademark rather than the generic or descriptive elements. Generic or descriptive elements of a trademark are presumptively available for the use of competitors and others, either because generic elements are not protected by trademark law or because descriptive elements are available under principles of trademark fair use. Consequently, generic and descriptive elements of a trademark are weighed less heavily in the court's analysis of this factor. Finally, the dominant use of a logo or house mark may dispel consumer confusion when coupled with a trademark, in cases that otherwise would be held to be confusing had the alleged use been made without the house mark.

a. Appearance (Sight)

A court will examine the mark to determine whether the trademark has dominant or significant characteristics, such as a color or combination of colors, shapes, font styles, or capitalization. A court will also consider whether the two trademarks have the same roots or similar combinations of alphanumeric characteristics. For example, in *Experience Hendrix, L.L.C. v. Hendrixlicensing.com, Ltd.*, 97 U.S.P.Q.2d 1364 (W.D. Wash. 2010), the court compared various trademarks that incorporated the name "Hendrix" in the mark (for the famed rock artist Jimi Hendrix), such as AUTHENTIC HENDRIX compared to HENDRIX ELECTRIC VODKA. The court found that the dominant characteristic in the marks was the word HENDRIX and that consumers would likely "'shrug off the difference[s] as an intentional modification identifying an ancillary division of the same company.'" *Id.* at 1373 (quoting *Dreamwerks Prod. Group, Inc. v. SKG Studio*, 142 F.3d 1127, 1131 (9th Cir. 1998)).

b. Sound

Many trademarks are encountered in the marketplace both orally and aurally. A consumer does not ask for a cola beverage by spelling it out with a "c"; instead, a consumer asks for a cola beverage. Consequently, while creative spellings, such as "kola" or "quola" for "cola" or "fone" for "phone," may not look the same as their dictionary counterparts, when spoken in the marketplace, they are pronounced the same and create the same aural impression. Similarly, while the spelling "CoLa" may create a different, non-similar appearance, it is still phonetically pronounced exactly as the word "cola." Furthermore, even more creative combinations such as quoke-quola are insufficiently different from Coca-Cola®. Thus, even though a consumer might easily distinguish the marks visually, the sound of the mark as perceived in the marketplace may still confuse consumers.

c. Meaning

If the trademarks are arbitrary and different in appearance and sound but have similar dictionary meanings, courts may find them similar. For example, the trademark CYCLONE was held to be an arbitrary mark for wire fencing. A competitor attempted to use the trademark TORNADO for another line of wire fencing. The court found that the words "cyclone" and "tornado" have similar dictionary meanings; thus, the mark TORNADO was similar to the mark CYCLONE. In another case, a court found that the marks ALPINE EMPEROR and MOUNTAIN KING for artificial Christmas trees were conceptually similar and created a likelihood of consumer confusion. Other examples of courts finding a likelihood of consumer confusion include the marks PLEDGE and PROMISE for furniture polish and WONDER MIX and MIRACLE WHIP for salad dressing.

4. Evidence of Actual Confusion

Evidence of actual confusion among a significant number of prudent consumers is strong evidence of a likelihood of consumer confusion. While it may seem that proof of actual confusion should be conclusive evidence of a likelihood of confusion, this is not the case. The reason is that the law does not require no confusion in the marketplace; some level of confusion is tolerated. Recall that for a finding of trademark infringement, plaintiff must show that an *appreciable number* of consumers are confused by the defendant's use of the mark. Thus, the fact that the plaintiff can show that *some* consumers are confused cannot be, in and of itself, sufficient for a finding of infringement.

Actual consumer confusion may be demonstrated through both anecdotal evidence and consumer survey evidence. Courts have recognized that there will always be some consumers who are confused, so the evidence of actual confusion must be significant before courts find the evidence probative. Courts will consider the number of instances of actual consumer confusion against the number of opportunities for confusion. But evidence of actual confusion is not limited solely to evidence of consumer confusion. Confusion among retailers or sales personnel is also relevant. In fact, in one case, the court found that an attorney's misspeaking at a judicial hearing constituted evidence of actual confusion.

Evidence of real-life, actual confusion is often difficult to obtain, so parties may introduce evidence of actual consumer confusion based on consumer surveys. Relying on a survey would not normally be considered direct evidence in other areas of the law. Still, for purposes of trademark infringement, many courts are prepared to accept a well-designed and well-conducted consumer survey as evidence of actual confusion.

Although proof of actual consumer confusion is not necessary to find a likelihood of consumer confusion, a lack of evidence of actual consumer confusion may be probative evidence of no confusion. For example, where the junior user's use of the mark is commercially significant, in the same or similar market or geographical location as the senior mark owner, and over a substantial period of time, and the plaintiff fails to introduce any evidence of actual confusion, under these circumstances, the junior user may argue the mark owner's lack of any evidence of real-life, actual consumer confusion demonstrates that there is no likelihood of consumer confusion.

5. Marketing Channels Used

For this element, the courts consider how the parties market and advertise their goods and how they distribute their products. Using similar or convergent marketing channels increases the likelihood of consumer confusion. The similarity of marketing channels becomes less significant as the channels become less obscure. Some older cases treated the internet as a single channel, but that has now changed. Since e-commerce is ubiquitous, the use of the internet as a marketing channel is given little weight. As noted by a court evaluating the sale of goods under the name of the deceased, famous rock guitarist Jimi Hendrix by different factions of his family via the internet:

> Advertising and selling goods on the internet does not necessarily indicate similar marketing channels when almost everything is available online. Here however, the similarity of the web sites, and the chances that consumers performing Jimi Hendrix related searches are likely to see both web sites, strongly indicates that the web-based marketing of both companies are related channels.

Experience Hendrix, LLC v. Electric Hendrix, LLC, No. C07-0338 TSZ, 2008 WL 3243896, *12 (W.D. Wash. Aug. 7, 2008).

6. Type of Goods and the Degree of Care Likely to Be Exercised by the Purchaser

Trademark law assumes that consumers behave rationally and prudently under the particular circumstances of how the products are sold. So, for inexpensive goods or impulse purchases, courts presume that consumers are unlikely to spend significant time or effort making purchasing decisions and are therefore more likely to be confused. As goods become more expensive, more specialized, or the consumer becomes more sophisticated, courts expect that prudent consumers will use a greater degree of care and so are less likely to be confused. At least one court has held that "[c]onsumers who use the internet for shopping are generally quite sophisticated about such matters." *Toyota Motor Sales v. Tabari*, 610 F.3d 1171, 1178 (9th Cir. 2010). However, considering the ubiquity of e-commerce and online consumer purchases, this observation is becoming less accurate with the passage of time.

7. Defendant's Intent in Selecting the Mark

If a junior user intentionally or knowingly adopts a trademark similar to a more senior user's trademark, courts are willing to presume that the use of the trademark was in bad faith and that the junior user accomplished its purpose, the deception of consumers. Frequently, this factor is given extraordinary weight by some circuit courts. Some courts even hold that where the alleged infringer had the intent to cause consumer confusion, the burden of proof is shifted from the plaintiff to prove confusion to the defendant to disprove confusion. This is the case in the Second and Ninth Circuits, among others. In the Third and Fifth Circuits, proof of intent only creates an inference of the likelihood of confusion, and the plaintiff still bears the burden of proof on the question of infringement.

Note that it is the intent to cause confusion or to deceive that is the issue, not merely the intent to copy. As explained in the Restatement, "if the actor reasonably believes that the other's designation is functional or that the actor's use is on goods sufficiently unrelated to the other's goods that confusion is unlikely, proof that the actor intentionally copied the other's designation does not justify an inference of confusion." Restatement § 22 cmt. c.

8. Likelihood of Expansion of the Product Lines

A trademark owner is protected against use of the trademark on competing goods, so a strong possibility of either party's expanding its business in a manner that will compete with the other party will weigh in favor of finding a likelihood of consumer confusion. This allows the senior user its natural zone of expansion in its products. Only the Second, Sixth, and Ninth Circuits include this element. Other circuit courts question the relevance of the likelihood-of-expansion factor to the ultimate question of the likelihood of consumer confusion. Note also that if the parties are already direct competitors, this factor is irrelevant.

9. Other Relevant Factors

The *Sleekcraft* factors are not exhaustive, and courts will apply other factors as the facts in the case warrant. Some courts will consider the quality of the alleged infringer's goods. For instance, the producer of low quality or shoddy goods (or even goods that are sold at a lower cost than the senior user's goods) may be trying to trade on the goodwill of the senior user. By comparison, a junior user with a high-quality product that is priced at a point comparable to or higher than the senior user's is more likely trying to develop its own goodwill, that is, it is not trying to free ride on the senior user's goodwill.

D. Passing Off, Reverse Passing Off, Post-Sale Confusion, Reverse Confusion, and Initial-Interest Confusion

The Lanham Act proscribes, in connection with goods, any false designation of origin which is "likely to cause confusion, or to cause mistake, or to deceive ... as to [their] origin[.]" Lanham Act § 43(a). Judicial interpretations of the Lanham Act extend well beyond the fraudulent passing off of a trademarked good and include the prohibition of many other modern forms of unfair business practices. The Lanham Act not only prohibits the literal false designation of a good but also prohibits the economic equivalents of passing off, including reverse passing off, initial-interest confusion, and post-sale confusion.

1. Passing Off

Much modern trademark law is based on the common law tort of "passing off," or "palming off." Passing off is a deceptive practice in which one trademark owner sells goods mislabeled with the trademark of another seller. Passing off may be either express or implied. Express passing off is when a business affirmatively labels its goods or services with another business's trademark or otherwise affirmatively misrepresents the source or origin of the goods or services. Implied passing off is when a business presents its product in such a manner as to suggest to the consumer that another business made its product.

2. Reverse Passing Off

A related practice is reverse passing off, which may also be expressed or implied. Express reverse passing off is when the plaintiff's trademark is removed from a product which is then sold by the defendant under a different trademark. Implied reverse passing off is removing the trademark and then selling the product without a trademark. Reverse passing off is prohibited because it deprives the actual manufacturer of the advertising and goodwill that should be associated with the product and creates the potential that consumers may be deceived about the true source of the goods.

The trademark doctrine of reverse passing off is severely limited in the context of copyrighted works that are now in the public domain. Reverse passing off will apply to a mismarked physical embodiment of the public domain work, but it will not apply to uses of the actual copyrighted work which are now in the public domain. In *Dastar Corp. v. Twentieth Century Fox Film Corp.*, 539 U.S. 23, 37 (2003), the Court held that the phrase "origin of goods" in the Lanham Act refers to "the producer of the tangible goods that are offered for sale, and not to the author of any idea, concept, or communication embodied in those goods"—in other words, the phrase means the source of the actual product and not the intellectual source of the copyrighted content.

3. Post-Sale Confusion

A post-sale confusion claim is based not on the confusion experienced by the actual point-of-sale purchaser but rather by subsequent observers of the infringing product, which is often a counterfeit product in the post-sale consumer confusion situation. Usually, post-sale confusion involves knock-off or counterfeit consumer luxury products. In the post-sale consumer confusion context, the confused consumer is presented with the product outside the marketplace and incorrectly associates the product with a trademark owner, and that false association later influences the other consumers' perception of the quality of the trademark owner's legitimate goods. Post-sale confusion is probably the best explanation for why fake luxury brand consumer goods injure the trademark owner. A related reason is that with some luxury brands, there are so many counterfeit products that a licensed product purchaser may avoid the brand to escape compliments on "how real" their presumed fake luxury good looks. Remember that one function of a luxury brand is to signal high social status. If the market is infiltrated with realistic-looking counterfeit products, the brand may come to signal the exact opposite of high social status, resulting in consumers' unwillingness to pay the goodwill premium for the exclusivity that the mark originally conveyed.

Generally, it is not the direct purchaser of the good that is confused. Rarely is anyone presented with luxury goods being sold on a street corner or from the back of an unmarked van at bargain-basement, fire-sale prices confused about whether they are purchasing a genuine, licensed luxury good. However, other legitimate consumers who see the purchaser wearing the counterfeit luxury good may be deceived into thinking that the low-quality fake is, in fact, a licensed product. When the fake fails to perform at the level of the licensed product, it may draw negative impressions about the luxury brand. In the context of post-sale confusion, courts often weigh the likelihood-of-consumer confusion factors differently; for example, marketing channels are usually irrelevant in the post-sale confusion context.

4. Reverse Confusion

Reverse confusion occurs when the junior user of the mark gains greater recognition for its trademark than the senior user. Thus, while the senior user has priority in the mark from having used the mark first and is thus protected against commercial uses that cause a likelihood of consumer confusion, it is the junior user that is perceived by consumers to be the mark owner. These reverse-confusion cases are sometimes described as "David v. Goliath" cases because the confusion may occur when the senior user is a smaller business. The larger junior user can supplant the senior user by extensively advertising its goods under the same mark.

Reverse likelihood-of-confusion cases are less common than traditional (or "forward") confusion cases, but they are not rare. A cause of action for reverse confusion is now recognized by many federal circuit courts and the Restatement (Third) of Unfair Competition (Restatement § 20 cmt. f). The classic situation is exemplified in the BIGFOOT tire case, where a smaller regional company, Big O, sold a tire under the BIGFOOT trademark. Goodyear, a national tire company, started marketing a new tire under the same mark and essentially swamped Big O's market for its BIGFOOT branded tire. *See Big O Tire Dealers, Inc. v. Goodyear Tire & Rubber Co.*, 561 F.2d 1365 (10th Cir. 1977). (Forward confusion, where the junior user is mistaken as being associated with the senior user, is discussed at the beginning of this chapter.)

Allowing a remedy for reverse confusion protects the senior user from losing control of its mark. Professor McCarthy refers to this situation as one where a larger company "rolls over" over the smaller senior user. McCarthy § 23:10. Courts recognize reverse confusion to protect the senior user's goodwill, prevent unjust enrichment of the junior user, and fulfill the primary intent of trademark law, which is minimizing consumer confusion by clearly showing a mark's source.

Although each circuit has its own likelihood-of-consumer-confusion test and may weigh factors differently, they nevertheless generally use the same likelihood-of-confusion factors in assessing reverse confusion. *Wreal, LLC v. Amazon.com*, 38 F.4th 114 (11th Cir. 2022), is illustrative of how a court might analyze the likelihood-of-consumer-confusion factors in a reverse-confusion case. In *Wreal*, the court applied standard likelihood-of-confusion factors to a reverse-confusion case where Wreal's senior FYRETV mark was allegedly infringed by Amazon's heavily marketed FIRETV. Though the products did not overlap in marketing or sales channels, some evidence showed consumers questioning an association between Wreal and Amazon, establishing potential reverse confusion despite differences between the marks and products. The court analyzed the case under the standard likelihood-of-confusion principles, showing that reverse confusion is assessed using the same factors. Nevertheless, in the context of the junior user's overshadowing the senior user's mark, the factors are weighed differently.

In reverse-confusion cases, the standard likelihood-of-confusion factors used in assessing trademark infringement are applied from the perspective of the smaller senior user's mark being infringed upon by the larger junior user, as opposed to the more typical scenario involving a larger senior user's mark being infringed by a smaller junior user. In analyzing such a case, courts may give different weights to each factor based on the marketplace's specifics, the parties' involved conduct, and the actual impact on consumers' perceptions. The ultimate goal is to assess the likelihood that an "appreciable number of ordinarily prudent purchasers" will be confused about the source of the goods or services because of the junior user's use of the mark.

a. Application of Likelihood-of-Confusion Factors

i. Strength of the Mark

In reverse confusion, the junior user's mark strength becomes crucial because a powerful mark from a larger company can overwhelm the senior user's mark, causing consumers to believe the senior user is the infringer. There is some disagreement over how to apply this factor. Some circuits focus on the relative strength of the junior user's mark compared to the senior user's mark. Others still consider the inherent strength of the senior user's mark. Professor McCarthy agrees it is appropriate to evaluate whether the junior user's stronger mark is overshadowing the senior user's weaker mark in the minds of consumers.

In *Wreal*, the strength analysis hinged on the reverse-confusion posture. In forward-confusion cases, the inherent distinctiveness of the plaintiff's mark is key since the junior user is trading on the senior user's goodwill. But in reverse confusion, like here, the issue is whether the junior user's commercial strength is eclipsing the senior user's identity. Amazon's extensive advertising and fireTV's market success showed the commercial strength of Amazon's mark, supporting Wreal's reverse-confusion claim and weighing this factor in its favor. To assess whether the junior user overshadows the senior user, proper analysis considers the relative strength of the marks in the marketplace.

ii. Similarity of the Marks

The similarity factor examines the marks' visual, auditory, and conceptual similarity. While important in both forward and reverse confusion, in reverse cases the focus is on whether the senior user's mark is being overshadowed or subsumed by the junior user's similar mark. The nearly identical nature of the marks here plays a critical role, as it does in forward confusion, but in reverse confusion, the concern is whether the public might believe the senior user's products come from the dominant junior user.

In reverse confusion, the similarity may lead consumers to think the senior user infringes on the junior user's mark, instead of the reverse. The overall similarity of the marks is vital since the senior user worries the junior user's commercial strength will dilute the senior mark's identity. In *Wreal*, the near phonetic identity and semantic similarity of "fire" in both marks established strong similarity despite spelling/style differences, and this similarity was compounded by use of the generic "TV," which did not differentiate the marks significantly.

Furthermore, unlike in forward confusion, a house mark like Amazon's does not necessarily dispel reverse confusion but may in fact worsen it. Amazon's use of its dominant house mark alongside FIRETV can reinforce the wrongful association between its product and Wreal's FYRETV mark, thereby increasing the likelihood of reverse confusion.

iii. Marketing Channels

In reverse-confusion cases, the junior user's extensive marketing may saturate the market, leading consumers to believe that the smaller senior user is an offshoot or imitator. Unlike forward confusion, where the focus is on the same consumers encountering both products, in reverse-confusion cases, the focus is on the extent of the junior user's marketing—the sheer scale of the junior user's marketing, not just overlapping promotion, is key in reverse-confusion analysis. In *Wreal*, Amazon's far-reaching marketing created reverse-confusion risks even though the companies promoted through different channels.

iv. Actual Confusion

In reverse-confusion cases, actual confusion evidence focuses on whether consumers associate the senior user with the junior user instead of the other way around, as occurs in typical forward-confusion cases. In *Wreal*, the court's analysis showed that at least a few consumers were confused by Amazon's mark. While forward-confusion evidence was useful in the case, direct reverse-confusion evidence was even more relevant: Wreal provided evidence that one of its customers had inquired whether Wreal merged with Amazon, and surveys by both parties indicated low rates of confusion. However, the court was reluctant to give significant weight to either type of evidence, keeping in mind an Amazon expert witness's claim that consumers of pornography are less likely to report their media consumption out of a sense of shame.

The court noted that even two instances of confusion can prove actual confusion based on context—here, despite only two reported cases indicating confusion, the expert witness's testimony as to pornography consumers' underreporting tendencies led the court to find there was sufficient triable evidence of actual confusion favoring Wreal. The court gave limited weight to the survey evidence, expressing its general skepticism of trademark surveys because of their inherent limitations and potential biases, and considered the specifically identified instances of actual consumer confusion more significant. This aligns with the circuit's broader tendency to be wary of survey evidence in trademark cases.

v. Consumer's Degree of Care

Reverse confusion can occur when a junior user's extensive marketing so swamps the senior user's reputation in the market that it affects consumer perceptions about the senior user's mark. In reverse-confusion cases, the dominant junior user's brand recognition and marketing reach shape consumers' view of the senior user's mark *over time*. A court's degree-of-care analysis will consider the products' nature and buyers' expected scrutiny, with a focus not on point-of-sale confusion but rather whether confusion has been caused by consumers' gradual association of the senior user's mark with the junior user's mark.

In *Wreal v. Amazon*, the court noted that the degree-of-care factor in reverse-confusion cases fundamentally differs from forward-confusion cases. The concern in *Wreal* was not confusion at the point of purchase; rather, the concern was whether Amazon's marketing saturation could potentially cause consumers to mistakenly associate Wreal with Amazon over time, even if buyers exercised care at the point of sale. In other words, Amazon's vast reach could shape consumer perceptions of Wreal's mark despite consumer care. The degree-of-care analysis accounts for this long-term associative confusion risk explicitly created by the junior user's influence in reverse-confusion situations.

vi. Defendant's Intent

Whether a defendant intentionally copied the senior mark to exploit its reputation is the key factor in forward-confusion cases. But in reverse-confusion cases, the more dominant junior user's intent to overwhelm the market and potentially subsume the senior user's mark in doing so can cause more subtle damage, even absent an intent to confuse. In *Wreal v. Amazon*, the court noted that the intent factor fundamentally differs between these types of cases: In forward-confusion cases, the defendant's intent to benefit from the plaintiff's reputation is pivotal. In reverse-confusion cases, however, the issue becomes whether the senior user's mark may be drowned out by the junior user's pervasive advertising, causing the public to mistakenly think the senior user's goods originate from the junior user.

The Ninth Circuit in *Marketquest Group, Inc. v. BIC Corp* has expressed a nuanced view of intent in reverse-confusion cases. Intent can be inferred from behaviors like willful ignorance of the senior user's mark, performing inadequate trademark searches, or demonstrating a general intent to dominate the market. This flexible approach acknowledges the reduced relevance of direct evidence of specific deceitful intent in the reverse-confusion context. *Marketquest Group, Inc. v. BIC Corp.*, 862 F.3d 927, 934 (9th Cir. 2017).

Applying the Ninth Circuit's standard in *Wreal*, the Eleventh Circuit found considerable evidence of problematic intent by Amazon. Its prior knowledge of Wreal's mark and later market-saturation strategy showed intent, supporting Wreal's reverse-confusion claim. The court concluded that Amazon likely intended to diminish the visibility of Wreal's mark, which shifted the intent factor in Wreal's favor, given the reverse-confusion posture.

vii. Likelihood of Expansion

In reverse-confusion cases, the potential for the larger junior user to expand and, in doing so, heighten the reverse-confusion risk is a key concern. Unlike in forward confusion, where the issue is the senior user's entering into the junior user's market, in reverse confusion, the issue is that the junior user's ability to expand can make it seem more plausible to consumers that the smaller senior user is infringing or exploiting the larger junior user's reputation. In *Wreal*, the appellate court noted that this expansion factor carries more weight in reverse-confusion cases. Amazon's demonstrated ability and intent to expand into many new markets increased the risk that it could overwhelm Wreal's mark if it entered Wreal's niche adult-streaming market. This expansion possibility increased the risk that Amazon could be perceived as the senior user while Wreal would be perceived as the infringing junior user riding on Amazon's coattails. The potential harms to Wreal included the misperception of Wreal as an infringer, loss of trademark value and corporate identity, and impeded market expansion.

b. Defenses in a Reverse-Confusion Case

While many defenses in reverse- and forward-confusion cases may overlap, there are some that are particularly relevant in the former. The following are some examples of such defenses: making a sophisticated-consumer argument showing that specific buyers are less likely to be confused even when the senior mark is obscure; emphasizing the mark users' different product/service markets, irrespective of the junior user's larger size; arguing that the goods/services bearing similar marks are noncompeting; demonstrating the use of prominent disclaimers distinguishing the junior user's products from the senior user's; making a niche market defense focusing on whether the junior user is overwhelming the senior user's specific market; demonstrating minimal commercial-activity overlap; and showing a lack of intent to confuse (though this is not needed). Overall, reverse-confusion defenses stress key contextual factors—niche markets, product differences, disclaimers, etc.—that may prevent the junior user from overshadowing the senior user, even if the marks are similar.

In reverse-confusion cases, the argument that infringement increased the senior user's brand value is generally ineffective. Though the senior user may see short-term attention or sales gains from the junior user's presence, this does not outweigh the long-term harm of reduced distinctiveness and loss of control over reputation/goodwill. The principal harm is not diverted sales but rather the senior mark's weakened identity. Even if the senior user experiences temporary economic benefits, reverse confusion can still dilute the uniqueness of the senior mark over time. Short-term gains do not address harm to the senior user's brand image if the junior user has inferior quality products/services or an incompatible reputation. Additionally, the goals of trademark law are to protect exclusive use rights and to minimize consumer confusion regarding product origins. The fact that infringement may incidentally benefit the senior user does not align with these purposes or negate marketplace confusion. Though this argument is unlikely to defend against liability, it may influence the damages awarded: courts may reduce monetary damages where the senior user did not suffer calculable losses. And injunctive relief would still be appropriate to stop ongoing confusion. See Chapter 12 for a discussion of general trademark infringement defenses.

c. Remedies in a Reverse-Confusion Case

Federal remedies aim to reestablish the senior user's commercial distinctiveness. The availability and extent of these remedies may depend on various factors, including the jurisdiction, the case's specific facts, and whether the infringement is intentional or willful. Injunctive relief, where a court orders the junior user to cease the activities causing confusion, is the most common remedy.

Another remedy is corrective advertising. Corrective advertising for a reasonable period may alleviate confusion by helping to re-establish the senior user's brand identity and clarify the distinction between the two marks for the public. In *Big O Tire Dealers, Inc. v. Goodyear Tire & Rubber Co.*, 561 F.2d 1365 (10th Cir. 1977), Big O, a regional tire distributor operating in fourteen states at the time of the case, sued Goodyear, the then-largest manufacturer of tires in the world, for infringement of Big O's BIGFOOT trademark. The jury found in favor of Big O, the senior user, and awarded significant damages for corrective advertising based on the amount of advertising Goodyear did nationally. The Tenth Circuit significantly reduced that award because the amount of corrective advertising needed was not proven to be based on Goodyear's total advertising budget, and Big O did not operate nationally.

Courts might also award the profits that the junior user wrongfully earned from the confusion, provide for the destruction or forfeiture of infringing items, and, in cases of willful infringement, award attorney fees and treble damages. Other remedies, such as punitive damages, may be available under state law. See Chapter 13 for a more detailed discussion of trademark remedies.

5. Initial-Interest Confusion

Initial-interest confusion is that which occurs at the earliest stages of the product-search process. Initial-interest confusion involves diversion of the consumer's interest from the trademarked product to a competing product, and it does not take into account whether the consumer is actually confused at the point of purchase. Initial-interest confusion is analogous to a bait-and-switch scheme, except that by the time the purchase is made, the purchaser is aware of the switch. Initial-interest confusion first came to prominence in *Mobil Oil Corp. v. Pegasus Petroleum Corp.*, 818 F.2d 254, 259 (2d Cir. 1987). In that case, an oil trader was using the word mark "Pegasus" for its business. Because one of Mobil Oil's trademarks is the image of Pegasus (the divine, winged horse in Greek mythology), other oil traders were contacting Pegasus Petroleum to engage in a transaction under the misapprehension that they were dealing with Mobil Oil. However, since the oil trading business is a small and discrete market where the traders are generally familiar with each other, no trader was actually confused at the time of entering into a contract to purchase oil. Nevertheless, the court concluded that Pegasus Petroleum had infringed Mobil Oil's flying horse trademark; Pegasus had made the sales as a result of the initial confusion created by their use of Mobil Oil's mark. *Id.* at 260.

Since *Pegasus Petroleum*, initial-interest confusion has developed into a theory often cited in infringement cases on the internet. The theory goes that when someone is directed to the wrong website, that is initial-interest confusion. However, courts have become generally more skeptical of any lasting harm in internet initial-interest cases, given how easy it is to correct the mistake. Initial interest on the internet and in the e-commerce context is discussed in Chapters 14 and 15.

E. Third-Party Liability or "Indirect Infringement"

Parties other than the direct infringer may be liable for trademark infringement, under generally recognized tort theories of indirect liability such as contributory and vicarious liability. Third-party liability is often useful since the direct infringers may be small, lack financial assets, and be challenging to locate and sue. A third party may be a flea market, website, or other party, and successful litigation against that third party may effectively prevent numerous acts of direct infringement.

1. Contributory Infringement

The test for contributory trademark infringement as initially formulated by the Supreme Court in *Inwood Laboratories, Inc. v. Ives Laboratories, Inc.*, 456 U.S. 844, 854 (1982), is as follows:

> [I]f a manufacturer or distributor intentionally induces another to infringe a trademark, or if it continues to supply its product to one whom it knows or has reason to know is engaging in trademark infringement, the manufacturer or distributor is contributorily responsible for any harm done as a result of the deceit.

This is narrower than liability for direct infringement, where proof of the defendant's intent is not necessary. To prove contributory infringement, the plaintiff must show either intent (for inducement) or knowledge (for continuing to supply). This latter category does permit a finding of liability for constructive knowledge under the "has reason to know" language.

By its terms, the Supreme Court's *Inwood* test applied to manufacturers or distributors of goods. Later, the test was expanded by lower courts to include liability for other third parties, including a theory of "landlord liability" often applied to owners of flea markets. Under this application of contributory liability, the owner of premises where infringing goods are sold may be liable if it knows or has reason to know that such goods are being sold on the premises. The court in *Hard Rock Cafe Licensing Corp. v. Concession Services, Inc.*, 955 F.2d 1143 (7th Cir. 1992), stated that a flea market owner could also be contributorily liable where it is guilty of "willful blindness," which the court held to be the equivalent of actual knowledge. To establish liability under willful blindness, the trademark owner must show that the defendant "suspect[ed] wrongdoing and deliberately fail[ed] to investigate." *Id.* at 1149.

The Second Circuit Court of Appeals stated that this theory can be extended to include websites like eBay. However, the court held in *Tiffany (NJ) Inc. v. eBay Inc.*, 600 F.3d 93 (2d Cir. 2010), that eBay could not be held contributorily liable where it only had generalized knowledge that counterfeit Tiffany products were being sold and acted to remove auctions of infringing goods when it was alerted to their existence.

If the defendant provides a service, then the plaintiff must show that the defendant had direct control of and monitored the service used to infringe the trademark. Actual knowledge is not required if the defendant is willfully blind. Regardless of the moral culpability of the third party, a third party cannot be held contributory liable unless there is a direct infringer and evidence of direct infringement.

2. Vicarious Infringement

To prove a claim of vicarious trademark infringement, the plaintiff must show that the defendant and the direct infringer have an actual or apparent partnership, that they have the authority to bind one another in transactions with third parties, or that they exercise joint ownership or control over the infringing product. So, if an authorized independent contractor (agent) concludes a transaction with a third party on behalf of the agent's principal, and if the principal benefits from the transaction, the principal may be vicariously liable for trademark infringement. The principal's liability is based on the agent's foreseeable infringing actions if a third party reasonably relied on the agent's representations and the third party has no notice that the representations were unauthorized.

F. Respondeat Superior and Employees

Under the doctrine of respondeat superior, a corporation or an employer may be liable for the trademark-infringing acts of its employees or officers. In addition, the employees and officers may be personally liable for their acts of trademark infringement. The fact that infringement occurs within the scope of an employee's employment does not shield the employee from personal liability. Accordingly, directors, officers, or managers who directly approve the infringing acts as well as ordinary employees who carry out their employer's trademark infringing policies, may be individually liable for trademark infringement, either directly or under principles of third-party liability.

G. Likelihood-of-Confusion Test and the First Amendment

In *Jack Daniel's Properties, Inc. v. VIP Prod. LLC*, 143 S. Ct. 1578 (2023), the Supreme Court considered whether the traditional test for likelihood of confusion was preempted by First Amendment free-speech considerations when a defendant alleged that its trademarks were parodies of the plaintiff's marks protected as an expressive use, and thus not subject to the traditional test. The Court held that if "a mark is used as a mark (except, potentially, in rare situations), the likelihood-of-confusion inquiry does enough work to account for the interest in free expression." *Id.* at 1591. Thus, no special First Amendment analysis is needed for situations where the defendant's use is of an allegedly infringing trademark.

The Court noted that the likelihood-of-confusion analysis could take account of the defendant's parody, which might lessen the likelihood that consumers would be confused. In this regard, the Supreme Court cited with approval *Louis Vuitton Malletier S. A. v. Haute Diggity Dog, LLC*, 507 F.3d 252 (4th Cir. 2007), in which the circuit court explained that the analysis of the likelihood-of-confusion factors should be modified to take account of the defendant's parodic use of the plaintiff's mark. The Fourth Circuit stated that if a parody is successful, that is, that consumers understand that the defendant is making fun of the plaintiff's mark, then the chance that consumers would believe the plaintiff was reduced. In particular, the Fourth Circuit noted that the more famous the plaintiff's trademark, the more likely source confusion would be all but eliminated.

CHECKPOINTS

- To prevail on a claim of trademark infringement under the Lanham Act, plaintiff must prove that (1) plaintiff has a protectable ownership interest in the mark, and (2) defendant's use of the mark is likely to cause consumer confusion.
- To determine whether a specific use creates a likelihood of consumer confusion, each federal circuit court, the PTO, and the individual state courts have established their own multi-factor tests. All tests

begin with the determination of who the relevant consumer is, and what the relevant consumer's standard of care is.

- The Ninth Circuit's test for the likelihood of confusion provides a good example of factors a court will consider: strength of the mark, proximity of the goods, the similarity of the marks, evidence of actual confusion, marketing channels used, type of goods and the degree of care likely to be exercised by the purchaser, defendant's intent in selecting the mark, the likelihood of expansion of the product lines, and other relevant factors.
- The likelihood-of-consumer-confusion factors are weighed differently in the reverse-confusion context.
- The Lanham Act not only prohibits the literal false designation of a good but also the economic equivalents of passing off, including reverse passing off, post-sale confusion, reverse confusion, and initial-interest confusion.
- Third-party liability is often useful since the direct infringers may be small, lack financial assets, and be difficult to locate and sue. Such third parties may be held liable under contributory and vicarious liability theories.
- Under the doctrine of respondeat superior, a corporation or an employer may be liable for the trademark-infringing acts of its employees or officers. Moreover, acts of trademark infringement under a corporate or business entity's guise do not shield individual officers or employees from personal liability.

CHAPTER 10

Trademark Infringement by Dilution

ROADMAP

- Infringement by dilution
- State law
- Federal law
- The elements of a dilution claim
- Dilution by blurring
- Dilution by tarnishment
- Federal preemption of state law dilution claims

A. Infringement by Trademark Dilution

While the origins of the traditional likelihood-of-confusion trademark infringement action can be traced back to ancient common law principles, trademark dilution is of recent statutory vintage, and its origins in the United States can be traced back to 1927. The concept of trademark dilution originated in England when a British court protected the trademark KODAK from being used on bicycles. In America, individual states, and then the federal government, recognized the need to provide additional protection for famous trademarks. Anti-dilution statutes have developed to correct traditional trademark infringement law's failure to stop the unauthorized use of trademarks where there is no likelihood of confusion.

The law of trademark dilution aims to protect the distinctive quality of a trademark from deterioration caused by its use on dissimilar products. Under this principle, famous trademarks have a more significant zone of protection than other trademarks. Like any other trademark, a famous trademark is protected from uses that are likely to cause consumer confusion. However, a famous mark is also protected against commercial uses that decrease the capacity of the famous trademark to serve as a single source identifier or commercial uses that tarnish the reputation of the trademark even without the likelihood of consumer confusion or competition between the famous mark owner and the entity using the famous mark. Since federal law generally does not preempt state trademark dilution laws, this is an area where the careful selection of a forum may convey a significant litigation advantage.

1. State Law Evolution

The theory of trademark dilution was first articulated in a 1927 law review article, Frank I. Schecter, *The Rational Basis of Trademark Protection*, 40 HARV. L. REV. 813 (1927). In 1947, Massachusetts was the first state to enact an anti-dilution statute. Today, roughly two-thirds of the states have some form of anti-dilution protection. Most states have created anti-dilution laws through statutes. Under many state anti-dilution statutes, a trademark owner may obtain protection if the alleged diluted trademark is distinctive (and there is a likelihood of dilution due to diminution in the uniqueness of the trademark), or if injury has resulted from use of the trademark in a manner that tarnishes or misappropriates the goodwill associated with the trademark. State protection encompasses distinctive as well as famous trademarks. A distinctive mark is strong but does not necessarily rise to the level of a famous trademark. A distinctive trademark is an arbitrary, a fanciful, a suggestive, or a descriptive mark that has, over time or through the efforts of the trademark owner, acquired strong secondary meaning. Thus, "Potato" for a line of personal computers may be a distinctive and arbitrary trademark—a very strong mark—but it would not be a famous mark. For a variety of reasons, state anti-dilution laws are rarely invoked and even more rarely result in liability. Even today, state anti-dilution claims often only receive cursory analysis and are erroneously treated by courts as synonymous with the federal dilution claim.

2. Federal Dilution Law

Two major federal laws have attempted to protect famous trademarks from dilution. The first, the Federal Trademark Dilution Act (FTDA), is generally considered a failure; the U.S. Supreme Court limited the scope of the FTDA to cases where there was proof of actual dilution because of how the statute was written. Congress had to step in and pass the Trademark Dilution Revision Act (TDRA) to resolve numerous intra-circuit conflicts and to clarify the scope of federal dilution protection.

a. The FTDA

The Federal Trademark Dilution Act (FTDA) was enacted in 1996 and excluded noncommercial uses, parody, satire, and editorial expression from its reach. The FTDA adopted much of its language from state statutes.

The significant differences are that the FTDA

- limited the dilution claim to famous trademarks;
- required proof of actual trademark dilution rather than likelihood of dilution;
- provided for nationwide injunctive relief;
- provided for monetary relief in cases of "willful" dilution; and
- recognized a new defense that defendant's ownership of a federal registration acts as a bar to plaintiff's claims based on state statutory or common law.

As a trademark law that was national in scope, the FTDA purported to provide a uniform federal law protecting famous marks, so that owners of famous marks did not have to rely on a patchwork of state laws to protect their trademarks from being "whittled away" by non-confusing uses from junior trademark owners.

Early cases under the FTDA needed to be clarified, but more importantly, they were conflicting. The U.S. circuit courts were split on whether the merchant needed to prove actual dilution or merely a likelihood that the alleged use of the famous mark diluted the famous mark. The circuits were also split on what constituted a famous mark since the FTDA did not define the term "famous." Some circuits recognized "niche" fame, where a trademark is famous in a geographical region or among a very select group of consumers. Moreover, it was unclear whether the FTDA protected only inherently distinctive famous marks, or if it also protected marks with acquired distinctiveness (those that had developed secondary meaning). In at least one circuit, the court interpreted the FTDA as requiring a famous and distinctive trademark. This court held that a mark that initially required proof of secondary meaning to function as a trademark was not protected under the FTDA, regardless of how "famous" it was; therefore, trademarks that were initially descriptive terms, regardless of their eventual acquisition of secondary meaning or indeed fame, would never be protected under the FDTA. In terms of creating a predictable and uniform national federal law prohibiting trademark dilution, the FTDA was a failure.

The intra-circuit conflicts came to a head in *Moseley v. V Secret Catalogue, Inc.*, 537 U.S. 418 (2003). The Moseleys ran a small business called Victor's Little Secret, that sold adult products including women's lingerie. The national chain Victoria's Secret objected and filed a complaint alleging, *inter alia*, likelihood of consumer confusion and trademark dilution. At summary judgment, the trial court found no likelihood of consumer confusion, which left only the claim of trademark dilution by blurring or tarnishment. The Supreme Court held that the FTDA did not protect against the likelihood of dilution, only actual dilution. There was nothing in the record to show actual dilution, and the *Moseley* case provided no guidance on how to prove actual dilution. *Moseley* dramatically reduced the effectiveness of the FTDA because owners of famous trademarks often wished to seek injunctive relief to prevent harm to such trademarks rather than to wait until a famous trademark was diluted and the goodwill associated with it had been harmed. Because of the Court's holding in *Moseley*, the intra-circuit splits on other issues, and other perceived faults in the FTDA, famous trademark owners and industry associations immediately began to lobby Congress for a new law protecting famous trademarks.

b. Moseley *and the Trademark Dilution Revision Act (TDRA)*

In 2006, Congress enacted the Trademark Dilution Revision Act (TDRA), codified as Lanham Act § 43(c). The TDRA corrected many of the perceived failings of the FTDA. For example, the TDRA legislatively overruled *Moseley* and established that a likelihood of dilution is sufficient for injunctive relief. The TDRA also rejected the concept of niche fame and defined a famous mark as "widely recognized by the general consuming public of the United States as a designation of source of the goods or services of the mark's owner." The TDRA formally recognized two forms of trademark dilution as actionable: dilution by blurring and dilution by tarnishment. Finally, under the TDRA, no distinction is made between marks that are inherently distinctive and those that have acquired distinctiveness. The TDRA is in effect today.

B. TDRA: Elements of a Trademark-Infringement-by-Dilution Case

The TDRA protects trademarks that are famous against commercial uses that are likely to cause dilution by blurring or dilution by tarnishment. First a court must determine whether the trademark is famous, Lanham Act § 43(c)(2)(A); then a court must determine if the challenged use of the famous mark either blurs the mark (lessens the capacity of the trademark to serve as a single source identifier), Lanham Act § 43(c)(2)(B), or tarnishes the mark (the challenged use injures the reputation or goodwill associated with the famous mark), Lanham Act § 43(c)(2)(C).

1. Famous Trademarks

The TDRA defines a famous mark as being "widely recognized by the general consuming public of the United States as a designation of source of the goods or services of the mark's owner." Lanham Act § 43(c)(2)(A). However, neither the TDRA nor the case law has established the degree of fame necessary under this definition to be protected as a famous trademark. One prominent treatise author suggested that between 50 percent and 75 percent (or more) of the trademark owner's consumers must be aware of the trademark before it could be considered famous. One court has described the level of fame as follows: "In other words, the mark must be a household name." *Board of Regents, Univ. of Texas Sys. v. KST Elec.*, 550 F. Supp. 2d 657, 674 (W.D. Tex. 2008).

The TDRA reduced from eight to four the factors that a court may consider to determine fame. Under the TDRA, a court may consider the following:

1. The duration, extent, and geographic reach of advertising and publicity of the trademark
2. The amount, volume, and geographic extent of sales of the goods or services offered under the trademark
3. The extent of actual recognition of the trademark
4. Federal registration of the trademark

The first three factors are obvious for a court to consider when determining whether a trademark is famous; each of these factors considers evidence relevant to the question of fame and measures the extent to which the consuming public has been exposed to the trademark. The first two factors consider indirect (circumstantial) evidence of fame. A famous mark is likely to be linked with a great deal of associated advertising and publicity, and to have achieved high sales. Even so, many marks are used on goods and services that have achieved national success but are not famous in the minds of consumers. For example, in considering the national prominence of the University of Texas's longhorn steer silhouette mark, which is well-known by viewers of college football, the court held that "it is not at all clear that if one is not a college football fan (or, to a much lesser extent, college baseball or basketball fan) would [*sic*] recognize the [longhorn steer logo] as being associated with [University of Texas], as all of the evidence relates to the use of the logo in sporting events." *Board of Regents, Univ. of Texas*, 550 F. Supp. 2d at 678.

The third factor, the extent of actual recognition of the mark, looks directly at consumer perceptions of the mark. Here, it is common for the plaintiff to introduce survey evidence to support the mark's fame. It is important that the surveys conducted reach a national audience. If only the plaintiff's local market is surveyed, then this would fail to establish that the mark is widely recognized by consumers nationally.

Inclusion of the fourth factor, whether the mark is federally registered, is not so obvious. Logically, if a trademark is genuinely famous, then it is valuable. The best way to protect a valuable trademark is through registration. Thus, if the trademark owner cannot be bothered to obtain a trademark registration, then the trademark is unlikely to be famous for the purposes of trademark dilution.

It is common for courts to be cursory in their review of evidence supporting the fame of the plaintiff's mark. For example, in evaluating whether STARBUCKS is a famous mark, one court noted while only a limited number of marks are famous under the TDRA, "that the Starbucks Marks are 'famous' within the meaning of 43(c) is not disputed by the parties in this case." *Starbucks Corp. v. Wolfe's Borough Coffee, Inc.*, 588 F.3d 97, 105 (2d Cir. 2009). The same court spent a scant two short paragraphs summarizing the evidence of STARBUCKS's fame in a subsequent appeal. *Starbucks Corp. v. Wolfe's Borough Coffee, Inc.*, 736 F.3d 198 (2d Cir. 2013). Similarly, in evaluating a dilution claim brought by Louis Vuitton Malletier S.A., another court stated simply that "LVM has adopted trademarks and trade dress that are well recognized and have become famous and distinct," noting that *Business Week* had ranked LOUIS VUITTON as the 17th best brand in the world. *Louis Vuitton Malletier S.A. v. Haute Diggity Dog, LLC*, 507 F.3d 252, 257 (4th Cir. 2007). Meanwhile, other courts have spent pages on the history of the mark, market size, the revenues associated with the mark, and other indicia of how the U.S. consuming public understands the mark.

2. Dilution by Blurring

The TDRA specifically recognizes dilution by blurring as actionable and establishes a six-factor test that courts may consider when determining whether an "association arising from the similarity between a mark or trade name and a famous mark that impairs the distinctiveness of the famous mark" arose. The six factors are

1. The degree of similarity between the non-famous and famous trademarks
2. The degree of inherent or acquired distinctiveness of the famous trademark
3. The extent to which the famous mark's owner is engaging in substantially exclusive use of the trademark
4. The degree of recognition of the famous trademark
5. Whether the use of the non-famous mark intended to create an association with the famous trademark
6. Whether there is any actual association between the non-famous mark and the famous trademark

Lanham Act § 43(c)(2)(B).

Under the first factor, a court compares the sight, sound, and meaning of the famous and non-famous trademarks. The more similar the two marks, the more likely it is that the court will find that this factor weighs in favor of the famous trademark owner. The Second Circuit has noted that the more recent version of § 43(c) under the TDRA does not require that the defendant's mark be substantially similar to be dilutive of the plaintiff's mark, and it has overturned its earlier precedent under the FTDA which held that the marks had to be substantially similar for there to be dilution.

The second factor requires the court to consider the famous trademark's strength. Famous trademarks that are arbitrary, fanciful, or suggestive are stronger than those that are descriptive with acquired secondary meaning. However, over time, a descriptive trademark, through long use, market position, advertising, or free publicity may become a strong mark. As the famous trademark becomes commercially stronger, this factor increasingly weighs in favor of the famous trademark owner.

The third factor requires that the court consider other uses of the famous trademark. For example, terms like Acme, American, United States, or Federal may be part of many famous trademarks, yet there are numerous legitimate users of these terms as parts of non-famous trademarks. The more frequently others use the famous mark, the less likely this factor will weigh in favor of the famous trademark's being blurred. However, the plaintiff's use need not be entirely exclusive; some use by others will be tolerated.

The fourth factor weighs the consuming public's recognition of the famous trademark. The more widely recognized the famous trademark, the more likely the use will blur it.

The fifth factor measures the intent of the owner of the non-famous trademark. If the non-famous trademark owner adopted its trademark to create an association between the two trademarks, the court will weigh this factor in favor of finding blurring. The Second Circuit has noted that proof of an intent to create an association is just a factor and does not create a presumption of actual association. If it did, that would read the final factor out of the statute. If the non-famous trademark owner adopted its trademark innocently or in good faith, the court will weigh this factor in favor of the non-famous trademark owner. With good faith, the court's focus is not on the lack of knowledge of the famous mark but on whether the junior user could have honestly believed that there was a legal basis on which it could appropriate the mark.

Finally, although not required, proof that there is an actual association between the famous trademark and the non-famous trademark weighs heavily in finding dilution by blurring.

3. Dilution by Tarnishment

To protect the reputations of famous marks from being harmed by negative associations with similar marks, regardless of whether the similar marks create a likelihood of consumer confusion, the TDRA prohibits dilution by tarnishment. Under theories of dilution by tarnishment, courts have enjoined uses of similar-looking trademarks that bring the famous mark into disrepute. For example, Geoffrey, LLC, the owner of the famous trademark TOYS 'R' US for children's toys, was able to enjoin the designation "Adults 'R' Us" for adult products. *See Geoffrey, Inc. v. Toys 'R Us, Inc.*, 756 F. Supp. 661 (D.P.R. 1991).

To illustrate the potential effects of dilution by tarnishment, think of your favorite famous national-brand beverage. Imagine that someone starts to sell toilet bowl cleaner using the same trademark. We can speculate that at least some consumers will feel "yucky" or experience discomfort when purchasing their favorite famous beverage because of the association with the toilet bowl cleaner. Now consider whether you would serve this beverage to guests at a party and the associated comments or jokes that may be made—would you be more or less likely to purchase this beverage again the next time you shop? Defenses to trademark dilution are discussed in Chapter 12, and remedies are discussed in Chapter 13.

4. Federal Registration Bars State Dilution Actions

Federal trademark registration on the Principal Register bars an action against the registered mark based on state statutory or common law dilution claims. Lanham Act § 43(c)(6).

CHECKPOINTS

- Trademark infringement by dilution aims to protect the distinctive quality of a trademark from deterioration caused by its use on dissimilar products, and protects trademarks even when consumer confusion does not exist.
- Trademark infringement by dilution is a creature of statute, enacted first by the states, and followed by the federal government.
- Early federal legislation, the FTDA, was a failure that resulted in confusion and split circuit court authority.
- Congress, acting in response to *Victoria's Secret*, enacted the TDRA in 2006; it remains in force today. It clarifies confusing points under the FTDA and provides causes of action for trademark infringement by blurring and tarnishment.
- There are two types of dilution: dilution by blurring and dilution by tarnishment.

- The prohibition against dilution by blurring seeks to prevent a famous mark's distinctiveness from being impaired by association with similar marks, something that is often referred to as the gradual "whittling away" of the mark's distinctiveness.
- Dilution by tarnishment occurs when an association is made between the famous mark and the diluting mark that harms the famous mark's reputation, for instance, when the famous mark is erroneously linked with goods of shoddy quality or an unwholesome portrayal of the mark.

CHAPTER 11

False or Deceptive Commercial Advertising

ROADMAP

- False or deceptive commercial advertising
- The elements of a § 43(a)(1)(B) claim
- False speech
- Commercial speech
- Materially influencing a consumer's decision
- Damages to the plaintiff
- Remedies
- Actual damages
- Defendant's profits
- Corrective advertising
- Goodwill
- Enhanced damages
- Attorney fees
- Defenses

A. False or Deceptive Commercial Advertising

Section 43(a)(1)(B) of the Lanham Act provides that "[a]ny person who ... in commercial advertising or promotion, misrepresents the nature, characteristics, qualities, or geographic origin of his or her or another person's goods, services, or commercial activities, shall be liable in a civil action by any person who believes that he or she is or is likely to be damaged by such act." Under the Lanham Act, a court will not review the truthfulness of speech relating to political, religious, or social issues unless that speech is associated with commercial speech. Section 43(a) does not encompass political speech or other expressive speech that is not of a commercial nature. The difference between commercial speech and political or religious speech will be discussed further in section B.2 of this chapter.

B. Standing

Although the Lanham Act refers to *any person*, courts have narrowly interpreted this language, limiting standing under § 43(a)(1)(B) to competitors or other commercial entities—individual consumers do not have standing to bring an action under this section. However, individual consumers may have standing to sue under other federal laws, state laws, or state mini-Federal Trade Commission Acts that prohibit unfair and deceptive commercial trade practices.

C. The Elements of a § 43(a)(1)(B) Claim

Under the Lanham Act, the four elements of a § 43(a)(1)(B) claim are as follows:

1. That the defendant made *false or misleading factual representations*
2. That the defendant used the false or misleading representations *in commerce*

3. That the *deceptions are material* and likely to influence consumer decisions
4. That the defendant's actions made the plaintiff believe that it is *likely to be damaged* by such false or misleading factual representations

1. First Element: False or Misleading Speech

Commercial speech may be honest and accurate, in which case it is constitutionally protected under the First Amendment, or the speech may be false or misleading. The First Amendment does not protect false or deceptive commercial speech. Courts have categorized false or deceptive speech as either explicitly or implicitly false. Explicitly and implicitly false statements are analyzed differently.

a. Explicitly or Literally False Statements

An explicit or literally false statement is a statement that is false on its face. For example, if a product is advertised as "100% cotton" when, in fact, the fabric is a "75% cotton/25% polyester blend," then that statement is literally false. If a court finds that a statement is literally or explicitly false, the court may enjoin the use of that statement without further considering the consumer perception or the impact on the consumer.

b. Implicitly False Statements

Implicitly false statements are more problematic. An implicitly false statement is a statement that is literally true but likely to mislead a significant portion of consumers. Before enjoining the advertisement, the court will require evidence of how reasonable consumers understand the message conveyed by the implicitly false statement. The plaintiff has to produce evidence that consumers were actually deceived, not that they may have been deceived. Often this requires that the plaintiff produce consumer surveys or other evidence of consumer perceptions of the advertisement. Courts have been unwilling or unable to establish a bright-line rule regarding how many consumers must be deceived. It is safe to say that if the results of the consumer surveys demonstrate that less than 15 percent of the relevant consumer population is deceived, a court is unlikely to find that the plaintiff met its burden of proof.

However, the plaintiff may avoid the need for consumer surveys if it can demonstrate that the defendant egregiously and intentionally set out to deceive the public. If so, then the court may presume that the public was, in fact, deceived. Once the court finds deceptive intent, the burden will then shift to the defendant to show that consumers were not, in fact, deceived.

c. Statements Based on Tests

A statement based on a test is literally false if the scientific test or study does not support the claims or if the test is not sufficiently scientifically reliable to support the claims. The Supreme Court established how courts should evaluate scientific data in *Daubert v. Merrell Dow Pharmaceuticals, Inc.*, 509 U.S. 579 (1993). The *Daubert* test is a standard employed by federal courts to evaluate the admissibility of expert witness testimony. It requires that scientific evidence be both relevant and reliable. Courts consider several factors: whether the theory or technique can be tested, has been subjected to peer review, has a known or potential error rate, adheres to standards controlling its operation, and has attained general acceptance within the relevant scientific community. Generally, a test is reliable if its methodology or results are accepted as such by experts in the field and are consistent with the weight of scientific authority or more recent research.

2. Second Element: Commercial Speech

The U.S. Supreme Court still needs to provide a bright-line test to distinguish between commercial and noncommercial speech. Courts have held the difference to be one of degree. Commercial speech, at its core, is speech that proposes or promotes commercial transactions. Courts have instructed that a commonsense test should be used to distinguish between commercial speech in areas historically regulated by the government and other varieties of speech entitled to a substantially higher level of First Amendment protection. Merely linking commercial speech to speech traditionally afforded a higher level of First Amendment protection does not insulate it from review by the courts. The Court has been willing to tolerate limited government regulation and impose civil liability for false commercial speech because

> commercial speakers have extensive knowledge of both the market and their products. Thus, they are well situated to evaluate the accuracy of their messages.... In addition, commercial speech, the offspring of economic self-interest, is a hardy breed of expression that is not 'particularly susceptible to being crushed by overbroad regulation.'

Central Hudson Gas & Elec. Corp. v. Pub. Serv. Comm'n, 447 U.S. 557, 564 n.6 (1980).

To determine whether speech is "commercial speech," courts consider three factors:

1. Whether the communication is an advertisement
2. Whether the communication refers to a specific product or service
3. Whether the speaker had an economic motive for the speech

These factors are not dispositive but do provide "strong support" that the speech in question is commercial speech. But because a court's determination of whether the challenged speech is commercial speech is often dispositive, it is necessary to understand how the courts understand these factors.

a. Whether the Communication Is an Advertisement

The concept of "advertisements" is not limited to billboards, television or radio advertisements, or similar formal communications to the public. In this context, advertising means speech that is communicated to the public or calculated to be communicated to the public. So, issuing a press release or spreading a rumor that one knows will be repeated or end up in the media may be considered an advertisement.

b. Whether the Communication Refers to a Specific Product or Service

A communication does not have to specifically name the product as long as the consuming public is aware of the product or service that the speech references. If a business has a significant market share, the product may not be mentioned at all. So, if a major fast-food hamburger chain with a significant market share were to run "public service announcements" falsely denigrating the health effects of fried chicken, this would be problematic. A court may find that by decreasing fried chicken sales, the hamburger chain will increase hamburger sales generally and profit from this general increase in hamburger sales, even if there is no mention of a specific fried chicken franchise or specific hamburger franchise.

c. Whether the Speaker Had an Economic Motive for the Speech

Under the third factor, courts are careful to distinguish between speech primarily motivated by religious or political reasons and speech merely proposing a commercial transaction. The mere fact that a speaker profits from the speech does not require a finding of an economic motivation. In *Procter & Gamble Co. v. Amway Corp.*, 242 F.3d 539, 553 n.28 (5th Cir. 2001), the court provided a hypothetical example involving an owner of a Christian book and music store who tells customers that they should only buy Christian rock music because the devil influences more mainstream rock music. A court evaluating her economic motivation would be influenced by whether she started the book and music store out of sincerely and strongly-held religious beliefs that Christian music was needed to combat the evils of mainstream culture. If so, this would be evidence of a primarily religious rather than economic motivation for the speech. On the other hand, if the record showed her to be an agnostic who only opened a Christian book and music store because it would be highly profitable, this would be evidence that her speech was economically motivated and thus commercial. If the speech was religiously motivated, it is protected regardless of its objective truth; however, if it was economically motivated and false, the speaker is subject to civil penalties under the Lanham Act.

3. Third Element: Materiality

Whether a statement is material is an intensively fact-specific question that asks whether the statement is one that an appreciable number of ordinary prudent consumers would rely on in purchasing decisions. The court must determine who is the ordinary prudent consumer, what factors would play a significant role in the consumer's decision-making process, and whether the false statement would be significant or germane to that process. Imagine a car commercial that offers a new vehicle for 25,000 bananas as part of the dealer's "Make a Monkey Out of Me Sale." Although price is clearly a significant factor in most new car purchasing decisions, it is not likely that an ordinary prudent consumer would show up at the dealership with a truckload of bananas as payment for the new car.

4. Fourth Element: Damages

The plaintiff must be able to prove that the false advertisements damaged him or her. Damages may consist of lost sales, lost profits, injury to the plaintiff's goodwill, or the expenses of running corrective advertisements to protect sales, market share, or goodwill.

D. Remedies

As in other trademark actions, a court may award the prevailing plaintiff actual damages, defendant's profits, corrective advertising, enhanced damages, and attorney fees (to either party in exceptional cases).

1. Actual Damages

If the statement is literally false or the plaintiff demonstrates that the defendant actually intended to deceive consumers, the court may award actual damages. The plaintiff must demonstrate that there is a causal relationship between the lost sales and the false advertising: after the false advertising commenced, the plaintiff lost sales. The defendant may respond by showing that there were intervening factors other than the false advertising that accounted for lost sales. For example, the defendant might show that lost sales were due to changes in public taste. In the case of comparative advertising, some courts presume a causal relationship.

2. Defendant's Profits

If the defendant's actions were willful or in bad faith, the court may award the defendant's profits to the plaintiff to prevent the defendant's unjust enrichment, to prevent damage to the plaintiff, or to deter future bad conduct. A defendant is unjustly enriched when it retains profits from its illicit conduct. Determining the gross value of the sales associated with the illicit activity and subtracting the reasonable costs associated with those sales is the method used to calculate the defendant's profits. The net sum yielded by this calculation is the reasonable profit available.

3. Corrective Advertising

If the plaintiff had to budget additional sums to respond to the false advertising, the court may award these additional advertising expenditures as damages. The plaintiff does not have to prove that the corrective advertising was directed solely at correcting the commercial impression of the false advertisement. Rather, the plaintiff merely has to prove that but for the false advertisement, these funds would not have been spent. The amount expended by the plaintiff merely has to be reasonable, so this amount may be higher than the defendant's advertising expenditures. Courts accept that a reasonably prudent businessperson may spend more on advertising to protect his or her brand image than the defendant spent in injuring the brand image.

4. Compensation for Loss of Goodwill

If the defendant's false advertising, usually in the context of comparative advertising, harms the commercial reputation (goodwill) of the plaintiff, then the court may award an amount to compensate for the damage to the plaintiff's goodwill. Harm to the plaintiff's goodwill may be difficult to prove. Often the plaintiff will show that its sales continued to decline or did not recover even after the false advertising ceased. Because calculating damage to the plaintiff's goodwill may be speculative or difficult, some courts have justified injury to the plaintiff's goodwill as a basis for enhanced damages.

5. Enhanced Damages

Under Lanham Act § 35, the judge may increase damages up to three times the amount of the actual damages. Enhanced damages serve as a form of compensation and may not be awarded as either a penalty, punitive damages, or to deter future bad conduct. The court will award enhanced damages when actual damages are difficult to quantify, for example, as when there is an injury to the plaintiff's goodwill. However, if the plaintiff also pled a *state common law unfair competition claim*, the plaintiff may be entitled to punitive damages under state law.

6. Attorney Fees

The Lanham Act has an attorney fees shifting provision. Generally, in the United States, each party pays his or her own attorney fees. However, Lanham Act § 35 permits the court in its sound discretion to award attorney fees to the prevailing party when equitable considerations justify such an award. Under the Lanham Act, either the plaintiff or the defendant may be the prevailing party for the purposes of the award of attorney fees. The prevailing party has the burden of showing that it is entitled to attorney fees by producing clear and convincing evidence of exceptional circumstances. Section 35 does not define the term "exceptional." Courts have found exceptional cases under the

Lanham Act if there was malicious, fraudulent, deliberate, or willful conduct or a showing that the losing party pursued groundless claims in bad faith or for purposes of harassment. Merely prevailing on the claim's merits is insufficient to demonstrate exceptional circumstances.

E. Defenses

Defenses to a § 43(a)(1)(B) false or deceptive advertising claim include that the speech was in fact truthful, that the speech was not commercial speech, or that the plaintiff was not in fact actually injured by the alleged misleading or false speech. However, the most common defense is "puffery." The truth or falsity of the statement is not an element of a puffery defense. Puffery refers to exaggerated or boastful statements about a product or service that are subjective rather than objective in nature, typically opinions that no reasonable person would take literally. These statements are not considered misleading in a legal sense because they are not quantifiable facts that can be proven true or false; in other words, they are merely opinions. An example of puffery would be a claim that a particular brand of coffee is "the best in the world." Such a statement is considered a subjective opinion that is not measurable or verifiable, and thus is not likely to mislead consumers in the way that a claim about the coffee's containing a specific percentage of a particular ingredient that it did not contain would. In false advertising cases under the Lanham Act, courts have consistently distinguished puffery from actionable misrepresentations. Other possible defenses are discussed in Chapter 12.

CHECKPOINTS

- The Lanham Act provides a cause of action for plaintiffs damaged by false advertising.
- The elements of the claim are (1) that the defendant made false or misleading material factual statements; (2) that the defendant used those misrepresentations in commerce; (3) that the misrepresentations are material; and (4) that the plaintiff believes that it is likely to be damaged by the false or misleading representations.

- There are a number of available types of damages, including actual damages, disgorgement of the defendant's profits, the cost of running corrective advertising, the value of damage to the plaintiff's goodwill, exceptional damages where the amount of damages is difficult to calculate, and attorney fees.
- Defenses to a false or misleading advertising claim are that the First Amendment protected the speech, the speech was not commercial, and that there was no actual damage to the plaintiff.
- The most common defense is puffery, or that the false claim was so outrageous that a reasonable consumer would not believe it or would not rely on the statement in making a purchasing decision.

CHAPTER 12

Defenses to Infringement

ROADMAP

- Senior-user or prior-user defense
- Junior-user defense (the "*Tea Rose-Rectanus*" doctrine)
- Fair use
- Statutory fair use
- Nominative fair use
- Parody and other First Amendment defenses
- Special concerns with dilution
- Genericism/merely descriptive marks
- Functionality
- Equitable defenses
- Statute of limitations
- Acquiescence/laches
- Unclean hands
- Antitrust/misuse

Generally, there are two types of trademark defenses: active and passive. An active defense challenges the validity of the mark itself. Passive defenses claim that the use of the mark is either legally excused or non-infringing because the challenged use creates no likelihood of consumer confusion.

A. Senior-User and Intermediate Junior-User Defenses

Note: For the discussion in Section A, where the plaintiff owns a registration for its mark, we will refer to them as the "registrant," rather than the "plaintiff," to highlight that they own the registered mark and to eliminate possible confusion. Typically, the registrant will be the party that sues the other trademark user for infringement, and so would be the plaintiff in the case.

1. Senior User

As discussed in Chapter 7, trademark rights are generally based on the legal principle of "first in time, first in right." A good faith, first in time, first in right, common law use of a trademark is a valid defense to a trademark infringement claim under Lanham Act § 32 based on infringement of a registered trademark. Such a defense can either result in the defendant's proving ultimate ownership of the mark instead of the registrant; divided ownership with the registrant in remote or differing markets; or the defendant's having rights subject to limitations imposed by the registrant's registration. This section will review the latter two concepts, particularly to the effect of the registrant's federal registration on the defendant's common law rights.

The Lanham Act recognizes the first principle as the senior-user defense. Obviously, if the parties each claim common law rights in their mark, the court will focus on who first developed trademark rights, as explained in Chapter 7. That person will then be determined to be the owner of the mark.

However, where the registrant (as noted for our purposes, the plaintiff) has registered its mark, the protections of the Lanham Act for registered marks will change the analysis.

The senior-user defense protects users who acquired valid common law trademark rights before the date of the registrant's application of the mark in its registration. This priority exists because the constructive-use benefit granted to the registrant under § 7(c) does not apply when the defendant's common law rights precede the date of the registrant's application. Lanham Act § 7(c)(1). If the defendant has absolute priority, that is, the defendant's first use precedes both the registrant's date of application and first use, then the defendant's common law rights might even trump the registrant's registration. Whether this is true will depend on whether the registrant's registration has become incontestable. See Chapter 8 for a discussion of incontestability.

If the registrant's registration is not incontestable, then it is subject to cancellation under Lanham Act § 14 by the defendant, the party with absolute common law priority. The parties will have to litigate to determine their respective rights in the mark based solely on common law rights and free of any benefits from the registrant's registration.

However, if the registrant's registration is incontestable under Lanham Act § 15, the registrant's ownership of the mark cannot be challenged by the defendant. Combining the registrant's lack of constructive-use rights under § 7(c)(1) with the incontestability of the registrant's rights to claim ownership under § 15 results in the registrant only having prima facie rights to the mark under § 7(b). Of course, the registrant will receive an evidentiary advantage, namely, that the registration is "prima facie evidence of the validity of the registered mark and of the registration of the mark, of the owner's ownership of the mark, and of the owner's exclusive right to use the registered mark in commerce on or in connection with the goods or services specified in the certificate...." Lanham Act § 7(b).

However, that evidentiary benefit is only prima facie and can be overcome by evidence submitted by the defendant. Thus, the registrant's right to use the mark will be subject to any common law rights provable by the defendant that are superior to the registrant's rights, limiting the registrant to only what it can prove at common law as well (since the registrant's rights are only prima facie valid, not conclusively valid). As a result, the registrant's rights could be reduced to effectively nothing.

2. Section 33(b)(5): Limited-Area Exception

Another circumstance exists where the defendant's first use date is after the registrant's first use date (that is, the registrant is the senior user in absolute terms). However, the defendant's use began before the registrant's Lanham constructive-use rights attached (before the registrant filed its application). Cases refer to this scenario as the limited area exception. Lanham Act § 33(b)(5) provides that the defendant who adopts and uses its mark in good faith and without knowledge of the registrant's prior use will possess circumscribed common law trademark rights. These rights are limited to the relevant goods or services in the area where the defendant used its mark in good faith sufficiently to establish trademark rights.

Because the limited area defense only protects the defendant's rights in the area where the defendant used its mark before the registrant's application, the defendant's rights are essentially frozen. The defendant cannot expand its use of the mark beyond the territory where it operated when the registrant filed its application. Some courts may be willing to grant the user a small natural zone of expansion in relationship to territory or types of goods or services protected by its common law trademark rights.

The limited-area-exception defense lasts only as long as the senior user continuously uses the mark and does not abandon it. The limited area defense may be asserted against the registrant even after the registrant's registered mark has become incontestable under the Lanham Act § 15.

3. Remote Intermediate Junior-User Defense— The "*Tea Rose-Rectanus*" Doctrine

Two pre-Lanham Act cases, *Hanover Star Milling Co. v. Metcalf ("Tea Rose")*, 240 U.S. 403 (1916), and *United Drug Co. v. Theodore Rectanus Co.*, 248 U.S. 90 (1918), are the basis for the common law trademark *Tea Rose-Rectanus* doctrine. The *Tea Rose-Rectanus* junior-user defense elements are that (1) the junior user's first use was in good faith and (2) its first use was in a remote area. The *Tea Rose-Rectanus* doctrine permits concurrent trademark rights by users in different geographically remote markets independently developed by the junior user if the junior user adopted the mark in good faith and the senior user has not yet developed consumer association for its mark in the junior user's territory.

Courts are unclear about whether *mere* knowledge of the senior user's use of the mark is sufficient by itself to support a finding of a bad-faith trademark adoption by the junior user. *See GTE Corp. v. Williams*, 904 F.2d 536 (10th Cir. 1990). The more persuasive line of cases holds that a junior user's mere knowledge of another's use of the mark is insufficient evidence to support a finding of bad faith. Instead, these cases hold that courts should focus on whether the junior user is attempting to benefit from the reputation of the senior user's mark.

If the junior user asserts the *Tea Rose-Rectanus* defense, the senior user must then show that its trademarked goods or services have penetrated the junior user's territory, causing a likelihood of consumer confusion. If the senior user successfully proves its common law rights in the junior user's area of doing business, the damages will be limited to the senior user's area of market penetration.

The *Tea Rose-Rectanus* doctrine has a significant limitation. It applies only if both users have common law trademarks, and it does not apply if the plaintiff's mark is registered because the Lanham Act provides that trademark registration constitutes nationwide constructive notice of the registrant's claim to the mark.

B. Fair Use

The fair use defense has two distinct forms: "classic" or statutory fair use and the newer "nominative" fair use. *New Kids on the Block v. News America Publ'g, Inc.*, 971 F.2d 302 (9th Cir. 1992). Classic fair use is distinguished from nominative fair use based on the nature of the allusion to the senior mark. Courts utilize the classic fair use analysis if a junior user has used the senior mark only to describe the junior user's product and not the senior user's product. Consider the following advertising example: "Island Hopper Airlines is an American airline that flies directly from the U.S. to vacation spots in the Caribbean." Here, the junior user is not referring to AMERICAN AIRLINES, the registered trademark of an existing airline. Rather, the term "American airline" describes the country of origin of Island Hopper Airlines. In contrast, a nominative fair use analysis is only appropriate when a merchant uses the trademark to describe the actual trademark owner's product. For example, a secondary manufacturer of peripherals for tablet computers, such as a battery charger, uses the Apple mark IPAD to identify its battery charger's compatibility with an Apple IPAD tablet computer by stating "iPad compatible" on the product's label. In this case, the defendant is using Apple's IPAD trademark to describe Apple's tablet computer.

1. Statutory Fair Use

Statutory fair use is codified at § 33(b)(4) of the Lanham Act, which provides: "the use of the name, term or device charged to be an infringement is a use, otherwise than as a mark ... of a term or device which is descriptive of and used fairly and in good faith only to describe the goods or services of such party, or their geographic origin." The statutory fair use defense is limited to the trademark's being used in its descriptive sense rather than as a trademark to distinguish among goods. Consequently, as a mark moves along the spectrum of distinctiveness from descriptive with secondary meaning to arbitrary or fanciful, a court is less likely to find a statutory fair use defense. Arguably, there may never be a statutory trademark fair use defense if the court finds that the trademark in dispute is fanciful; because the trademark owner created the fanciful trademark term, it has no independent meaning apart from the trademark and the associated goodwill. For example, there would be no trademark fair use for the fanciful trademark KODAK except to refer to products made by the owner or a licensee of the KODAK trademark.

The leading case, *Zatarains, Inc. v. Oak Grove Smokehouse,* Inc., 698 F.2d 786 (5th Cir. 1983), involved the mark FISH-FRI. FISH-FRI was the trademark for a seasoned corn-flour batter mix used for frying fish and other seafood. However, the similar term "fish fry" refers to a meal featuring battered or breaded fried fish as the main course. Therefore, competitors needed to use the common term "fish fry" to describe their competing batter mix products for seafood. The court found that this descriptive use of the term "fish fry" was a fair use by Zatarains's competitors, holding that the purpose of the statutory fair use defense is to prevent a trademark owner from using trademark law to appropriate descriptive terms that are necessary to accurately describe competing products. Consequently, owners of trademarks do not have the legal right to prevent others from using the mark in its primary, descriptive, or ordinary meaning sense.

The risk of creating some likelihood of consumer confusion is consistent with a statutory fair use defense. The Supreme Court in *KP Permanent Make-Up, Inc. v. Lasting Impression I, Inc.,* 543 U.S. 111, 121 (2004), expressly held that "some possibility of consumer confusion must be compatible with fair use." However, the Court did not address how much consumer confusion is compatible with a finding of statutory fair use, nor did it address the relevance of the presentation or prominence of the descriptive use of the trademarked term as an element of creating a likelihood of consumer confusion.

2. Nominative Fair Use

If a trademark is not being used in its primary, descriptive sense, then the statutory fair use defense is inapplicable, and courts may consider whether the challenged use falls within the nominative fair use defense. The nominative fair use defense is often used in the comparative advertising context to justify the use of a trademark when two products are being evaluated or compared. Nominative fair use is also appropriate when the defendant used the plaintiff's mark to refer to the plaintiff's product, even though the defendant's ultimate goal was to describe its own product, for example, a restaurant honestly stating that its tuna salad contains a trademarked national brand of tuna fish and mayonnaise. The nominative fair use doctrine provides that using a trademark to identify not the defendant's goods or services but rather the plaintiff's goods or services is not an infringement so long as there is no likelihood of confusion.

The nominative fair use test balances the trademark owner's interests in protecting its goodwill from the likelihood of consumer confusion against competitors' or other's legitimate communicative uses that identify their products. Imagine distinguishing between competing cola beverages without using trademarks ("Do you prefer the cola beverage manufactured by the company headquartered in Atlanta, Georgia, or the cola beverage from the company headquartered in Purchase, New York?").

In *New Kids on the Block v. News America Publishing, Inc.*, 971 F.2d 302 (9th Cir. 1992), *USA Today* conducted a public opinion poll in which it asked readers to choose their favorite member of the music group New Kids on the Block. The survey instructed readers to call a "1-900" number, which imposed a charge. New Kids on the Block sued, alleging unauthorized commercial use of their trademarked name. The court established the principle of nominative fair use and developed a three-part test. Under this test, to find nominative fair use, the court must do the following:

1. First, consider whether the product or service is not readily identifiable without the use of the trademark.
2. Second, determine whether the defendant used more of the mark than was reasonably necessary to identify the product or service.
3. Third, decide whether the user had done anything suggesting sponsorship or endorsement by the trademark owner in conjunction with the mark.

Applying this test, the Ninth Circuit found that *USA Today*'s use was a nominative fair use of the NEW KIDS ON THE BLOCK trademark.

In *Century 21 Real Estate Corp. v. LendingTree, Inc.*, 425 F.3d 211 (3d Cir. 2005), the Third Circuit took a different approach to nominative fair use. The Ninth Circuit has held that its test for nominative fair use in *New Kids on the Block* replaces the standard likelihood-of-confusion analysis. By comparison, the Third Circuit held in *LendingTree* that a plaintiff-mark owner must first establish that there is a likelihood of confusion. The court stated that the likelihood-of-confusion factors most relevant in nominative fair use cases are

- the price of the goods and other factors indicative of the care and attention expected of consumers when making a purchase;
- the length of time the defendant has used the mark without evidence of actual confusion;
- the intent of the defendant in adopting the mark; and
- the evidence of actual confusion.

Only if the plaintiff can show that there is a likelihood of confusion does the burden then shift to the defendant to establish that its use of the plaintiff's mark is a nominative fair use. The Third Circuit used a modified three-part test for a nominative fair use defense that considers

- the price of the goods and other factors indicative of the care and attention expected of consumers when making a purchase;
- the length of time the defendant has used the mark without evidence of actual confusion; and
- the intent of the defendant in adopting the mark.

The *LendingTree* case is also interesting because the Third Circuit applied nominative fair use in the context of the internet. LendingTree operated an online, consumer-oriented referral business that included referrals to real estate brokers participating in its referral network. While the brokers had contracted with Lending Tree, the various real estate franchising companies to which the brokers belonged, such as Century 21, had not, and these companies sued to stop LendingTree from displaying the companies' trademarks on its website.

Nominative fair use has limits, as the court held in *Pebble Beach Co. v. Tour 18 I, Ltd.*, 155 F.3d 526 (5th Cir. 1998). In that case, the Fifth Circuit applied the *New Kids on the Block* test to a golf course that consisted of a collection of replicas of golf holes from famous courses and which identified the holes by using the names of the famous golf courses it copied them from. The Fifth Circuit affirmed the district court's finding that the defendant's use of the marks was not merely nominative. The court recognized that "one can use another's mark truthfully to identify another's goods or services in order to describe or compare its product to the mark owner's product.... [However,] the defendant cannot use the mark to identify its goods because this would not be a nominative use, and it would also suggest affiliation, sponsorship, or endorsement." *Id.* at 545–46. Because the district court had correctly found that the defendant had used the plaintiffs' marks to refer to its own products, the Fifth Circuit denied the defendant the defense of nominative fair use.

C. Parody and Other First Amendment Defenses

The First Amendment protects expressive uses of marks. However, First Amendment rights are not absolute and must be balanced with the Lanham Act's goal of protecting consumers against deception. The most frequently litigated First Amendment cases involve trademark parodies or the defense to a claim of trademark infringement that the mark was being used to comment in some way on the mark owner or its business practices. Other often-challenged expressive uses include marks in artistic works, motion pictures, or video games. Courts often construe the Lanham Act narrowly in the context of parodies and other expressive works, thereby balancing the need to protect the trademark owner's interest in the trademark, the consuming public's interest in avoiding consumer confusion, and society's interest in protecting robust free speech.

1. Trademark Parody

This section analyzes the parody defense when the defendant is using a designation as a mark to parody the plaintiff's mark. The next section considers the defendant's use of the plaintiff's mark in an artistic work in a non-trademark sense.

It is important to remember that merely being a parody is not enough to prevail in a trademark infringement case. The context and meaning of the parody are essential considerations in determining whether the parody will be permitted. In the recent Supreme Court case *Jack Daniel's Properties, Inc. v. VIP Products, LLC*, 143 S. Ct. 1578 (2023), the Court considered whether a manufacturer of parody dog toys was protected against trademark infringement actions based on the claim that the company's toys were protected parodies. In the case, the Court said it was important to distinguish situations where the parodist used the mark as a source identifier. VIP Products had adapted the Jack Daniel's trademarks humorously, using the term "Bad Spaniels" instead of "Jack Daniel's" on a dog toy designed to look like the well-known Jack Daniel's bottle. The Court focused on the fact that VIP Products had used its "Bad Spaniels" term as a source identifier, that is, as a trademark, and such use necessitated applying traditional trademark infringement analysis to determine the likelihood of confusion. The Court specifically rejected the argument that free-speech concerns necessitated that courts apply the *Rogers* test as a First Amendment "filter" when the defendant claims parody. (*Rogers v. Grimaldi* is discussed in greater detail in the next section.) The Court also noted Professor McCarthy's criticism: "As a leading treatise puts the point, the Ninth Circuit's expansion of *Rogers* 'potentially encompasses just about everything' because names, phrases, symbols, designs, and their varied combinations often 'contain some "expressive" message' unrelated to source. 6 McCarthy § 31:144.50." *VIP Products*, 143 S. Ct. at 1590.

Thus, where the alleged infringer uses a designation as a mark similar to the mark owner, the trial court should apply the local circuit court's test for the likelihood of consumer confusion. The Supreme Court noted that, while "[t]here is no threshold test working to kick out all cases involving 'expressive works[,]' ... a trademark's expressive message—particularly a parodic one, as VIP asserts—may properly figure in assessing the likelihood of confusion." *Id.* at 1591. Thus, a trial court should weigh the likelihood-of-consumer-confusion factors in context, perhaps giving less weight to factors such as similarities between the trademarks and intentional copying and more weight to those that emphasize that the alleged infringer is not the trademark owner. As explained by the Court,

> A parody must "conjure up" "enough of [an] original to make the object of its critical wit recognizable." Yet to succeed, the parody must also create contrasts, so that its message of ridicule or pointed humor comes clear. And once that is done (if that is done), a parody is not often likely to create confusion.

Id. (citations omitted).

A trademark parody "'juxtapos[es] the irreverent representation of the trademark with the idealized image created by the mark's owner.' ... A parody must 'convey two simultaneous—and contradictory—messages: that it is the original, but also that it is *not* the original and is instead a parody.'" *People for the Ethical Treatment of Animals v. Doughney*, 263 F.3d 359 (4th Cir. 2001). The second message (commentary on the mark itself) distinguishes the parody from the original and conveys the parodist's protected speech. Often this commentary is by way of ridicule or satire. In *Jordache Enterprises, Inc. v. Hogg*

Wyld, Ltd., 828 F.2d 1482, 1486 (10th Cir. 1987), the court found that the mark LARDASHE for jeans marketed toward full-figured women was a permissible parody of JORDACHE jeans, which were not.

A defendant cannot merely use another's trademark to avoid the labor of creating something new and fresh. The use of that trademark is permitted because there is a need to evoke it to communicate a message. If the defendant uses the trademark in a parody to avoid the drudgery of creating her own work—even if the parody is quite amusing—a court is unlikely to find that such a use is fair use. Thus, using a trademark to comment on the trademark, the product, or the trademark owner is more likely to be found to be a non-infringing, fair use.

Conversely, using a humorous or expressive trademark that does not comment on the trademark, the product, or the trademark owner is likely to be an infringing use. Once the parodist comments on the trademark, the parodist is then free to use it to comment on more significant social issues or engage in other expressive uses. These significant social comments are sometimes called satire. The essential legal difference between parody and satire is that parody requires using the mark to communicate, but satire does not. These concepts of satire and parody originated in copyright fair-use cases but are often generally applicable to trademark analysis.

Parodies are often commercial in that they may be attached to products, such as t-shirts, or compiled into a book or magazine format and sold in the marketplace. As noted by the Supreme Court, courts have held even parodies contained in advertisements for products to be lawful. In *Jack Daniel's Properties, Inc. v. VIP Products, LLC*, 143 S. Ct. 1578 (2023), the Court cited approvingly to *Louis Vuitton Malletier S.A. v. Haute Diggity Dog, LLC*, 507 F.3d 252 (4th Cir. 2007), where the circuit court found that Haute Diggity Dog's line of extremely inexpensive "designer" chew toys for dogs was a legal commercial parody of Louis Vuitton, internationally famous as a mark for luxury leather goods such as handbags and accessories. The Fourth Circuit noted and distinguished between the registered trademark and the alleged infringing mark, concluding that "[t]he dog toy irreverently presents haute couture as an object for casual canine destruction. The satire is unmistakable. The dog toy comments on the rich and famous, the LOUIS VUITTON name and related marks, and conspicuous consumption in general. This parody is enhanced by the fact that 'Chewy Vuiton' dog toys are sold with similar parodies of other famous and expensive brands—'Chewnel No. 5' targeting 'Chanel No. 5'; 'Dog

Perignon' targeting 'Dom Perignon'; and 'Sniffany & Co.' targeting 'Tiffany & Co.'" *Id.* at 261.

In the case of a parody or an expressive use defense, the court focuses on the parodist's expressive intent rather than on her free-riding on the goodwill of the trademark. A parodist desires to sell her own product; therefore, a legitimate parody should not confuse an ordinary prudent consumer. A legitimate parody may momentarily call to mind the trademark, but the context in which the parody trademark is presented should immediately dispel any lingering consumer confusion. For example, in *Haute Diggity Dog*, the court found that "[t]he differences [between the dog toy and the LVM products] are immediate, beginning with the fact that the 'Chewy Vuiton' product is a dog toy, not an expensive, luxury LOUIS VUITTON handbag. The toy is smaller, it is plush, and virtually all of its designs differ. Thus, 'Chewy Vuiton' is not LOUIS VUITTON ('Chewy' is not 'LOUIS' and 'Vuiton' is not 'VUITTON,' with its two Ts); CV is not LV; the designs on the dog toy are simplified and crude, not detailed and distinguished." 507 F.3d at 260. The case law involving parody and expressive uses of a trademark is extremely fact- and context-specific. While there is no bright-line rule, a very rough rule of thumb may be that, if the judge or factfinder "gets" the "joke" (the parody), the expressive use is more likely to be found to be protected and excused as a non-infringing use. However, if the factfinder does not understand the message being conveyed with trademark, then the trademark's use is unlikely to be excused as an expressive trademark use.

One using the trademark of another for expressive purposes should take reasonable efforts to minimize the likelihood of consumer confusion, for example, only using those limited portions of the mark that are necessary for the communicative purpose, providing a disclaimer, using the trademark in traditionally expressive First Amendment protected media (a court is more likely to find a use in a magazine or on a television program an expressive use than the same use on a t-shirt or other product that is sold in the marketplace) or using the mark in a clearly noncommercial manner. Reasonable efforts to dispel or minimize consumer confusion coupled with a clear expressive message will reduce the likelihood of consumer confusion as well as the possibility that a court will find an infringing commercial use.

2. Artistic or Other Creative Expressive Uses of a Mark

This section considers uses of trademarks by the defendant in artistic works in a non-trademark fashion. Courts have developed a significant body of caselaw applying the First Amendment protections developed in the seminal Second Circuit case *Rogers v. Grimaldi*, 875 F.2d 994 (2d Cir. 1989). While the Supreme Court did not have cause to consider the use of the plaintiff's mark in a non-trademark sense in *VIP Products*, it nevertheless intimated in both its majority and concurring opinions that existing caselaw applying the *Rogers* test might be somewhat problematic even in non-trademark use cases. As Justice Gorsuch noted in his concurrence, "[W]e necessarily leave much about *Rogers* unaddressed. For example, it is not entirely clear where the *Rogers* test comes from—is it commanded by the First Amendment, or is it merely gloss on the Lanham Act, perhaps inspired by constitutional-avoidance doctrine? [*Rogers v. Grimaldi*, 875 F.2d] at 998. For another thing, it is not obvious that *Rogers* is correct in all its particulars...." *VIP Products*, 143 S. Ct. at 1594.

Therefore, while this section summarizes the caselaw as it currently stands, there is a possibility that lower courts will adjust their analyses to attempt to conform to the concerns expressed by the Supreme Court in *VIP Products*.

Before the *VIP Products* decision, trademarks were frequently incorporated into artistic works. Perhaps the most famous example is Andy Warhol's 1962 silkscreen painting *Campbell's Soup Can (Tomato)*. The Warhol painting consists solely of a realistic, true-to-life rendition of a Campbell's tomato soup can. A district court carefully weighing its circuit's likelihood-of-consumer-confusion factors is likely to find that no reasonable consumer of Campbell's soup products would be likely to be confused as to source, origin, or sponsorship of a museum-quality work of art (a set of 32 flavors of these Warhol soup cans is owned by New York's Museum of Modern Art). However, it may become a closer case when a trademarked product is featured in a motion picture or video game, where advertisers often pay to sponsor product placement. It would not be unreasonable for a consumer of Campbell's tomato soup to assume that Campbell's in some way endorsed a motion picture if the soup is a featured consumable in the motion picture. Interestingly, Campbell contacted Andy Warhol to express concern regarding his use of Campbell's trademarks.

Courts have addressed the use of a mark in an artistic work using three approaches: (a) the likelihood-of-consumer-confusion test; (b) the alternative-avenues test; and (c) the *Rogers* no-artistic-relevance test. *See Parks v. LaFace Records*, 329 F.3d 437, 447 (6th Cir. 2003).

a. *Traditional Likelihood of Consumer Confusion*

Under the traditional trademark infringement test, the court does not give any particular weight to the First Amendment defense. It is assumed that the circuit's traditional likelihood-of-consumer-confusion factors are sufficiently nuanced so that the factfinder can separate artistic expression uses from other uses likely to cause consumer confusion. For example, an artistic-expressive use may not be a trademark use, or if it is a trademark use, the relevant factors weigh against a finding of the likelihood of consumer confusion. Furthermore, some confusion in the marketplace is acceptable. A court will usually only find a likelihood of consumer confusion when 15 percent or more of the ordinary prudent consumers of the junior user's product are confused. So, in this case, 15 percent of the artist's consumers would have to be confused—it would be a far stretch to assume that 15 percent of the consumers of avant-garde art, such as that created by Andy Warhol, would confuse his art with the rather pedestrian products of the Cambell's soup line of products. One may conclude that the First Amendment is not a defense to trademark infringement under this test.

The test has been criticized because it treats artistic-expressive works protected under the First Amendment as merely other commercial articles in commerce. The public's interest in the free exchange of ideas is as strong as, if not stronger than, its interest in avoiding consumer confusion.

The continued viability of this test is in question: It is occasionally still used, with some reservations, in the Ninth and Tenth Circuits. In the Ninth Circuit, recent cases have applied the *Rogers* no-artistic-relevance test. However, some Justices in the even more recent *VIP Products* case have questioned the *Rogers* test.

b. *Adequate Alternative Avenues*

Under the adequate alternative avenues test, once a likelihood of consumer confusion is found, then, if there are sufficient alternative means for an artist to convey his or her idea, the First Amendment defense fails. This test is used in the Eighth Circuit and is based on a false analogy to real property law. Just as a shopping mall can prevent speakers from using its real property to express ideas if adequate alternative venues exist, mark owners can prevent others from using their marks if there are alternative ways to communicate the same idea. This distinction in the Eighth Circuit might be analogized to the problem in copyright law of distinguishing between parody and satire. Parody requires the use of the copyrighted work to communicate a message about the copyrighted work, while satire does not. Courts applying the alternative avenues test find themselves needlessly entangled in determining whether the artist's use of a mark is artistic and thus necessary to convey an idea, or whether the artist could have chosen another non-trademark means to convey the same idea. As the *Rogers* court stated, "[W]e cannot indulge the facile assumption that one can forbid particular words without running a substantial risk of suppressing ideas in the process." 875 F.2d at 999.

c. *No Artistic Relevance* (Rogers v. Grimaldi)

Finally, based on the holding in *Rogers v. Grimaldi*, 875 F.2d 994 (2d Cir. 1989), the no-artistic-relevance test is most solicitous to First Amendment values of free artistic expression. Although the *Rogers* case involved use of the first name of a famous actress, Ginger Rogers, in the title of a motion picture, *Fred and Ginger*, its holding has been expanded to artistic uses of trademarks. *See, e.g., Twin Peaks Prods., Inc. v. Publishing Int'l, Ltd.*, 996 F.2d 1366, 1379 (2d Cir. 1993). Following the analysis in *Rogers*, the rights of a trademark owner will not supersede free expression concerns unless (1) the title has no artistic relevance to the underlying work whatsoever, or, (2) if it has some artistic relevance, unless the title explicitly misleads as to the source or content of the work. The *Rogers* test appears to be the "majority rule" and has been applied in the Second, Fifth, Sixth, and Ninth Circuits.

Professor McCarthy has criticized the *Rogers* approach because it requires that the court make complex judgments regarding artistic relevance of the content instead of focusing on whether the user is free-riding on the goodwill of the mark. *See* McCarthy § 10:31.

Nevertheless, an argument can be made that the artistic relevance test seems no more problematic than others used by the courts daily, including tests for trademark fair use, trademark nominative fair use, and other nuanced tests.

The most significant element under the *Rogers* test is whether there is artistic relevance. In *Parks v. LaFace Records*, 329 F.3d 437 (6th Cir. 2003), the defendants, the hip-hop music duo OutKast, and the record producer LaFace Records, titled their hit single *Rosa Parks*. The lyrics contained lines like "Everybody move to the back of the bus" and "She got off the bus, the conversation lingered in my head for hours." *Id.* at 442–43. The plaintiff, civil-rights icon Ms. Rosa Parks, alleged that using her name constituted false advertising under Lanham Act § 43(a) because consumers would believe that the song was about her or that she was affiliated with the defendants. The court considered the issue of artistic relevance. Despite the phrase "move to the back of the bus" in the lyrics, the court found that in the context of the song's lyrics, the phrase had nothing to do with Ms. Parks. One lyricist admitted, "We (OutKast) never intended the song to be about Rosa Parks or the civil rights movement." *Id.* at 452. The court concluded that Ms. Parks's name had no artistic relevance to the song by the defendants; rather, its use was solely as a hook to sell records.

One may conclude that the use of the mark must be true to the content of the artistic work. In the cases where the *Rogers* defense has been successfully asserted, the use of the mark was clearly related to the artistic work's communicative message. That is, it is the artist's target audience that determines the artistic relevance of the artist's use of the mark rather than the likelihood of confusion of the mark owner's consuming public. *See, e.g., Parks*, 329 F.3d 437; *Mattel, Inc. v. MCA Records, Inc.*, 296 F.3d 894 (9th Cir. 2002). The more pronounced the relationship between the mark and the message, the more likely a court will find that the First Amendment protects artistic use. Although outside the scope of this book, be aware that the use of marks in artistic works often raises copyright issues and state law tort claims based on rights of publicity, defamation, or false light.

As noted above, the Supreme Court appears, at best, to be ambivalent about the relevance of the analysis in *Rogers v. Grimaldi*. The Court stated explicitly in the *VIP Products* case that it took no position on the applicability of the *Rogers* test and noted that it is a "cabined doctrine." Nevertheless, the Court did review several cases applying the *Rogers* test for non-trademark uses of a mark in artistic works as described above. This supports the argument that at least the policy concerns expressed in *Rogers*, that non-trademark uses of a mark in an artistic work should receive some First Amendment protections, should be considered.

The authors note that the problem may be that the *Rogers* test itself was originally moored in the case's specific facts. However, later courts increasingly watered down the *Rogers* test to the point where the mere assertion of an artistic use is sufficient to insulate the use from any consideration of the likelihood of consumer confusion.

D. Dilution

The Trademark Dilution Revision Act (TDRA) made dilution by blurring and dilution by tarnishment actionable and is discussed in detail in Chapter 10. While the TDRA provides the same categories of defenses for dilution as those discussed above, because trademark dilution does not require that the court find a likelihood of consumer confusion, trademark dilution defenses are applied somewhat differently from the same defenses in a traditional trademark infringement action.

The first defense to a trademark dilution infringement action is based upon the provision for an injunction. Specifically, Lanham Act § 43(c)(1) states that the owner of a famous mark cannot obtain an injunction where the defendant commenced use of its mark before the plaintiff's mark became famous. The only legal protection of the mark that the famous mark owner would lose is the ability to obtain an injunction preventing the defendant from using its mark in a manner that dilutes the distinctive character of the famous mark. This temporal limitation makes sense because the vast majority of marks will never become famous, and trademark law permits the coexistence of marks as long as there is no likelihood of consumer confusion. To permit a newly emergent famous mark to destroy existing well-settled rights would have been a dramatic elimination of previously protectable trademark property rights.

In addition to this defense, Lanham Act § 43(c)(3) provides for the following enumerated defenses to trademark dilution: fair use (both nominative and descriptive); advertising; parody, criticism, or commentary on the goods or the famous trademark owner; news reporting; and any noncommercial use of the mark. It should be noted that while these speech-related defenses are statutory for infringement based on trademark dilution, they are common law defenses based on the likelihood of consumer confusion. These defenses are relatively straightforward and easily applied if the defendant's expressive use of a famous mark is not on the defendant's own goods or services. Thus, if a defendant uses a famous mark in a parody or as part of criticism of the plaintiff's business or its marks, these statutory defenses should be relatively easy to establish.

These statutory defenses become problematic when the defendant uses a famous mark on its own goods or services. The Supreme Court stated unequivocally in *VIP Products* that the text of § 43(c)(3) makes it clear that a parody defense is unavailable where the defendant uses the plaintiff's mark as a source identifier. Importantly, the Court merely held that the automatic defense to blurring by parodying is eliminated if the defendant's use is as a mark; it did not conclude that dilution was automatic or presumed. Therefore, using marks in a parodying sense may still be permitted if the use does not blur the plaintiff's mark. One of the leading cases involving trademark dilution and expressive use of the famous mark is *Louis Vuitton Malletier S.A. v. Haute Diggity Dog*, 507 F.3d 252 (4th Cir. 2007), discussed above. In the case, Louis Vuitton alleged that Haute Diggity Dog was blurring Louis Vuitton's famous mark by selling its goods (dog chew toys) incorporating a humorous allusion to the LOUIS VUITTON mark (luxury goods), namely including the term "chewey vuiton" and similar designs on the toy.

The *Vuitton* court refused to automatically apply the Lanham Act § 43(c)(3) parody defense because Haute Diggity Dog was using the disputed famous trademark in connection with its own products. Instead, the court used trademark parody as one of the relevant factors in determining whether the famous LOUIS VUITTON trademark was being diluted either by blurring or by tarnishment. The court noted that there must be an evocation of the famous mark by the speaker. Nevertheless, the parody or satire must also immediately remind the audience that it is not the famous mark. The court then held that a successful parody or satire can actually enhance the famous mark's distinctiveness. In *Vuitton*, the court concluded that because the defendant used the accused mark on its own products, it was not entitled to a Lanham Act § 43(c)(3) fair use defense, but because the parody was successful, there was no dilution by blurring because the use did not weaken the association with the mark—calling to mind is not the same as blurring. Because there was no evidence of tarnishment, the court summarily dismissed this claim without much discussion.

E. Genericism/Merely Descriptive

A designation must be capable of distinguishing the source or origin among competing goods and services if it is to function as a trademark. A common defense against trademark infringement is to argue that the mark is not distinctive, either because it is merely descriptive or because it is generic. (Distinctiveness is discussed in detail in Chapter 3, with respect to when a designation can be protected as a trademark. Chapter 3 presents a full discussion about determining if a designation is merely descriptive or a generic term, or when a descriptive term may be protected as a mark. This section only discusses how issues of descriptiveness and genericness are raised as defenses to infringement.)

Whether a trademark is either merely descriptive or generic and thus not protectable or is a descriptive term that has developed secondary meaning will be raised differently in a trademark infringement action depending on whether the plaintiff's mark is federally registered or is a common law trademark. In a trademark infringement action where the plaintiff's mark is unregistered, the plaintiff has the burden of proving that it owns a valid trademark. The plaintiff must prove that it owns an inherently distinctive mark or that its descriptive mark has developed a secondary meaning. By extension, the plaintiff also carries the burden of proving its mark is not generic. Thus, in a dispute between a company that prepared the multistate bar exam and a company that offered a course to prepare law school graduates to take the bar exam successfully, the court held that "[b]ecause the alleged trademark [MULTISTATE BAR EXAMINATION] in this case is unregistered, plaintiffs had the burden of proving that its mark was not an unprotectible generic mark." *National Conference of Bar Examiners v. Multistate Legal Studies, Inc.*, 692 F.2d 478, 488 (7th Cir. 1982).

If the plaintiff's mark is federally registered, the court will apply the various protections for registered marks. First, under Lanham Act § 7(b), a federal registration is "prima facie evidence of the validity of the registered mark." Courts interpret this language to mean that the burden of proof in a Lanham Act § 32(1) trademark infringement action shifts to the defendant, and the defendant has the burden to establish either that the mark is merely descriptive or generic. The legal presumption of prima facie validity only relates to the goods or services for which the mark has been registered. The mark owner would still have the burden of proof regarding trademark rights claimed in goods and services beyond those listed in the registration. The effect of this burden-shifting is to turn the issue of descriptiveness and genericness into an affirmative defense in the case of registered marks.

In addition to Lanham Act § 7(b), the registrant also receives the benefit of the five-year statute of limitations contained in Lanham Act § 14(1) (note that § 14(1) is not referred to as a statute of limitations in the Lanham Act, but effectively operates as one for specific actions challenging a registration). Section 14(1) states that, for marks that have been used for fewer than five years, a party may seek to cancel a registration if it "believes that [it] is or will be damaged ... by the registration of a mark on the principal register." This allows the defendant to challenge the registration on any basis, including mere descriptiveness or genericness, during the first five years after the mark has been registered.

By comparison, if a registration is more than five years old, then under Lanham Act § 14(3), the kinds of available challenges diminish, including the ability to challenge the mark as being merely descriptive. However, under § 14(3), a defendant may challenge a registration "[a]t any time if the registered mark becomes the generic name for the goods or services, or a portion thereof, for which it is registered...." This does not change the burden of proof but allows the defense of genericness to be asserted at any time during the life of the mark. This is true even if the registrant has successfully filed an affidavit claiming incontestable status under Lanham Act § 15.

Since the issue of whether a mark is a generic term can be raised at any time, one aspect of genericness is important: Over time, many strong brands end up no longer being able to serve a trademark function because consumers use the trademark term as the name for the product itself rather than as a trademark to indicate the source or origin of a product. As was discussed in Chapter 4, because of the way aspirin was introduced into the U.S. marketplace, the term "aspirin" no longer serves as a source identifier under U.S. trademark law. In the United States (unlike the rest of the world), the designation aspirin is merely a common name or generic term for acetylsalicylic acid. In most other countries, however, ASPIRIN is the registered trademark of Bayer Healthcare Pharmaceuticals, and it indicates to consumers a specific source or manufacturer of acetylsalicylic acid.

Whether a trademark is generic is a question of fact. To determine whether a trademark is generic or merely descriptive for a product or service, a court must determine the primary significance of the mark in the minds of the relevant consumers. The court must determine whether consumers understand the disputed trademark to refer either to the goods themselves or to a particular producer's goods. Sometimes, this is called the "who-are-you" versus "what-are-you" test. A valid trademark tells the consumer who is the source or origin of the goods. By comparison, a generic term tells the consumer what the goods are without indicating the origin of the goods. If the primary significance of the formerly valid trademark in the mind of the consumer is to describe the product rather than indicate the producer of the product, then the trademark has become a generic term and no longer serves to function as a trademark. This process of a trademark's becoming a generic term is sometimes called "genericism" or "genericide." It most commonly occurs with very well-known marks where consumers refer to the product solely by its trademark. As discussed in Chapter 4, this happened to the ASPIRIN mark: consumers only referred to acetylsalicylic acid by the brand name, thus causing the term "aspirin" to lose any trademark significance among consumers. The Xerox Corporation has combatted this problem concerning its well-known mark XEROX for photocopiers. Other famous or well-known trademarks that have become generic include cellophane, dry ice, escalator, thermos, and trampoline.

F. Functionality

The functionality doctrine is discussed in detail in Chapter 5. Please refer to that chapter for a full explanation of how the doctrine is applied to trade dress. Functionality can be raised in litigation, but there are unique procedural issues relating to whether the trade dress in question is registered with the USPTO. Under Lanham Act § 43(a)(3) the burden of proving the non-functionality of *unregistered* trade dress rests on the party asserting trademark protection for the unregistered trade dress. Thus it must be part of the plaintiff's case in chief. However, if the trade dress is registered, then the registrant is entitled to a presumption of validity of its registered trade dress. This shifts the burden of proving the functionality of the trade dress to the alleged infringer. In other words, functionality becomes an affirmative defense when infringement of registered trade dress is claimed. This burden-shifting is similar to proof of descriptiveness and genericness.

One additional nuance is that functionality can be raised at any time as a defense to infringement of a registered mark, even if that registration is incontestable, Lanham Act § 33(b)(8), and is a statutory ground for canceling a registration at any time, Lanham Act § 14(3). Since this defense can be raised anytime, functionality is similar to a claim that the mark is (or has become) generic.

G. Statute of Limitations and Equitable Defenses

Two types of affirmative defenses that can be raised but are not specific to trademark law are the statute of limitations and equitable defenses. The assertion of a statute of limitations is generally relatively circumscribed in trademark lawsuits, given the ongoing harm from trademark infringement. By comparison, equitable defenses are more easily asserted.

Equitable defenses in trademark law are affirmative defenses in which the defendant asserts that the trademark owner engaged in some inequitable or unfair conduct that was sufficiently egregious that the court should deny the trademark owner damages or injunctive relief. The equitable defenses that are most often asserted in a trademark case are laches, acquiescence, unclean hands, and antitrust/trademark misuse.

1. Statute of Limitations

The burden of proving that the statute of limitations has run is on the defendant. The defendant must show both (1) a lack of diligence by plaintiffs and (2) resulting prejudice to the defendant. The Lanham Act does not have a specific statute of limitations provision, and the 1990 federal four-year catchall statute of limitations provision most likely does not apply to actions brought under the Lanham Act. The Federal Trademark Dilution Act (FTDA) and the Anticybersquatting Consumer Protection Act (ACPA), which were enacted in 1996 and 1999, respectively, may be exceptions since they were enacted after the federal four-year catchall statute of limitations. However, no federal court has applied the catchall statute to an action brought under § 1125(c) or (d).

Almost all the federal courts considering the question of a statute of limitations under the Lanham Act have looked to analogous state law. Some federal courts have found that a violation of Lanham Act § 43(a) is comparable to a state fraud claim and so used the state fraud statute of limitations period. Other federal courts have found other state statute of limitations periods more relevant in determining the federal limitations period. In some states, trademark infringement is a continuous wrong, and as long as the trademark infringement continues, the statute of limitations does not run. The statute of limitations commences when the last act of infringement occurs. Perhaps the only bright-line rule is that under the Lanham Act, the period of the statute of limitations must be determined on a jurisdiction-by-jurisdiction basis, if it is applied at all.

Courts have used a state statute of limitations to assist in determining whether a delay in asserting trademark rights was reasonable under the doctrine of laches, which is discussed in the next section.

2. Acquiescence or Laches

Both the acquiescence and laches defenses imply consent by the trademark owner. The acquiescence defense suggests active consent to the infringement of the trademark, while the laches defense suggests passive consent. The three elements needed to prove acquiescence are as follows:

- the senior user actively represented that it would not assert a right or a claim;
- the delay between the active representation and assertion of the right or claim was not excusable; and
- the delay caused the defendant undue prejudice.

A court may find active consent if the trademark owner's conduct was sufficient to assure the defendant that the trademark owner would not assert its trademark rights.

In the case of laches, the court interprets the plaintiff's unreasonable delay to imply consent to the defendant's conduct. The elements of laches are

- knowledge of the defendant's trademark use;
- inexcusable delay in commencing the trademark infringement action; and
- the defendant will be prejudiced if the plaintiff is now allowed to bring the action (frequently, this means that the defendant relied on the plaintiff's prior inaction).

A court will often find that periods spent in settlement negotiations or in litigation against other infringers, where the initial infringement is minor, constitute excusable delays in commencing the trademark infringement action against the defendant.

As to the third element, if the defendant has relied on the trademark owner's delay to its detriment—for example, because of the delay, the defendant has made a significant investment in producing the alleged infringing trademarked goods—a court is likely to find prejudice against the defendant. However, because of the substantial public interest in preventing consumer confusion such acquiescence or laches is often insufficient to bar equitable remedies. Thus, even if monetary damages are barred, a court may often still award injunctive relief or another equitable remedy to the mark owner to protect the public interest.

3. Unclean Hands

In trademark cases, the doctrine of "unclean hands" is an affirmative defense that prevents a court "from granting relief to a plaintiff no better than the defendant he is suing." 5 McCarthy § 31:45. In an unclean hands defense, the defendant usually alleges that the mark owner committed acts constituting fraud, deceit, unconscionability, or bad faith relating to the alleged infringed trademark. For the defendant to invoke the unclean hands doctrine, the mark owner must engage in some inequitable action related to the trademark infringement. Bad conduct that does not relate to the ligation of the trademark dispute before the court is not relevant to the unclean hands defense. Moreover, if the plaintiff has washed its hands and ceased engaging in the inequitable conduct, the defendant's unclean hands defense may not apply.

Two types of conduct are often found in trademark cases that justify the application of the unclean hands doctrine: inequitable conduct toward the public and misuse of the trademark itself. In the case of inequitable conduct involving harm to the public, the trademark owner uses the trademark to deceive the public. The unclean hands defense requires that a court find that the mark owner engaged in egregious misconduct detrimental to the public's interest. This misconduct does not have to have harmed the defendant. Intentionally misrepresenting the nature or qualities of the product, deceptively using the mark, or misusing the trademark registration symbol are all examples of egregious misconduct. Because equity requires the court to consider the public interest when granting or denying an injunction, courts often require clear and convincing evidence of the misconduct and are reluctant to strictly apply the equitable doctrine of unclean hands between the parties if the application of the unclean hands doctrine would result in likelihood of consumer confusion or deception in the marketplace. Therefore, some courts will reject the unclean hands defense if it implicates the public's interest in preventing deception or will wait until the mark owner has washed its hands (is no longer engaging in misconduct) before granting the injunction.

4. Antitrust/Trademark Misuse

The trademark misuse doctrine is distinguishable from patent or copyright misuse. In the case of patent or copyright misuse, the owner of intellectual property rights attempts to expand the scope of the patent or copyright exclusivity beyond that granted by law. For example, a patent owner may attempt to extend the scope of the limited patent monopoly to cover an unpatented product. Courts have rejected this concept of misuse as applied to trademarks because of the fundamental differences between patent or copyright and trademark law. A patent or copyright represents a limited statutory monopoly. In contrast, a trademark creates no monopoly rights. *See Door Sys., Inc. v. Pro-Line Door Sys., Inc.*, 83 F.3d 169, 173 (7th Cir. 1996). Consequently, while unlawful assertions of patents or copyrights hinder competition and frustrate their constitutional purpose to promote the progress of science and the useful arts, trademark rights do not exclude others from competing in the marketplace.

The caselaw is unclear as to the existence of the equitable defense of trademark misuse. Some courts have applied the doctrine of trademark misuse at least rhetorically in the context of an allegation of the violation of antitrust laws. Although the courts are unsettled about whether the defense of "trademark misuse" even exists, it has been applied where a defendant can show that a plaintiff has used its marks in violation of the antitrust laws or has made false or misleading representations in an attempt to increase the scope of its marks. Further, the role of trademark misuse as a claim separate and apart from an antitrust claim is further confounded because some courts have found that if the trademark owner used the mark to achieve the violation of the antitrust laws, then the court may recognize a separate unclean hands defense. The judicial focus is not on whether the trademark was used in association with goods, services, or other collateral business activities but rather on whether the trademark itself was an instrument used to violate antitrust laws.

5. Bad Faith and Sham Litigation

A relatively common trademark misuse defense in trademark infringement litigation is that the litigation is merely a sham and was brought in bad faith. The plaintiff will assert its rights under the *Noerr-Pennington* doctrine to counter this allegation. *Eastern Railroad Presidents Conf. v. Noerr Motor Freight, Inc.*, 365 U.S. 127, 135 (1961); *United Mine Workers v. Pennington*,

381 U.S. 657, 670 (1965). The *Noerr-Pennington* doctrine holds that the First Amendment to the Constitution permits companies to petition the courts to redress grievances and that such suits are not a form of anticompetitive activity. There is a limitation on the *Noerr-Pennington* right to pursue litigation if the litigation is a sham designed to harm competition. Sham litigation must be objectively baseless, and the litigation must be aimed at interfering with competition by abusing the courts or government processes.

Though a review of antitrust law is outside the scope of this book, suffice it to say that one essential element of an antitrust violation claim requires that the alleged monopolist have market power in the relevant market. Rarely will trademark rights convey market power, and the courts have held that the relevant market cannot be the goods or services identified with a single trademark owner; otherwise, a trademark owner would be a "monopolist" in its legally controlled marks. Usually, courts find that restrictive trademark licenses are pro-competitive under the rule of reason test. For example, in *1-800-Contacts, Inc. v. FTC*, 1 F.4th 102, 119 (2d Cir. 2021), the court held that "[t]rademarks are by their nature non-exclusionary, and agreements to protect trademark interests are 'common, and favored, under the law.' As a result, 'it is difficult to show that an unfavorable trademark agreement creates antitrust concerns.' This is true even though trademark agreements inherently prevent competitors 'from competing as effectively as [they] otherwise might[.]'" (internal citations omitted). The court concluded that "'trademark agreements are favored in the law as a means by which parties agree to market products in a way that reduces the likelihood of consumer confusion and avoids time-consuming litigation.'" *Id.* at 119–20.

Finally, the abuse of some certification marks may raise antitrust issues. However, requiring a certification mark to be licensed to all eligible users should ameliorate most of these potential difficulties. If the owner of a certification mark refuses to permit its use by an eligible merchant, this abuse of the certification mark may be challenged under trademark law.

CHECKPOINTS

- There are several defenses available in a trademark infringement case. The first is that the challenged use is a "fair use." There are two types of fair use: statutory fair use, where the use of the word or words in the mark are necessary in the course of communication, and nominative fair use—which is often found in comparative advertising—where the defendant must use the mark to compare its product.

- First Amendment defenses exist, most notably parody or satire, where the defendant uses the plaintiff's mark to comment on it or society as a whole.
- In artistic expression cases, there is an affirmative First Amendment defense in some circuits. There is no trademark infringement unless (1) the mark has no artistic relevance to the underlying work whatsoever, or, (2) if it has some artistic relevance, unless the use of the mark explicitly misleads as to the source or the content of the work.
- Statutory fair use in trademark dilution claims does not permit the use of the famous mark on the defendant's goods.
- Parody may be considered as an element of determining whether the mark is being blurred.
- A parody use may, under some circumstances, strengthen a famous mark.
- Defendant may claim that its use of a mark identical or similar to the plaintiff's famous mark was used in commerce before it became famous.
- Defendant may claim that the mark is generic or merely descriptive and thus either not protectable under the Lanham Act or requires proof of secondary meaning to achieve protection. The defense that the mark is generic may be made at any time during the life of the mark.
- The plaintiff has the burden of proving the non-functionality of its trade dress where the trade dress is unregistered. However, if the trade dress is registered, the defendant must raise the issue as an affirmative defense.
- Defendant may also make equitable defenses, among them, laches—that the plaintiff knew of the defendant's infringement and waited to act to prevent it, to the detriment of the defendant; unclean hands—that the plaintiff somehow engaged in inequitable conduct concerning the mark; or that the statute of limitations has run on the claim. Statute of limitations defenses are very state-specific, and federal courts often look to state law to determine the available time period, as the Lanham Act has no statute of limitations.

- Defendant may seek to claim that the mark itself violates antitrust law or that the litigation is a sham initiated solely to gain a competitive advantage. This abuse of the courts is an exception to the *Noerr-Pennington* doctrine, which protects businesses from liability under the antitrust laws for lobbying for or attempting to enforce laws that have anticompetitive effects.

CHAPTER 13

Trademark Remedies

ROADMAP

- Injunctions
- Damages
- Defendant's profits
- Plaintiff's actual damages
- Attorney fees
- Statutory damages in counterfeiting
- Barring importation to the United States

Remedies available in trademark infringement actions include injunctive relief; actual damages; profits; corrective advertising damages; attorney fees; costs; cancellation of the marks; statutory damages in counterfeiting actions; barring infringing products from being imported into the United States; and punitive damages, if available under state law. Because rights in trademarks are property rights, courts are more comfortable in granting equitable remedies, such as injunctions, in addition to monetary damages. Most monetary awards for trademark infringement are equitable, rather than legal, remedies, requiring different kinds of proof than typical damages in a tort or contract action.

A. Injunctions

Because trademark infringement involves the likelihood of consumer confusion, it will often occur before there has been any actual monetary damage to the mark. Therefore, obtaining an injunction preventing the defendant's use of the mark is a very effective remedy for the mark owner since it forces the defendant to stop using the mark. This makes an injunction the primary remedy for trademark infringement.

In trademark cases, injunctions may be either preliminary, issued before decisions on the merits, or final, granted by a court after adjudication of the trademark infringement actions on the merits. An injunction can be prohibitory, such as prohibiting the sale of infringing goods or using the mark in advertising, or it can be mandatory, such as ordering a recall of infringing goods, ordering corrective advertising, requiring disclaimers on the infringing product, or requiring use of disclaimers in advertising the product. Under Lanham Act § 34(a), courts have the power "to prevent the violation of any right of the registrant of a mark ... or to prevent a violation of § 43(a) of the Lanham Act." At the close of the trial on the merits, if the trademark owner has proven trademark infringement, the district court will generally issue a permanent injunction.

Trademark owners desire to stop infringing activities at the earliest possible opportunity, so the court is often asked for a preliminary injunction early in the case. Generally, the purpose of a preliminary injunction is to protect the interests of the parties before a decision on the merits. Each of the 13 federal circuits has articulated the test for a preliminary injunction somewhat differently. 5 McCarthy § 3:32. This area of equity practice requires careful reading of the various judicial articulations of the equitable standards applied in the relevant federal circuit or state court. To obtain a preliminary injunction, generally, the plaintiff bears the clear burden of showing (1) a likelihood of success on the merits; (2) irreparable injury; (3) that such injury outweighs any harm to the defendant; and (4) that the injunction would not harm the public interest. Professor McCarthy notes that some courts also consider whether the preliminary injunction would preserve the status quo as a factor. 5 McCarthy § 3:31.

1. Likelihood of Success on the Merits

First, the court must find that there is a likelihood of success on the merits. The senior trademark owner may prove a likelihood of success on the merits by showing that the it has prior rights in the mark and that the junior user adopted a mark that was the same or confusingly similar to the senior mark, such that consumers are likely to confuse the two marks, and that the mark was used in commerce. Often, the likelihood of success on the merits is an analysis using a likelihood-of-consumer-confusion test. If there is a likelihood of consumer confusion, then there is a likelihood of success on the merits, assuming that the plaintiff can establish the other elements of a prima facie trademark infringement case. See Chapters 9 and 10 for discussions on establishing trademark infringement.

2. Irreparable Harm

Second, the court must determine if the plaintiff will suffer irreparable harm as a result of allowing the defendant to continue to use its infringing mark. Irreparable harm is a finding by the court that monetary damages are inadequate to make the trademark owner whole if the continued infringement of the mark is not immediately stopped. Because a trademark is the symbolic representation of the trademark owners' goodwill, once that goodwill is dissipated or diluted by an infringer, the infringer cannot compensate the trademark owner by buying back that goodwill.

Section 34(a) was amended in 2020 to reverse cases where federal courts had inappropriately applied the Supreme Court's holding in *eBay Inc. v. MercExchange*, 547 U.S. 388 (2006), to trademark disputes. In *eBay*, the Court held that there was no presumption of irreparable harm in a patent infringement suit in determining whether to issue a permanent injunction. Despite the differences in the nature of infringement of a trademark compared to a patent, some lower courts held that *eBay*'s reasoning applied to trademark disputes. *Compare People's United Bank v. Peoplesbank*, No. 3:08cv01858 (PCD), 2010 WL 2521069 (D. Conn. June 17, 2010) (declining to indulge in the presumption of irreparable harm in a trademark case), with *Nationwide Payment Solutions, LLC v. Plunkett*, 697 F. Supp. 2d 165 (D. Me. 2010) (indulging in a presumption of irreparable harm).

Congress overruled those decisions that held the *eBay* case precluded a rebuttable presumption of irreparable harm by amending § 34(a) to add the following second sentence:

> A plaintiff seeking any such injunction shall be entitled to a rebuttable presumption of irreparable harm upon a finding of a violation identified in this subsection in the case of a motion for a permanent injunction or upon a finding of likelihood of success on the merits for a violation identified in this subsection in the case of a motion for a preliminary injunction or temporary restraining order.

Thus, this amendment restored the presumption of irreparable harm in determining whether to grant an injunction to the plaintiff. This presumption applies to any case brought for infringement of a registered mark under § 32 or an unregistered mark under § 43(a), or for dilution or cybersquatting under §§ 43(c) and 43(d), respectively.

3. Balance of the Hardships

Third, a balancing of the hardships requires the court to weigh the injury to the senior trademark owner if the junior user's alleged infringing activities are allowed to continue during the litigation, against the damages to the junior user if it is prohibited from continuing to use the mark while the litigation is pending. This factor may be weighed in light of the other three preliminary injunction factors. A strong finding of a likelihood of success on the merits or irreparable harm may lead the court to conclude that a balance of the hardships weighs in favor of the senior trademark owner. However, if other factors do not favor, or only weakly favor, the senior trademark owner, then the court may weigh this factor in favor of the junior user.

4. Public Interest

Finally, since trademark law aims to protect the public against consumer confusion, granting a preliminary injunction to prevent a likelihood of consumer confusion is usually in the public interest. On the rare occasion where there is a defense of fair use, nominative fair use, or other First Amendment concerns, the court may delicately balance the relevant commercial-speech or free-speech interests of the public with the need to protect the goodwill of the mark owner.

5. Other Factors

Another articulation of the preliminary injunction test, which is widely used, is that of the Second Circuit, which has held that a preliminary injunction should be issued upon a clear showing of either (1) probable success on the merits and possible irreparable injury or (2) sufficiently serious questions going to the merits to make them a fair ground for litigation and a balance of hardships tipping decidedly toward the party requesting the preliminary relief. The Sixth, Eighth, and Ninth Circuits have, to some degree, also adopted the Second Circuit's test. *See Fennell v. Butler*, 570 F.2d. 263, 264 (8th Cir. 1978).

6. Permanent Injunctions Compared to Preliminary Injunctions

The main difference in analysis between a permanent and a preliminary injunction is that, in the case of the former, the plaintiff has established infringement by winning its case, showing that confusion is likely (or that dilution is likely, if it is a cause of action brought under § 43(c)). Thus, irreparable harm would result from allowing the defendant to continue to use its mark despite a finding that consumers would be confused or the distinctive character of the plaintiff's mark would be diluted. Although granting of an injunction is not automatic, given the rebuttable presumption of irreparable harm, courts typically hold that granting a permanent injunction is the preferred remedy for trademark infringement. This is so even if a monetary award (damages) is also granted, since this type of award provides a remedy for past harm but cannot adequately compensate for future harm should the defendant be allowed to continue using its infringing mark.

B. Damages

The ability to obtain an award of damages is not automatic under trademark law. This is because an award of damages is "subject to the principles of equity," Lanham Act § 35(a), meaning that a court has some discretion in deciding when and how much to award. Damages under the Lanham Act may include the defendant's profits, the plaintiff's damages, and costs. If the plaintiff also brought a state law trademark cause of action, the plaintiff may also receive punitive damages under state law.

1. Defendant's Profits

If the plaintiff proves that the defendant is liable for trademark infringement, the court may award the plaintiff the defendant's profits to compensate the plaintiff for lost sales and to deter future infringement. Such an award is in the nature of an accounting granted under equity, so it is not automatically granted. Thus, the Supreme Court has upheld the denial of an accounting for profits where there was trademark infringement but no fraud or palming-off was proven. *Champion Spark Plug Co. v. Sanders,* 331 U.S. 125 (1947) (holding that an injunction was sufficient).

The circuit courts had been split on whether the plaintiff must show either intentional or willful infringement as a prerequisite for awarding profits. The Supreme Court resolved this dispute by holding that, while willfulness is a highly important consideration in awarding profits under § 35(a), it is not an absolute precondition to obtaining an accounting for profits. *Romag Fasteners, Inc. v. Fossil Group, Inc.*, 140 S. Ct. 1492 (2020). But what "willful" means is not entirely clear. As noted by Prof. McCarthy, "[c]ourts have defined a 'willful' state of mind using a variety of descriptions, ranging from deliberate and knowing to reckless and indifferent. It is difficult to get any clear picture of the state of mind judges are looking for." McCarthy § 30:62.

Courts also disagree on whether profits are appropriate only when the goods are competitive, or whether profits may be awarded under an unjust enrichment theory or to deter future infringement. The case for disgorgement of profits is clear if diverted sales can be established; however, many courts believe that avoiding unjust enrichment is appropriate even without direct competition because it serves the purposes of trademark law by making willful infringement unprofitable.

Pursuant to Lanham Act § 35(a), the plaintiff only has to show the defendant's gross sales to determine lost profits. The defendant may then deduct ordinary business expenses and those profits that are not attributed to the trademark infringement; the remainder, if any, is the defendant's profit. Finally, the court may adjust the award if it is inadequate or excessive, "as the court shall find to be just."

2. Plaintiff's Actual Damages

Actual damages may consist of lost sales, lost royalties, and the costs of corrective advertising to dissipate consumer confusion. Plaintiff's damages may be awarded in addition to the defendant's profits, so long as this does not result in double recovery. Actual damages compensate the plaintiff for the injuries caused by the trademark infringement. Usually, the plaintiff will have to show either actual consumer confusion or sufficient evidence of the defendant's intent to deceive so that the court may presume that there was actual confusion. The plaintiff must introduce evidence that the infringement was a material cause of the injury to show that the damage award is not too speculative.

a. Lost Profits by Plaintiff

The plaintiff may prove damages in the form of its lost profits (as distinguished from an accounting of the defendant's profits) by showing that it did not meet reasonable target goals. The defendant may respond by showing that factors other than the trademark infringement account for the loss of profits. For example, the plaintiff's loss of profits might be attributed to the plaintiff's poor management or to changes in consumer tastes rather than to the defendant's infringement of the mark.

b. Reasonable Royalty

The plaintiff may show by previous negotiations, other trademark licensees, or the custom and usage of the trade the amount of royalties that it would have been entitled to in an arm's length transaction but for the trademark infringement. Often in intentional or willful trademark infringement cases, if the measure of damages is a reasonable royalty, a court will also award the infringer's profits because, otherwise, the infringer could still profit from the trademark infringement.

c. Corrective Advertising

Usually, corrective advertising is awarded in reverse-infringement cases. A reverse-infringement case is where the junior user (infringer) is a large corporation infringing the trademark of a much smaller business. Ordinarily, the plaintiff may recover the costs of responsive advertising commenced before or during the pendency of the litigation to dispel or dissipate consumer confusion. The costs of the responsive advertising must be proportionate to the amount spent by the trademark infringer. Such an award is problematic if the plaintiff has not yet determined the amount necessary to run the corrective advertising. The goal of corrective advertising damages is to restore the goodwill associated with the trademark and to dissipate lingering consumer confusion. The senior trademark owner must demonstrate to the court that mending the reputation and goodwill of the senior mark, rather than adopting a new mark, is the most cost-effective remedy.

Corrective advertisement awards have been criticized by leading scholars because of the potential that they may be disproportionate to any actual injury to the senior user and will result in a windfall to the senior user. However, courts have been very solicitous to this concern. In *Big O Tire Dealers, Inc. v. Goodyear Tire & Rubber Co.*, 561 F.2d 1365 (10th Cir. 1977), the court found that dispelling consumer confusion did not require dollar-for-dollar expenditures. Instead, the court took the amount spent by the infringer on advertising in all 50 states, determined the number of states in which the senior user did business, and then discounted that amount by 75 percent, following the Federal Trade Commission's practice of ordering businesses engaging in misleading advertising practices to spend 25 percent of their advertising budgets on corrective advertising. The formula used by the court resulted in a final award of approximately $680,000 to Big O Tire Dealers that it could spend on running corrective advertising, reduced from a jury award of $2.8 million. If the actual damages are not speculative, then an award for corrective advertising should not exceed actual damages, and in no case should the value of the corrective advertising exceed the value of the infringed trademark.

3. Treble Damages

Under Lanham Act § 35(b), a court may increase the award of actual damages in a trademark infringement action up to three times (treble damages); however, the trial court may not award treble damages under the Lanham Act as a form of penalty. *See La Quinta Corp. v. Heartland Corp.*, 603 F.3d 327 (6th Cir. 2010). This creates some tension. And although the Lanham Act provides the trial court with almost no guidance in awarding treble damages, trial courts have considered the following equitable factors:

1. The defendant's intent to deceive
2. The plaintiff's lost sales
3. The adequacy of other remedies
4. The plaintiff's unreasonable delay in bringing the case
5. The public's interest in making the conduct "unprofitable"

6. Whether the plaintiff was "palming off" its goods
7. Whether an imprecise damages calculation may fail to do justice
8. Whether the defendant's actions cause the difficulties calculating the damage award

Because Congress, in the Lanham Act, left the issue of treble damages to the trial court's sound discretion on a case-by-case basis, an award of treble damages is unlikely to be modified on appeal unless the appellate court find that an award was punitive in nature or an abuse of discretion.

4. Punitive Damages under State Law

Punitive damages are not available under the Lanham Act. However, punitive damages may be available under state law if the defendant's conduct was especially egregious and when actual damages are not an adequate remedy. Statutory damages are not an adequate basis on which to predicate punitive damages. Punitive damages must bear a reasonable relationship to the injury and be sufficient to punish the defendant. Judges will often reduce punitive damages if the amount shocks the judicial conscience. Moreover, excessive or unreasonable punitive damages may constitute an unconstitutional deprivation of property without due process of law.

5. Attorney Fees

Under the Lanham Act, the court may award attorney fees to the prevailing party in exceptional cases. The prevailing party may be either the plaintiff or the defendant. The court usually will find an "exceptional case" if

- the plaintiff proves the defendant's deliberate or willful infringement of the mark,
- the defendant's conduct was fraudulent, or
- the defendant used the mark after being denied permission.

Defendants are often awarded attorney fees if the plaintiff commenced the case in bad faith, was frivolous, or brought the case for strategic competitive reasons rather than to seek justice. Attorney fees are mandatory in trademark counterfeiting cases.

To calculate a reasonable attorney's fee, the party requesting the fee must document the time spent involved in the litigation. The court will then multiply a reasonable number of hours by a reasonable hourly rate to calculate the fees awarded. The court may award attorney fees for work on unsuccessful claims that ultimately lead to the party's prevailing.

6. Rebuttable Presumption of Willfulness for False Domain Name Registration

Under Lanham Act § 35(e), whenever proof of willfulness is required to obtain a monetary award, there is presumption of willfulness when the defendant has knowingly provided false information to a domain name registrar or registry, whether for obtaining, maintaining, or renewing a domain name registration. This is particularly useful for cases brought under § 43(d) for cybersquatting.

C. Statutory Damages

In a trademark counterfeiting case, under Lanham Act § 35(c), the plaintiff may be awarded statutory damages instead of actual damages. This election must be made before the final entry of judgment. Statutory damages do not require a finding of actual damages. Accordingly, many attorneys will wait until the jury has returned a verdict or the judge has stated the amount of damages it intends to award, then elect the better of the two remedies. Statutory damages range from $500 to $100,000 for each counterfeit mark on each different type of goods. If the court finds that the counterfeiting is willful, the court may impose statutory damages of up to $1 million. The amount of statutory damages is an amount that the court deems just. In determining an award of statutory damages, a court may consider whether the infringement was willful or intentional, whether the defendant cooperated by producing evidence from which actual damages could be determined, the potential deterrent effect on the defendant or others, and the methods used to market the infringing products. Some courts have considered use of the internet to market counterfeit goods as an aggravating factor in determining the amount of statutory damages.

In addition to counterfeiting, under Lanham Act § 35(d), the plaintiff may be awarded statutory damages instead of actual damages in the case of cybersquatting brought under § 43(d)(1). As with counterfeiting, a party may elect statutory damages for cybersquatting at any time before final judgment. Such statutory damages can be "of not less than $1,000 and not more than $100,000 per domain name, as the court considers just." Lanham Act § 35(d).

D. Barring Importation into the United States

The owner of a federally registered mark may record that mark with the U.S. Bureau of Customs and Border Protection (formerly the U.S. Customs Service). Customs will endeavor to keep goods that infringe the federally registered mark from entering the United States without the trademark owner's consent. Goods with a similar mark likely to cause consumer confusion may be returned to their place of origin or permitted to enter the United States if the infringing mark is removed. Goods with a counterfeit mark may be destroyed, transferred to the U.S. government, or either sold at auction or given to charity after removing the counterfeit mark.

CHECKPOINTS

- The primary remedy for trademark infringement is an injunction. It is common for courts to grant preliminary injunctions in trademark infringement cases.
- While the elements for a preliminary injunction vary somewhat between the circuit courts, generally, to obtain a preliminary injunction, a trademark owner must show (1) a likelihood of success on the merits; (2) irreparable injury; (3) that such injury outweighs any harm to the defendant; and (4) that the injunction would not harm the public interest.
- While not automatic under the Lanham Act, successful plaintiffs may obtain damage awards for lost profits, the cost of corrective advertising, a reasonable royalty, treble damages, and punitive damages under state law claims.
- Damages awards of a defendant's profits and reasonable attorney fees are also available.

- In counterfeiting cases, statutory damages are also available, but the plaintiff must elect to receive statutory damages before a final judgment has been entered.
- Finally, plaintiffs may seek to bar entry of goods with a similar mark into the United States—through the U.S. Bureau of Customs and Border Protection.

CHAPTER 14

Domain Names and Trademark Law

ROADMAP

- The history of domain names as trademarks
- The Federal Trademark Dilution Act (FTDA)
- The Anticybersquatting Consumer Protection Act (ACPA)
- The Uniform Domain Name Resolution Policy (UDRP)

This chapter will discuss some legal issues associated with internet domain names containing trademarks. At the dawn of the internet age, domain names did not clearly fit into the existing body of trademark law. Courts responded to the challenges posed by applying trademark law when a trademark was being used as part of an internet domain name, with limited success. They decided domain name disputes under the pre-existing body of trademark law, which did not adequately account for such uses of trademarks. Congress responded by enacting new laws to remedy a trademark-like use of a domain name by someone other than a trademark owner. In addition, new sui generis private institutions were established to resolve domain name disputes.

A. History

Starting in the late 1980s, the then-new technologies of the Internet began to present serious challenges to the practice of trademark law. One such challenge revolved around the ownership of internet domain names. Computers on the internet communicate using a numeric internet protocol (IP) address. This early IPv4 address consisted of four numbers (each of no more than three digits) separated by a period.[1] This is commonly referred to as a "dotted quad." For example, to get to the website owned by AT&T, one could enter http://144.160.155.43 into a browser address line. However, these numeric sequences are challenging for many people to remember. Therefore, the engineers who designed the internet created a system that translates an easy-to-remember domain name into its numeric IP address equivalent. This is called the Domain Name System, or DNS for short, and a computer that does the translating is called a domain name server. Thus, the DNS equivalent for 144.160.155.43 is att.com.

Domain names are divided into two parts: the top-level domain, such as .com, and the second-level domain, such as the "att" in att.com. The top-level domains were originally divided into two categories: country code domains, such as .us for the United States or .cn for China, and generic top-level domains. The generic top-level domains consisted of .com, .net, .org, .gov, .mil, and .edu, for commercial, internet, non-profit, government, military, and education domain names, respectively. Thus, only one top-level domain was initially assigned to all commercial websites. Since there can be only one domain name consisting of a particular combination of letters, and there was initially only one top-level domain dedicated to commercial use, only one party could register a particular .com domain name.

The system was further complicated by the fact that the DNS system was initially maintained by Network Solutions, Inc. (NSI), a private Virginia company under contract with the U.S. National Science Foundation, a government agency. Under this contract, NSI had sole authority to issue domain names. Because any given IP address can only be associated with a single domain name, and since the system only allowed one version of a domain name under a given top-level domain, NSI had great power to determine who was granted a particular domain. It wielded this power by granting domain names on a

1. There is a newer form of IP address known as IPv6. The difference between IPv4 and IPv6 is not relevant for a trademark analysis. IPv4 is a 32-byte address and IPv6 is a 128-byte address.

first-come, first-served basis, without considering whether the domain name incorporated a trademark or whether the registrant had any rights in the mark. Further, when NSI initially began registering domain names, it had no mechanism to resolve disputes about rights to domain names. As a result, NSI was usually a named defendant in lawsuits about rights to particular domains. It later added an arbitration provision to its registration contract, but this still required NSI to be involved in domain disputes at some level.

Further, in the early days of the internet, search engines were primitive or non-existent. If a user did not know the domain name of the site she wanted, then the user had to guess and enter various "names" or relevant terms that might be associated with the desired website. Therefore, having a recognizable or memorable domain name was a valuable asset to have to build an e-business.

Because of the DNS structure, internet domain names were the gold rush of the 1980s. Early adopters or sophisticated users staked out territory on the internet by registering both generic words and trademarks. The trademark owners of many famous brand names were latecomers to the internet. They arrived ready to do business on the internet and found that cybersquatters or cyber-entrepreneurs had already registered domain names that corresponded to their real-world trademarks. This first-to-register system led to competing claims for the domain name space between the registrant under NSI's first-to-register policy and trademark owners having rights under various national laws, including under the Lanham Act, state trademark law, or common law.

B. Federal Trademark Dilution Act (FTDA) Cases

Early domain name cases were brought under trademark infringement and dilution theories. Until 1999, when Congress passed the Anticybersquatting Consumer Protection Act (ACPA), no specific legislation clearly prohibited the bad-faith registration of domain names. Therefore, plaintiffs in these early pre-ACPA cases had to bring their claims to the domain name based upon existing trademark infringement theories that were not designed to address the challenges posed by the internet and cybersquatters. In particular, plaintiffs in these early cases faced several problems. First, under the traditional likelihood-of-consumer-confusion theories of trademark law, using an identical trademark to one previously used by another party does not always result in liability. There are innumerable examples of very similar trademarks that co-exist in the marketplace and do not create a likelihood of confusion among consumers. For example, DELTA as a trademark or service mark for airlines, travel services, plumbing fixtures, and dental insurance does not result in a likelihood of consumers confusing DELTA AIRLINES with DELTA DENTAL INSURANCE. Nevertheless, all of these companies may desire to use the internet domain name delta.com. Therefore, just because a domain name incorporates another entity's trademark does not mean that the domain name's registrant is liable for trademark infringement absent evidence of consumer confusion. Further, the domain name delta.com might be used noncommercially, for example, by an environmental website using the term delta to refer to a river delta.

In 1996, with the enactment of the Federal Trademark Dilution Act (FTDA), the burden of showing the likelihood of consumer confusion was eliminated for owners of famous marks. A more detailed discussion of the FTDA and trademark dilution is presented in Chapter 10. Because the FTDA created a cause of action that did not require proof of the likelihood of consumer confusion, this eliminated the need to produce evidence of the likelihood of consumer confusion. Once the plaintiff proved that its mark was famous, that the defendant's mark (here the domain name) was sufficiently similar to the plaintiff's mark, and that the use (here the registration of the domain name, or at the least, the posting of a website associated with the domain name) began after the plaintiff's mark became famous, the owner of a famous mark was entitled to have the domain name transferred from the alleged cybersquatter to the owner of the famous mark.

Of course, the FTDA only protected legally famous marks. Even so, the FTDA, as initially enacted, was vague about the level of fame that a mark must possess to be protected from trademark dilution. Some circuits recognized a concept of niche fame under the FTDA. A mark famous in a niche is merely famous in a narrow geographical region or among a specialized subset of consumers but is not generally famous among the general consuming population of the United States. In *Times Mirror Magazines, Inc. v. Las Vegas Sports News, L.L.C.*, 212 F.3d 157 (3d Cir. 2000), the court held that the trademark THE SPORTING NEWS for a weekly sports publication was famous in the narrow niche market of sports periodicals, although, outside the narrow market of sports publications, this mark might not have been found to be a famous mark. So the FTDA was an available remedy, if not a robust one, for the owners of well-known, if not technically legally famous, marks. This judicial understanding of niche fame satisfying the FTDA's requirement that the mark be famous is also consistent with the Restatement. *See* Restatement § 25 cmt. e. In 2006, Congress passed the TDRA, rejecting the concept of niche fame and legislatively overruling these cases in favor of a national standard for fame among the general consuming public. *See* Chapter 10.

The second problem trademark owners faced is that Congress may only regulate trademarks in the context of its Commerce Clause powers. Consequently, the FTDA did not create automatic liability for cybersquatters because plaintiffs had difficulty in proving that the mere registration of a domain name without an additional element of some actual use was sufficient to be legally a use in commerce under the Lanham Act. This posed a problem because most cybersquatters merely registered domain names which incorporated well-known or famous marks; they did not use them to sell goods or services but instead used the registration of those domains to keep others from acquiring them. The mere act of registering a domain name did not cleanly fit into the existing concepts of "use" in commerce because the cybersquatter was not trying to sell a product or offer a service but merely reserving the right to use the domain name later. The fact that the cybersquatter's registration of the domain name prevented the trademark owner from registering a domain name associated with its mark did not create liability under either the likelihood of confusion or dilution.

In order to deal with this second problem, courts went through various machinations to find commercial use, holding that some registrations were sufficiently commercial where the registration was made with an intent to sell the domain to the mark owner. Probably the most infamous cases to be litigated under the FTDA based on cybersquatting were Dennis Toeppen's domain name registrations for intermatic.com and panavision.com. Toeppen represented the classic breed of early "cyber-entrepreneurs." Toeppen registered hundreds of domain names that incorporated well-known or famous brands, including deltaairlines.com, crateandbarrel.com, and eddiebauer.com. After registering the domain names, he would offer to transfer the domain names to the trademark owner for a payment, often in the range of thousands of dollars.

In both *Intermatic Inc. v. Toeppen*, 947 F. Supp. 1227 (N.D. Ill. 1996), and *Panavision International v. Toeppen*, 141 F.3d 1316 (9th Cir. 1998), the courts held that the marks were famous. The more difficult issue was whether Toeppen actually was using the marks in commerce. The courts held that Toeppen's act of registering hundreds of marks as domain names and then trying to sell the domain names to the mark owners was itself a use in commerce. Since the marks were famous (according to the courts), Toeppen was ordered to transfer the domain names to the trademark owners.

After Toeppen and others lost some of those early cases in the 1990s, cybersquatters became more sophisticated. First, they would not contact the businesses but instead wait to be contacted by the mark owners. Then, they would not offer to sell the domain name but instead offer to settle the dispute about the right to the domain name. Because under Federal Rule of Evidence 408, offers of litigation settlement cannot be used as proof of liability, the cybersquatter could contend that he or she was not offering the domain name for sale, just offering to settle the claim.

Some cybersquatters contended that their use (registration) of the domain name was noncommercial. The FTDA had a specific exception for noncommercial uses of trademarks. Toeppen made a form of this argument in the *Panavision* case. He set up a website under the panavision.com domain name, which contained pictures of Pana, Illinois. The website did not refer to Panavision, Inc., the trademark owner. The court rejected this argument because it found that Toeppen had a business of reselling domain names. However, without such striking evidence, it would be hard to make out a case of trademark dilution.

Unfortunately, the cases finding liability for cybersquatters under both trademark infringement and trademark dilution required the courts to stretch existing trademark law to the limits of what was intended to be prohibited activity under those laws. For example, the "use in commerce" idea under trademark law had been one where a party had used the mark to sell other goods or services under the mark. Selling a domain name registration containing the mark does not clearly fit into this understanding of trademark usage. The closest analogs under trademark law were the cases holding a defendant liable for selling cloth patches containing the plaintiff's marks as products that would later be attached to clothing, hats, or bags. However, in the leading case, *Boston Professional Hockey Association, Inc. v. Dallas Cap & Emblem Manufacturing, Inc.*, 510 F.2d 1004 (5th Cir. 1975), the Bruins hockey club did have a history of selling merchandise with the BRUINS mark.

C. Anticybersquatting Consumer Protection Act (ACPA)

While traditional trademark infringement and dilution laws were stretched to meet the needs of trademark owners, the Clinton administration recognized the need for an inexpensive, fast, and multi-jurisdictional method of resolving domain name disputes. Finally, Congress enacted the Anticybersquatting Consumer Protection Act of 1999, Lanham Act § 43(d). Congress added § 43(d) to provide a federal cause of action with two types of claims for cybersquatting: a direct cause of action against a person who registers, traffics in, or uses a domain name in bad faith; and an in rem cause of action against a domain name that violates one of the protections for registered and unregistered trademarks under the Lanham Act.

The direct cause of action requires proof that the domain name registrant had a bad-faith intent to profit from the registration, trafficking in, or use of a domain name that is identical or confusingly similar to a trademark that is either distinctive or famous. Also protected is an individual personal name that functions as a mark, and it prohibits the use of domain names that dilute a famous mark. Section 43(d) now provides trademark owners with a cause of action for the mere bad-faith registration of a domain name which incorporates a trademark. Under the ACPA, it is no longer necessary to prove that consumer confusion or dilution is likely. Although those other trademark causes of action are still available, this change means that trademark owners and courts do not have to use strained logic or distort trademark law principles to protect valuable trademarks from cybersquatting.

The key to a § 43(d) cause of action is showing proof that the domain name registration was filed in bad faith. Section 43(d) provides a non-exhaustive list of nine factors that may be considered by a court to determine if the registrant acted in bad faith, including

1. Whether the defendant has any intellectual property rights [including trademark rights] in the domain
2. Whether the domain consists of the plaintiff's name
3. Whether the defendant has made prior use of the domain to offer goods or services
4. Whether the defendant has made any bona fide noncommercial or fair use of the mark on the site

5. Whether the defendant has the intent to confuse consumers or dilute the mark
6. Whether the defendant has offered to sell the domain name
7. Whether the defendant used any false or misleading information when registering the domain
8. If applicable, whether the defendant has multiple registrations of other domain names that incorporate third parties' marks
9. Whether the plaintiff's mark is distinctive or famous

The first case to apply the ACPA was *Sporty's Farm L.L.C. v. Sportsman's Market, Inc.*, 202 F.3d 489 (2d Cir. 2000), in which the defendant had registered the domain sportys.com, which allegedly incorporated the trademark of an aviation merchandise company, SPORTY'S. The court found that the mark SPORTY'S was distinctive (see discussion of distinctiveness in Chapter 3), so the court did not reach the issue of whether SPORTY'S was also a famous mark. While not identical, the marks SPORTYS.COM and SPORTY'S were confusingly similar. The court discounted the apostrophe as a difference because grammatical symbols cannot be used in domain names. Further, the court found the ".com" element was also irrelevant to its similarity analysis. The court then evaluated the nine bad-faith factors and found in favor of the trademark owner. Except for the first factor, the factors are mainly self-explanatory. Congress used the term "intellectual property rights" rather than "trademark rights," in the first factor. Accordingly, if the defendant has some other rights in the domain name, for example, if the owner of a copyrighted work such as a song, movie, book, etc., registered as a domain name the title of that work, that would weigh against a finding of bad faith on the first factor. In *Sporty's Farm L.L.C.*, the court held that because the defendant company was not formed until nine months after the domain name was registered, and did not begin using the domain until after that, the defendant had no intellectual property rights in the domain.

Several other cases have considered the scope of the ACPA. In *Lamparello v. Falwell*, 420 F.3d 309 (4th Cir. 2005), the court held that the use of a domain name that incorporated a person's name to maintain a website critical of that person was a noncommercial use and thus did not meet the requirements of a "bad faith intent to profit." The court noted that "gripe sites" (websites using domain names of company's names plus some variation of the word "sucks," such as bestbuysux.com) have been determined to be noncommercial critiques of those sites. The court distinguished *People for the Ethical Treatment of Animals v. Doughney*, 263 F.3d 359, 367 (4th Cir. 2001), where the defendant had registered 50 or 60 domain names and had offered to settle that case for payment of money. In that case, the court found these actions to run afoul of factors six and eight listed in § 43(d).

In *DSPT International, Inc. v. Nahum*, 624 F.3d 1213 (9th Cir. 2010), the Ninth Circuit concluded that the bad-faith intent to profit can arise after the registration of a domain name. In that case, the business owner brought his friend into his business and had the friend set up his website, which included registering the business's domain name. After the relationship soured, the friend left to work for a competitor and refused to transfer the domain name to the business owner. The court held that holding the business owner's domain name "for ransom" evidenced a bad-faith intent to profit from the domain name, consistent with factor six noted above, even though the acts occurred after domain name registration. The court held this act to fall under the prohibition against using or trafficking in a domain name.

D. Uniform Domain Name Resolution Policy (UDRP)

While trademark rights are national or territorial in scope, the internet is a global resource. As discussed above, the DNS was managed initially by a private Virginia-based company, NSI. By the late 1990s, it became clear that having a single private company manage the DNS and oversee the distribution of domain names was not workable. In response to criticism of the system, the U.S. government encouraged the creation of a non-profit company to oversee the management of the allocation of IP addresses and the DNS while shifting to a decentralized system for registering domain names. The company created to oversee this system is Internet Corporation for Assigned Names and Numbers, or ICANN. ICANN manages the computers that operate the top-level domain system (the root name servers). ICANN does not provide registration services for domain names but instead licenses other companies, such as Go Daddy, Name, Namecheap, and Gandi, to do so. This provides competition in the business of domain name registration.

No one jurisdiction can adequately police the domain name system. Cybersquatters may not be amenable to the jurisdiction of the national courts of the trademark owner, and litigation in foreign courts may be inordinately complex, time-consuming, and expensive. Consequently, no one country's laws could adequately protect the interests of trademark owners in domain names. In May 1997, the Internet Assigned Number Authority (IANA) and the Internet Society (ISOC) entered into a Memorandum of Understanding on the Generic Top-level Domain Name Space of the Internet Domain Name System (gTLD-MoU). Under the gTLD-MoU, establishing an alternative dispute resolution system also accompanied the creation of the seven generic top-level domain names. Because the process of granting domain names is done by private organizations licensed by ICANN, an administrative system analogous to nonbinding arbitration has been developed to provide an alternative to litigation in the courts. The major difference between arbitration and a URDP administrative proceeding is that arbitration is final and binding on the parties and may be challenged in court on only a very limited number of grounds. If a party is dissatisfied with a UDRP panelist's decision, the aggrieved party may file a complaint in court and the entire proceedings are de novo. The panelist's decision is entitled to little if any weight, and at best is treated as persuasive authority on par with a law review or similar publication.

In order to become a domain name registrar, the registrar-applicant must agree in its contract with ICANN to transfer a domain name upon the request of the domain name registrant, receipt of an order from a court or arbitral tribunal, or receipt of a decision by an UDRP Administrative Panel. The domain name registrar then must impose similar contractual obligations to comply with the UDRP on each domain name registrant. A significant provision of the UDRP is that it simplifies some jurisdictional questions. Challenges to the award may be brought in a "Mutual Jurisdiction," which "means a court jurisdiction at the location of either (a) the principal office of the Registrar (provided the domain-name registrant has submitted in its Registration Agreement to that jurisdiction for court adjudication of disputes concerning or arising from the use of the domain name), or (b) the domain-name registrant's address as shown for the registration of the domain name in the Registrar's Whois database at the time the complaint is submitted to the Provider." ICANN, Rules for Uniform Domain Dispute Resolution Policy ¶ 1. A registrant may find that a domain name registrar in a distant nation provides registration at a lower cost. However, the registrant may also find that the dispute may be litigated in a distant forum. Further, the UDRP default is that the language used in the Registration Agreement is the language that will be used to adjudicate the dispute. Consequently, the choice of the registrar should not be made solely on the cost of registering the domain name.

An administrative panel is a sui generis proceeding under the UDRP. ICANN has recognized several providers of dispute resolution services. In a UDRP proceeding, the administrative dispute-resolution service provider is analogous to the court clerk's office. It accepts the various fees, processes the paperwork, identifies the administrative panelist (arbitrator), and publishes the panelist's decision. The provider also assures that the parties and administrative panelist(s) comply with the rules governing the UDRP and with the provider's supplemental rules. All UDRP decisions are published and available on the web or on legal research databases. The complainant may choose any ICANN-approved provider, and the ICANN-approved providers compete for business. Some providers have a reputation earned or unearned for having more pro-complainant biased panelists. Accordingly, forum shopping among approved providers is alive and well in the UDRP process. Each UDRP provider may also have supplemental rules that may provide a strategic advantage depending on the facts of the dispute. The process from complaint to panelist's decision usually takes under six weeks. A panelist may find for the complainant and transfer the domain name and cancel the registration, or it may find for the respondent. The panelist has no other authority regarding the disposition of the dispute. The panelist is obligated to ensure that the proceedings comply with the Rules for the Uniform Domain Name Dispute Resolution Policy and that the parties to the dispute are treated fairly. Generally, the entire process is done electronically, and the parties do not personally appear before the panel. The panelist is free to use the substantive trademark law of any country in analyzing the dispute as long as the chosen body of law does not conflict with the requirements of the UDRP.

The complainant must select a provider, file a complaint, and pay the appropriate fees. The respondent may then elect to expand the panel from a single panelist to three panelists. In that case, the additional fees are split evenly between the parties. There is some suggestion in the literature analyzing UDRP decisions that three-panelist panels are more "respondent friendly" than a single-panelist panel or that they are better able to consider disputes requiring a subtle understanding of the principles of trademark law.

The complainant trademark owner must demonstrate the following elements:

1. The owner has rights in the trademark and the domain name is identical or confusingly similar.
2. The respondent has no rights or legitimate interests in the domain name.
3. The domain name was registered or is being used in bad faith.

A U.S. trademark owner relying on common law rights acquired through trademark use may find it more challenging to prove interest in the trademark than a trademark owner relying on a trademark registration. So-called gripe sites present an interesting issue on the question of substantial similarity. These sites are often highly critical of the trademark owner, its products, or its policies. In a gripe site domain name dispute, the registrant registers the trademark plus a negative term to create a website to comment on the trademark owner (trademarksucks.com). This type of use is analogous to nominative fair use, discussed in Chapter 12. There is a debate among UDRP panelists whether "trademark + sucks" (or other negative term) is confusingly similar or whether the derogatory term negates a finding of trademark similarity. A 2005 analysis of UDRP panel decisions found the majority rule among panelists was that even when the trademark is presented in the context of a negative term such as "sucks," the trademark and domain name trademarksucks.com are similar. The articulated justification for this interpretation of the domain name is that for many internet users, English is not their primary language and many do not recognize the significance or connotations of the associated derogatory or negative term. The minority rule is that using a negative term in association with a trademark in a domain name results in a domain name that is not confusingly similar.

The complainant may prove bad faith by showing that the respondent acquired the domain name to sell it, to prevent a competitor from using it, or to create a likelihood of consumer confusion that the respondent then profited from. The respondent may establish rights in the domain name by having prepared to use the domain name, prior to the dispute, for a legitimate purpose; by showing that the respondent is generally known by the disputed trademark, even if the respondent has no trademark rights in the domain name; or, finally, by showing that the respondent is making noncommercial or fair use of the domain name without intending to mislead consumers.

While the language of the UDRP suggests that the burden of proof is on the complainant, there is a de facto presumption that since the UDRP does not provide for discovery, in practice, the actual burden is on the respondent to show a legitimate interest in the domain name. Whether the "registration and use in bad faith" element should be read as requiring both "registration" *and* "use in bad faith," or as "registration" *or* "use in bad faith" depends on the panelist. Most panelists interpret the word "and" as a disjunctive "or"; therefore, bad faith at any point is sufficient for the panelist to transfer the domain name. However, a few panelists will require both that the registration be made in bad faith and that the registrant's use continues to be a bad-faith use.

Finally, the panelist must consider legitimate noncommercial use or fair use of the domain name under the UDRP. These uses are often referred to as trademarksucks.com or gripe-site cases. Some panelists, often from countries with civil law traditions, seem to read the noncommercial use provision out of the UDRP and assume that any use other than by the trademark owner is illegitimate. Other panelists, often from common law countries, tend to give greater weight to legitimate fair uses of the trademark, especially nominative fair uses. The evidentiary rule that negotiations attempting to settle a dispute are inadmissible does not apply to UDRP proceedings. Sophisticated counsel for the plaintiff may attempt to bait the respondent into demanding to settle the dispute and then use that demand as evidence of bad faith. Some panelists have used clear rhetorical responses such as, "I would not sell the domain name for a million dollars," as evidence of bad faith. A respondent negotiating a settlement should be very careful when communicating counter-offers or demands as part of the settlement negotiations. Consider whether there should be a formal agreement with the complainant that settlement discussions will not be used as part of any subsequent UDRP domain name dispute resolution.

If either party is dissatisfied with the panel's decision, it may commence an action in a court in any mutual jurisdiction, which will then place the panel proceedings on hold until the matter is finally adjudicated by a court of law. Alternatively, since a panel's decision has no res judicata effect, either party may commence another UDRP proceeding to attempt to reach a different result. The party who won the first proceedings may then argue its persuasive effect to a subsequent panel, but prior panel decisions do not necessarily bind subsequent panels. In the United States, proceedings to challenge a panelist's award will often be brought under the ACPA, which was discussed previously in this chapter.

CHECKPOINTS

- Some early internet users registered numerous trademarks as domain names that they then warehoused for later sale to trademark owners. This practice was called cybersquatting.
- The technological architecture of the internet did not anticipate trademark issues.
- In the early days of the internet, domain names were given out on a first-come, first-served basis, without regard to existing trademark rights.
- Trademark law was initially unclear whether the mere registration of a domain name constituted a trademark used in commerce.
- Early cases were brought under theories of trademark dilution and so only protected well-known marks under state law or famous marks under federal law.
- The Anticybersquatting Consumer Protection Act (ACPA) protects against bad-faith registration of a domain name that is the same as or similar to a trademark.
- The ACPA provides for federal court jurisdiction and in rem proceedings if the court does not have personal jurisdiction over the parties.
- The Uniform Domain Name Resolution Policy (UDRP) is a fast, inexpensive method of resolving domain name disputes.
- UDRP provides for an arbitration-like proceeding in which a panelist may order a domain name transferred to the trademark owner if the domain name is the same or confusingly similar to the owner's trademark and the domain name was registered or used in bad faith.
- UDRP panel decisions may be challenged in court.

CHAPTER 15

Trademarks and the Internet

ROADMAP

- Domain name as an email address
- Search engine liability
- Meta tags
- Wallpaper/watermarks
- Keyword advertising
- Sponsored or banner advertising
- Website "third-party" liability
- Linking
- Phishing
- Trademarks in virtual worlds and games

The use of marks on the internet presents many novel questions that require careful consideration of the principles of trademark law. Chapter 14 discussed the unique problems caused by domain name cybersquatting. This chapter will discuss some emerging issues involving trademark use on the internet. These issues are discussed in a separate chapter not because the law governing trademark use on the internet is somehow different but rather because they require some discussion of the relevant technology.

A. Domain Name Used as Email Address

One of the significant problems facing internet users is spam or unwanted bulk commercial email. Spammers often use fake email addresses to avoid their victims' wrath. In *America Online, Inc. v. IMS*, 24 F. Supp. 2d 548 (E.D. Va. 1998), the issue was whether a false sender email address domain name violated the Lanham Act. Two of the claims in the complaint relate to trademark law. America Online (AOL) alleged false designation of origin under Lanham Act § 43(a) and trademark dilution by tarnishment under Lanham Act § 43(c). After being notified to cease sending bulk emails, defendant IMS allegedly sent out, over the course of about ten months, more than 60 million unauthorized emails using aol.com in the email header. The novel issue before the court was whether the use of AOL's registered trademark in an email header as part of the "return address" was a designation of origin.

To understand the historical context of the case, one must remember that it was one of the first spam cases in the early days of the internet; it involved using primitive email technology. The email header contains primary data relating to the routing of the email, the "to," "from," "subject," and "date" fields, for example. The header may be analogized to the information printed on an envelope. At summary judgment, the district court held that any email recipient could logically assume that the spam email originated from the aol.com domain. *IMS* is an interesting case because the trademark issue is that the designation of origin indicated that the email originated from an AOL server. So perhaps consumers believed that AOL had in some way endorsed or tacitly approved spam email by permitting alleged spammers to use AOL's servers. Internet users' relative lack of sophistication in 1998 may have made this assumption reasonable. Now that the use of email is commonplace (as is, unfortunately, an email user's experience with spam), it needs to be clarified that the result would be the same today. Perhaps a new case will resolve consumer confusion regarding the source of a bulk email's contents.

Trademark dilution by tarnishment was the second count alleged by AOL. The court found that AOL was a famous mark and that having the AOL mark associated with junk email created a negative association in the consumer's mind. Accordingly, the court granted summary judgment to AOL on both counts. Consequently, the improper use of a mark as part of an email-address domain name may be a sufficient trademark use for a court to find liability under the Lanham Act.

B. Search Engine Liability

Web search engines are critical to the efficient use of the internet. As was discussed in Chapter 14, in the early days of the internet, there was no easy way of locating a merchant's website if you did not know the domain name. As a result, many users would type the main trademark name associated with the merchant or product in the address bar along with the ".com" top level domain in an attempt to locate the merchant's website. Before businesses became savvy about using the internet to market their goods and services, unscrupulous competitors and enterprising cybersquatters often hijacked such domain names by registering the trademark as a domain name first. This resulted in a fair amount of confusion about a given merchant's domain name. Since the advent of web search engines, consumers may quickly locate the relevant site regardless of the domain name used, significantly reducing the importance of knowing the exact domain name of the company being searched.

The new arena for trademark disputes is the search engine. For example, competitors have often used another competitor's trademark to increase the visibility of their products with comparative advertising. This naturally led to whether this permits merchants to use their competitors' trademarks to drive traffic to their own websites under the guise of comparative advertising. Further, as was discussed in Chapter 14, internet users often use trademarks as shorthand for the product itself. In the physical world, some shoppers may ask, "Where do I find Coke?" when the information they want is "Where do I find soft drinks?" The internet analogy is that some searchers enter a well-known brand as a proxy for the generic name of the product they seek. While web search engines may have slightly decreased the need for a specific domain name, they have also presented numerous legal questions of trademark law—usually relating to whether the new online use created an impermissible likelihood of initial-interest confusion. Initial-interest confusion is discussed in greater detail in Chapter 9.

1. Meta Tags and Wallpaper

Few individuals look beyond the first few websites in a search engine results list. Accordingly, as search engines became more popular, website owners strived to be listed higher in the search results. The algorithm used by some early search engines assumed that the more frequently a search term was used on a website, even when it appeared on the wallpaper, the more relevant the website was to the individual searching. Other algorithms prioritized the descriptive terms used by the website owner in the meta tags in ranking the search results. Technically, trademark use in a meta tag or as wallpaper does not constitute web search engine use and does not create search engine liability. However, trademarks are often used in these contexts to manipulate search engine results.

a. Meta Tags

Meta tags are hypertext markup language (HTML) tags that provide information about the website or web document without being automatically displayed to the website user. The meta tags are usually in the header of the web page. Two frequently used meta-tag attributes or fields that raise trademark issues are "keywords" and "descriptions."

The meta keywords tag contains important terms selected by the website owner relating to the contents of a website or web page. A meta tag for keywords that might be associated with a website for this book may look like this:

> <meta name="keywords" content="trademark study aid Lanham Dilution FTDA Smith Gibbons"/>

Between 1995 and 1997, early search engines such as Infoseek and AltaVista relied on these terms in the keyword meta-tag field in ranking search results. However, by 2002, search engines were no longer heavily weighting the data in the keyword meta tag. Currently, some search engines, such as Google, give keywords no weight, while others, such as Yahoo, have assigned the keywords the lowest weight as a ranking signal.

The meta description tag contains information about the website or page. For example, the meta description tag for a website about this book might look like this:

> <meta name="description" content="A book for lawyers and law students covering both the common law trademarks and Lanham Act, the basics of modern trademark law, and the dilution of famous trademarks."/>

Unlike the meta keywords tag, some search engines such as Yahoo and Bing still rely on the meta description tag to some degree. Other popular search engines, such as Google, sometimes use the meta description tag, although less frequently. Therefore, the meta description tag may still be a viable way to manipulate search engine results.

Website creators attempted to optimize their websites for different search engines by manipulating the data in the meta-tag fields. One optimization method was to select and include in both the keywords and the description key terms that were likely to be used by a prospective searcher. The selected terms used in the meta fields often were trademarks associated with competitors. This is only commonsense marketing. If a searcher were looking for a specific brand-name product, competitors would like to make that searcher aware of competing products. Stores do this all the time by forcing shoppers to go past competing products (often at the end of the shopping aisle) to reach the desired premium national brands in the center of the aisle.

In *Brookfield Communications, Inc. v. West Coast Entertainment Corp.*, 174 F.3d 1036 (9th Cir. 1999), an early leading case on this topic, the court held that web surfers looking for Brookfield Communications would be led astray by the search engine. If the competitor's services were sufficiently similar to those offered on Brookfield's website, the web surfer might decide to use the services provided on the competitor's website. There was no source confusion because the web surfers knew they were not on the Brookfield Communications website; however, West Coast Entertainment benefited from Brookfield Communications' goodwill in the mark. Judge Berzon, in her concurrence in *Playboy Enterprises, Inc. v. Netscape Communications Corp.*, 354 F.3d 1020 (9th Cir. 2004), called into question the continued viability of the holding in *Brookfield Communications* regarding the use of meta tags to create a likelihood of consumer confusion. The trial courts in other circuits have declined to follow *Brookfield Communications. See, e.g., Site Pro-1, Inc. v. Better Metal, LLC*, 506 F. Supp. 2d 123 (E.D.N.Y. 2007); *J.G. Wentworth, S.S.C. Ltd. P'ship v. Settlement Funding LLC*, No. 06-0597, 2007 WL 30115 (E.D. Pa. Jan. 04, 2007).

Courts have found that using a trademark in the meta-data fields may be a fair use. In *Playboy Enterprises, Inc. v. Welles*, 279 F.3d 796 (9th Cir. 2002), the court held that a former "Playmate of the Year" could use Playboy's trademarks of PLAYMATE and PLAYBOY as meta tags as a classic trademark fair use. The defendant was the 1981 Playboy Playmate. The court found that the defendant was using Playboy's trademarks in a descriptive sense, to describe her modeling services and for the sale of her personal photographs. The court also found that the defendant minimized her use of the plaintiff's trademarks, used disclaimers, and did not attempt to deceive visitors to her website. The website clearly stated that Playboy Enterprises, Inc., did not endorse it, and she did not use the distinctive stylized Playboy font. The court concluded that the defendant's use was in good faith to index the contents of her website. The fact that the meta tags were not visible to site users was irrelevant to her classic or traditional trademark fair use defense.

The *Playboy Enterprises* court also considered the trademark nominative fair use defense. The court found no descriptive substitutes for Playboy Enterprise's trademarks. The court held that the defendant did not have to go to absurd lengths, such as to use a phrase like "nude model selected by Mr. Hefner's magazine as its number-one prototypical woman for the year 1981." *Id.* at 802. Moreover, no web surfer looking for the 1981 Playboy Playmate of the Year would attempt such an absurd search. As a factor in favor of good-faith fair use, the court also observed that the defendant neither repeatedly used Playboy's trademarks in her meta tags nor extensively used them so that her website would be at the top of the search results. The court stated that its decision might have been different if the defendant had used the trademarked terms so extensively as to appear above the trademark owner in search engine results regularly.

Because a large part of the defendant's website discussed her association with Playboy Enterprises over the years, using trademarks like PLAYBOY in the meta description tag was appropriate. The court concluded that "[p]recluding the use of trademarks would hinder the free flow of information on the internet." *Id.* at 804.

Courts may have to tweak judicial interpretations of trademark law developed in the context of physical goods or weigh the likelihood-of-consumer-confusion or fair-use factors differently. However, based on the limited case law, it may be safe to assume that traditional principles of trademark law, including the two fair use defenses, apply to using a competitor's trademark on a website. But, because of the evolution of web search engine technology, which no longer relies heavily on data provided in the meta tags, these early cases may be limited to their specific facts then.

b. Wallpaper

A website's background images and text are sometimes called "wallpaper." Such wallpaper can be designed with a virtually limitless collection of images and text. Relying on this, some enterprising website developers figured out that a site's wallpaper could be used to affect search engine results. They did so by incorporating competitors' trademarks into the website's wallpaper. Such use worked because several of the early search engines used the frequency of a term's use on a website as a proxy for relevance and did not distinguish between terms that appeared in a text box and text that was incorporated into the wallpaper. The algorithm used by these web search engines ranked the results on the assumption that the more often a search term was used on a website, the more relevant the website was to the searcher. So, using a competitor's trademark in the wallpaper could result in higher rankings in web search engine results. Moreover, the use of marks in the wallpaper did not have to be visible to the web surfer. White text on a white background is invisible to the human eye but detectable by the search engine and thus highly relevant to the index function of an early search engine.

The *Playboy Enterprises* case discussed above considered using a mark in a website's wallpaper. In the case, the defendant visibly used the acronym for Playmate of the Year, "PMOY '81," repeatedly in the wallpaper of her website. Welles argued that her use of this term was a nominative fair use. The first prong of this test required Welles to demonstrate that the fact that she was a Playmate was not readily identifiable without the use of the "PMOY '81" designation. Although the court had held that Welles did have a limited right to say "Playboy Playmate of the Year 1981" on her website, the court found that the repeated use of "PMOY '81" in the website's wallpaper was not necessary and thus failed the first prong of the trademark nominative fair use defense. Her use of the "PMOY '81" designation in the wallpaper was an infringement. Based on this case, it is highly likely that repeated use of a competitor's trademark on a website in wallpaper or as a watermark, especially if the mark is not visible to the website visitor, is likely to fail the nominative fair use defense because the defendant used more of the plaintiff's mark than was reasonably necessary to identify the plaintiff's product or service.

2. Keyword Advertising, Banner Advertising, or Sponsored Advertising

Web search engine advertising is effective and profitable because it immediately targets the searcher's current interests with products or services that meet their needs. Individuals conducting searches related to foreign travel may receive focused advertisements for travel-related services or tours of a desired destination on the page displaying the search results. Generally, this is fine. If a searcher is looking for information on Louisville, Kentucky, there is no reason why a web search engine could not present advertisements for the Kentucky Derby or fine bourbon. However, some web search engines permitted advertisers to license the right to have their advertisements appear when an individual searched using a competitor's mark.

a. Keyword Advertising

Web search engines use databases of terms to link search queries to responsive advertising. Often these databases contain marks as search terms. As discussed in Chapter 3, a mark may be a strong arbitrary mark, for example, APPLE for consumer electronics and software. Simultaneously, the mark may be generic, for example, apple for fruit. Also, more than one business may use the same mark for different goods. For example, APPLE for consumer electronics and software and APPLE for a music-recording label. Consequently, merely including the term *apple* in a database is not, per se, trademark infringement. Trademark infringement (or dilution) would only occur when the database term is then linked to the goods or services of a competitor, causing a likelihood of consumer confusion or being used in a manner that dilutes the goodwill associated with a famous mark.

The three essential elements of trademark infringement (see Chapter 9) are (1) plaintiff's ownership of a mark, (2) use of the mark in commerce by a defendant, (3) and a likelihood of consumer confusion. In most cases, there is no dispute about the first element, ownership of the mark. The web search engine cases tend to cluster around the second and third elements. The second element, "use in commerce," tends to be very fact- and technology-specific. Two cases discussed in the following section, *1-800 Contacts, Inc. v. WhenU. Com, Inc.*, and *Rescuecom Corp. v. Google Inc.*, nicely frame the issues.

i. *1-800 Contacts, Inc. v. WhenU.Com, Inc.*

In *1-800 Contacts, Inc. v. WhenU.Com, Inc.*, 414 F.3d 400 (2d Cir. 2005), the court considered whether the defendant's use of a trademark to trigger pop-up advertisements was a use in commerce under the Lanham Act. This is a technology-specific case. The defendant provided proprietary software, which computer users voluntarily downloaded and installed on their computers. Once installed, the software responded to a consumer's internet computer use by generating contextually relevant, clearly labeled pop-up advertisement windows. A pop-up advertisement is displayed in a new web browser window, as contrasted with a banner advertisement, which is displayed as part of the currently active window. The software had an internal database of approximately 32,000 website addresses, 29,000 search terms, and 1,200 keyword algorithms corresponding to consumer interests. When the software identified that the consumer was interested in a term that appeared in its database, it randomly delivered a selected advertisement from the related category. So, in theory, a user searching for eyeglasses might receive advertisements for anything from opticians or optometrists to defogging lens cleaning supplies or contact lenses.

For this section's purposes, only the use of the mark in the directory is relevant. The plaintiff alleged that this conduct infringed its trademarks and created a likelihood of consumer confusion. In this case, the defendant did not reproduce or display the plaintiff's mark. Instead, only after the computer user entered the web address "1800contacts.com" did the software deliver contextually relevant pop-up advertisements. The court found that the bracketing of the mark 1-800CONTACTS with *www.* and *.com* converted the trademark into an unprotected web address. A computer user could not trigger a pop-up advertisement by merely typing 1-800CONTACTS. The user was required to type the *www.1800contacts.com* web address before a pop-up advertisement was delivered to the user's screen. Further, the defendant did not sell the trigger words or keywords to its advertisers. The court found that the defendant did not "use" the mark in commerce as required under the Lanham Act when the address was used in the database to trigger pop-up advertisements.

According to the *1-800 Contacts* case, use in commerce requires that the infringed mark be placed on a good or service to pass it off as an authorized product or service. The *1-800 Contacts* court concluded that "[a] company's internal utilization of a trademark in a way that does not communicate it to the public is analogous to a[n] individual's private thoughts about a trademark. Such conduct does not violate the Lanham Act, which is concerned with the use of trademarks in connection with the sale of goods or services in a manner likely to lead to consumer confusion...." *Id.* at 409. Moreover, this case involved a web address, www.1800contacts.com, and not the trademark 1-800CONTACTS. Dicta in this case suggested that had there been an actual trademark at issue, the results might have been different.

ii. *Rescuecom Corp. v. Google, Inc.*

Three years later, the Second Circuit was squarely faced with keyword advertising and limited the court's holding in *1-800 Contacts.* In *Rescuecom Corp. v. Google Inc.*, 562 F.3d 123 (2d Cir. 2009), with a bit of understatement, the court described the defendant Google as operating a "popular internet search engine" that permitted a user to search the web by entering a query based on the searcher's selection of terms. These terms could include trademarks or generic terms or a mixture of both. The defendant then responded to the search in two ways. The defendant provided a list of relevant websites ranked according to its proprietary software in order of relevance. The defendant also displayed relevant context-based advertising concerning the search terms.

The defendant, Google, had two advertising programs: AdWords and Keyword Suggestion Tool. AdWords was Google's program that permitted advertisers to purchase keywords which, when used as search terms, would trigger advertisements. Google also offered a Keyword Suggestion Tool, recommending keywords to prospective advertisers. Some of the keywords the Keyword Suggestion Tool recommended as advertising terms might include a competitor's mark.

As will be discussed in detail in the next section, this process results in the display of a sponsored or banner advertisement in the context of the search results. Google was then paid for each click-through on the displayed advertisement. The plaintiff claimed that 97 percent of Google's revenue was associated with the AdWords program.

Following *1-800 Contacts*, the district court dismissed the complaint for failure to state a claim. The question before the court on appeal was whether the defendant's use of the mark was a use in commerce under the Lanham Act. On appeal, the circuit court vacated the district court's judgment, and remanded. The *Rescuecom* court distinguished the facts in the *Rescuecom* case from those in *1-800 Contacts*. First, in *1-800 Contacts*, the court stressed that the defendant made no use of the plaintiff's mark, while in *Rescuecom*, the defendant was recommending and selling the plaintiff's mark to its advertisers. Second, the defendant in *1-800 Contacts* did not "use or display" the plaintiff's mark, unlike in *Rescuecom*, where the defendant displayed, offered, and sold the plaintiff's mark and encouraged the purchase of the defendant's marks as keyword search terms through its Keyword Suggestion Tool program. Therefore, the defendant's use of the plaintiff's mark in *Rescuecom* clearly fit within the literal terms of the Lanham Act.

The *Rescuecom* court in dicta reasoned that the phrase "use in commerce," as defined in Lanham Act § 45, was for the purpose of obtaining trademark rights and that, although the identical phrase is employed in Lanham Act §§ 32(1) and 43(a) (trademark infringement), Congress could not have intended the same standard to apply. The *Rescuecom* decision suggests that the use-in-commerce standard for trademark infringement is broader than the types of uses in commerce that invest a merchant with trademark rights.

In this case, Google (and a distinguished group of amici) contended that the *1-800 Contacts* case stood for the proposition that including a trademark in an internal computer database cannot constitute trademark use. The *Res-*

cuecom court rejected this as an overbroad reading of *1-800 Contacts*. In *Rescuecom*, the defendant did more than merely use the trademark in a database. The defendant recommended and sold the trademark to advertisers. Also, *1-800 Contacts* did not involve using a trademark but rather a World Wide Web address. Finally, as a matter of public policy, the court held that insulating internal database use of a mark from liability under the Lanham Act would permit operators of web search engines to create business models that deceive the public. The court then speculated on the parade of trademark-infringing activities that an unscrupulous web search engine could engage in if internal use of a mark was not a per se use under the Lanham Act.

Google and the distinguished amici then contended that the defendant's web search engine's use of a mark was, by analogy, the digital equivalent of product placement in the real world. An example of product placement is a supermarket's placing its house brand product next to a national brand product so that a customer looking for the national brand product may consider purchasing the house brand as a substitute. The *Rescuecom* court cut short this argument by finding that characterizing conduct as product placement is not a talisman against trademark infringement and that product placement creating a likelihood of consumer confusion is also prohibited conduct under the Lanham Act.

So, despite suggestions in earlier cases, internal use of a mark in a database may be a sufficient use in commerce to satisfy the "use in commerce" element of trademark infringement. However, whether internal use, or more specifically, Google's use, is a "use in commerce" for the purposes of trademark infringement under the Lanham Act is still an open question in other circuits, *see Rosetta Stone Ltd. v. Google, Inc.*, 676 F.3d 144 (4th Cir. 2012), and has been rejected by some trial courts, *see Government Employees Ins. Co. v. Google, Inc.*, No. 1:04cv507, 2005 WL 1903128 (E.D. Va. Aug. 8, 2005).

Because this was an appeal from the district court's grant of a dismissal of the action under Rule 12(b)(6) of the Federal Rules of Civil Procedure for failure to state a claim upon which relief could be granted, the court did not have to reach the third element: the question of whether banner advertising created a likelihood of consumer confusion.

b. Banner Advertising or Sponsored Advertising

The third element of a trademark infringement claim is whether the challenged use creates a likelihood of consumer confusion. This section will discuss banner or sponsored advertising in the context of alleged trademark infringement. There are two frequently used methods of presenting advertising on the web. One discussed earlier is pop-up advertising, in which a new window opens, and the advertisement appears in the new window. Pop-up advertisements are less frequent now that most web browsers have pop-up blockers that make this advertising cumbersome and ineffective.

The second common type of internet advertising is banner advertising or sponsored advertising. Banner advertising or sponsored advertising is often associated with web search engines. Any website may present a banner or sponsored advertising. Although the terms are often used as synonyms, some relevant differences exist. Banner advertisements are, as their name suggests, similar to ads presented on a physical page. In appearance, banner advertisements are usually quite distinct from the other content on the page, often appearing along the top part of the Web page and containing content controlled by the advertiser.

In contrast, web search engines offer sponsored advertisements. Sponsored advertisements often appear immediately before the organic results of a search and in separate columns on the search results page. Sometimes sponsored results are set-off by having a slightly different-colored background or a phrase like "sponsored results" or "sponsored advertising" in small print before these advertisements.

i. Banner Advertising

In *Playboy Enterprises, Inc. v. Netscape Communications Corp.*, 354 F.3d 1020 (9th Cir. 2004), Netscape (Netscape distributed Navigator, a leading web browser in the 1990s) had a list of 400 terms to which an advertiser could key its advertisements. Two of these terms were "playboy" and "playmate." Netscape required advertisers offering adult products to key to these two terms. So, when a searcher entered "playboy" as a query, in addition to the search results for the query "playboy," the search results page would also sometimes display sexually explicit banner advertising for other allegedly more vulgar or offensive adult products. The banner advertisements were labeled "click here," and the searcher was then linked to the advertiser's competing website. The banner advertisements did not disclaim any association with Playboy Enterprises, Inc.

Playboy contended that the searcher was arguably confused initially at the point of the "click" because these banner advertisements were presented because of typing in "playboy" as a query. The court did not decide this issue but did suggest that had the banner advertisements been clearly labeled as advertisements and had Netscape taken other opportunities to minimize the likelihood of consumer confusion, this form of keyword advertising might have been permissible. The court also noted that it was not resolving the use of the keyword "playboy" in some form of comparative advertising, such as "if you are interested in Playboy, you may also be interested in the following message from [a different named company]." *Id.* at 1030.

Judge Berzon, in her concurrence, distinguished hijacking a user to another website by making the user believe that he or she is going to the trademark owner's website from merely presenting the user with choices other than that of the trademark owner. The concurrence suggests that this latter use, if properly labeled, is analogous to product placement, for example, a customer in a store asks for Playboy and is sent to the adult section of the store where there are other adult magazines placed in front of Playboy magazine. This would not violate Playboy's trademark rights, even if the competing magazines paid the storeowner for prominent placement of their magazines near Playboy.

ii. Sponsored Advertising

Sponsored search results look similar to the organic search results except that a sponsored advertisement will often have a different background color and a small print tagline indicating that it is a sponsored ad. Google displays up to three sponsored advertisements above the organic search results. This placement is important because web search engine users will generally click on links higher up on the search page.

The Google AdWords business model was discussed earlier in this chapter. Advertisers purchase keywords to display their advertisements above the search results, or near the right side of the web page. Google's current policy permits the limited use of trademarks as keywords if the sponsor is a reseller, makes or sells components for the trademark product, offers compatible parts, or provides information about the trademarked product. Google's technology is apparently able to verify these four conditions for using a trademark designation as part of its keyword-advertising program.

The court in *Government Employees Insurance Co. (GEICO) v. Google, Inc.*, No. 1:04cv507, 2005 WL 1903128 (E.D. Va. Aug. 8, 2005), also considered Google's liability for sponsored advertising. The court recognized that initial-interest confusion is different on the web because once the user recognizes that he or she has arrived at the wrong website, that error can be instantaneously corrected. In the real world, there is a time or financial cost to correct initial-interest confusion. The court found that the use of the plaintiff's marks in the heading or text of advertisements keyed to the plaintiff's marks might have violated the Lanham Act. However, the court rejected the plaintiff's survey evidence that sponsored links that do not reference the plaintiff's marks created a likelihood of consumer confusion.

In *J.G. Wentworth, S.S.C. LP v. Settlement Funding LLC*, No. 06-0597, 2007 WL 30115 (E.D. Pa. Jan. 4, 2007), a case brought against a non-web search engine defendant using Google's AdWords to advertise on Google, the defendant, apparently learning from the holding in *GEICO*, did not incorporate the plaintiff's marks in its sponsored advertising. The court found that

> [a]t no point are potential consumers "taken by a search engine" to defendant's website due to defendant's use of plaintiff's marks in meta-tags. Rather, as in the present case, a link to defendant's website appears on the search results page as one of many choices for the potential consumer to investigate. As stated above, the links to defendant's website always appear as independent and distinct links on the search result pages regardless of whether they are generated through Google's AdWords program or search of the keyword meta-tags of defendant's website. Further, plaintiff does not allege that defendant's advertisements and links incorporate plaintiff's marks in any way discernable [*sic*] to internet users and potential customers.

Id. at *7.

The court then held that "[d]ue to the separate and distinct nature of the links created on any of the search results pages in question, potential consumers have no opportunity to confuse defendant's services, goods, advertisements, links or websites for those of plaintiff. Therefore ... initial interest protection does not apply here." *Id.* at *8.

In *Rosetta Stone v. Google, Inc.*, 676 F.3d 144 (4th Cir. 2012), Rosetta Stone alleged that Google's use of its trademark ROSETTA STONE as a keyword in its AdWords program and in the context of advertisements constituted direct trademark infringement. The court in *Rosetta Stone* accepted on procedural grounds that the trademark infringement elements of "use" and "in connection with the sale, offering for sale ... of any goods or services" were not on appeal before it. So the only issue remaining on appeal was whether Google's use of the ROSETTA STONE mark created a likelihood of consumer confusion. The court rejected the mechanical application of the circuit's nine-factor likelihood-of-consumer-confusion test. It approved, under the facts of this case, the district court's focus on three specific factors: defendant's intent, evidence of actual confusion, and the consuming public's sophistication. The other six factors were not especially relevant because of the nature of the internet and Google's referential use of the mark. The appeals court vacated the district court's grant of summary judgment on the direct infringement claim and remanded for further proceedings.

On the first factor, the defendant's intent, Google was aware, based on internal studies, that there was significant confusion among internet surfers when trademarks were used in the title or body of advertisements. This was sufficient to create a question of material fact. On the second factor, evidence of actual confusion, there was a survey and other evidence of actual consumer confusion. On the third factor, the consuming public's sophistication, the court cited an internal Google study that "even well educated, seasoned internet consumers are confused by the nature of Google's sponsored links and are sometimes even unaware that sponsored links are, in actuality, advertisements." *Id.* at 160.

Google raised the trademark functionality defense. As discussed in Chapter 12, the functionality defense prevents a mark owner from protecting (under trademark law) the functional, practical, or useful feature of a product or its packaging. The functionality defense is the line that separates patent law protection (useful features) from trademark law protection (source signaling function of a mark). The *Rosetta Stone* court rejected the district court's analysis. The district court did not focus on whether the mark was functional based on Rosetta Stone's own use. Instead, the district court focused on whether the mark, once entered into Google's AdWords program, became functional. The functionality doctrine does not apply to this use of a mark. Rosetta Stone's own use of the mark was solely as a source identifier; this is the classic and approved use of a mark. The mark ROSETTA STONE is not relevant for language-learning programs. The fact that its use made Google's AdWords program or any computer program more efficient does not transform a source identifier into a functional mark.

In *Tiffany (NJ) Inc. v. eBay, Inc.*, 600 F.3d 93 (2d Cir. 2010), plaintiff Tiffany alleged that defendant eBay directly infringed its mark by using it on the eBay website and by purchasing sponsored links on Google and Yahoo!. While citing with approval the line of cases applying the nominative fair use doctrine, the *Tiffany* court declined to address the doctrine of nominative fair use. Instead, the court limited its holding to the narrower ground that a defendant may use the plaintiff's trademark (1) if it is necessary to describe the plaintiff's product and (2) does not mislead the public that there is some affiliation or endorsement by the plaintiff. A trademark owner has no right to stop the sale of genuine goods bearing a true trademark, even if the sale is unauthorized by the trademark owner. No law prevents the truthful and non-deceptive use of a trademark. The plaintiff then tried to expand traditional principles of trademark law by asserting that even if the "truthful and non-deceptive" use defense applied to the genuine Tiffany goods that were sold on the eBay website, it could not be extended to protect the defendant eBay because eBay knew that some counterfeit Tiffany-branded goods were also sold on its site. Tiffany's contention was that the defense was limited to the need to advertise genuine Tiffany-branded products; therefore, the defense could not be asserted if any counterfeit products were sold on the eBay website. The court rejected this proposed limitation on the defense. It was sufficient that eBay used the Tiffany marks to describe genuine products, and the fact that some sellers were also selling counterfeit Tiffany products did not preclude the defense.

The court limited the role of eBay's knowledge to whether eBay contributed to the direct infringement of the Tiffany mark by the sellers providing counterfeit goods. The court also noted that eBay removed listings that Tiffany claimed were for counterfeit goods and took other affirmative steps to prevent or remove listings for counterfeit goods. To impose liability on eBay because it could not guarantee that all the goods offered on eBay bearing the Tiffany mark were genuine would "unduly inhibit the lawful resale of genuine Tiffany goods." *Id.* at 103.

The state of the law regarding holding search engines liable under the Lanham Act is muddy. The cases tend to be very fact-specific. Because the relevant law is unclear, it is difficult for the district court to determine which facts are material; therefore, these cases involving new technologies or new uses of existing technologies are sometimes prematurely decided on summary judgment motions. What does appear clear is that there is no per se trademark immunity for search engines, and except for the *Tiffany* case, appellate courts have been reluctant so far to address the issue of nominative fair use as a defense to sponsored advertising. The lesson from the case law may be that courts considering allegations of direct infringement by search engines will apply the relevant principles of trademark law to the disputes. If the use by the search engine creates a likelihood of consumer confusion or violates other sections of the Lanham Act, the search engine will be found liable. Prudent search engine providers should take affirmative steps to minimize the likelihood of consumer confusion. Also, this body of case law determining which facts give rise to a likelihood of consumer confusion will evolve over time as internet consumers become more sophisticated in their use of searching and browsing technologies and are exposed to new internet services, such as social media and new ways of presenting advertising.

C. Website Liability for Third-Party Trademark Infringement

Trademark infringement on the web is endemic, and it is often difficult for trademark owners to obtain jurisdiction over the direct infringers who may live in another country or to commence cost-effective litigation against numerous judgment-proof small infringers. Some trademark owners have instead proceeded against the web search engines, auction sites, or other e-commerce sites that allegedly facilitate trademark infringement. Chapter 9 discusses third-party liability in greater detail.

1. Search Engines

Search engines are an obvious target for imposing third-party liability since they host the alleged infringing advertisements. To prevail under the *Inwood* test for contributory infringement, a trademark owner must establish that a defendant intentionally induced trademark infringement or continued to supply a product to an entity that it knows or had reason to know was engaged in infringing activity. In *Rosetta Stone v. Google, Inc.*, 676 F.3d 144 (4th Cir. 2012), in addition to its direct trademark infringement claims discussed above, Rosetta Stone alleged that Google's use of its trademark ROSETTA STONE as a keyword in its AdWords program and in the context of sponsored advertisements constituted contributory trademark infringement. The court held that mere knowledge that some users were engaged in infringing activity is not enough. To be liable, the defendant must supply its products or services to specific individuals that it knows or has reason to know are engaged in trademark infringement. The court applied the *Inwood* test for trademark infringement without discussing whether it was the appropriate contributory infringement test for a provider of online services. The application of *Inwood* to a provider of online services is discussed in detail in section 2 of this chapter.

According to its infringement-prevention policy, Google removed sponsored advertisements and links when Rosetta Stone notified it that a linked website sold counterfeit ROSETTA STONE products. However, Google did not remove sponsored advertising and associated links to other websites by the same advertiser. The district court in *Rosetta Stone* had looked at the issues raised in the *Tiffany* case. The appeals court distinguished *Rosetta Stone*, which was before the district court on a summary judgment motion, and *Tiffany*, which had been decided after a lengthy bench trial. The court of appeals in *Rosetta Stone* vacated the district court's order granting summary judgment on the contributory trademark infringement claim, stating that the district court had misapplied the Federal Rule of Civil Procedure 56 summary-judgment standard. One could wonder, had Google not only removed sponsored links but also terminated the other advertisements by alleged trademark infringers, whether summary judgment might have been appropriate.

Rosetta Stone also alleged vicarious trademark infringement. To prove vicarious infringement, Rosetta Stone had to show that Google and the alleged direct infringers had an apparent or actual partnership, had the authority to bind one another in transactions with third parties, or exercised joint ownership or control over the infringing product. 676 F.3d at 165. The court rejected Rosetta Stone's contention that, since Google and the alleged direct infringers jointly controlled the appearance of the sponsored advertisement or sponsored links on Google's search engine results page, they were partners or were exercising joint control of the infringing product. Rosetta Stone seemed to ask the court to find that the advertisements or the sponsored links themselves were the infringing product rather than the counterfeit copies of Rosetta Stone's products being sold by the direct infringer. Control over the advertisement is not the same as control over the advertised product, at least for the purposes of vicarious trademark liability. On the vicarious infringement claim, the appeals court affirmed the district court's grant of summary judgment in favor of Google. However, one could speculate that if the advertisements themselves were directly infringing, false, or misleading, the result may have been different.

2. Auction Sites

Trademark owners have also tried to hold auction sites liable for the trademark-infringing activities conducted by site users. Typically this involves selling counterfeit goods or genuine goods through unauthorized distribution channels (often called gray market goods). Sometimes the unstated goal of the trademark owner is to stop the sale of used, second-hand products or lawfully produced trademarked products that are being sold on terms or conditions inconsistent with the trademark owner's preferred brand image. In some sense, these disputes are merely a continuation of the third-party liability imposed on real-world flea markets and auction houses for the infringing activities of their users. Third-party liability for trademark infringement is further discussed in Chapter 9. However, virtual internet auction sites are legally distinguishable from real-world auction houses.

The term "auction site" is often a misnomer. Many of these sites do not provide auction services, as the phrase is commonly understood to mean the public sale of property to the highest bidder. These sites do not conduct auctions, nor are they auctioneers. Instead, they merely provide a venue where a willing buyer and a willing seller may reach an agreement. Courts have found the leading auction site eBay is not an auctioneer because it is not an "individual" and that "eBay does not conduct 'auctions' within the meaning of the [California Auction Act] because the sale does not culminate by the acceptance of the auctioneer of the highest offer but rather at the expiration of the fixed period designated by the seller." *Ewert v. eBay, Inc.*, No. C-07-02198 RMW, 2008 WL 906162, at 1–2 (N.D. Cal. Mar. 31, 2008).

In *Tiffany (NJ), Inc. v. eBay, Inc.*, 600 F.3d 93 (2d Cir. 2010), Tiffany, in addition to its direct infringement claim, also alleged that eBay was liable for contributory infringement because it culpably facilitated the infringement of Tiffany marks by the eBay sellers' offering counterfeit Tiffany-branded products. This case was supposed to be the first case to address whether the Supreme Court's test for contributory liability, set out in *Inwood Laboratories v. Ives Laboratories*, 456 U.S. 844 (1982), applied to online providers of services. The *Inwood* test had been designed for manufacturers or distributors of physical products. Inexplicably, on appeal, eBay no longer maintained that it was not subject to the *Inwood* test. 600 F.3d at 105.

The circuit court in *Tiffany* observed in dicta that courts have applied *Inwood* to contributory infringement claims against flea markets, swap meets, and even domain name registrars, such as in *Lockheed Martin Corp. v. Network Solutions, Inc.*, 194 F.3d 980 (9th Cir. 1999). The district court adopted the Ninth Circuit's *Lockheed Martin* test. It concluded that *Inwood* applied to a service provider who exercises sufficient control over the means of the infringing conduct and that eBay had significant control over the transactions, listing, and sales conduct using its website. eBay should have pressed the issue of whether the application of *Inwood* to providers of online services was appropriate.

The amici argued that *Inwood* does "not govern where, as here, the alleged contributory infringer has no direct means to establish whether there is any act of direct infringement in the first place." This argument focuses on the fact that contributory trademark infringement usually is imposed on a service provider, for example, a landlord or the owner of a flea market, who not only has notice that trademark infringing activities are taking place but who also has physical access to the alleged counterfeit goods for inspection. eBay at no time is in possession of or has access for inspection of the goods being sold on its website. The court declined to consider this issue because it was not pressed on appeal by eBay, and then it assumed without deciding that *Inwood* applied. Consequently, it is still an open question as to whether *Inwood*'s contributory trademark infringement test applies to online providers of services.

Tiffany did not contend that eBay induced trademark infringement. Therefore, the only remaining basis for finding eBay liable was because it provided or continued to provide services to vendors it knew or should have known were selling counterfeit products. Concerning providing services, eBay immediately terminated bidding and reversed sales when it was notified that the products in question were counterfeit; it warned buyers and sellers and returned any fees that it earned from the transaction. Applying *Inwood*, it is clear that eBay had general knowledge of infringing activities. However, when eBay was provided with specific knowledge of infringement, it immediately took steps to halt bidding and to reverse the sales. Tiffany argued for creating a new duty, that eBay should be liable because eBay was on notice that there was "a substantial problem" and it failed to act. The trial and appellate courts rejected the novel "substantial problem" test.

One of the principle benefits the providers of online services offer is the disintermediation of the supply chain. Many years ago, individuals interested in purchasing an airplane ticket had to use a licensed intermediary or a travel agent to do so. Today, prospective passengers can buy airplane tickets directly from the airlines. Online services, such as eBay, add value because they aggregate willing buyers and sellers and provide a platform that provides information that facilitates transactions at low cost. These services facilitate numerous honest transactions and add value. However, some users will engage in unlawful activities. From the perspective of trademark owners, platforms such as eBay facilitate trademark infringement on a massive scale, and little can be done about it. Often, the alleged sellers of counterfeit products are either outside the jurisdiction of U.S. courts or are judgment-proof. Hence, trademark owners view large online platforms such as eBay as being in the best place to deter trademark counterfeiting. Whether this proves to be a correct assessment of the future direction of trademark law is an open question, although it seems clear that the courts will need to reconsider the *Inwood* test, especially the knowledge element, in light of available technologies to minimize counterfeit sales, and the other realities of e-commerce.

D. Linking

The World Wide Web (WWW) is composed of numerous uniform resource locators (URLs) that link (reference) other documents using HTML code. Often the links consist of text or domain names that incorporate trademarks. When such linking is done without the trademark owner's permission, the possibility of a trademark infringement claim is raised. However, such claims are generally rejected. For example, in *Knight-McConnell v. Cummins*, No. 03 Civ. 5035 (NRB), 2004 WL 1713824 (S.D.N.Y. Jul. 29, 2004), the court held that "[t]he mere appearance on a website of a hyperlink to another site will not lead a web-user to conclude that the owner of the site he is visiting is associated with the owner of the linked site."

Also, the placement of a trademark in a post-top-level domain (TLD) path of a URL (e.g., after the .com, .net, .org, etc.) is not a trademark violation because it is merely an address to locate web content and does not function as a trademark. So, if a competitor of the trademark-owner Acme uses *www.acme.com* as a domain name, that will likely be an infringing use. However, the use of the trademark ACME by a competitor in the link *www.competitor.com/goods/service/Acme* is not a trademark use of the designation ACME because consumers do not understand this use of *Acme* as a signal indicating source, origin, or sponsorship of a good or service, *see Interactive Products Corp. v. a2z Mobile Office Solutions, Inc.*, 326 F.3d 687 (6th Cir. 2003), nor is it actionable under the UDRP or Lanham Act § 43(d).

Sometimes links are created not to the trademark owner's homepage but to another page maintained at a site. This is referred to as "deep linking." Deep linking, in and of itself, should not create liability. For example, in *Ticketmaster Corp. v. Tickets.com, Inc.*, No. CV99-7654-HLH (BQRx), 2000 WL 1887522 (C.D. Cal Aug. 10, 2000), Ticketmaster alleged that Tickets.com's practice of deep linking to individual web pages within Ticketmaster's website rather than Ticketmaster's homepage created a likelihood of consumer confusion. The court rejected this argument. Under the facts of the case, Tickets.com did not deep link to venues or performances for which it was selling tickets, and Ticketmaster's dominant branding of each deep-linked page dispelled the likelihood of consumer confusion. Further, the court analogized the use of deep links to a library catalog to reference other information.

"Inline linking" is the use of content of one website appearing on another. Sometimes this is called "framing" because while the content is located on a different site, the website's viewer may perceive the other website's content as being on the website he or she is currently viewing. There needs to be more case law addressing framing. The complaint filed in *Washington Post Co. v. TotalNews, Inc.*, No. 97 Civ. 1190 (PKL) (S.D.N.Y., filed Feb. 2, 1997), alleged trademark infringement and trademark dilution. The defendant in the case allegedly created a website with links to news services so that when a user clicked on the links he or she would see content provided by the news service framed by TotalNews's advertisements and content. The plaintiff alleged that TotalNews's framing of content that included the news service's marks created a danger that users may believe there is some sponsorship or affiliation between the news service and TotalNews. Fortunately for the parties to the litigation, but unfortunately for trademark practitioners, students, and scholars, the *TotalNews* case was settled before a judgment on the merits.

In *Jones Day v. Blockshopper LLC*, 89 U.S.P.Q.2d 1623 (N.D. Ill. 2008), the defendant allegedly deep-linked articles on its website to the plaintiff's website regarding residential real estate transactions by the Jones Day law firm associates. Among the claims by the plaintiff, it alleged that the links to its website created the false impression that the plaintiff was affiliated with or approved, sponsored, or endorsed the defendant's business and that the defendant's use diluted the distinctive character of the plaintiff's mark. The plaintiff also alleged that the defendant's use of its mark on the defendant's website created a likelihood of consumer confusion. The trial judge denied the defendant's Federal Rule of Civil Procedure 12(b)(6) motion to dismiss for its failure to state a claim on which relief could be granted. The case was ultimately disposed by a stipulated dismissal. At a bare minimum, this case argues that deep linking may support a claim under the Lanham Act.

The trademark law governing linking needs to be clarified and developed. However, a deep link or inline link may be presented in such a manner that will create a colorable claim of trademark infringement or trademark dilution. When linking or framing, website creators should be careful to minimize the likelihood of consumer confusion and ensure that the use is a fair use under trademark law or, in the case of famous marks, falls within the statutory defenses.

E. Phishing

Phishing is an attempt to discover confidential information by impersonating a reliable source. In *Yahoo! Inc. v. XYZ Companies*, 872 F. Supp. 2d 300 (S.D.N.Y. 2011), Yahoo! asserted that the defendants perpetuated the Yahoo! Lottery Fraud, which consisted of the defendants' sending out hoax emails to individuals informing them that they had won lotteries that these individuals had never entered. If the victim was naïve enough to respond to one of the defendants' emails, the defendant would then use Yahoo!'s name to obtain identity and financial information. The court found for the purposes of a default judgment that the defendants' alleged use of the Yahoo! trademarks misled the email recipients into believing that Yahoo! sent the email. Courts have also found that phishing is evidence of a bad-faith intent to profit from an owner's trademark for the purposes of the Anticybersquatting Consumer Protection Act (ACPA), Lanham Act § 43(d).

F. Trademarks in Virtual Worlds and Games

One of the most exciting areas of law is the application of trademark law principles within the context of virtual worlds and computer games. Virtual worlds and computer games are commercially significant. Many real-world companies are advertising and participating in virtual worlds, and inhabitants of virtual worlds often assume that the brand name "products" that appear digitally in the virtual world are affiliated with the real-world analog. However, there are relatively few cases on point. In *E.S.S. Entertainment 2000, Inc. v. Rock Star Videos, Inc.*, 547 F.3d 1095 (9th Cir. 2008), the owner of a strip club with the name "Play Pen Gentlemen's Club" sued the producer of the *Grand Theft Auto* series of video games. The creators of Grand Theft Auto created a fictional community, Los Santos, based on Los Angeles, California, as part of the game *Grand Theft Auto: San Andreas*. The plaintiff alleged that depicting a fictional East Los Santos strip club called "Pig Pen" as part of the game infringed on its marks and associated trade dress. The court found that the nominative fair use defense did not apply because the marks and trade dress were not identical.

The court then considered the intersection of trademark law and the First Amendment. Courts construe the Lanham Act to apply to artistic words only when the public interest in avoiding consumer confusion outweighs the public interest in free expression. This is often called the *Rogers* or *Grimaldi* test. *See Rogers v. Grimaldi*, 875 F.2d 994, 999 (2d Cir. 1989). (The various approaches used by the different circuits considering the First Amendment and the likelihood of consumer confusion are discussed in greater detail in Chapter 12.) The *Rogers* test has two prongs: The first prong is that an artistic trademark use is excused unless it has no artistic relevance to the underlying work. The second prong is, if it has artistic relevance, whether the use explicitly misleads the public as to the source or content of the work. The court found in *Rock Star Videos* that a computer game was artistic. The defendant argued that the defense should fail because the game was not about his club; therefore, there was no artistic relevance. The court found that any artistic relevance above zero would suffice to meet the *Rogers* test. The game's goal was to replicate the look and feel of a seedy Los Angeles neighborhood. Using some real buildings to create an authentic feel was sufficient to show "some artistic relevance."

The defendant then contended that the use of the mark PIG PEN in the game explicitly misled the public about the source of the work. The court found that the relevant question was whether players of *Grand Theft Auto* would be confused into thinking that the plaintiff's strip club somehow sponsored the defendant's game. The mere use of a trademark is not enough to meet this prong. The court's choice of language is telling.

> Both San Andreas and the Play Pen offer a form of low-brow entertainment; besides this general similarity, they have nothing in common. The San Andreas Game is not complementary to the Play Pen; video games and strip clubs do not go together like a horse and carriage or, perish the thought, love and marriage. Nothing indicates that the buying public would reasonably have believed that ESS produced the video game or, for that matter, that Rockstar operated a strip club.

Rock Star Videos, 547 F.3d at 1100.

Finally, the plaintiff argued that players can ignore the storyline and spend as much time as they like in the virtual strip club; therefore, the virtual Pig Pen could be considered a significant part of the game, leading to confusion. The court rejected this contention, reiterating the finding that a chance to visit a virtual strip club is not the game's main selling point.

Rock Star Videos suggests that there could be liability for the use of marks in virtual environments and computer games; however, imposing such liability under the Lanham Act raises significant First Amendment concerns.

CHECKPOINTS

- The domain name portion of an email address can indicate source, origin, or sponsorship and constitute a false designation of origin for an email that did not originate from that service provider.
- Use of a mark in web page meta tags and keyword advertising, banner or sponsored advertising, or pop-up advertising may constitute a use in commerce and create liability under the Lanham Act.
- Often, confusion on the internet is initial-interest confusion, which is usually dispelled before the point of purchase.
- The good-faith use of a competitor's trademark in meta tags or on a website may be excused under classic or traditional fair use or as nominative fair use.
- The use of a trademark as a keyword for internet advertising is a use in commerce under the Lanham Act.
- Banner or sponsored advertising as part of a web search engine results page may create a likelihood of consumer confusion, depending on how the mark is presented to the consumer.
- Inline linking, deep linking, or framing may constitute trademark infringement if the link is presented on the originating website in such a manner as to cause a likelihood of consumer confusion.
- The use of a trademark as part of a URL address (not the domain name) is generally not a use under trademark law.
- The use of trademarks in phishing schemes may constitute trademark infringement.

- The use of a trademark in a virtual world or within a computer game may support a cause of action for trademark infringement or trademark dilution.
- The use of trademarks in virtual worlds or games often raises serious First Amendment concerns that must be considered as a defense to claims of trademark infringement.

CHAPTER 16

Introduction to International Trademark Law

ROADMAP

- Background of international trademark law
- Paris Convention for the Protection of Industrial Property
- Madrid System for the International Registration of Marks
- Nice Agreement on International Classification and Services
- Other Multilateral Regional Agreements
- Agreement on Trade-Related Aspects of Intellectual Property Rights (TRIPS Agreement)
- Internationally recognized trademark subject matter
- Trademarks
- Geographical indications
- Registration, use, and priority
- Use and priority date
- Well-known marks
- Ownership and trademark rights
- Minimum levels of trademark enforcement
- Remedies
- Criminal penalties
- Extraterritorial application of the Lanham Act

There is no such thing as an international trademark or international trademark rights. Trademark rights are legal rights created and granted under the laws of each country. Despite there being no such thing as an international trademark or international trademark law, a body of international treaties provides for the harmonization of national laws, the facilitation of trademark registration on a multinational basis, and international trademark enforcement. The core and most economically significant trademark rights from registration to enforcement are protected in most countries under that nation's interpretation of its obligations under the Agreement on Trade-Related Aspects of Intellectual Property Rights (TRIPS Agreement), which is an obligation of each World Trade Organization (WTO) member state. This chapter limits its discussion to international trademark law as practiced in light of the TRIPS Agreement, the Trademark Law Treaty, and the Madrid System for Registration of Marks (Madrid System).

A. U.S. Trademark Law and Its Relationship to U.S. Treaty Law

Applying treaties governing trademark rights may be problematic in the United States because of the U.S. federal system of government and its common law legal traditions. Under the Supremacy Clause of the Constitution, upon ratification by the Senate, treaties become the supreme law of the land. However, not all treaties are self-executing. If a treaty is not self-executing, Congress must pass appropriate legislation to conform to federal law to satisfy the United States' treaty obligations. Federal courts will not create causes of action, recognize defenses, or grant rights or remedies under a non-self-executing treaty. Whether a treaty is self-executing is often subject to great debate and disagreement between various courts interpreting the treaty or parties trying to obtain rights under a treaty that Congress still needs to enact into positive domestic law. A further complicating factor is that a state may recognize trademark rights as a matter of its common law of trademark equivalent to those recognized under a treaty without relying on the treaty or any change in federal law. Students and practitioners should always compare the treaty language and the positive enactments into U.S. law through legislation or agency regulations to determine the trademark law currently in effect in the United States and consider state common law as an additional source of rights.

As discussed in Chapter 13, trademark causes of action under federal law will often plead causes of action under state law in the same complaint.

B. Background of International Trademark Law

During the 19th century, common law countries led by the United Kingdom started to develop a body of trademark law based on common law fraud or the passing-off in commerce of goods or services. In continental European civil code countries, trademark protection evolved out of principles of unfair competition. By the end of the 19th century, most Western countries had established a trademark registration system. Differing bodies of trademark law within both common law and civil law jurisdictions hindered international trade, and often trademark protection was only available based on reciprocity. By 1880, the then-developed industrialized nations realized the necessity for some limited harmonization of their domestic trademark laws.

The first significant treaty addressing international intellectual property, the Paris Convention for the Protection of Industrial Property (Paris Convention), was concluded in 1883. Since 1883, the Paris Convention has been revised or amended at least six times. Other significant trademark treaties include the 1891 Madrid Agreement Concerning the International Registration of Marks and the 1989 Madrid Protocol (collectively these two treaties are referred to as the "Madrid System for the International Registration of Marks" or "Madrid System"). In addition to the Paris Convention and the Madrid System, other significant trademark treaties include the TRIPS Agreement and the Nice Agreement on International Classification. The Trademark Law Treaty only required minor tecnical amendments to U.S. Law.

1. Paris Convention for the Protection of Industrial Property

The Paris Convention for the Protection of Industrial Property of 1883 was the first major international intellectual property treaty. The Paris Convention is significant today since it is the floor on which international principles of trademark protection are based. In fact, the great advancement of this treaty is that it imposed a duty of "national treatment" by member states on the nationals of other member states. Stated simply, member states may not treat foreign mark owners worse than the member state's own citizens. The Paris Convention first recognizes this in Article 6, which states that registration of a mark in one country (including the country of the trademark owner, referred to as the country of origin) is not dispositive of that mark's status in other member states of the Paris Convention ("Paris Convention countries"). This provision prevents member states from prohibiting registration of a mark because of the status of that mark in the country of origin. This prevents member states from disadvantaging mark owners from other states.

In addition, the Paris Convention imposes some minimum requirements on member states. For example, under Article 6*bis*, Paris Convention countries must provide a minimal level of protection for well-known marks. Further, Paris Convention Article 6*ter* provides protection for governmental or intergovernmental emblems, flags, and similar symbols. Paris Convention Article 9 provides for the seizures of goods bearing counterfeit marks. Finally, Paris Convention Article 10 has general provisions against various forms of unfair competition. Subsequent treaties, in particular the TRIPS Agreement, explicitly incorporate provisions of the Paris Convention or exist as special unions under the Paris Convention.

2. Madrid System for the International Registration of Marks

The Madrid System for the International Registration of Marks consists of the 1891 Madrid Agreement Concerning the International Registration of Marks, the 1989 Protocol Relating to the Madrid Agreement, and the Common Regulations under the Agreement and Protocol. The International Bureau of the World Intellectual Property Organization (WIPO) administers the Madrid System. International registration under the Madrid System has several advantages to the trademark registrant. The trademark holder only has to file one application, in one language, and pay one combined fee. Absent the Madrid System, the trademark holder would have to file numerous applications in many different languages and pay separate fees to each trademark office. The trademark holder would then have to await the approval of each trademark office. Under the Madrid System, the mark is registered if the trademark office does not issue a timely provisional rejection. The trademark holder may renew its trademark registration in all designated countries directly through the International Bureau.

The 1989 Madrid Protocol was created partly to address the United States' issues with the Madrid Agreement. There are some differences between the two treaties. Still, the essence of the two treaties is to create an international mechanism for filing trademark applications in many different countries simultaneously by only filing a single application (subject to the payment of a fee for each designated country). Differences between the treaties include the following:

- the time a national trademark office may take to review an application (Protocol: 18 months; Agreement: 12 months);
- the language the application must be filed in (Protocol: French, English, or Spanish; Agreement: French only); and
- the right to convert to separate national applications if the original application is rejected, withdrawn, or abandoned (Protocol).

Any member state of the Paris Convention may become a contracting party to either treaty the Madrid System comprises. Any natural or legal person with a commercial presence in, or is a national or domiciliary of, a member state of the Madrid System is eligible to file an international application. Generally, a mark eligible for an international application has already been registered or is subject to an application for registration in the trademark office of a member state. The application is processed through the Office of Origin (the trademark office where the mark is registered or subject to a trademark application). The Office of Origin will then forward the international trademark application to the WIPO International Bureau. An international application requires the payment of a basic fee, a fee for each designated country, and fees for each Nice Classification for goods and services beyond the first three unless the designated country charges a separate individual fee.

At a minimum, the international application must contain a reproduction of the mark as it was filed with the Office of Origin for the national registration and using the International Classification of Goods and Services (Nice Classification system), a list of goods or services for which the mark is being registered. The Office of Origin must certify that the mark in the international application is the same as the mark in the basic registration, and that the list of goods or services in the basic registration is the same as the list of goods or services in the international registration. Under Article 4 of the Paris Convention, the applicant may claim up to a six-month priority date based on a prior trademark registration in the Paris Convention or

WTO country. If the International Bureau receives the properly completed application within two months of the date that the Office of Origin received the request for the international application, then that is the date of the international registration.

The applicant must designate in which contracting countries it is seeking protection. If the application needs to be completed or there are other problems, the applicant has three months to correct the problems or the International Bureau will treat the application as abandoned. If the application is complete and complies with the relevant provisions of the Madrid System, then the trademark is registered and published in the *WIPO Gazette of International Marks.*

Designated country trademark offices examine the international application for registration as if it had been filed directly with that country's trademark office. The designated trademark office will either notify the International Bureau that there are no grounds to deny or, if there are grounds to deny the application, that it is issuing a provisional refusal. If the application is provisionally refused, all subsequent responses to the provisional refusal are entirely between the applicant and the designated trademark office. The designated trademark office will notify the International Bureau of its final action on the trademark application, which will be published in the *WIPO Gazette of International Marks.*

3. Nice Agreement on International Classification and Services

The Nice Agreement on the International Classification of Goods facilitates the registration of goods in different trademark registration offices because the same good or service has the same classification number in each office. For example, class 45, which covers "Legal services; security services for the protection of property and individuals; personal and social services rendered by others to meet the needs of individuals," would be the same in every country that is a party to the Nice Agreement (also referred to as the Nice Classification system). Also, because the classification numbers are available in several languages, the cost of translating the trademark application is reduced. The Nice Classification system currently has 34 classes of goods and 11 classes of services. To keep it current, the classifications are updated on an ongoing basis. While the updates had been every five years, that process has been changed. The current classification is the 11th edition, which took effect on

January 1, 2022. That classification will be in effect for six years. Thereafter, the Nice Classifications will be issued every three years. *See* TMEP § 1401.02(a).

4. ARIPO, OAPI, Andean Pact, MERCOSUR, NAFTA, Pan-American Convention, and the European Community Trademark

In addition to the major international treaties, agreements, protocols, or conventions that address trademark rights, other multilateral regional agreements, such as the African Regional Intellectual Property Organization (ARIPO) and the Organisation Africaine de la Propriété Intellectuelle (OAPI) in Africa, the Andean Pact and MERCOSUR in South America, the North American Free Trade Agreement (NAFTA), the Pan-American Convention, and the European Community Trade Mark (ECTM), facilitate trademark registration and the enforcement of trademark rights. Probably the most economically significant of these regional trademark treaties is the European Union Community Trademark system. These specialized trademark treaty regimes are outside the scope of this book.

5. Agreement on Trade-Related Aspects of Intellectual Property Rights (TRIPS Agreement)

By the 1980s, many developed nations sought to modernize and extend the existing intellectual property treaties, such as the Paris Convention. However, some member nations that were hostile to the expansion of intellectual property, particularly patents, refused to negotiate on revisions to the existing treaties. As a result, the developed nations switched strategies. They decided to include intellectual property rights as part of the then-ongoing General Agreement on Tariffs and Trade (GATT) treaty negations, in which those same nations were participating. The developed nations then conditioned the expansion of global trade and access to markets promised under GATT on those nations adopting the TRIPS Agreement as an adjunct to GATT (referred to as GATT-TRIPS). The developed nations were successful in achieving their aim. GATT created the WTO, which now plays a role in international intellectual property enforcement.

The TRIPS Agreement established modern international trademark standards. TRIPS Article 2(1) requires member nations of the WTO to comply with Articles 1 through 12 and Article 19 of the Paris Convention (1967), and places additional requirements for the protection of marks and quasi-marks in Articles 15 through 24 of the TRIPS Agreement. Consequently, for most purposes, the international law of trademark is the body of trademark law agreed to by WTO member states as expressed in the TRIPS Agreement. However, the TRIPS Agreement represents only the floor of trademark law protection that WTO member states must offer other member states' trademark owners. Member states may offer less protection to their domestic trademark owners, and some member states may have bilateral or multilateral agreements that provide trademark rights above the minimum level of protection required under the TRIPS Agreement. For example, Article 17.2.6 of the Australia-United States Free Trade Agreement requires both nations to extend protection for well-known marks under Article 6*bis* of the Paris Convention to goods and services that are not identical or similar. Article 6*bis* of the Paris Convention limits its application to identical or similar goods.

The TRIPS Agreement is sometimes referred to as "Paris-Plus," since it expands on some obligations and includes several provisions not contained in the Paris Convention. For example, in Article 4, the TRIPS Agreement requires that when a member state extends protection for intellectual property to the citizens of another member state, such protection must extend to citizens of all other member states; Article 15(1) includes a uniform definition of what constitutes a trademark; and Article 16 applies certain provisions of the Paris Convention to services that had only previously applied to marks for goods. Some of the other increases in protection are described below.

C. Internationally Recognized Trademark Subject Matter

Trademarks and other types of marks are protected under various treaties, the most important of which are the Paris Convention and the TRIPS Agreement. The signaling function of a sign as a source identifier may fall under two major classification schemes. They may be treated as trademarks, the norm in the United States and many other countries. In these countries, the general principles of trademark law govern all source-identifying signals. Unlike the

United States, some other countries have created a sui generis body of law governing the use of signs that identify the geographical region that is the source of the product. Geographical indications are treated differently from traditional trademarks in both domestic law and international agreements. This section will discuss the trademarks and geographical indications under the Paris Convention and the TRIPS Agreement.

1. Trademarks

The TRIPS Agreement Article 15(1) defines a trademark as "[a]ny sign ... capable of distinguishing the goods or services of one undertaking from those of other undertakings." Article 15(1) further defines "signs" as "words, personal names, letters, numerals, figurative elements, combinations of colors, as well as any combination of such signs." Member states may but are not required to register single-color marks, sound marks, or scent marks. Consequently, since the United States has a more robust definition of a mark, some marks which are protectable in the United States, such as scent marks or single-color marks, may not be eligible for registration or protection in some other WTO countries.

2. Geographical Indications

A geographical indication (GI) is a signal used on goods originating in a specific geographical region and possessing qualities, reputation, or characteristics that are uniquely tied to the geographical place of origin. TRIPS Article 22. GIs are protected under a variety of laws. Often a GI is associated with an agricultural product, such as wine, which is influenced by local geographical factors, for example, soil, climate, or traditional methods of preparation. Frequently a geographical indication is identical to the geographical name of the region from which the product originates. For example, a sparkling white wine that is produced by inducing in-bottle secondary fermentation of the wine to effect carbonation using primarily chardonnay, pinot meunier, or pinot noir grapes grown and processed in the Champagne region of France is commonly called by the GI "champagne."

A specialized type of GI is an appellation of origin (AO). An AO usually consists of a geographical name, or a traditional designation used on products whose characteristics or qualities are uniquely tied to the specific geographical environment in which they are produced. So the term "champagne" is both a

GI and an AO for a type of white sparkling wine. Some geographical regions have valuable reputations for producing agricultural products of extraordinary quality. Producers of products similar-in-type or inferior products may desire to trade on these reputations, thus damaging the reputations of legitimate producers and deceiving consumers.

A GI and a trademark serve similar but distinct functions. A trademark is potentially any signal used by a business to distinguish among the qualities and characteristics of its goods and services from those of others. Traditional trademark law merely grants the trademark owner the right to police the mark by preventing uses that cause a likelihood of consumer confusion. In contrast, a geographical indication informs the public that a product was made in a specific geographical region, often through the use of some traditional production method. Any producer in the relevant geographical region who produces the product using the traditional method is entitled to use the geographical indication. In this sense, a GI is roughly analogous to a certification mark in the United States. While trademarks tend to be owned and supervised by the private owners or private associations of producers, geographical indications tend to be supervised by governmental agencies. GI protection often grants broader rights than trademark law, for example, even if there is no likelihood of consumer confusion, producers of other products may not truthfully advertise that their products are like or similar to a GI or produced using the same process as the GI-protected product. And, in some countries, rights in a later-granted GI may trump private-owner rights in an earlier trademark.

The status of GIs in international law is hotly debated. In the United States, GIs are functionally protected under the Lanham Act as either certification or collective marks. GIs may also be protected under unfair competition laws, consumer protection laws, or under sui generis or ad hoc laws protecting individual GIs. In the European Union, GIs are generally protected under a comprehensive regime of special laws. Internationally, GIs are protected under several treaties including the Paris Convention, and the Lisbon Agreement for the Protection of Appellations of Origin and Their International Registration. In addition, Articles 22 to 24 of the TRIPS Agreement cover the minimum standards of international protection of geographical indications within the framework of the WTO.

a. Paris Convention for the Protection of Industrial Property of 1883

Geographic indications are a form of industrial property under Article 1(2) of the Paris Convention. The Paris Convention, under principles of national treatment, requires signatory nations to protect foreign geographical indications on the same basis as it protects domestic geographical indications. Articles 9 and 10 require that signatory nations take appropriate measures to prevent the deceptive use of source identifiers and to prevent unfair competition. There is no affirmative requirement in the Paris Convention to create a sui generis legal regime to protect geographical indications outside the rubric of trademark protection. As will be discussed later in this chapter, the TRIPS Agreement provides for additional mandatory protections for some geographical indications relating to wines and spirits.

b. Lisbon Agreement for the Protection of Appellations of Origin and Their International Registration of 1958

The Lisbon Agreement for the Protection of Appellations of Origin and Their International Registration of 1958 (Lisbon Agreement) is a special union established under Article 19 of the Paris Convention to regulate and protect geographical indications. Members of the Lisbon Agreement grant priority to later-occurring geographical indications over earlier trademarks and must phase out trademarks that conflict with geographical indications. Only a few countries have joined the Lisbon Agreement, and of those few, only a tiny minority has either a significant number of geographical indications or geographical indications that have either global notoriety or are even economically very significant. Some commentators consider the Lisbon Agreement to be a failure, and it has largely been replaced or supplemented by provisions of the TRIPS Agreement. Some provisions of the Lisbon Agreement arguably conflict with its member nations' obligations under the TRIPS Agreement as WTO members. However, the Lisbon Agreement provides superior protection to geographical indications in comparison to the TRIPS Agreement or Paris Convention, and the mere existence of a GI, even one that is recognized after the priority date of a trademark, may create significant difficulties for the trademark owner.

c. TRIPS Agreement's Geographical Indication Provisions

TRIPS Agreement Article 22 defines geographical indications as "indications which identify a good as originating in the territory of a Member, or a region or locality in that territory, where a given quality, reputation or other characteristic of the good is essentially attributable to its geographical origin." Under TRIPS, member states must permit interested parties to prevent "the designation or presentation of a good that indicates or suggests that the good in question originates in a geographical area other than the true place of origin in a manner which misleads the public as to the geographical origin of the good" or any use that constitutes unfair competition under Article 10*bis* of the Paris Convention. Interested parties have the right to invalidate the registration of trademarks that mislead the public by using a geographical indication for goods that do not originate in the relevant geographical territory. The TRIPS Agreement also prohibits the use of geographical terms that may be literally true but which mislead the public as to the true place of origin—for example, Havana Cigars made in Havana, Ohio, since prudent cigar consumers would assume the cigars originate in Havana, Cuba.

As part of the compromise that led to the adoption of TRIPS, Article 23 of the TRIPS Agreement has special provisions protecting the geographical indications for wines and spirits. All WTO member states must protect the geographical indications associated with wines and spirits. This protection is required even if there are adequate disclaimers or the market context clearly dispels any likelihood of consumer confusion or deception. For example, if a U.S. wine uses a French GI for wine in very small print, and in much larger print states "MADE IN CALIFORNIA, USA," this is illegal, even if no one believes the wine comes from a particular region of France. Moreover, a GI may not be used even if it is used in translation or there are clear expressions such as "kind," "type," "style," "imitation," or the like that would dispel consumer confusion. Thus, a manufacturer may not use a GI in the trademark fair use sense to indicate that one product is similar to another even when such advertising is both truthful and does not result in a likelihood of consumer confusion. Interested parties have a right to invalidate a trademark registration that contains or consists of a geographical indication for wine or spirits.

To accomplish this goal of protecting geographical indications for wine and spirits, WTO member states were supposed to undertake negotiations regarding a multilateral system of notification and registration of eligible GIs. While these negotiations did take place, there has been no progress on creating such a registration system. There is a significant divide between new-world countries such as the United States and old-world countries such as France on the process by which a GI could be registered and the legal effect once the GI has been registered. The European Union wants a registration system with mandatory effect that would be binding on national trademark offices unless they objected to the registration in a relatively short period of time. The U.S. proposal is that the registration system would be for informational purposes only and would merely be one source that local trademark registration offices may consider when examining a trademark.

D. Registration, Use, and Priority

Under the TRIPS Agreement, a member state must grant trademark protection, but it may also grant trademark rights only upon actual use and provide for trademark rights to senior users that continue to exist even after the junior user had registered the mark. Most civil law countries protect trademark rights almost entirely by registration. Common law countries, on the other hand, often will provide some limited rights based solely on trademark use. While the TRIPS Agreement appears to presume a registration-based system, there are sufficient flexibilities for members with a use-based trademark system to achieve their national priorities.

1. Registration

TRIPS Article 15 contains several requirements regarding trademark registration. Member states may limit trademark registration to marks that have secondary meaning, and they may require descriptive marks to have a requisite level of acquired distinctiveness or secondary meaning through use. Member states cannot reject an application for trademark registration solely because the mark was not used within three years of the application date. The nature of the goods or services on which the mark is being used is not grounds to deny trademark registration. Member states must publish a trademark application and provide an opportunity for interested parties to file an opposition either before the trademark registration is granted or shortly thereafter. The initial trademark registration term cannot be less than seven years and is indefinitely renewable.

Under TRIPS Article 19, if continued use of a trademark is required to maintain or renew the trademark registration, the registration may be canceled if the registrant or its licensee without a valid excuse ceases to use the mark for a period of at least three years. Circumstances outside the control of the trademark owner such as import restrictions or other government requirements for goods or services protected by the trademark are recognized excuses for the non-use of the registered mark.

2. Use and Priority Date

Under TRIPS Article 15(3), member states may require that the trademark be actually used in commerce, but prior use cannot be a prerequisite to applying for trademark registration. In the United States, Lanham Act §§ 1(b) and 44 implement TRIPS Article 15(3). Section 1(b) is the intent-to-use provision as a basis to apply for a U.S trademark, and § 44 permits a non-U.S. trademark holder to use its pending foreign application for a registered trademark as a basis to apply for a U.S. trademark. The foreign applicant can "backdate" its U.S. application and claim the priority date of its earlier filed foreign application, so long as that foreign date of filing occurs no more than six months prior to the U.S. filing date.

3. Well-Known Marks

Under Article 6*bis* of the Paris Convention as incorporated through the TRIPS Agreement, a member state must refuse to register, cancel the registration, or prohibit the use of a mark that is well-known in that country even if the trademark is not registered in the country. There is no generally accepted definition of a well-known mark. Suffice to say, it may be useful to look at the definition of a famous trademark in the United States and then apply the relevant factors by analogy as part of the process of determining whether a mark is a well-known mark. However, the level of notoriety required to be a well-known mark is lower than that required to be a famous mark under trademark dilution. In determining whether a trademark is well-known, TRIPS requires that members consider the knowledge of the trademark among the relevant public sectors and to consider whether this knowledge is a result of promotion of the trademark. Perhaps the pre-TDRA caselaw finding niche fame or levels of fame below that which is currently required under the TDRA may be instructive.

The application of the TRIPS well-known-marks provision in the United States is in a state of confusion. The U.S. circuit courts are split on this issue.

Compare *ITC Ltd. v. Punchgini, Inc.*, 482 F.3d 135 (2d Cir. 2007) (rejecting the well-known mark exception), with *Grupo Gigante, SA v. Dallo & Co, Inc.*, 391 F.3d 1088 (9th Cir. 2002) (recognizing the well-known mark exception to the territoriality principle). Moreover, even if a federal circuit court of appeals does not recognize the TRIPS well-known-mark article under federal law, some states, as a matter of state law or state common law, will recognize and protect well-known marks since the unauthorized use of the well-known mark is likely to create consumer confusion. Consequently, a deftly pleaded complaint should assert both state and federal rights so that the district court may protect the well-known mark under state-law provisions.

More recently, in *Belmora LLC v. Bayer Consumer Care AG*, 819 F.3d 697 (4th Cir. 2016), the Fourth Circuit considered whether the owner of a foreign mark that had not used the mark in U.S. commerce had standing to challenge a competitor's use and registration of that well-known foreign mark in the United States. Without relying on the Paris Convention Article 6*bis* directly, the court held that the use by Belmora in the United States of Bayer's FLANAX mark, which Bayer only used in Latin America and Mexico, fell within the zone of interests protected under §§ 43(a) and 14(3). The court held that these sections, which create liability for false association and false advertising, on the one hand, and grounds for cancellation, on the other, allow a plaintiff to bring suit if it would be damaged by the use or registration of a mark, without requiring proof of use of the plaintiff's mark in the United States. The court applied the Supreme Court's reasoning from *Lexmark International, Inc. v. Static Control Components, Inc.*, 572 U.S. 118 (2014), in which it held that under the Lanham Act, a court should determine standing based on whether the plaintiff's claimed rights fall within the zone of interests protected by the statute and whether violations of the statute proximately cause the harms.

E. Ownership and Trademark Rights

Under TRIPS Article 16, the owner of a registered trademark has the exclusive right to prevent third parties from using identical or similar marks for goods or services that are identical or similar to the registered mark and the goods or services for which the mark is registered when the unauthorized use results in a likelihood of consumer confusion. In the case of identical marks, there is a legal presumption of consumer confusion.

WTO member states may create limited exceptions to the trademark owner's rights, for example, a fair use defense to the use of the mark as a descriptive term. But member states must consider both the legitimate interests of the trademark owner and third parties in creating limited exceptions to the trademark owner's rights.

F. Minimum Levels of Process for the Enforcement of Trademark Rights

Under Part III of the TRIPS Agreement, WTO member states are not required to create a special judicial or administrative system for the enforcement of trademark rights. However, member states must have enforcement mechanisms that are effective, expeditious, and deter continued trademark infringement. Judicial and civil administrative enforcement procedures should be fair, equitable, simple, and expeditious. A defendant must receive timely detailed written notice of the allegations against her. Parties may be represented by independent legal counsel and allowed to present relevant evidence. Judicial authorities may order the production of evidence in the possession of a party, and if that party fails to produce evidence in its possession, the court may draw reasonable inferences from the party's failure to produce the evidence. The judicial decision in a trademark dispute should be in writing, available to the parties to the dispute, based on evidence produced before the tribunal, and the parties to the dispute must have an opportunity to be heard regarding the evidence. In civil cases, there must be some form of judicial review of final administrative decisions and decisions by trial courts. However, there is no obligation to provide for a review of an acquittal in a criminal case.

G. Remedies

1. Equitable Remedies

TRIPS Article 44 requires civil law judges to have the authority to grant remedies analogous to equitable remedies in the common law system. Judges may order a party to cease infringing activities, preserve evidence, and prevent infringing goods from entering the stream of commerce; they may order infringing goods to be seized immediately after customs clearance; and they may condition such orders upon payment of a bond or provision of other such security to compensate an innocent alleged infringer. While typically a part of a common-law judge's inherent authority, these rights are not universal, especially in some civil law jurisdictions. Therefore, in some civil law countries, these remedies may be available if one pleads a violation of rights under the TRIPS Agreement, but not in other related domestic civil law trademark actions.

2. Damages

TRIPS Article 45 requires that courts have authority to order a trademark infringer to pay the trademark rights holder adequate damages. The language of Article 45 seems to suggest that this right could be conditioned on the court's finding that either the infringer knew or had grounds to know that the act constituted trademark infringement. The court may also order the infringer to pay the trademark owner's attorney fees and other expenses. Member states may permit judicial authorities to order the recovery of profits or statutory damages even if the infringer did not knowingly or willfully infringe the trademark.

3. Other Remedies

TRIPS Article 46 states that judicial authorities may order infringing goods to be disposed of outside the normal stream of commerce and without any compensation to the trademark infringer, in such a manner as to not harm the interests of the trademark owner, or they may order them to be destroyed. The court may also order the destruction or other disposition without compensation of the goods, products, or machinery that predominantly contributed to the infringement of the trademark. Judicial authorities shall balance the seriousness of the remedy and the infringement proportionally with the interests of third parties. Merely removing the infringing trademark from the counterfeit goods is generally an inadequate remedy except in the rarest of circumstances.

4. Border-Control Measures

TRIPS Articles 51 through 59 require that WTO member states have border-control procedures so that they can prevent entry of such goods if they are notified regarding the shipment of infringing goods. The trademark owner must notify the customs agency, demonstrate a prima facie case of trademark infringement under the importing country's laws, and provide the customs authorities with sufficient information to identify the alleged infringing articles. The customs authorities may require the trademark owner to post a reasonable bond or provide other reasonably adequate security to protect the importer and legal authorities. After the goods are seized, the parties are notified, and the importer may commence proceedings to release the goods. In the case of wrongful detention of the goods, authorities may order the trademark holder to pay appropriate compensation to the importer of the goods. Customs officials may also act on their own initiative to detain counterfeit or trademark-infringing goods.

5. De Minimis Imports

TRIPS Article 60 provides that WTO member states may provide limited exceptions to border-control measures for de minimis imports of counterfeit trademark or infringing goods, which are clearly for personal and noncommercial use. Usually, these goods will accompany the traveler and are contained within the traveler's luggage.

H. Criminal Penalties

Under TRIPS Article 61, WTO member states must provide for criminal penalties in the case of willful trademark counterfeiting on a commercial scale. The TRIPS Agreement requires that the penalties include imprisonment, fines, and the forfeiture and destruction of infringing goods and products that have as their primary use the purposes of trademark infringement. The TRIPS Agreement does not specify the length of time of imprisonment or the amount of the fines, but they must be sufficient to deter the offense and comparable to the "penalties applied for crimes of a corresponding gravity."

I. Reach of Lanham Act to Foreign Activity

The Supreme Court has long held that there is a presumption against the extraterritorial application of U.S. law to foreign activities. The Court has considered the application of the Lanham Act to foreign conduct in light of this presumption on two occasions. First, in 1952, the Supreme Court held that the activities of the defendant in Mexico, himself a U.S. citizen, could subject the defendant to liability under the Lanham Act because some harm occurred in the United States. Specifically, the defendant manufactured and sold watches branded with the Bulova mark in Mexico, a trademark registered in the United States by the Bulova Watch Company. Some of those watches made it into the U.S. market as a consequence, and the Court held that the defendant could be liable for trademark infringement under the Lanham Act. *Steele v. Bulova Watch Co.*, 344 U.S. 280 (1952).

Seventy-one years later, the Court decided *Abitron Austria GmbH v. Hetronic International, Inc.*, 600 U.S. 412, 143 S. Ct. 2522 (2023). Abitron, a German company that had licensed Hetronic's trademarks, rejected the license after determining it actually owned the marks in question outside of the United States. Hetronic sued Abitron in the United States for trademark infringement under Lanham Act §§ 32(1)(a) and 43(a)(1)(A), winning a $96 million verdict, which included damages for infringing activities outside of the United States, and obtaining a world-wide injunction. Abitron appealed, claiming that these remedies were an unlawful extraterritorial application of the Lanham Act.

The Court in *Abitron* noted that since the *Steele* case was decided in 1952, the Court had developed a two-step analysis to determine if a U.S. law applies to conduct outside the United States despite the presumption against extraterritoriality. Under step one, a court considers whether Congress affirmatively and unmistakably legislated that the relevant provision of U.S. law applies extraterritorially. If the answer to step one is yes, then the law applies to the extraterritorial activity. The Court unanimously held in *Abitron* that the Lanham Act did not contain a clear, affirmative indication that §§ 32(a) and 43(a) were to apply extraterritorially. The Court noted that mentioning foreign commerce in a statute does not make the statute extraterritorial.

Where the answer to step one is no, then step two requires that the court determine "whether the suit seeks a (permissible) domestic or (impermissible) foreign application of the provision [of the law]." 143 S. Ct. at 2528. This requires a court to consider the statutory focus of the legislation and whether the conduct is relevant to the statutory focus occurred in the United States. Here, a majority of the Justices distinguished the *Steele* case, noting it was "narrow and factbound," as it dealt with a defendant whose actions which "when viewed as a whole" occurred in both the United States and Mexico. The Court said the relevant conduct that forms the statutory focus of §§ 32 and 43 of the Lanham Act is a use in commerce, as defined in the Act itself. The Court distinguished between the focus of the theory of liability (here, likelihood of confusion) and "the location of the conduct relevant to the focus," which the Court said had to be the use of the marks in commerce in the United States.

The Court rejected the dissent's view that foreign conduct which could result in likelihood of confusion in the United States fell under the Lanham Act. The majority said this confused the legislation's statutory focus with the relevant conduct's location. Even if confusion might occur in the United States, if the conduct was not based on a use in commerce in the United States, then the Lanham Act did not apply to that conduct.

CHECKPOINTS

- Trademark rights are created and granted by each country. Various treaties, including particularly the Paris Convention and the TRIPS Agreement, have been negotiated to harmonize protection of trademarks internationally.
- The Paris Convention of 1883 was the first such treaty, and it established the floor on which international principles of trademark protection are based. The Paris Convention has been amended six times.
- The Madrid System provides an international system where a trademark holder only must file one application in one language and pay one fee to register its mark internationally.
- The TRIPS Agreement harmonized and expanded the obligations of member nations to protect trademarks. The TRIPS Agreement includes the following obligations:
    - A member state may restrict trademark rights to only actual use and protect senior trademark users even after a junior user has registered the mark.

  - A member state must refuse to register, cancel the registration, or prohibit the use of marks that are well-known in that country even if the trademark is not yet registered in the country.
  - The owner of a registered trademark has the exclusive right to prevent third parties from using identical or similar marks for goods or services that are identical or similar to the registered mark and the goods or services for which the mark is registered when the unauthorized use results in a likelihood of consumer confusion.
  - Member states are not required to create a special judicial or administrative system to enforce trademark rights. However, member states must have enforcement mechanisms that are "effective, expeditious, and deter continued trademark infringement."
  - Civil law judges must have the authority to grant remedies that are analogous to equitable remedies in the common law system.
  - Judicial authorities must have the authority to order a trademark infringer to pay the trademark rights holder adequate damages.
  - Judicial authorities may order infringing goods to be disposed of outside the normal stream of commerce without any compensation to the trademark infringer, in such a manner so as to not harm the interests of the trademark owner, or they may order them to be destroyed.
  - Member states must have border-control procedures so that if they are notified regarding a shipment of infringing goods, they can prevent its entry.
  - Member states may provide for limited exceptions to border-control measures for de minimis imports of counterfeit trademark or infringing goods that are clearly for personal use and noncommercial use.
  - A member state must provide for criminal penalties in the case of willful trademark counterfeiting on a commercial scale.
- The Lanham Act's provisions do not apply extraterritorially, and the relevant conduct creating liability for trademark infringement must occur in the U.S.

Mastering Trademark and Unfair Competition Law Master Checklist

The following checklist reflects topics covered in each chapter. A good understanding of the overall material would require a detailed knowledge of each of these topics.

CHAPTER 1 • INTRODUCTION TO TRADEMARK LAW

- ☐ Value and role of trademarks
- ☐ Use of trademarks
- ☐ Sources of law and persuasive authority
- ☐ Trademark terminology

CHAPTER 2 • HISTORICAL DEVELOPMENT OF TRADEMARK LAW

- ☐ Trademark use in history
- ☐ Early trademark law
- ☐ Federal legislation

CHAPTER 3 • WHAT IS A MARK?

- ☐ Marks as source identifiers
- ☐ Types of marks

- ☐ Inherent versus acquired distinctiveness

CHAPTER 4 • PROTECTING GOODWILL

- ☐ Maintaining a mark
- ☐ Loss of trademark rights
- ☐ Residual goodwill

CHAPTER 5 • TRADE DRESS

- ☐ Distinctiveness of trade dress
- ☐ Trade dress and functionality
- ☐ Trade dress and patent law

CHAPTER 6 • GEOGRAPHIC INDICATORS AND OTHER QUASI MARKS

- ☐ Geographic indicators
- ☐ Quasi marks

CHAPTER 7 • OWNERSHIP AND DEVELOPMENT OF RIGHTS IN A MARK

- ☐ Ownership of a trademark
- ☐ Obtaining rights in a mark
- ☐ The creation of common-law rights
- ☐ The extent of common-law rights

CHAPTER 8 • TRADEMARK REGISTRATION

- ☐ State vs. federal registration
- ☐ The registration process
- ☐ Limits on registration
- ☐ Post-registration matters
- ☐ The Madrid Protocol

CHAPTER 9 • TRADITIONAL TRADEMARK INFRINGEMENT

- ☐ The elements of trademark infringement
- ☐ The traditional trademark-infringement test
- ☐ Likelihood of confusion and its factors
- ☐ Non-traditional theories of trademark infringement
- ☐ Third-party liability

CHAPTER 10 • TRADEMARK INFRINGEMENT BY DILUTION

- ☐ Infringement by dilution (state and federal law)
- ☐ The elements of a dilution claim

CHAPTER 11 • FALSE OR DECEPTIVE COMMERCIAL ADVERTISING

- ☐ The elements of a § 43(a)(1)(B) claim
- ☐ Remedies
- ☐ Defenses

CHAPTER 12 • DEFENSES TO INFRINGEMENT

- ☐ Senior- or prior-user defense
- ☐ Junior-user defense: The "*Tea Rose-Rectanus*" Doctrine
- ☐ Fair use: statutory and nominative
- ☐ Parody and other First Amendment defenses
- ☐ Genericism/merely descriptive marks
- ☐ Functionality
- ☐ Equitable defenses

CHAPTER 13 • TRADEMARK REMEDIES

- ☐ Injunctions
- ☐ Damages

☐ Statutory damages in counterfeiting

☐ Barring importation to the United States

CHAPTER 14 • DOMAIN NAMES AND TRADEMARK LAW

☐ The history of domain names as trademarks

☐ The Federal Trademark Dilution Act (FTDA)

☐ The Anticybersquatting Consumer Protection Act (ACPA)

☐ The Uniform Domain Name Resolution Policy (UDRP)

CHAPTER 15 • TRADEMARKS AND THE INTERNET

☐ Domain name as an email address

☐ Search-engine liability

☐ Website "third-party" liability

☐ Linking

CHAPTER 16 • INTRODUCTION TO INTERNATIONAL TRADEMARK LAW

☐ Paris Convention for the Protection of Industrial Property

☐ Madrid System for the International Registration of Marks

☐ Agreement on Trade-Related Aspects of Intellectual Property Rights (TRIPS)

☐ Internationally recognized trademark subject matter

☐ Registration, use, and priority

☐ Minimum levels of trademark enforcement

☐ Remedies

☐ Criminal penalties

APPENDIX 1

Trademark Application and Post-Registration Process Timelines

---

ROADMAP

- Section 1(a) timeline: Application based on use in commerce
- Section 1(b) timeline: Application based on intent to use
- Section 44(d) timeline: Application based on foreign application
- Section 44(e) timeline: Application based on a foreign registration
- Section 66(a) timeline: Application based on the Madrid Protocol
- Post-registration timeline for all registrations except Madrid Protocol-based registrations
- Post-registration timeline for Madrid Protocol-based registrations

---

This Appendix contains timelines to provide you with an overview of the process, steps, and timeframes for filing a trademark application with a particular filing basis and for maintaining a trademark registration. It is based upon timelines prepared by the PTO, available at http://www.uspto.gov/trademarks/process/tm_timeline.jsp (these are U.S. Government works not protected by U.S. copyright). No copyright claim is made to U.S. government works.

Section 1(a) Timeline

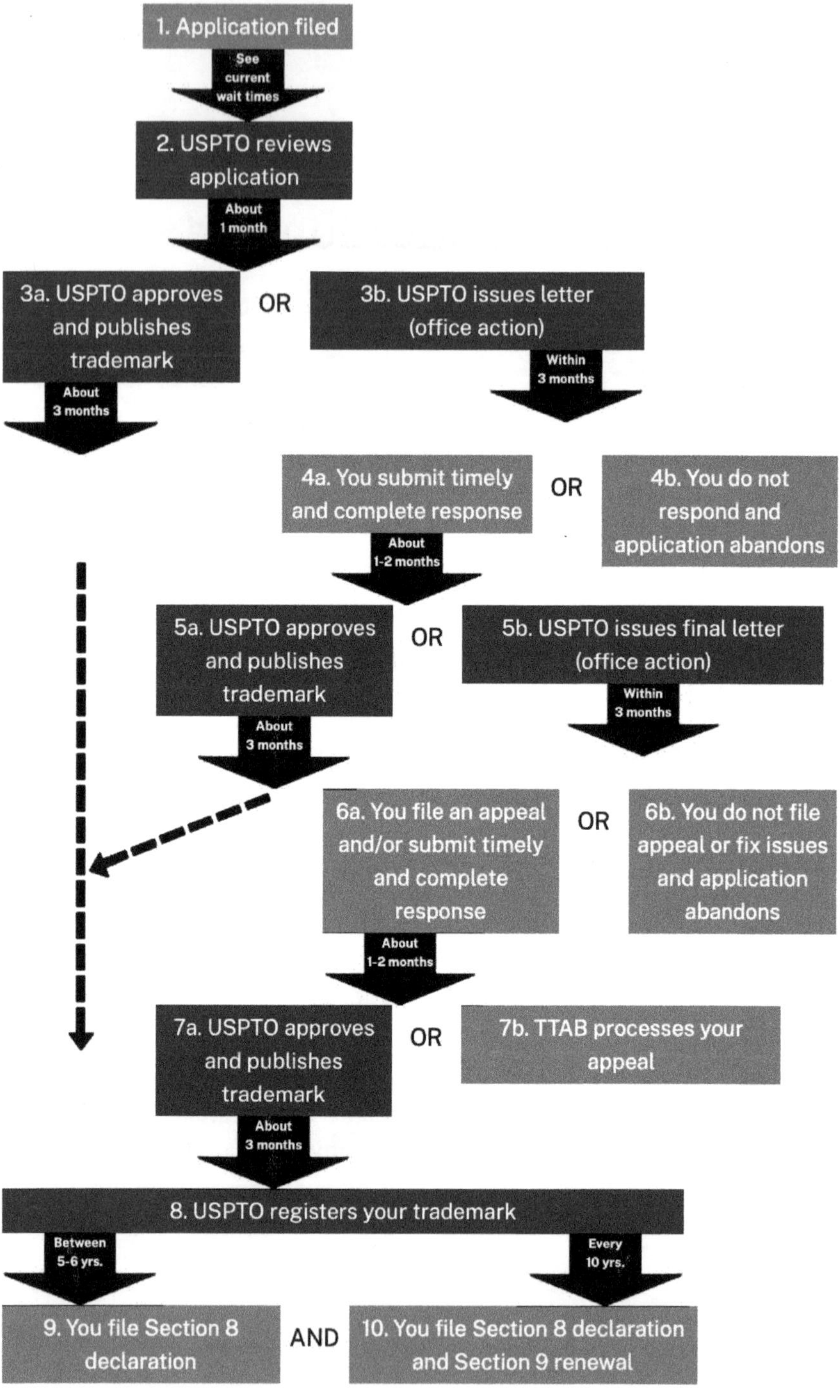

Step 1. Application filed. You file an application based on use of your trademark in commerce. Your application is given a USPTO serial number. You can check the status of your application by entering the serial number in the Trademark Status and Document Retrieval (TSDR) system or calling the trademark status line at 571-272-5400, or toll-free at 1-800-786-9199 (select option 1, then option 2). In about six to nine months go to step 2.

Step 2. USPTO reviews application. If your application meets the filing requirements, it's assigned to an examining attorney, who reviews it to determine whether federal law permits registration of your trademark. Filing fees are generally not refunded, even if your application is later refused registration. In about one month go to step 3a or step 3b.

Step 3a. USPTO approves trademark and publishes it for opposition. If the examining attorney does not find grounds for refusing to register your trademark, and your application satisfies all legal requirements, your trademark will be approved for publication in the USPTO's Trademark Official Gazette (TMOG). The TMOG, a weekly online publication, gives advance notice to the public that the USPTO plans to register your trademark. Approximately one month after approval, your trademark will publish in the TMOG.

Within 30 days of the publishing date, anyone who believes their business will be harmed if we register your trademark may file an objection (or "opposition"). An opposition is similar to a federal court proceeding, but is held before the Trademark Trial and Appeal Board (TTAB), a panel of administrative judges who review and decide these matters. An opposition can extend the time between publication of your trademark in the TMOG and registration of your trademark. If someone files an opposition against your trademark, we will let you know. You may want to hire a U.S.-licensed attorney, as oppositions are complex proceedings. No further action is taken to register your trademark until the 30-day opposition period has expired and any oppositions are resolved. In about three months go to step 8.

Step 3b. USPTO issues letter (office action). If the examining attorney finds grounds for refusing to register your trademark, or if your application does not satisfy all legal requirements, the examining attorney issues a letter (office action) explaining those refusals and/or requirements. You must respond to the office action within three months of the date it was issued. Within three months go to step 4a or step 4b.

Step 4a. You submit a timely and complete response to the office action. To avoid abandonment of your application, you must timely submit a response that overcomes each refusal and/or satisfies each requirement in the office action. The examining attorney will review your response. For information on how to respond to an office action, see our webpage on responding to office actions, and our video, "Response to Office Action." In about one to two months go to step 5a or step 5b.

Step 4b. You do not respond and your application abandons. If you don't respond within three months of the date the office action was issued, your application is abandoned. An optional three-month extension can be requested for a fee. After expiration of the response deadline, we send you a Notice of Abandonment. We can no longer process your application and your trademark will not register. In this situation, filing fees are not refunded. To restart the processing of your application, you must file a petition to revive the application within two months of the date the Notice of Abandonment issued. You must also submit the petition fee. If the petition is filed later than two months after the abandonment date, the petition will be denied as untimely and your only option is to file a new application with new fees. For information on filing a petition to revive your application, see our petition to revive information sheet and the Petitions video.

Step 5a. USPTO approves trademark and publishes it for opposition. If the examining attorney does not find grounds for refusing to register your trademark, and your application meets all legal requirements, your trademark will be approved for publication in the TMOG. The TMOG, a weekly online publication, gives advance notice to the public that we will be registering your trademark. Approximately one month after approval, your trademark will publish in the TMOG.

Within 30 days of the publishing date, anyone who believes their business will be harmed if we register your trademark may file an objection (or "opposition"). An opposition is similar to a federal court proceeding, but is held before the TTAB, a panel of administrative judges who review and decide these matters. An opposition can extend the time between publication of your trademark in the TMOG and registration of your trademark. If someone files an opposition against your trademark, we will let you know. You may want to hire a U.S.-licensed attorney, as oppositions are complex proceedings. No further action is taken to register your trademark until the 30-day opposition period has expired and any oppositions are resolved. In about three months go to Step 8.

Step 5b. USPTO issues final letter (office action). If your response does not overcome all refusals and/or satisfy all requirements, the examining attorney will issue a "final" refusal letter (final office action) that makes final any remaining refusals and/or requirements. You may appeal the examining attorney's decision by filing an appeal with the TTAB. You may also submit a response to the final letter that overcomes the remaining refusals and satisfies the remaining requirements. And in limited circumstances you may file a Petition to Director. For more information on appeals, visit the TTAB webpage and see the TTAB video. Within three months go to step 6a or step 6b.

Step 6a. You file an appeal and/or submit a timely and complete response to final letter. To avoid abandoning your application, you must timely file a Notice of Appeal to the TTAB. You may also submit a response to the final letter (office action) to the examining attorney, who will review it to see if it overcomes all final refusals and/or satisfies all final requirements. If not, and you did not file a Notice of Appeal, your application will be abandoned and your trademark will not register. In this situation, filing fees are not refunded. For information on how to respond to an office action, see our webpage on responding to office actions, and the Response to Office Action video. In about one to two months go to step 7a or step 7b.

Step 6b. You do not file an appeal or fix remaining issues and your application abandons. If you don't file an appeal or otherwise fix all the remaining issues within three months of the date the office action was issued, your application is abandoned. An optional three-month extension can be requested for a fee. After expiration of the response deadline, we send you a Notice of Abandonment. We can no longer process your application and your trademark will not register. In this situation, filing fees are not refunded. To restart the processing of your application, you must file a petition to revive the application within two months of the date the Notice of Abandonment issued. You must also submit the petition fee. If the petition is filed later than two months after the abandonment date, the petition will be denied as untimely and your only option is to file a new application with new fees. For information on filing a petition to revive your application, see our petition to revive information sheet and the Petitions video.

Step 7a. USPTO approves trademark and publishes it for opposition. If the examining attorney does not find grounds for refusing to register your trademark, and your application satisfies all legal requirements, your trademark will be approved for publication in the TMOG. The TMOG, a weekly online publication, gives advance notice to the public that the USPTO plans to register your trademark. Approximately one month after approval, your trademark will publish in the TMOG.

Within 30 days of the publishing date, anyone who believes their business will be harmed if we register your trademark may file an objection (or "opposition "). An opposition is similar to a federal court proceeding, but is held before the TTAB, a panel of administrative judges who review and decide these matters. An opposition can extend the time between publication of your trademark in the TMOG and registration of your trademark. If someone files an opposition against your trademark, we will let you know. You may want to hire a U.S.-licensed attorney, as oppositions are complex proceedings. No further action is taken to register your trademark until the 30-day opposition period has expired and any oppositions are resolved. In about three months go to step 8.

Step 7b. TTAB processes your appeal. If your response does not overcome all final refusals and/or satisfy all final requirements and you filed a Notice of Appeal with the Trademark Trial and Appeal Board (TTAB), the appeal will be processed and instituted by the TTAB. For more information on appeals, visit the TTAB webpage and see the TTAB video.

Step 8. USPTO registers your trademark. Within about three months after your trademark publishes in the TMOG, if no opposition was filed, we register your trademark. If an opposition was filed but was unsuccessful, we will register your trademark after the TTAB dismisses the opposition. After your trademark registers, you must periodically file maintenance documents and fees within specific time frames to keep the registration active. For information on keeping your registration active, as well as the optional Section 15 filing to enhance the legal strength of your registration, see the Post-Registration Issues video. Between five to six years go to step 9 and every 10 years go to step 10.

Step 9. You file a Section 8 declaration. Before the end of the first six-year period after the registration date, or within six months of the expiration of the sixth year with an additional fee, you must file a Declaration of Use or Excusable Nonuse under Section 8 and pay applicable fees. This declaration must include a verified statement that your trademark is in use in commerce, along with evidence showing that use. If you don't file this declaration, your registration will be canceled.

Step 10. You file a Section 8 declaration and Section 9 renewal. Within one year before the end of every 10-year period after the registration date, or within six months of the end of the 10-year period, you must file a Combined Declaration of Use or Excusable Nonuse/Application for Renewal under Sections 8 and 9 and pay applicable fees. This declaration generally must include a verified statement that your trademark is in use in commerce, along with evidence showing that use, and the renewal is a statement requesting that the USPTO renew your registration. If you don't file this combined declaration, your registration will be canceled and expire.

Section 1(b) Timeline

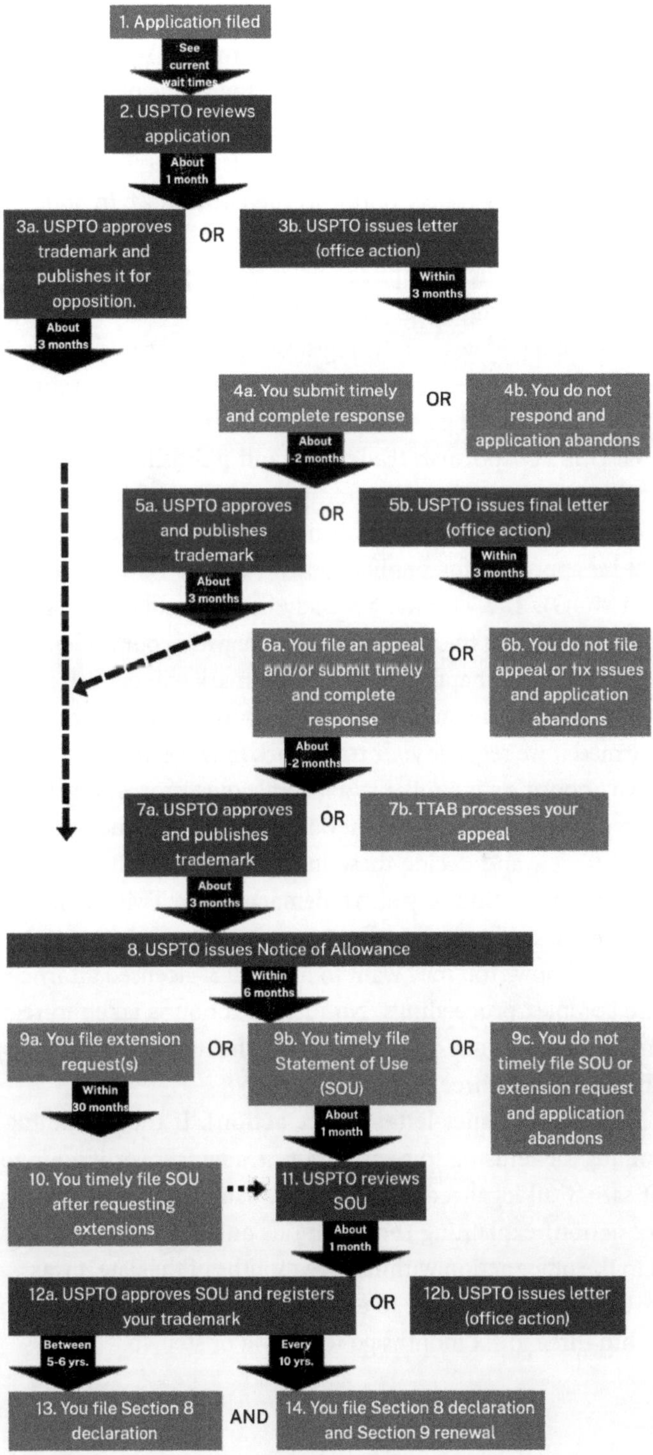

Step 1. Application filed. You file an application based on your bona fide intention to use your trademark in commerce. Your application is given a USPTO serial number. You can check the status of your application by entering the serial number in the Trademark Status and Document Retrieval (TSDR) system or calling the trademark status line at 571-272-5400, or toll-free at 1-800-786-9199 (select option 1, then option 2). In about six to nine months go to step 2.

Step 2. USPTO reviews application. If your application meets the filing requirements, it's assigned to an examining attorney, who reviews it to determine whether federal law permits registration of your trademark. Filing fees are generally not refunded, even if your application is later refused registration. In about one month go to step 3a or step 3b.

Step 3a. USPTO approves trademark and publishes it for opposition. If the examining attorney does not find grounds for refusing to register your trademark, and your application satisfies all legal requirements, your trademark will be approved for publication in the USPTO's Trademark Official Gazette (TMOG). The TMOG, a weekly online publication, gives advance notice to the public that the USPTO plans to register your trademark. Approximately one month after approval, your trademark will publish in the TMOG.

Within 30 days of the publishing date, anyone who believes their business will be harmed if we register your trademark may file an objection (or "opposition"). An opposition is similar to a federal court proceeding, but is held before the Trademark Trial and Appeal Board (TTAB), a panel of administrative judges who review and decide these matters. An opposition can extend the time between publication of your trademark in the TMOG and registration of your trademark. If someone files an opposition against your trademark, we will let you know. You may want to hire a U.S.-licensed attorney, as oppositions are complex proceedings. No further action is taken to register your trademark until the 30-day opposition period has expired and any oppositions are resolved. In about three months go to step 8.

Step 3b. USPTO issues letter (office action). If the examining attorney finds grounds for refusing to register your trademark, or if your application does not satisfy all legal requirements, the examining attorney issues a letter (office action) explaining those refusals and/or requirements. You must respond to the office action within three months of the date it was issued. You also have the option to request to extend the deadline for three months, with a fee. Within three to six months go to step 4a or step 4b.

Step 4a. You submit a timely and complete response to the office action. To avoid abandonment of your application, you must timely submit a response that overcomes each refusal and/or satisfies each requirement in the office action. The examining attorney will review your response. For information on how to respond to an office action, see our webpage on responding to office actions, and the Response to Office Action video. In about one to two months go to step 5a or step 5b.

Step 4b. You do not respond and your application abandons. If you don't request an extension of the response deadline or don't respond within three months of the date the office action was issued, your application is abandoned. After expiration of the response deadline, we send you a Notice of Abandonment. We can no longer process your application and your trademark will not register. In this situation, filing fees are not refunded. To restart the processing of your application, you must file a petition to revive the application within two months of the date the Notice of Abandonment issued. You must also submit the petition fee. If the petition is filed later than two months after the abandonment date, the petition will be denied as untimely and your only option is to file a new application with new fees. For information on filing a petition to revive your application, see our petition to revive information sheet and the Petitions video.

Step 5a. USPTO approves trademark and publishes it for opposition. If the examining attorney does not find grounds for refusing to register your trademark, and your application meets all legal requirements, your trademark will be approved for publication in the TMOG. The TMOG, a weekly online publication, gives advance notice to the public that we will be registering your trademark. Approximately one month after approval, your trademark will publish in the TMOG.

Within 30 days of the publishing date, anyone who believes their business will be harmed if we register your trademark may file an objection (or "opposition"). An opposition is similar to a federal court proceeding, but is held before the TTAB, a panel of administrative judges who review and decide these matters. An opposition can extend the time between publication of your trademark in the TMOG and registration of your trademark. If someone files an opposition against your trademark, we will let you know. You may want to hire a U.S.-licensed attorney, as oppositions are complex proceedings. No further action is taken to register your trademark until the 30-day opposition period has expired and any oppositions are resolved. In about three months go to step 8.

Step 5b. USPTO issues final letter (office action). If your response does not overcome all refusals and/or satisfy all requirements, the examining attorney will issue a "final" refusal letter (final office action) that makes final any remaining refusals and/or requirements. You may appeal the examining attorney's decision by filing an appeal with the Trademark Trial and Appeal Board (TTAB). You may also submit a response to the final letter that overcomes the remaining refusals and satisfies the remaining requirements. You must take either action within three months from the issue date of the final office action. You have the option to request to extend this deadline by three additional months, for a fee. In limited circumstances you may have the option to file a Petition to Director. For more information on appeals, visit the TTAB webpage and see the TTAB video. Within three to six months go to step 6a or step 6b.

Step 6a. You file an appeal and/or submit a timely and complete response to final letter. To avoid abandoning your application, you must timely file a Notice of Appeal to the TTAB. You may also submit a response to the final letter (office action) to the examining attorney, who will review it to see if it overcomes all final refusals and/or satisfies all final requirements. If not, and you did not file a Notice of Appeal, your application will be abandoned and your trademark will not register. In this situation, filing fees are not refunded. For information on how to respond to an office action, see our webpage on responding to office actions, and the Response to Office Action video. In about one to two months go to step 7a or step 7b.

Step 6b. You do not file an appeal or fix remaining issues and your application abandons. If you don't file an appeal or otherwise fix all the remaining issues within three months of the date the office action was issued, or within six months of the issue date of the final office action if you filed and were granted a three month extension of the deadline, your application is abandoned. After the expiration of the response deadline, we send you a Notice of Abandonment. We can no longer process your application and your trademark will not register. In this situation, filing fees are not refunded. To restart the processing of your application, you must file a petition to revive the application within two months of the date the Notice of Abandonment issued. You must also submit the petition fee. If the petition is filed later than two months after the abandonment date, the petition will be denied as untimely and your only option is to file a new application with new fees. For information on filing a petition to revive your application, see our petition to revive information sheet and the Petitions video.

Step 7a. USPTO approves trademark and publishes it for opposition. If the examining attorney does not find grounds for refusing to register your trademark, and your application satisfies all legal requirements, your trademark will be approved for publication in the USPTO's Trademark Official Gazette (TMOG). The TMOG, a weekly online publication, gives advance notice to the public that the USPTO plans to register your trademark. Approximately one month after approval, your trademark will publish in the TMOG.

Within 30 days of the publishing date, anyone who believes their business will be harmed if we register your trademark may file an objection (or "opposition"). An opposition is similar to a federal court proceeding, but is held before the TTAB, a panel of administrative judges who review and decide these matters. An opposition can extend the time between publication of your trademark in the TMOG and registration of your trademark. If someone files an opposition against your trademark, we will let you know. You may want to hire a U.S.-licensed attorney, as oppositions are complex proceedings. No further action is taken to register your trademark until the 30-day opposition period has expired and any oppositions are resolved. In about three months go to step 8.

Step 7b. TTAB processes your appeal. If your response does not overcome all final refusals and/or satisfy all final requirements and you filed a Notice of Appeal with the TTAB, the appeal will be processed and instituted by the TTAB. For more information on appeals, visit the TTAB webpage and see the TTAB video.

Step 8. USPTO issues Notice of Allowance (NOA). We issue a NOA (pronounced "noah") within two months after the trademark publishes in the TMOG. A NOA is not a registration, but means that your trademark made it through the 30-day opposition period and will be allowed to register after you timely file an acceptable Statement of Use (SOU). The deadline to file an SOU or request for extension of time to file an SOU (extension request) is calculated from the date the NOA issued. If you don't file an SOU or extension request within six months of the NOA date, your application will abandon. Within six months go to step 9a or step 9bor step 9c.

Step 9a. You file extension request(s). If you are not yet using the trademark in commerce on all the goods and/or services listed in the NOA, you must timely file an extension request and pay the required fees to avoid your application abandoning. Because each granted extension request lasts only six months, you must continue to file extension requests every six months, during an unexpired extension period. You can file a total of five extension requests. You must file the first request within six months of the NOA date and you must file all subsequent requests before the expiration of a previously granted extension. Within 30 months of the date of the first extension request, you must go to step 10.

Step 9b. You timely file Statement of Use (SOU). If you are using the trademark in commerce on all of the goods and/or services listed in the NOA, you must submit an SOU and the required fees within six months of the NOA date to avoid abandonment. You cannot withdraw the SOU, but you can file one extension request with or after the SOU to get more time to address any deficiencies in the SOU. For information on when to submit the SOU, and what you need to provide with it, see the Statement of Use video. In about one to two months go to step 11.

Step 9c. You do not timely file SOU or extension request and your application abandons. If you don't file an SOU or extension request within six months of the NOA date, we send you a Notice of Abandonment. We can no longer process your application and your trademark will not register. In this situation, filing fees are not refunded. To restart the processing of your application, you must file a petition to revive the application within two months of the date the Notice of Abandonment issued. You must also submit the petition fee. If the petition is filed later than two months after the abandonment date, the petition will be denied as untimely and your only option is to file a new application with new fees. For information on filing a petition to revive your application, see our petition to revive information sheet and the Petitions video.

Step 10. You timely file SOU after requesting extensions. If you are using the trademark in commerce on all the goods and/or services listed in the NOA, you must submit an SOU and the required fees within six months of the previous granted extension to avoid abandonment. You cannot withdraw the SOU, but you can file one extension request with or after the SOU to get more time to address any deficiencies in the SOU (usually specimen issues). Get a list of SOU minimum filing requirements. Go to step 11.

Step 11. USPTO reviews SOU. If your SOU meets the minimum filing requirements, the SOU is forwarded to an examining attorney, who determines whether federal law permits registration. You cannot withdraw the SOU and the filing fees will not be refunded, even if the application is later refused registration on legal grounds. In about one month go to step 12a or step 12b.

Step 12a. USPTO approves SOU and registers your trademark. If the examining attorney does not find grounds for refusal, and your application meets all legal requirements, your SOU will be approved. Within about two months after the SOU is approved, we register your trademark. You must periodically file maintenance documents and fees within specific time frames to keep the registration active. For information on keeping your registration active, as well as the optional Section 15 filing to enhance the legal strength of your registration, see the Post-Registration Issues video. Between five to six years go to step 13 and every 10 years go to step 14.

Step 12b. USPTO issues letter (office action). If the examining attorney finds grounds for refusing to register your trademark, or if your application does not satisfy all legal requirements, the examining attorney issues a letter (office action) explaining those refusals and/or requirements. You must respond to the office action within six months of the date it was issued. This is the same process that occurs before the trademark is published if the examining attorney determines that legal requirements must be met (see step 3b). The process and timeframes remain the same, except that if you successfully address the issues with your SOU and it is approved, we issue a registration within about two months. If not all issues are successfully addressed, the application will abandon.

Step 13. You file a Section 8 declaration. Before the end of the first six-year period after the registration date, or within six months of the expiration of the sixth year with an additional fee, you must file a Declaration of Use or Excusable Nonuse under Section 8 and pay applicable fees. This declaration must include a verified statement that your trademark is in use in commerce, along with evidence showing that use. If you don't file this declaration, your registration will be canceled.

Step 14. You file a Section 8 declaration and Section 9 renewal. Within one year before the end of every 10-year period after the registration date, or within six months of the end of the 10-year period, you must file a Combined Declaration of Use or Excusable Nonuse/Application for Renewal under Sections 8 and 9 and pay applicable fees. This declaration generally must include a verified statement that your trademark is in use in commerce, along with evidence showing that use, and the renewal is a statement requesting that the USPTO renew your registration. If you don't file this combined declaration, your registration will be canceled and expire.

Section 44(d) Timeline

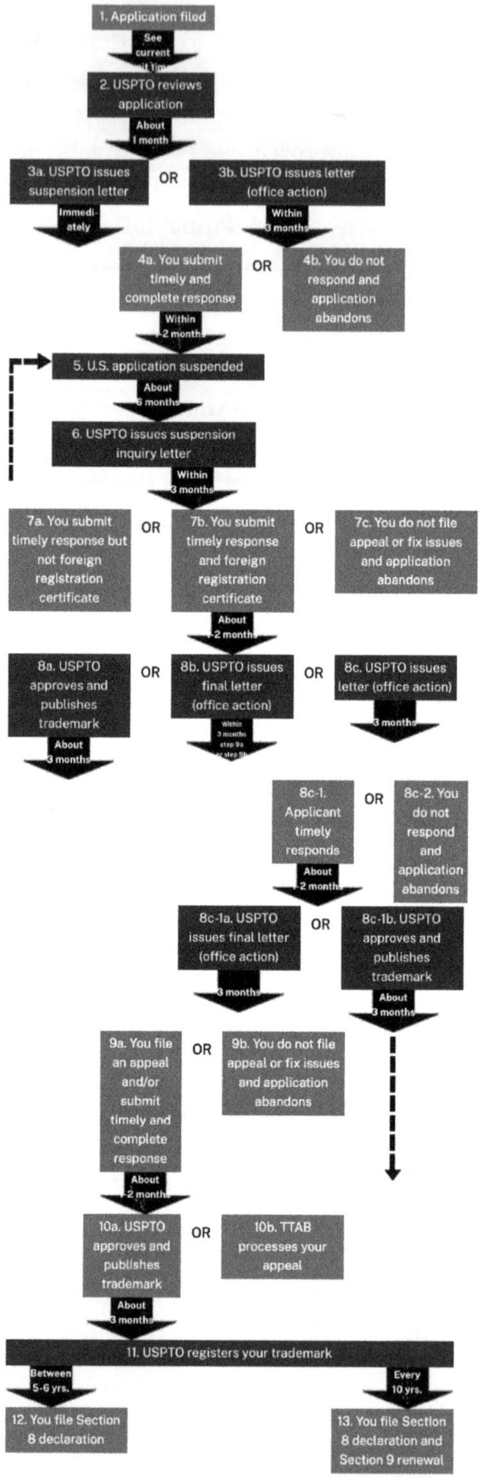

Step 1. U.S. and foreign applications filed. You file a U.S. application with the USPTO within six months of filing a foreign application for the same trademark and same goods and/or services in a country that is party to a treaty or international agreement with the United States. Your country of origin must also be a party to a treaty or international agreement with the United States. However, the foreign application does not have to be from your country of origin unless it is also being used for a Section 44(e) basis (based on a foreign registration for the same trademark and goods and/or services). Section 44(d) alone does not provide a basis for registration so you must also provide a valid basis under Section 44(e) and/or Section 1. Most people who apply for a trademark based on a foreign application will also claim the Section 44(e) basis for registration. This timeline assumes a Section 44(e) registration basis. In about six to nine months go to step 2.

Step 2. USPTO reviews application. If your U.S. application meets the filing requirements, it's given a USPTO serial number. Your application is assigned to an examining attorney, who reviews it to determine whether federal law permits registration of your trademark. Filing fees are generally not refunded, even if the application is later refused registration. In about one month go to step 3a or step 3b.

Step 3a. USPTO issues suspension letter. If the examining attorney does not find grounds for refusing to register your trademark, and your application satisfies all legal requirements, he or she issues a suspension letter stating that no further action will be taken on the application until we receive the foreign registration certificate, as required for a Section 44(e) registration basis. Go to step 5.

Step 3b. USPTO issues letter (office action). If the examining attorney finds grounds for refusing to register your trademark, or if your application does not satisfy all legal requirements, the examining attorney issues a letter (office action) explaining those refusals and/or requirements. You must respond to the office action or request a single three-month extension of the response deadline within three months of the date it was issued. There is a fee for an extension request. Within three to six months go to step 4a or step 4b.

Step 4a. You submit a timely and complete response to the office action. To avoid abandonment of your application, you must timely submit a response that overcomes each refusal and/or satisfies each requirement in the office action. The examining attorney will review your response. For information on how to respond to an office action, see our webpage on responding to office actions, and the Response to Office Action video. In about one to two months go to step 5.

Step 4b. You do not respond and your application abandons. If you don't respond within three months of the date the office action was issued, or within six months of the issue date if you filed and were granted an extension of the deadline, your application is abandoned. An optional three month extension can be requested for a fee. After the six months from the date of the office action was issued, we send you a Notice of Abandonment. We can no longer process your application and your trademark will not register. In this situation, filing fees are not refunded. To restart the processing of your application, you must file a petition to revive the application within two months of the date the Notice of Abandonment issued. You must also submit the petition fee. If the petition is filed later than two months after the abandonment date, the petition will be denied as untimely and your only option is to file a new application with new fees. For information on filing a petition to revive your application, see our petition to revive information sheet and the Petitions video.

Step 5. U.S. application is suspended. The examining attorney issues a letter suspending action on the application until we receive the foreign registration certificate and restating any refusals and/or requirements. You do not need to respond to the suspension letter, but you should check the status of your U.S. application every three to four months using the TSDR database. Your U.S. application is suspended until the examining attorney issues a letter inquiring about the status of the foreign application. In about six months go to step 6.

Step 6. USPTO issues suspension inquiry letter. If we have not received the required foreign registration certificate for the Section 44(e) basis, the examining attorney will issue a letter inquiring about the status of the foreign application (whether it has registered yet). A suspension inquiry letter will be issued every six months until you submit the foreign registration certificate. For information on how to respond to a suspension inquiry letter, see our webpage on responding to office actions, and the Response to Office Action video. Within three months go to step 7a or step 7b or step 7c.

Step 7a. You submit a timely response but do not submit the foreign registration certificate. To avoid abandonment of your application, you must submit a timely response specifying the status of the foreign application. If the foreign application is still pending, the examining attorney will issue you a letter re-suspending the U.S. application. Go to step 5.

Step 7b. You submit a timely response as well as the foreign registration certificate. When we receive the foreign registration certificate, the examining attorney takes your U.S. application out of suspension and reviews the foreign registration to determine if the trademark, owner, and goods and/or services are the same as those in your U.S. application. In about one to two months go to step 8a or step 8b or step 8c.

Step 7c. You do not respond and your application abandons. If you don't respond within three months of the date the suspension inquiry letter was issued, your application is abandoned. An optional three month extension can be requested for a fee. After the six months from the date of the office action was issued, we send you a Notice of Abandonment. We can no longer process your application and your trademark will not register. In this situation, filing fees are not refunded. To restart the processing of your application, you must file a petition to revive the application within two months of the date the Notice of Abandonment issued. You must also submit the petition fee. If the petition is filed later than two months after the abandonment date, the petition will be denied as untimely and your only option is to file a new application with new fees. For information on filing a petition to revive information sheet and the Petitions video.

Step 8a. USPTO approves trademark and publishes it for opposition. If the examining attorney does not find grounds for refusing to register your trademark, and your application satisfies all legal requirements, your trademark will be approved for publication in the USPTO's Trademark Official Gazette (TMOG). The TMOG, a weekly online publication, gives advance notice to the public that the USPTO plans to register your trademark. Approximately one month after approval, your trademark will publish in the TMOG.

Within 30 days of the publishing date, anyone who believes his or her business will be harmed if we register your trademark may file an objection (or "opposition"). An opposition is similar to a federal court proceeding, but is held before the Trademark Trial and Appeal Board (TTAB), a panel of administrative judges who review and decide these matters. An opposition can extend the time between publication of your trademark in the TMOG and registration of your trademark. If someone files an opposition against your trademark, we will let you know. You may want to hire a U.S.-licensed attorney, as oppositions are complex proceedings. No further action is taken to register your trademark until the 30-day opposition period has expired and any oppositions are resolved. In about three months go to step 11.

Step 8b. USPTO issues final letter (office action). If the foreign registration certificate is acceptable, but you have not yet overcome the refusals and/or satisfied the requirements raised by the examining attorney, the examining attorney will issue a "final" office action that makes final any remaining refusals and/or requirements. You may appeal the examining attorney's decision by filing an appeal with the TTAB. You may also submit a response to the final letter that overcomes the remaining refusals and satisfies the remaining requirements. You must take either action within three months from the issue date of the final office action. You have the option to request to extend this deadline by three additional months, for a fee. In limited circumstances you may file a Petition to Director. For more information on appeals, visit the TTAB webpage and see the TTAB video." Within three months go to step 9a or step 9b.

Step 8c. USPTO issues letter (office action). If the foreign registration is not acceptable, the examining attorney will issue a letter (office action) stating why. You must respond to the office action within three months of the date it was issued. You also have the option to request to extend the response deadline for three months, with a fee. Within three to six months go to step 8c-1 or step 8c-2.

Step 8c-1. You submit a timely and complete response to the office action. To avoid abandonment of your application, you must timely submit a response that overcomes each refusal and/or satisfies each requirement in the office action. The examining attorney will review your response. For information on how to respond to an office action, see our webpage on responding to office actions, and the Response to Office Action video. In about one to two months go to step 8c-1a or step 8c-1b.

Step 8c-2. You do not respond and your application abandons. If you don't respond within three months of the date the office action was issued, your application is abandoned. An optional three month extension can be requested for a fee. After expiration of the response deadline, we send you a Notice of Abandonment. We can no longer process your application and your trademark will not register. In this situation, filing fees are not refunded. To restart the processing of your application, you must file a petition to revive the application within two months of the date the Notice of Abandonment issued. You must also submit the petition fee. If the petition is filed later than two months after the abandonment date, the petition will be denied as untimely and your only option is to file a new application with new fees. For information on filing a petition to revive your application, see our petition to revive information sheet and the Petitions video.

Step 8c-1a. USPTO issues final letter (office action). If the foreign registration certificate is acceptable, but you have not yet overcome the refusals and/or satisfied the requirements raised by the examining attorney, the examining attorney will issue a "final" office action that makes final any remaining refusals and/or requirements. You may appeal the examining attorney's decision by filing an appeal with the TTAB. You may also submit a response to the final letter that overcomes the remaining refusals and satisfies the remaining requirements. You must take either action within three months from the issue date of the final office action. You have the option to request to extend this deadline by three additional months, for a fee. In limited circumstances you may file a Petition to Director. For more information on appeals, visit the TTAB webpage and the TTAB video. Within three to six months go to step 9a or step 9b.

Step 8c-1b. USPTO approves trademark and publishes it for opposition. If the examining attorney does not find grounds for refusing to register your trademark, and your application satisfies all legal requirements, your trademark will be approved for publication in the TMOG. The TMOG, a weekly online publication, gives advance notice to the public that the USPTO plans to register your trademark. Approximately one month after approval, your trademark will publish in the TMOG.

Within 30 days of the publishing date, anyone who believes his or her business will be harmed if we register your trademark may file an objection (or "opposition"). An opposition is similar to a federal court proceeding, but is held before the TTAB, a panel of administrative judges who review and decide these matters. An opposition can extend the time between publication of your trademark in the TMOG and registration of your trademark. If someone files an opposition against your trademark, we will let you know. You may want to hire a U.S.-licensed attorney, as oppositions are complex proceedings. No further action is taken to register your trademark until the 30-day opposition period has expired and any oppositions are resolved. In about three months go to step 11.

Step 9a. You file an appeal and/or submit a timely and complete response to final letter. To avoid abandoning your application, you must timely file a Notice of Appeal to the TTAB. You may also submit a response to the final letter (office action) to the examining attorney, who will review it to see if it overcomes all final refusals and/or satisfies all final requirements. If not, and you did not file a Notice of Appeal, your application will be abandoned and your trademark will not register. In this situation, filing fees are not refunded. For information on how to respond to an office action, see our webpage on responding to office actions, and the Response to Office Action video." In about one to two months go to step 10a or step 10b.

Step 9b. You do not respond to final letter and your application abandons. If you don't respond within three months of the date the office action was issued, or within six months of the issue date of the final office action if you filed and were granted a three-month extension of the deadline, your application is abandoned. An optional three month extension can be requested for a fee. After the six months from the date of the office action was issued, we send you a Notice of Abandonment. We can no longer process your application and your trademark will not register. In this situation, filing fees are not refunded. To restart the processing of your application, you must file a petition to revive the application within two months of the date the Notice of Abandonment issued. You must also submit the petition fee. If the petition is filed later than two months after the abandonment date, the petition will be denied as untimely and your only option is to file a new application with new fees. For information on filing a petition to revive your application, see our petition to revive information sheet and the Petitions video.

Step 10a. USPTO approves trademark and publishes it for opposition. If the examining attorney does not find grounds for refusing to register your trademark, and your application satisfies all legal requirements, your trademark will be approved for publication in the TMOG. The TMOG, a weekly online publication, gives advance notice to the public that the USPTO plans to register your trademark. Approximately one month after approval, your trademark will publish in the TMOG.

Within 30 days of the publishing date, anyone who believes his or her business will be harmed if we register your trademark may file an objection (or "opposition"). An opposition is similar to a federal court proceeding, but is held before the TTAB, a panel of administrative judges who review and decide these matters. An opposition can extend the time between publication of your trademark in the TMOG and registration of your trademark. If someone files an opposition against your trademark, we will let you know. You may want to hire a U.S.-licensed attorney, as oppositions are complex proceedings. No further action is taken to register your trademark until the 30-day opposition period has expired and any oppositions are resolved. In about three months go to step 11.

Step 10b. TTAB processes your appeal. If your response does not overcome all final refusals and/or satisfy all final requirements and you filed a Notice of Appeal with the Trademark Trial and Appeal Board (TTAB), the appeal will be processed and instituted by the TTAB. For more information on appeals, visit the TTAB webpage and see the TTAB video.

Step 11. USPTO registers your trademark. Within about three months after your trademark publishes in the TMOG, if no opposition was filed, we register your trademark. If an opposition was filed but was unsuccessful, we will register your trademark after the Trademark Trial and Appeal Board dismisses the opposition. After your trademark registers, you must periodically file maintenance documents and fees within specific time frames to keep the registration active. For information on keeping your registration active, as well as the optional Section 15 filing to enhance the legal strength of your registration, see the Post-Registration Issues video. Between five to six years go to step 12 or every 10 years go to step 13.

Step 12. You file a Section 8 declaration. Before the end of the first six-year period after the registration date, or within six months of the expiration of the sixth year with an additional fee, you must file a Declaration of Use or Excusable Nonuse under Section 8 and pay applicable fees. This declaration must include a verified statement that your trademark is in use in commerce, along with evidence showing that use. If you don't file this declaration, your registration will be canceled.

Step 13. You file a Section 8 declaration and Section 9 renewal. Within one year before the end of every 10-year period after the registration date, or within six months of the end of the 10-year period, you must file a Combined Declaration of Use or Excusable Nonuse/Application for Renewal under Sections 8 and 9 and pay applicable fees. This declaration generally must include a verified statement that your trademark is in use in commerce, along with evidence showing that use, and the renewal is a statement requesting that the USPTO renew your registration. If you don't file this combined declaration, your registration will be canceled and expire.

Section 44(e) Timeline

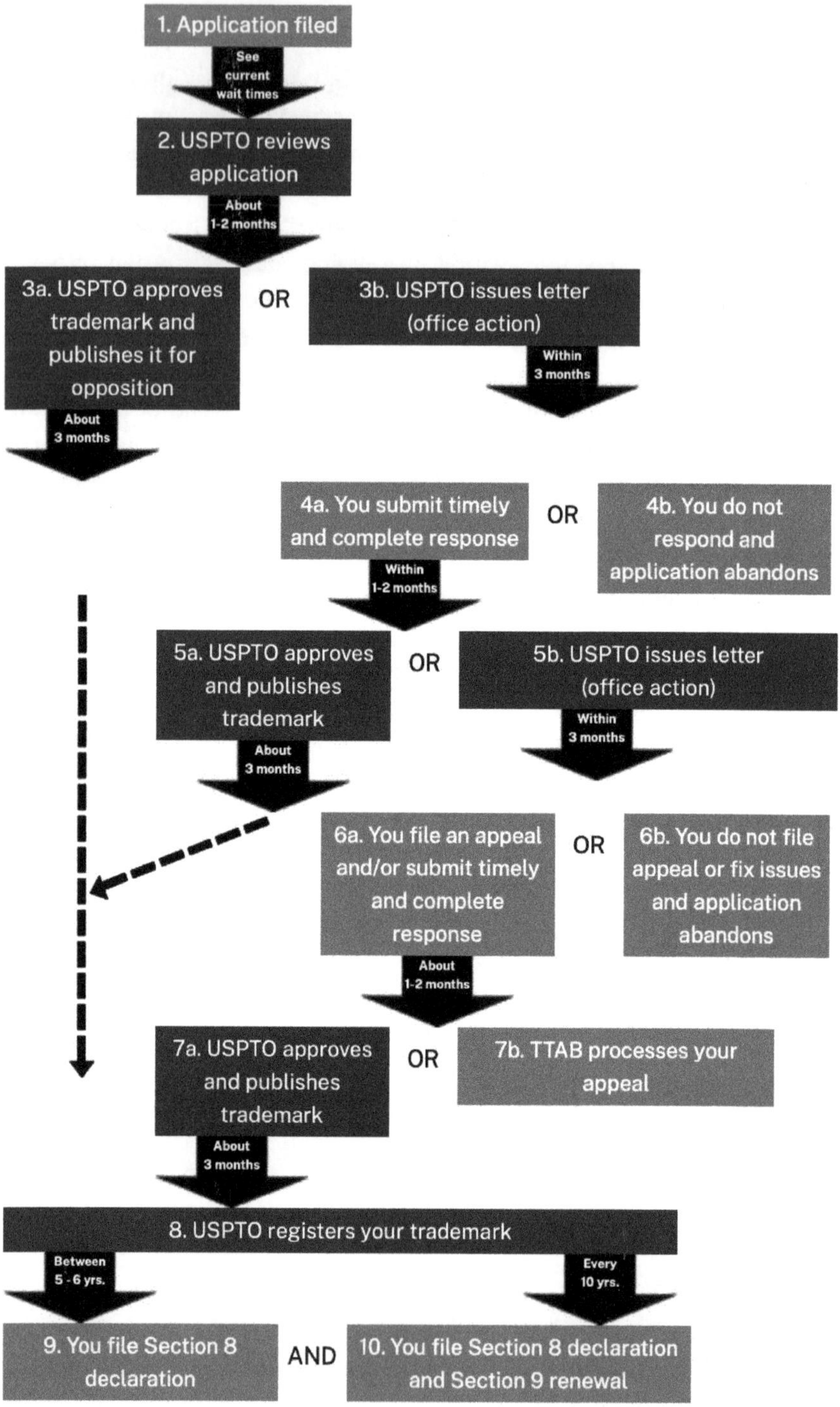

Step 1. Application filed. You file a U.S. application and rely on ownership of a foreign registration for the same trademark and same goods and/or services. The foreign registration does not have to be included in your U.S. application, but must be submitted before registration. The foreign registration must be issued by a country that is a party to a treaty or international agreement with the United States. The foreign registration must also be from your country of origin, must be owned by you, the same named applicant who filed the U.S. application, and must be for the same trademark as in the U.S. application and for goods and/or services that are the same as or encompass the goods and/or services in the U.S. application. In about three months go to step 2.

Step 2. USPTO reviews application. If your U.S. application meets the filing requirements, it's given a USPTO serial number. Your application is assigned to an examining attorney, who reviews it to determine whether federal law permits registration of your trademark. Filing fees are generally not refunded, even if the application is later refused registration. In about one month go to step 3a or step 3b.

Step 3a. USPTO approves trademark and publishes it for opposition. If the examining attorney does not find grounds for refusing to register your trademark, and your application satisfies all legal requirements, your trademark will be approved for publication in the USPTO's Trademark Official Gazette (TMOG). The TMOG, a weekly online publication, gives advance notice to the public that the USPTO plans to register your trademark. Approximately one month after approval, your trademark will publish in the TMOG.

Within 30 days of the publishing date, anyone who believes their business will be harmed if we register your trademark may file an objection (or "opposition"). An opposition is similar to a federal court proceeding, but is held before the Trademark Trial and Appeal Board (TTAB), a panel of administrative judges who review and decide these matters. An opposition can extend the time between publication of your trademark in the TMOG and registration of your trademark. If someone files an opposition against your trademark, we will let you know. You may want to hire a U.S.-licensed attorney, as oppositions are complex proceedings. No further action is taken to register your trademark until the 30-day opposition period has expired and any oppositions are resolved. In about three months go to step 8.

Step 3b. USPTO issues letter (office action). If the examining attorney finds grounds for refusing to register your trademark, or if your application does not satisfy all legal requirements, the examining attorney issues a letter (office action) explaining those refusals and/or requirements. You must respond to the office action within three months of the date it was issued, or within six months if you filed and were granted a request to extend the response deadline. We do not suspend review of your application to wait for you to submit a copy of the foreign registration certificate except under extraordinary circumstances (e.g., war or natural disaster). Within three to six months go to step 4a or step 4b.

Step 4a. You submit a timely and complete response to the office action. To avoid abandonment of your application, you must timely submit a response that overcomes each refusal and/or satisfies each requirement in the office action. The examining attorney will review your response. For information on how to respond to an office action, see our webpage on responding to office actions, and the Response to Office Action video. In about one to two months go to step 5a or step 5b.

Step 4b. You do not respond and your application abandons. If you don't respond within three months of the date the office action was issued, or within six months of the issue date of the final office action if you filed and were granted a three-month extension of the deadline, your application is abandoned. An optional three-month extension can be requested for a fee. After the six months from the date of the office action was issued, we send you a Notice of Abandonment. We can no longer process your application and your trademark will not register. In this situation, filing fees are not refunded. To restart the processing of your application, you must file a petition to revive the application within two months of the date the Notice of Abandonment issued. You must also submit the petition fee. If the petition is filed later than two months after the abandonment date, the petition will be denied as untimely and your only option is to file a new application with new fees. For information on filing a petition to revive your application, see our petition to revive information sheet and the Petitions video.

Step 5a. USPTO approves trademark and publishes it for opposition. If the examining attorney does not find grounds for refusing to register your trademark, and your application satisfies all legal requirements, your trademark will be approved for publication in the TMOG. The TMOG, a weekly online publication, gives advance notice to the public that the USPTO plans to register your trademark. Approximately one month after approval, your trademark will publish in the TMOG.

Within 30 days of the publishing date, anyone who believes their business will be harmed if we register your trademark may file an objection (or "opposition"). An opposition is similar to a federal court proceeding, but is held before the TTAB, a panel of administrative judges who review and decide these matters. An opposition can extend the time between publication of your trademark in the TMOG and registration of your trademark. If someone files an opposition against your trademark, we will let you know. You may want to hire a U.S.-licensed attorney, as oppositions are complex proceedings. No further action is taken to register your trademark until the 30-day opposition period has expired and any oppositions are resolved. In about three months go to step 8.

Step 5b. USPTO issues final letter (office action). If your response does not overcome all refusals and/or satisfy all requirements, the examining attorney will issue a "final" refusal letter (final office action) that makes final any remaining refusals and/or requirements. You may appeal the examining attorney's decision by filing an appeal with the TTAB. You may also submit a response to the final letter that overcomes the remaining refusals and satisfies the remaining requirements. You must take either action within three months from the issue date of the final office action. You have the option to request to extend this deadline by three additional months, for a fee. In limited circumstances you may file a Petition to Director. For more information on appeals, visit the TTAB webpage and see the TTAB video. Within three to six months go to step 6a or step 6b.

Step 6a. You file an appeal and/or submit a timely and complete response to final letter. To avoid abandoning your application, you must timely file a Notice of Appeal to the TTAB. You may also submit a response to the final letter (office action) to the examining attorney, who will review it to see if it overcomes all final refusals and/or satisfies all final requirements. If not, and you did not file a Notice of Appeal, your application will be abandoned and your trademark will not register. In this situation, filing fees are not refunded. For information on how to respond to an office action, see our webpage on responding to office actions, and the Response to Office Action video. In about one to two months go to step 7a or step 7b.

Step 6b. You do not file an appeal or fix remaining issues and your application abandons. If you don't respond within three months of the date the office action was issued, or within six months of the issue date of the final office action if you filed and were granted a three-month extension of the deadline, your application is abandoned. After expiration of the response deadline, we send you a Notice of Abandonment. We can no longer process your application and your trademark will not register. In this situation, filing fees are not refunded. To restart the processing of your application, you must file a petition to revive the application within two months of the date the Notice of Abandonment issued. You must also submit the petition fee. If the petition is filed later than two months after the abandonment date, the petition will be denied as untimely and your only option is to file a new application with new fees. For information on filing a petition to revive your application, see our petition to revive information sheet and the Petitions video.

Step 7a. USPTO approves trademark and publishes it for opposition. If the examining attorney does not find grounds for refusing to register your trademark, and your application satisfies all legal requirements, your trademark will be approved for publication in the TMOG. The TMOG, a weekly online publication, gives advance notice to the public that the USPTO plans to register your trademark. Approximately one month after approval, your trademark will publish in the TMOG.

Within 30 days of the publishing date, anyone who believes their business will be harmed if we register your trademark may file an objection (or "opposition"). An opposition is similar to a federal court proceeding, but is held before the TTAB, a panel of administrative judges who review and decide these matters. An opposition can extend the time between publication of your trademark in the TMOG and registration of your trademark. If someone files an opposition against your trademark, we will let you know. You may want to hire a U.S.-licensed attorney, as oppositions are complex proceedings. No further action is taken to register your trademark until the 30-day opposition period has expired and any oppositions are resolved. In about three months go to step 8.

Step 7b. TTAB processes your appeal. If your response does not overcome all final refusals and/or satisfy all final requirements and you filed a Notice of Appeal with the Trademark Trial and Appeal Board (TTAB), the appeal will be processed and instituted by the TTAB. For more information on appeals, visit the TTAB webpage and see the TTAB video.

Step 8. USPTO registers your trademark. Within about three months after your trademark publishes in the TMOG, if no opposition was filed, we register your trademark. If an opposition was filed but was unsuccessful, we will register your trademark after the Trademark Trial and Appeal Board dismisses the opposition. After your trademark registers, you must periodically file maintenance documents and fees within specific time frames to keep the registration active. For information on keeping your registration active, as well as the optional Section 15 filing to enhance the legal strength of your registration, see the Post-Registration Issues video. Between five to six years go to step 9 or every 10 years go to step 10.

Step 9. You file a Section 8 declaration. Before the end of the first six-year period after the registration date, or within six months of the expiration of the sixth year with an additional fee, you must file a Declaration of Use or Excusable Nonuse under Section 8 and pay applicable fees. This declaration must include a verified statement that your trademark is in use in commerce, along with evidence showing that use. If you don't file this declaration, your registration will be canceled.

Step 10. You file a Section 8 declaration and Section 9 renewal. Within one year before the end of every 10-year period after the registration date, or within six months of the end of the 10-year period, you must file a Combined Declaration of Use or Excusable Nonuse/Application for Renewal under Sections 8 and 9 and pay applicable fees. This declaration generally must include a verified statement that your trademark is in use in commerce, along with evidence showing that use, and the renewal is a statement requesting that the USPTO renew your registration. If you don't file this combined declaration, your registration will be canceled and expire.

Section 66(a) Timeline

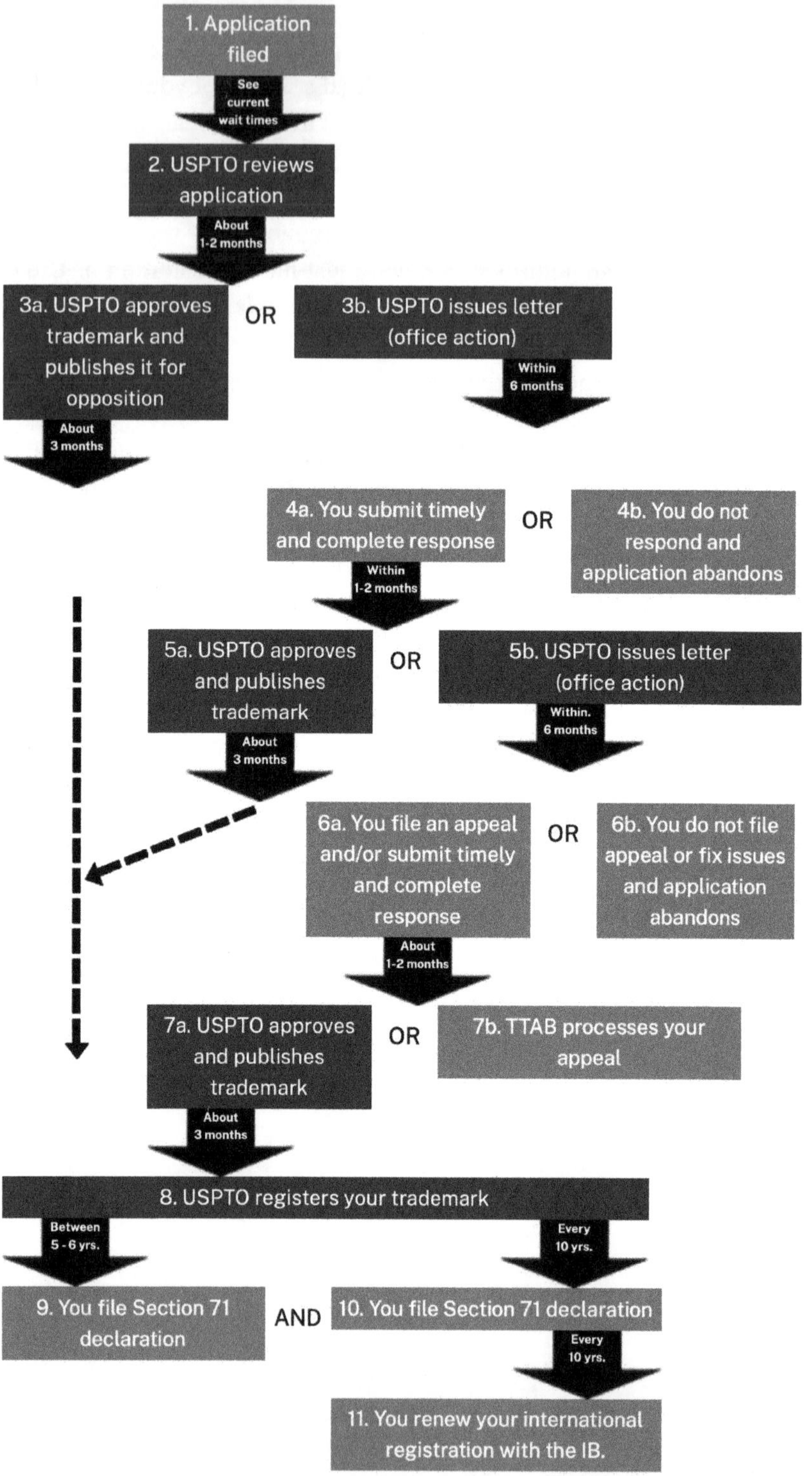

Step 1. Application filed. You filed a request for extension of protection of an international registration by designating the United States in your international application or in a subsequent designation form that is filed with the International Bureau (IB). Once we receive your request from the IB, it is given a USPTO application serial number and put in queue to be examined as U.S. application. You can check the status of your application by entering the serial number in the Trademark Status and Document Retrieval (TSDR) system. In about six to nine months go to step 2.

Step 2. USPTO reviews application. If your U.S. application meets the filing requirements, it's given a USPTO serial number. Your application is assigned to an examining attorney, who reviews it to determine whether federal law permits registration of your trademark. Filing fees are generally not refunded, even if the application is later refused registration. In about one month go to step 3a or step 3b.

Step 3a. USPTO approves trademark and publishes it for opposition. If the examining attorney does not find grounds for refusing to register your trademark, and your application satisfies all legal requirements, your trademark will be approved for publication in the USPTO's Trademark Official Gazette (TMOG). The TMOG, a weekly online publication, gives advance notice to the public that the USPTO plans to register your trademark. Approximately one month after approval, your trademark will publish in the TMOG.

Within 30 days of the publishing date, anyone who believes their business will be harmed if we register your trademark may file an objection (or "opposition"). An opposition is similar to a federal court proceeding, but is held before the Trademark Trial and Appeal Board (TTAB), a panel of administrative judges who review and decide these matters. An opposition can extend the time between publication of your trademark in the TMOG and registration of your trademark. If someone files an opposition against your trademark, we will let you know. You may want to hire a U.S.-licensed attorney, as oppositions are complex proceedings. No further action is taken to register your trademark until the 30-day opposition period has expired and any oppositions are resolved. In about three months go to step 8.

Step 3b. USPTO issues letter (office action). If the examining attorney finds grounds for refusing to register your trademark, or if your application does not satisfy all legal requirements, the examining attorney issues a letter (office action) to you via the IB, explaining those refusals and/or requirements. The IB records the office action, publishes notice of the refusal(s), and forwards the office action to the applicant/holder. You must respond to the office action within six months of the date it issued to the IB, as indicated on the letter. Within six months go to step 4a or step 4b.

Step 4a. You submit a timely and complete response to the office action. To avoid abandonment of your application, you must timely submit a response that overcomes each refusal and/or satisfies each requirement in the office action. The examining attorney will review your response. For information on how to respond to an office action, see our webpage on responding to office actions, and the Response to Office Action video. In about one to two months go to step 5a or step 5b.

Step 4b. You do not respond and your application abandons. If you don't respond within six months of the date the office action was issued, your application is abandoned. After the six months, we send you a Notice of Abandonment. We can no longer process your application and your trademark will not register. In this situation, filing fees are not refunded. To restart the processing of your application, you must file a petition to revive the application within two months of the date the Notice of Abandonment issued. You must also submit the petition fee. If the petition is filed later than two months after the abandonment date, the petition will be denied as untimely and your only option is to file a new application with new fees. For information on filing a petition to revive your application, see our petition to revive information sheet and the Petitions video.

Step 5a. USPTO approves trademark and publishes it for opposition. If the examining attorney does not find grounds for refusing to register your trademark, and your application satisfies all legal requirements, your trademark will be approved for publication in the TMOG. The TMOG, a weekly online publication, gives advance notice to the public that the USPTO plans to register your trademark. Approximately one month after approval, your trademark will publish in the TMOG.

Within 30 days of the publishing date, anyone who believes their business will be harmed if we register your trademark may file an objection (or "opposition"). An opposition is similar to a federal court proceeding, but is held before the TTAB, a panel of administrative judges who review and decide these matters. An opposition can extend the time between publication of your trademark in the TMOG and registration of your trademark. If someone files an opposition against your trademark, we will let you know. You may want to hire a U.S.-licensed attorney, as oppositions are complex proceedings. No further action is taken to register your trademark until the 30-day opposition period has expired and any oppositions are resolved. In about three months go to step 8.

Step 5b. USPTO issues final letter (office action). If your response does not overcome all refusals and/or satisfy all requirements, the examining attorney will issue a "final" refusal letter (final office action) to you directly (not to the IB) that makes final any remaining refusals and/or requirements. You may appeal the examining attorney's decision by filing an appeal with the Trademark Trial and Appeal Board (TTAB). You may also submit a response to the final letter that overcomes the remaining refusals and satisfies the remaining requirements. And in limited circumstances you may file a Petition to Director. For more information on appeals, visit the TTAB webpage and see the TTAB video. Within six months go to step 6a or step 6b.

Step 6a. You file an appeal and/or submit a timely and complete response to final letter. To avoid abandoning your application, you must timely file a Notice of Appeal to the Trademark Trial and Appeal Board (TTAB). You may also submit a response to the final letter (office action) to the examining attorney, who will review it to see if it overcomes all final refusals and/or satisfies all final requirements. If not, and you did not file a Notice of Appeal, your application will be abandoned and your trademark will not register. In this situation, filing fees are not refunded. For information on how to respond to an office action, see our webpage on responding to office actions, and the Response to Office Action video. In about one to two months go to step 7a or step 7b.

Step 6b. You do not file an appeal or fix remaining issues and your application abandons. If you don't respond within six months of the date the office action was issued, your application is abandoned. After the six months, we send you a Notice of Abandonment. We can no longer process your application and your trademark will not register. In this situation, filing fees are not refunded. To restart the processing of your application, you must file a petition to revive the application within two months of the date the Notice of Abandonment issued. You must also submit the petition fee. If the petition is filed later than two months after the abandonment date, the petition will be denied as untimely and your only option is to file a new application with new fees. For information on filing a petition to revive your application, see our petition to revive information sheet and the Petitions video.

Step 7a. USPTO approves trademark and publishes it for opposition. If the examining attorney does not find grounds for refusing to register your trademark, and your application satisfies all legal requirements, your trademark will be approved for publication in the TMOG. The TMOG, a weekly online publication, gives advance notice to the public that the USPTO plans to register your trademark. Approximately one month after approval, your trademark will publish in the TMOG.

Within 30 days of the publishing date, anyone who believes their business will be harmed if we register your trademark may file an objection (or "opposition"). An opposition is similar to a federal court proceeding, but is held before the TTAB, a panel of administrative judges who review and decide these matters. An opposition can extend the time between publication of your trademark in the TMOG and registration of your trademark. If someone files an opposition against your trademark, we will let you know. You may want to hire a U.S.-licensed attorney, as oppositions are complex proceedings. No further action is taken to register your trademark until the 30-day opposition period has expired and any oppositions are resolved. In about three months go to step 8.

Step 7b. TTAB processes your appeal. If your response does not overcome all final refusals and/or satisfy all final requirements and you filed a Notice of Appeal with the Trademark Trial and Appeal Board (TTAB), the appeal will be processed and instituted by the TTAB. For more information on appeals, visit the TTAB webpage and see the TTAB video.

Step 8. USPTO registers your trademark. Within about three months after your trademark publishes in the Trademark Official Gazette, if no opposition was filed, we register your trademark. If an opposition was filed but was unsuccessful, we will register your trademark after the Trademark Trial and Appeal Board dismisses the opposition. After your trademark registers, you must periodically file maintenance documents and fees within specific time frames to keep the registration active. For information on keeping your registration active, as well as the optional Section 15 filing to enhance the legal strength of your registration, see the Post-Registration Issues video. Between five to six years go to step 9 or every 10 years go to step 10.

Step 9. You file a Section 71 declaration. Before the end of the first six-year period after the registration date, or within six months of the expiration of the sixth year with an additional fee, you must file a Declaration of Use or Excusable Nonuse under Section 71 and pay applicable fees. This declaration must include a verified statement that your trademark is in use in commerce, along with evidence showing that use. If you don't file this declaration, your registration will be canceled. The USPTO will then notify the International

Bureau that your trademark's protection in the United States is invalidated. If your registration cancels, your only options are to file a new application with new fees with the USPTO or file a Subsequent Designation with the IB, designating the United States for protection again.

Step 10. You file additional Section 71 declarations periodically. Within one year before the end of every 10-year period after the registration date, or within six months of the end of the 10-year period, you must file a Section 71 declaration and pay applicable fees. This declaration generally must include a verified statement that your trademark is in use in commerce, along with evidence showing that use. If you don't file this declaration, your registration will be canceled. The USPTO will then notify the IB of the cancellation. If your registration cancels, your only options are to file a new application with new fees with the USPTO or file a Subsequent Designation with the IB, designating the United States for protection again.

Step 11. You renew your international registration periodically. In addition to periodically filing the Section 71 declaration with the USPTO in step 10, you must also renew your underlying international registration with the International Bureau every 10 years from the date of international registration. If you do not continue to renew the international registration, the IB will cancel it and notify us to cancel your related U.S. registration.

Post-registration Timeline:
For all registrations except those under section 66(a)

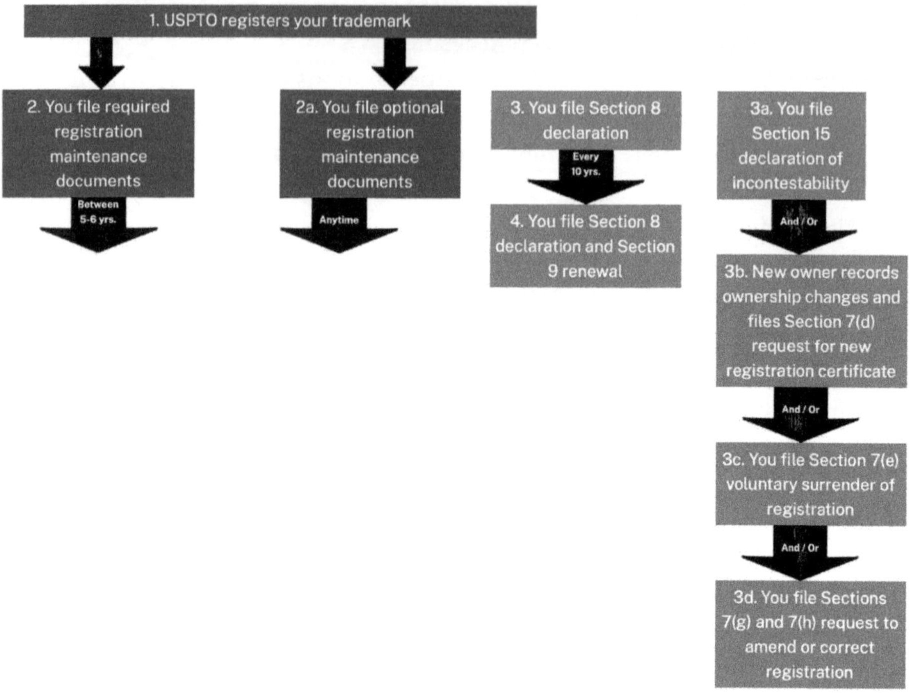

This timeline does not cover every scenario. If you are well outside the timeframes, call the trademark examiner at the phone number on the office action, or contact the Trademark Assistance Center (TAC) at 571-272-9250 (press 0), toll-free at 1-800-786-9199 (select option 1), or email TrademarkAssistanceCenter@uspto.gov.

Step 1. USPTO registers your trademark. After you receive your registration certificate, you must file specific registration maintenance documents and pay fees at regular intervals to keep your registration active. The deadlines for filing these documents are calculated from the registration date shown on the registration certificate. If you don't file these documents by the deadlines, your registration will expire or be canceled and cannot be reinstated. Your only option is to file a new application. Go to step 2 for required post registration documents and go to step 2a for optional post registration documents.

Step 2. You file required registration maintenance documents. You must timely file these documents to maintain your registration. Between five and six years go to step 3.

Step 2a. You file optional registration maintenance documents. You are not required to file any of these documents to maintain a registration. For optional documents that may be filed at least five years after the registration date, go to step 3a and for optional documents that may be filed any time, go to steps 3b-3d.

Step 3. You file a Section 8 declaration. Before the end of the first six-year period after the registration date, or within six months of the expiration of the sixth year with an additional fee, you must file a Declaration of Use or Excusable Nonuse under Section 8 and pay applicable fees. This declaration must include a verified statement that your trademark is in use in commerce, along with evidence showing that use. If you don't file this declaration, your registration will be canceled. The Section 8 declaration may be filed combined with the optional Section 15 declaration of incontestability (see step 3a for more information about this optional filing). Every 10 years go to step 4.

Step 3a. You file Section 15 declaration of incontestability. You may file a Section 15 declaration only if the trademark meets these criteria: 1) the trademark is registered on the Principal Register 2) the trademark has been in continuous use in commerce for at least five years after the registration date, and 3) there are no adverse legal decisions or pending legal proceedings involving rights in the registered trademark. A registration that is "incontestable" is a stronger registration that is easier to legally protect. A fee is required for this filing.

Step 3b. A new owner records ownership changes and files Section 7(d) request for new registration certificate. If you transfer or assign your registered trademark to a new owner, and the new owner wants a new registration certificate with their name on it, they must record the assignment with the USPTO and submit a Section 7(d) request form for a new registration certificate stating that the assignment has been recorded with the USPTO. A fee is required for recording the assignment and for a new certificate.

Step 3c. You file Section 7(e) voluntary surrender of registration. As the trademark registration owner, you may voluntarily surrender your registration for cancellation for all or only some of the goods and/or services. No fee is required.

Step 3d. You file Sections 7(g) and 7(h) request to amend or correct your registration. You may amend or correct the information in your registration by filing a Section 7(g) request to amend your registration or a Section 7(h) request to correct your registration. If you need to amend or correct the registered trademark itself, the changes must be minor and nonmaterial; we do not permit changes that will materially alter the trademark. And if you need to amend or correct the goods and/or services, you may only narrow or limit them; we do not permit changes that broaden the goods and/or services. A fee is required for requesting amendment or correction, except for corrections due to our error.

Step 4. You file a Section 8 declaration and Section 9 renewal. Within one year before the end of every 10-year period after the registration date, or within six months of the end of the 10-year period, you must file a Combined Declaration of Use or Excusable Nonuse Application for Renewal under Sections 8 and 9 and pay applicable fees. This declaration generally must include a verified statement that your trademark is in use in commerce, along with evidence showing that use, and the renewal is a statement requesting that the USPTO renew your registration. If you don't file this combined declaration, your registration will be canceled and expire.

Post-registration Timeline:
Section 66(a): For registrations based on the Madrid Protocol

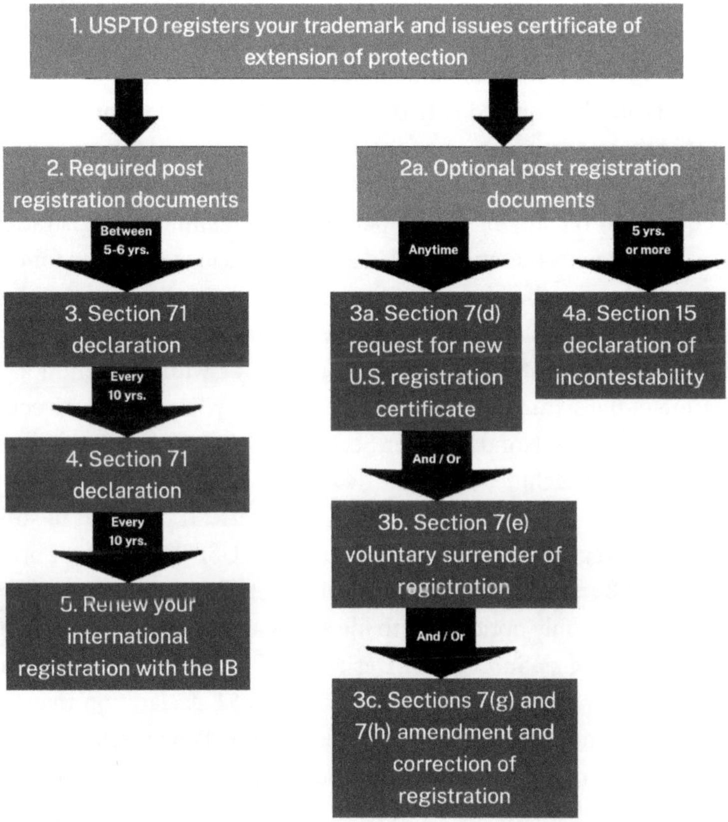

This timeline does not cover every scenario. If you are well outside the timeframes, call the trademark examiner at the phone number on the office action, or contact the Trademark Assistance Center (TAC) at 571-272-9250 (press 0), toll-free at 1-800-786-9199 (select option 1), or email TrademarkAssistanceCenter@uspto.gov.

Step 1. USPTO registers your trademark and issues certificate of extension of protection. After a U.S. registration issues, you must file specific registration maintenance documents and pay fees at regular intervals to keep your registration active. The deadlines for filing Section 71 declarations of use and excusable nonuse are calculated from the registration date shown on the U.S. registration certificate. However, the deadlines for renewing the international registration with the International Bureau of the World Intellectual Property Organization (IB) are calculated from the international registration date. If you don't file both of these documents, your U.S. registration will be canceled. Go to step 2 for required registration maintenance documents and go to step 2a for optional registration maintenance documents.

Step 2. You file required registration maintenance documents. You must timely file these documents to maintain your registration. Go to step 3.

Step 2a. You file optional registration maintenance documents. You are not required to file any of these documents to maintain a registration. For optional documents that may be filed any time, go to step 3a and for optional documents that may be filed every five years or more go to step 4a.

Step 3. You file your first Section 71 declaration. Before the end of the first six-year period after the registration date, or within six months of the expiration of the sixth year with an additional fee, you must file a Declaration of Use or Excusable Nonuse under Section 71 and pay applicable fees. This declaration must include a verified statement that your trademark is in use in commerce, along with evidence showing that use. If you don't file this declaration, your registration will be canceled. The USPTO will then notify the International Bureau that your trademark's protection in the United States is invalidated. Your only options are to file a new application with new fees with the USPTO or file a "Subsequent Designation" with the IB, designating the United States for protection again. The Section 71 declaration may be filed combined with the optional Section 15 declaration of incontestability (see step 4a for more information about this optional filing). Every 10 years go to step 4.

Step 3a. A new owner files a Section 7(d) request for new U.S. registration certificate. The owner of a registered extension of protection to the U.S. may request a new U.S. registration certificate only for the unexpired part of the registration period after filing the appropriate change request with the International Bureau of the World Intellectual Property Organization (IB). Any change in ownership—such as by assignment, transfer, or change of name—must first be recorded at the IB. The IB will notify the USPTO of any ownership changes, including partial changes of ownership of only some of the goods and/or services. After you file the Section 7(d) request and pay the required fee, the USPTO will update its electronic records to reflect the ownership change and issue a new registration certificate. Go to step 3b.

Step 3b. You file a Section 7(e) voluntary surrender of U.S. registration. You may voluntarily surrender your U.S. registration, in its entirety or for a portion of the goods and/or services. No fee is required. Go to step 3c.

Step 3c. You file Sections 7(g) and 7(h) amendment and correction of U.S. registration. You may file a request to amend or correct your U.S. registration at any time, but only in limited circumstances where the change will affect only the extension of protection to the United States. You cannot make any amendments to the trademark or broaden the goods and/or services. A fee is required for amendments and corrections, except for corrections due to USPTO error.

Step 4. You file additional Section 71 declarations periodically. Within one year before the end of every 10-year period after the registration date, or within six months of the end of the 10-year period, you must file a Section 71 declaration and pay applicable fees. This declaration generally must include a verified statement that your trademark is in use in commerce, along with evidence showing that use. If you don't file this declaration, your registration will be canceled. The USPTO will then notify the IB of the cancellation. Your only options are to file a new application with new fees with the USPTO or file a "Subsequent Designation" with the IB, designating the United States for protection again.

Step 4a. You file Section 15 declaration of incontestability. You may file a Section 15 declaration for a trademark on the Principal Register that has been in continuous use in commerce for a period of five years after the date of the U.S. registration when there is no adverse decision or pending proceeding involving rights in the trademark. "Incontestability" enhances the legal presumptions the U.S. registration receives. This declaration requires a fee.

Step 5. You renew your international trademark registration periodically. In addition to periodically filing the Section 71 declaration with the USPTO in step 4, you must also renew your underlying international registration with the International Bureau every 10 years from the date of international registration. If you do not continue to renew the international registration, the IB will cancel it and notify us to cancel your related U.S. registration.

APPENDIX 2

Procedural Issues before the PTO and on Appeal

ROADMAP

- Examination process at PTO
- Office actions
- Appeal to Trademark Trial and Appeal Board (TTAB)
- Appeal to Director, PTO
- Judicial appeals
- U.S. Court of Appeals for the Federal Circuit
- U.S. District Court

This appendix will discuss the procedural aspects of prosecuting a trademark from the initial filing with the PTO as well as subsequent administrative and judicial proceedings to challenge the PTO's granting or denial of a federal registration.

A. Examination Process at PTO

During the trademark application examination process, if the examining attorney has any questions regarding the application, the examining attorney may issue a formal office action (a letter requesting more information from the applicant) or informally contact the applicant by telephone or email. As these proceedings are ex parte, it is appropriate for the examining attorney to directly contact the applicant's attorney if legal counsel represents the applicant. Although not frequent, a telephone call or other informal communication by an examining attorney is not uncommon. A formal office action is quite common and is expected in most trademark prosecutions. A response to the PTO's office action should be candid and usually only address the questions actually raised by the examiner. Generally, experienced trademark practitioners will not volunteer answers to unasked questions and raise issues in their responses not initially raised by the examiner. The applicant must respond to the office action within six months or the PTO will consider the application abandoned. An abandoned application is no longer actively pending before the PTO and will not mature into a trademark registration.

If the application is unintentionally abandoned, the applicant may file a petition to revive the application with the PTO. A petition to revive an application must be filed within two months of the mailing date of the notice of abandonment or within two months of the applicant's learning that the application was deemed abandoned if the applicant did not get notice. Only diligent applicants may claim that they have yet to receive notice. A diligent applicant is an applicant who checks on the status of the application at least every six months. *See generally* TMEP § 1714.

However, if the application is diligently pursued and the applicant files all responses in a timely manner, the presumption is that an application will eventually mature into a registration; therefore, the burden of producing evidence justifying the denial of a trademark application is on the examiner and the PTO. The proceedings before the PTO are usually ex parte. The PTO has no independent fact-finding ability. Consequently, it will usually rely on public records, such as prior trademark registrations, or published sources, such as dictionaries, encyclopedias, or the internet. If the examiner allows the application, a notice of allowance is issued, and the trademark is published in the Official Gazette for opposition. If the application is denied, the applicant may appeal to the Trademark Trial and Appeal Board (TTAB). If an opposition is filed, the applicant or the opposer may appeal to the TTAB. If there is no opposition, then the PTO issues the trademark registration.

B. Trademark Trial and Appeal Board (TTAB)

If an appeal is filed, the Lanham Act governs a proceeding before the TTAB. The TTAB is the administrative court of the PTO. The TTAB by statute may only determine registrability. Lanham Act §§ 17, 18, and 20. The TTAB does not have the jurisdiction to determine whether the use of the mark challenged in the registration is infringing, damages, injunctive relief, violation of state anti-dilution laws, etc. Further, as an article I administrative court, the TTAB cannot determine whether any act of Congress is unconstitutional or other issues outside of the registrability of the mark under the Lanham Act. However, parties should raise all issues including those outside the jurisdiction of the TTAB to avoid waiving them in subsequent appeals. Also, despite not having jurisdiction to decide constitutional and other issues outside the scope of the Lanham Act, the TTAB may address threshold issues or make factual determinations underlying the issue which may alleviate the constitutional concerns. The TTAB generally follows the Federal Rules of Evidence and Civil Procedure. In addition, the TTAB has its own procedural manual, Trademark Trial and Appeal Board Manual of Procedure (TBMP). Attorneys prosecuting trademark applications or representing clients before the TTAB should be very familiar with the TBMP. However, the federal rules are slightly modified because these are proceedings before an administrative agency and not a court. The TTAB issues two types of decisions: precedential and non-precedential. Only precedential decisions may be cited by the TTAB as mandatory authority. A non-precedential TTAB opinion may be cited for whatever persuasive value it may have to the panel or under principles of res judicata or collateral estoppel. Suppose a party cites a non-precedential opinion that is not readily available from a public source, such as the United States Patent Quarterly (USPQ) or the PTO electronic database. In that case, the party should attach a copy of the non-precedential opinion to the brief or other filing. Parties may introduce new evidence that was unavailable to the examining attorney before the TTAB. The advantage of an appeal to the TTAB is that the attorney may fully develop the record, raise legal or factual issues that the examiner should have considered, and prepare the record for possible appellate review by the Federal Circuit.

C. Director of the PTO

At any point in the administrative proceedings before the PTO, a dissatisfied party may appeal to the Director of the PTO or the director's designee (Director). Before the PTO's reorganization, this procedure was called a Petition to the Commissioner. Appeals to the Director usually involve disputes over whether the PTO is following its regulations or policies or whether there is an extraordinary situation where justice requires that the Director suspend or waive one of the PTO's regulations. The Director may not waive statutory requirements.

D. Judicial Appeals

Any party dissatisfied with the final decision of the TTAB or the Director's decision may appeal from the final decision of either the TTAB or the Director. A final decision by an examining attorney that has yet to be reviewed by the TTAB or the Director or an interlocutory decision or order of the TTAB may not be challenged in federal court. But as was discussed in section C of this Appendix, a party may petition the Director to review interlocutory procedural decisions of the TTAB. There is one additional subject matter jurisdictional procedural hurdle regarding Lanham Act § 1(b) intent-to-use applications. In the case involving a Lanham Act § 1(b) intent-to-use application, the TTAB will not enter a final judgment in favor of an applicant until the applicant shows actual use. TBMP § 901.02(b).

There are two primary but mutually exclusive avenues of judicial appeal. TBMP § 900. First, Lanham Act § 21 provides that within two months from the date of the decision of the TTAB or the Director,

> any applicant for registration, or any party to an interference, opposition, or cancellation proceeding or any party to an application to register as a concurrent user, hereinafter referred to as *inter partes* proceedings, who is dissatisfied with the decision of the Trademark Trial and Appeal Board and any registrant who has filed an affidavit or declaration under

section 8 of the Act or who has filed an application for renewal and is dissatisfied with the decision of the Director, may appeal to the U.S. Court of Appeals for the Federal Circuit.

Second, in the alternative, Lanham Act § 21(b) provides that the dissatisfied party to a TTAB decision may file a civil action in a U.S. District Court, requesting the court to "adjudge that an applicant is entitled to a registration upon the application involved, that a registration involved should be canceled, or such other matter as the issues in the proceeding require, as the facts in the case may appeal." Ultimately, a dissatisfied party may file a petition for a *writ of certiori* to the U.S. Supreme Court from the judgment of the regional circuit court of appeals.

1. United States Court of Appeals for the Federal Circuit

The appeal to the Federal Circuit is based solely on the factual and legal record that was developed before the PTO. Lanham Act § 21(a)(4). This is why it is crucial for counsel to fully develop the record that they wish the TTAB to consider because on appeal they will have very limited ability to augment the factual record or to raise new legal issues that could have been initially raised before the TTAB. For example, the TTAB sustained an opposition to register a mark based on a comparison between the opposer's stylized "H" letter mark and the applicant's mark. On appeal to the Federal Circuit, applicant attempted to argue that its mark was sufficiently distinct from opposer's broader "composite common law mark" which incorporated additional features to the stylized "H" considered by the TTAB. The Federal Circuit held that arguing its mark should be compared to a broader version of the opposer's mark was waived by the applicant because it never raised the issue to the TTAB. *Hylete LLC v. Hybrid Athletics, LLC*, 931 F.3d 1170, 1173 (Fed. Cir., 2019).

On appeal, the standard of review is bifurcated. The Federal Circuit gives the TTAB's legal conclusions plenary review; however, the Federal Circuit reviews the TTAB's findings of fact to determine whether the findings are supported by substantial evidence. The decisions of the TTAB or Director are reviewed according to the substantial evidence standard of the Administrative Procedures Act. The substantial evidence standard requires that the reviewing court determine whether a reasonable person might find that the evidentiary record supports the agency's conclusion and is less deferential to the agency than the "arbitrary" or "capricious" standard of review. Merely because there are sufficient facts so that reasonable minds may weigh the facts differently or differ on the legal conclusions drawn from the facts does not mean that the PTO's decision was not based on substantial evidence. The Federal Circuit, on an appeal from a TTAB decision, may not grant injunctive relief or damages, and it is limited to determining the trademark registration status.

2. United States District Court

Proceedings before the U.S. district court are much more robust and permit parties to seek equitable relief. As developed by individual circuits, the trademark law of the United States is fertile ground for forum shopping. The defendant in a district court action is the party who won before the TTAB. Consequently, since venue is usually proper where the defendant resides, it is essential to research the law of the defendant's circuit. The trial before the district court is de novo, and there is no Seventh Amendment right to a jury trial. However, in trademark cases, "de novo" merely means that the parties are entitled to introduce new evidence. The district court must accept the TTAB's factual findings as controlling "unless the contrary is established by testimony which in character and amount carries thorough conviction." *Fleetwood Co. v. Hazel Bishop, Inc.*, 352 F.2d 841, 844 (7th Cir. 1965).

> The new evidence must itself be considered *de novo* by the district court—in the sense of being fairly weighed without placing a thumb on the scales or dismissing it out of hand. The evidence must then be weighed against the Board's findings under the thorough conviction standard. Unless the new evidence leads to a thorough conviction that a finding of the Board is incorrect, that finding is controlling.

Spraying Systems Co. v. Delavan, Inc., 975 F.2d 387, 391 (7th Cir. 1992).

The law is unclear whether issues that could have been raised before the TTAB may be raised for the first time before the district court. District courts will rarely consider evidence that was deliberately concealed from the TTAB.

Parties before the district court may introduce new evidence. For example, the additional time between the TTAB's decision and the district court's proceedings may allow a party to commission a well-designed survey to support that party's position. Some significant strategic differences between appeals to the Federal Circuit and appeals to the district court are that the Federal Circuit treats the TTAB's finding of the likelihood of consumer confusion as a question of law subject to de novo review, while many of its sister circuits (and their lower courts) treat a determination of the likelihood of consumer confusion as a question of fact and review it under the clearly erroneous standard. Finally, the district court grants a second opportunity for appellate review to that district court's regional circuit court of appeals. Choosing the appropriate forum to challenge a decision by the TTAB is a strategic decision based on the case's individual facts. A skilled attorney will analyze both the relevant law of the Federal Circuit and the laws of its sister circuits to determine whether to take an appeal to the Federal Circuit or in which district court to file proceedings based on the laws of that circuit court.

E. Appeals Process

Appeals of Decisions of the PTO

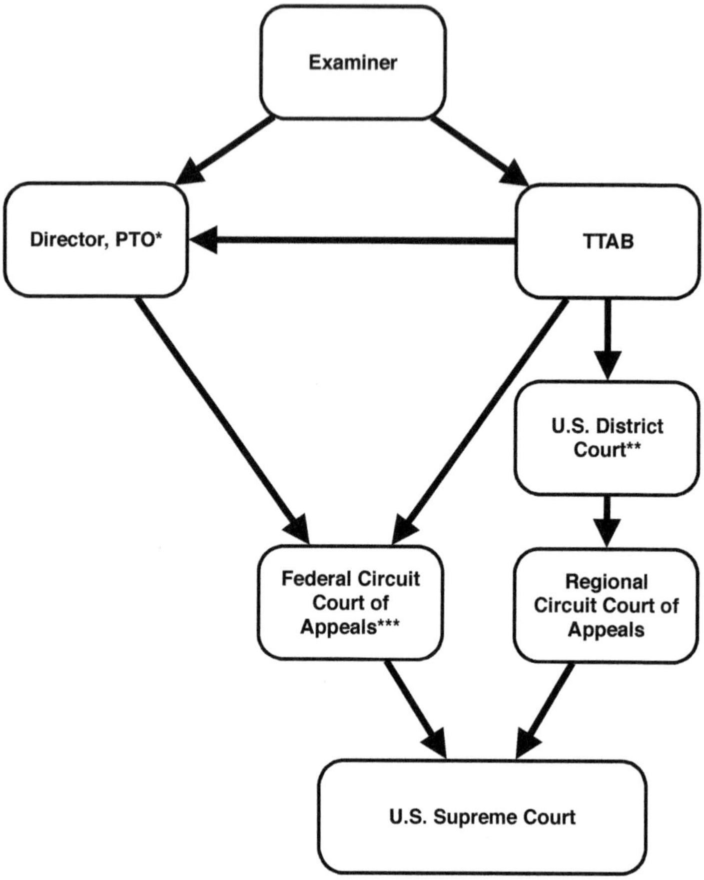

Standard of Review:

* Petition to the Director, clear error or an abuse of discretion review

** U.S. District Court, modified de novo review

*** Federal Circuit Court of Appeals, Administrative Procedures Act §706(2)(E) "Substantial evidence" review

APPENDIX 3

Trademark Searching

ROADMAP

- Importance and Process of Trademark Searching
- Traditional Methods
- WIPO Global Search
- Domain Names
- Social Media
- International and Translation Considerations
- Trademark Opinion Letter/Clearance

A. Introduction

In the intricate landscape of trademark law, the task of establishing a distinctive and legally protectable mark is both critical and complex. As businesses expand their reach into new markets and digital domains, the importance of conducting thorough trademark searches has never been more pronounced. Trademark screening not only aids in avoiding legal conflicts but also ensures the robustness and uniqueness of a brand in a crowded marketplace.

The process of selecting a trademark extends beyond mere registration; it is about crafting a brand's identity that is not only unique but also devoid of potential legal encumbrances. This begins with a detailed trademark search, which, while not a legal requirement, serves as a fundamental proactive step in trademark acquisition. Today's savvy businesses must navigate not only the traditional realms of commerce but also the expansive digital landscape, including domain names and social media, making the integration of these elements into trademark strategies essential.

This document aims to guide practitioners through the nuances of effective trademark searches, including the assessment of domain names and social media presence, which are pivotal in today's digital age. By understanding the intersection of these elements, businesses can secure a comprehensive legal and commercial footing, ensuring their mark not only resonates with consumers but is also fortified against potential infringements.

As we delve into the complexities of trademark screening and digital presence, we emphasize the synergy between legal foresight and strategic business planning. This approach not only minimizes the risk of trademark disputes but also enhances the brand's visibility and protection across multiple platforms, establishing a strong, defensible, and cohesive brand identity.

B. Trademark Searching

The journey to trademark registration begins with a crucial step: the trademark search. This process is instrumental in determining the availability and viability of a proposed mark, providing the groundwork for a strong, defendable trademark that aligns with both legal standards and business objectives.

1. Importance of Trademark Searches

While not mandated by law, performing a trademark search is a strategic move that can prevent significant legal and financial setbacks in the future. By identifying pre-existing marks that are similar or identical, businesses can avoid potential infringement issues, which could lead to costly litigation and damage to the brand's reputation. A thorough search not only identifies potential roadblocks in the registration process but also illuminates the competitive landscape, offering insights that could influence branding strategies.

2. The Process of Trademark Searching

A comprehensive trademark search involves several layers, starting with the Preliminary PTO database search to identify federally registered trademarks and pending applications. However, this alone is insufficient. Businesses must extend their searches to include common law sources where unregistered trademarks may exist, which are equally protected under U.S. trademark law. Utilizing professional search services like CompuMark or CoreSearch can provide access to extensive databases that cover trademarks in use across multiple channels, including online platforms, business directories, and more.

3. Digital Dimensions of Trademark Searches

In today's digital era, a trademark search extends beyond traditional databases. Potential registrants must consider domain names, social media handles, and even e-commerce platforms where similar marks might be in use. This is vital as digital presences are often the first interaction a consumer has with a brand. Securing a consistent domain name and social media identity that aligns with the trademark not only strengthens brand recognition but also protects against cybersquatting and unauthorized use online.

4. Strategic Considerations

Conducting a trademark search is a strategic component of brand management. It allows businesses to assess the distinctiveness of their mark, understand its potential for registration, and foresee any challenges that might arise during the registration process. The search results provide a foundation for informed decision-making, enabling businesses to either proceed with confidence, make necessary adjustments to their mark, or consider alternative branding strategies if significant conflicts exist.

5. Legal and Business Implications

The implications of a thorough trademark search are profound. Legally, it prepares the business for a smoother registration process with fewer objections from trademark offices or opposition from third parties. From a business perspective, it aids in building a resilient brand that is legally protectable and commercially viable. Furthermore, understanding the nuances of international trademark laws and considering global availability and protection are crucial for businesses looking to expand beyond domestic markets.

C. Searching Trademarks Using Traditional Methods

Traditional trademark searching methods involve systematic inquiries into databases maintained by trademark offices such as the United States Patent and Trademark Office (USPTO) and the World Intellectual Property Organization (WIPO). These platforms provide crucial resources for identifying registered trademarks and pending applications, which are essential for assessing the viability of a proposed trademark.

1. Accessing the USPTO Database

The USPTO's online search system, known as the Trademark Search System, is an essential tool for anyone performing trademark searches in the United States. To use this system effectively:

1. **Navigate to the USPTO website:** Start at the USPTO's official webpage dedicated to the trademark search system. The trademark search engine at the USPTO website is accessible at this website: https://tmsearch.uspto.gov/search/search-information.
2. **Select a Search Option:** The USPTO's trademark search system offers several search options, including Basic, Structured, and Free Form. Beginners may prefer the Basic search for simplicity, while more experienced users can utilize the Structured or Free Form searches for more complex queries.
3. **Conduct the Search:** Enter the proposed trademark or relevant keywords. It's advisable to search for phonetic equivalents and similar spellings to ensure a comprehensive search.
4. **Analyze the Results:** Review the records for any trademarks that are identical or confusingly similar to the proposed mark, taking note of their registration status, goods and services classifications, and any design elements.

2. Utilizing the WIPO Global Brand Database

For international trademark searches, the WIPO Global Brand Database is an invaluable resource that provides access to trademarks from multiple national and international sources. To conduct a search on WIPO:

1. **Access the WIPO Brand Database:** Go directly to the WIPO brand database website. The trademark search engine at the WIPO website is accessible at this website: https://branddb.wipo.int/.

2. **Perform a Search:** Input the trademark or associated keywords. The database allows filtering by country, status, and class of goods and services, which can refine the search results.

3. **Evaluate the Results:** Examine the trademarks for similarities in visual, phonetic, and conceptual elements. Also, assess the geographical scope and protection class of each relevant entry to understand potential international conflicts.

3. Best Practices for Traditional Searches

— **Broad and Narrow Searches:** Start with broad searches to capture any direct hits and gradually narrow down the search parameters to identify similar marks in related categories.

— **Regular Updates:** Trademark databases are regularly updated. Repeat searches at different stages of the trademark development process to catch any new applications that could pose a risk.

— **Document Findings:** Keep a detailed record of all search queries and results. This documentation will be valuable during the trademark application process and in any potential legal challenges.

4. Strategic Use of Traditional Search Methods

While online tools and professional search services offer comprehensive insights, traditional methods remain a cornerstone of trademark research. They provide first-hand information straight from authoritative sources, ensuring that businesses and legal professionals can rely on the accuracy of the data for making critical decisions about trademark registration and enforcement.

The professional trademark search firms provide search tools that expand beyond what is available with the USPTO and WIPO. Their services also include comprehensive common-law databases, including searches of databases including domain names and other social media services, described below.

D. Searching for Domain Names and Integration with Trademark Registries

As businesses increasingly operate online, securing a domain name that aligns with the business's trademark becomes crucial. Domain name searches are integral to trademark strategy, ensuring that the digital presence resonates with the trademark and enhances brand recognition.

1. Importance of Domain Name Searches

A domain name functions as a crucial brand identifier on the internet and often serves as the first point of contact for customers. Ensuring that a domain name does not infringe on existing trademarks is as critical as ensuring that it is available and aligns with the brand's identity. A comprehensive search helps mitigate risks of trademark infringement and cybersquatting, where third parties register domain names using well-known trademarks to profit from the brand's reputation.

2. How to Conduct Domain Name Searches

1. **Use of Domain Registrars:** Start with domain name registrars such as GoDaddy, Network Solutions, or Google Domains. These platforms provide search tools to check the availability of desired domain names instantly.
2. **Check Trademark Registries:** Alongside checking domain availability, consult trademark registries to ensure that the domain name does not infringe on registered trademarks. This can be done by using the search methods outlined in the sections on USPTO and WIPO database searches.
3. **Consider Variations and Extensions:** Search for variations of the proposed domain name and different domain extensions (.com, .net, .biz, etc.). This helps understand the landscape and avoid potential conflicts with similar names in different top-level domains (TLDs).
4. **International Considerations:** For businesses planning to operate internationally, consider searching domain names in country-specific TLDs (like .uk, .de, etc.) and integrating searches with international trademark databases to cover both bases.

— **Alignment with Trademarks:** Ensure that the chosen domain name can be used as a trademark if needed, reinforcing brand identity across different mediums.

— **Defensive Registrations:** Consider registering variations and common misspellings of the domain name to protect the brand from cybersquatters and competitors.

— **Legal Precautions:** If a desirable domain name is already taken but not yet a trademark, legal advice may be needed to determine the feasibility of acquiring it or negotiating with the current owner.

3. Best Practices for Domain Name Searches

— **Regular Monitoring:** Continuously monitor the availability of domain names and existing trademarks, especially as new domain extensions become available.

— **Professional Assistance:** Utilize professional search services that can provide more detailed checks across multiple databases, including domain name registries and social media handles.

— **Documentation:** Keep records of all searches and registrations, which can be crucial in any future trademark or domain disputes.

4. Integrating Domain Name Searches with Trademark Strategy

Integrating domain name searches with broader trademark strategies is essential for cohesive brand protection. This integration ensures that all aspects of a brand's online and offline presence are legally secure and aligned, offering comprehensive protection and enhancing the overall brand strategy.

E. Searching Social Media Sites for Trademark Protection

Building on the foundation of trademark and domain name searches, searching social media sites is another critical component for protecting a brand's intellectual property in today's digital age. This section will discuss how to effectively search social media platforms to ensure that a trademark is not only available but also protected from potential infringement and misuse online.

Social media platforms play a significant role in brand recognition and engagement, making them critical areas for trademark searches. These searches help ensure that a brand's name or logo is not already in use, and can also protect against potential infringements that could dilute a brand's reputation.

1. Importance of Social Media Searches

As social media continues to influence consumer behavior, the presence of a brand's trademark on these platforms can significantly impact its visibility and consumer perception. Conducting thorough searches across various social media platforms helps prevent unauthorized use of a trademark, which can lead to confusion among consumers and dilute the brand's value.

2. How to Conduct Social Media Searches

1. **Platform-Specific Searches:** Begin by searching for the trademark on major social media platforms like Facebook, Instagram, Twitter, LinkedIn, and TikTok. Use the search functions on each platform to look for exact matches, similar names, and variations of the trademark.
2. **Use of Advanced Search Tools:** Many social media platforms offer advanced search tools that allow users to refine their searches by location, language, and other parameters. These tools can help pinpoint potential trademark infringements more accurately.
3. **Monitoring Usernames and Hashtags:** Apart from searching for the trademark itself, check for usernames, handles, and hashtags that include the trademark or similar terms. This will help identify accounts that might be impersonating the brand or using the trademark without authorization.

3. Strategic Considerations in Social Media Searches

— **Proactive Registration:** If a trademark is available on social media, consider registering accounts under that trademark, even if there are no immediate plans to use them. This can prevent others from acquiring these valuable digital assets and using them inappropriately.

— **Regular Monitoring:** Set up alerts or use social media monitoring tools to keep track of any new mentions or uses of the trademark on these platforms. Ongoing monitoring is crucial for early detection of potential infringements.

—**Legal Actions:** If infringement is detected, take appropriate legal action. This may involve contacting the infringer to request the removal of the infringing content or escalating the matter through the platform's reporting system or legal channels.

4. Best Practices for Social Media Searches

—**Comprehensive Coverage:** Extend searches beyond the most popular platforms to include emerging social media sites and those popular in other regions or countries, particularly if the brand operates internationally.

—**Documentation:** Maintain detailed records of all search results and actions taken. This documentation will be valuable if legal steps become necessary to enforce the trademark.

—**Integration with Overall Trademark Strategy:** Ensure that social media searches are integrated with broader trademark protection strategies, including domain name and traditional trademark searches, to provide holistic protection.

5. Challenges in Social Media Searches

Navigating social media for trademark protection presents unique challenges, such as rapidly changing platform policies and the sheer volume of user-generated content. Adaptability and responsiveness are key in effectively managing a brand's presence on these dynamic platforms.

F. International Considerations and Translation Issues in Trademark Registration

In the global marketplace, the registration and use of trademarks are not confined by national borders. Companies looking to establish and protect their brand internationally must consider various linguistic, cultural, and legal factors that could affect their trademark's effectiveness and legality. One of the most critical aspects of international trademark registration is addressing translation issues that might alter a trademark's perception and potential acceptance in different regions.

1. Understanding Linguistic Challenges

Trademarks often include words or phrases that carry specific connotations or meanings in one language but may translate poorly or offensively in another. The implications of a poorly translated trademark can range from brand alienation to legal barriers in registration:

— **Direct Translation Risks:** Some trademark terms may translate into inappropriate or undesirable words in other languages. For example, a brand name that is catchy and positive in English might translate into a term that is humorous, offensive, or derogatory in another language, as famously seen with global brands in the past. For example, Entrepreneur Magazine reports that Mercedes Benz initially adopted the name "Bensi" for its brand in China. Unfortunately, one possible pronunciation of this expression in Mandarin is "rush to die," a less than auspicious name for a car company.[1]

— **Cultural Sensitivity:** Beyond the direct translation, the cultural context of words or symbols must be considered. What is considered benign in one culture can be controversial or have negative associations in another. This cultural sensitivity is crucial for maintaining a positive brand image.

2. Legal Implications of Translation

From a legal perspective, the translatability of a trademark into the languages of target markets can affect its registrability and the scope of its protection:

— **Registrability:** In many jurisdictions, the transliteration of a trademark into the local script can be necessary for registration. This transliteration must still meet the criteria of distinctiveness and non-deceptiveness as the original trademark.

— **Scope of Protection:** A trademark that is a generic term in one language but distinctive in another can have different levels of protection in respective jurisdictions. For instance, a term that is descriptive in English might be unfamiliar and distinctive in another language, providing broader scope for trademark protection in that country.

1. https://www.entrepreneur.com/growing-a-business/learn-from-mercedes-benzs-reputation-damaging-mistake-in/368807.

3. Strategic Recommendations for International Trademark Registration

To navigate these complexities, companies should adopt a proactive approach in their international trademark strategy:

— **Preliminary Multi-Lingual Research:** Conduct thorough research on the proposed trademarks in all target languages and relevant dialects to identify possible negative connotations or existing similar trademarks.

— **Use of Local Experts:** Engage with linguistic and cultural experts or local trademark attorneys who understand the nuances of the language and legal environment in each target market. This can help refine the trademark to avoid negative implications while maintaining the brand's core message.

— **Monitoring and Enforcement:** Regular monitoring of trademark use in international markets is necessary to ensure that the trademark's integrity is maintained and not diluted or misrepresented due to translation issues.

— **Flexible Branding Strategy:** Consider developing a flexible branding strategy that allows for variations of the trademark to suit different languages and cultures, thus optimizing both legal protection and market acceptance.

Addressing translation issues and cultural sensitivities is indispensable for businesses aiming to secure robust and effective trademark protection globally. By understanding and strategically managing linguistic challenges, companies can enhance their brand's international appeal and avoid potential legal and reputational pitfalls.

G. Essential Elements of a Trademark Opinion Letter

When drafting a trademark opinion letter, particularly in the context of the complex issues described above—including international considerations and translation issues—an attorney must ensure that the letter is comprehensive, well-structured, and provides clear guidance based on thorough research and legal analysis.

Here's how to cover the essential elements effectively:

1. Introduction and Purpose

— **Context Setting:** Begin with a brief introduction that sets the context for the client, outlining the purpose of the letter and the scope of the trademark search that was conducted.

— **Client's Request:** Clearly state the client's request or the trademark proposed for registration, ensuring that the purpose of the opinion letter aligns with the client's expectations and legal needs.

2. Description of the Search Process

— **Search Details:** Describe the databases and sources searched, including national and international trademark databases, domain name registries, and social media platforms. Mention any specific tools or services used, such as the USPTO's trademark search system, WIPO's Global Brand Database, or third-party search firms.

— **Scope of the Search:** Specify the geographical and digital scope of the search, explaining if searches were conducted on a local, national, or international level. This section should also address whether searches included direct translations, transliterations, and cultural sensitivity checks.

3. Analysis of Search Results

— **Findings Summary:** Provide a detailed summary of the search results, highlighting any existing trademarks that could potentially conflict with the proposed mark. Include an analysis of similar marks, the likelihood of confusion, and any relevant legal precedents or case law, as well as the distinctiveness of the proposed or existing mark to determine its inherent or acquired distinctiveness. Furthermore, the geographical scope of protection and potential conflicts should be considered, considering the intended use of the mark nationally, internationally, or in specific regions.

— **Domain and Social Media Findings:** Summarize findings from domain name and social media searches, explaining the implications of any conflicts or pre-existing uses of the proposed mark online.

4. Legal Opinion and Risk Assessment

— **Opinion on Registrability:** Offer a clear legal opinion on the registrability of the proposed trademark based on the search results. Discuss the trademark's distinctiveness, any descriptive or generic issues, and potential bars to registration.

— **Risk Evaluation:** Assess the risk of infringement and potential legal disputes if the trademark is used in commerce. This evaluation should consider both domestic and international risks, especially considering translation and cultural issues. Ownership and prior use of the mark must be verified to identify any conflicting rights or prior use that may impact its validity or enforceability. If a potentially conflicting mark has been identified, then ownership and prior use of such mark must be verified to identify any conflicting rights or prior use that may impact its validity or enforceability.

Potential issues related to dilution, infringement, or deceptive marks should be assessed. Market research or surveys can be conducted to gather empirical data on consumer perception and potential confusion. Based on these factors, a comprehensive risk assessment should be provided, evaluating the likelihood of successful registration, potential challenges or objections, and the risk of infringement or dilution.

— **Cultural and Linguistic Considerations:** Specifically address any international concerns related to translation and cultural appropriateness of the trademark, particularly if the brand plans to enter or expand in foreign markets.

5. Recommendations and Strategic Advice

— **Mitigation Strategies:** Provide strategic advice on how to mitigate any identified risks, such as modifying the trademark, seeking coexistence agreements, or abandoning the mark in favor of a more viable alternative.

— **Future Monitoring and Enforcement:** Suggest ongoing monitoring strategies for trademark usage and enforcement, particularly in digital and international arenas, to protect the trademark's integrity and value.

— **Next Steps:** Outline clear next steps the client should consider based on the opinion provided. This may include preparing for trademark application, engaging in negotiations, or enhancing monitoring mechanisms.

6. Conclusion

— **Summary of Key Points:** Conclude with a summary of the key points made throughout the letter, reiterating the main advice and recommendations.

— **Availability for Further Assistance:** Indicate your availability to discuss the contents of the letter in more detail or to provide further assistance as the client moves forward with their trademark strategy.

7. Considerations for Drafting

— **Clarity and Precision:** Use clear and precise language to ensure that the client understands the potential legal and business implications of the trademark registration.

— **Client-Specific Tailoring:** Tailor the letter to the client's specific business context, industry, and plans for brand expansion, ensuring that the advice is relevant and actionable.

— **Comprehensive Coverage:** Cover all necessary legal bases and potential scenarios to arm the client with all the information needed to make informed decisions.

This structured approach to writing a trademark opinion letter ensures that the attorney provides thorough and actionable legal advice tailored to the client's needs, considering all relevant trademark, digital, and international issues.

INDEX

A

abandonment through assignment-in-gross, 41
abandonment through conduct, 31, 36–37
Abandonment through genericism, 37–39
Abandonment through naked licensing, 39
Abandonment through non-use, 31, 33–36
Abandonment, quality control provisions, 40
Acquired distinctiveness, 13, 20, 24–26, 29, 46, 56, 69, 70, 72, 74, 77, 78, 89, 90, 108, 111, 112, 118, 151, 153, 155, 261, 272, 334
Acquisition of common law rights, 21, 62–77
Advertising, false or deceptive, 167
Anti-dissection rule, composite marks and the, 28, 129–130
Anticybersquatting Consumer Protection Act treatment of domain names, 211, 215, 222
Assignment-in-gross, 41, 44

B

Banner advertising or sponsored advertising and search engine liability, 230, 233–235
Barring importation, 197, 207, 274
Blurring, dilution by, 112, 149, 152, 153, 155–158, 185, 186
Brand, 3, 4, 14, 16–18, 28, 34, 35, 47, 126, 136, 137, 140, 142, 143, 155, 166, 167, 175, 189, 211, 225, 233, 241, 245, 323–336

C

Cancellation of registration, 114
Certification marks, 13, 17, 19, 20, 29, 57–59, 194
Changing the mark or the goods, 41–42
Collective marks, 13, 17, 19, 20, 29, 58, 258
Common law rights, 21, 43, 63, 65, 66, 69, 71, 73, 74, 76, 77, 80–82, 84–87, 93, 98, 170–172, 220
Common law rights, acquisition of, 21, 62–77
Common law rights, extent of, 76
Common law rights, priority based on, 21, 69, 71, 77–82, 84, 170–172

Composite marks and the anti-dissection rule, 28, 129–130
Composite marks, 13, 28
Constitutional limitations on use, 65
Constructive notice, priority and, 80
Constructive notice, priority based on registration and, 80
Constructive use, priority and, 80–81
Constructive use, priority based on registration and, 80–81
Consumer confusion, likelihood of, 10, 11, 48, 99, 106, 119, 122–124, 127–129, 131–134, 137, 147, 150, 152, 156, 169, 172, 174, 175, 178, 180, 182, 184, 185, 192, 194, 198–200, 212, 220, 227, 230, 231, 233, 235, 236, 238, 244–247, 258, 260, 263, 269, 320, 321
Counterfeit goods and auction websites, 240–241
Counterfeit goods, statutory damages and, 197, 206–208
Counterfeit goods, barring importation, 207
Counterfeit goods, De minimis imports and, 269
Counterfeit goods and post-sale confusion, 135–137
Counterfeit goods and search engines, 239–240
Counterfeit goods and other remedies under TRIPS, 265
Criminal penalties, international law and, 266

D

Damages, 143, 159, 164–166, 168, 172, 190, 192, 197, 199–201, 203–208, 265, 267, 269, 273, 274, 317, 320
Dawn Donut Rule, 83, 86
De facto secondary meaning, 27
Defense to infringement, fair use, 173–177
Defense to infringement, functionality, 189
Defense to infringement, genericism, 186–189
Defense to infringement, parody, 177–180
Defenses to dilution, 185–186
Defenses to false advertising, 167
Defenses to infringement, generally, 169–194
Defenses to infringement, junior user, 172–173
Defenses to infringement, senior user, 170–172
Descriptive marks, 24, 25, 27, 77, 85, 89, 169, 261, 273
Dilution by blurring, 112, 149, 152, 153, 155–158, 185, 186
Dilution by tarnishment, 149, 152, 153, 156–158, 185, 224
Dilution, defenses to, 185–186
Distinctiveness classification of marks, 20–23
Distinctiveness, trade dress and, 46
Domain name used as email address, 224
Domain names, Anticybersquatting Consumer Protection Act treatment of, 211, 215, 222
Domain names, Federal Trademark Dilution Act treatment of, 211–214

Domain names, generally, 209–211
Domain names, history of, 209, 274
Domain names, Uniform Domain Name Resolution Policy treatment of, 217–221

E

Elements of a claim of false advertising, 160–164
Email address, domain name used as, 224
Equitable defenses, acquiescence, 191–192
Equitable defenses, antitrust/ trademark misuse, 193
Equitable defenses, bad faith and sham litigation, 193–194
Equitable defenses, laches, 191–192
Equitable defenses, statute of limitations, 169
Equitable defenses, unclean hands, 190, 192
Equitable defenses to infringement, 191–193
Equitable defenses, generally, 190
Extent of common law rights, 76

F

Fair use defense to infringement, 173–177
False advertising, defenses to, 167
False advertising, elements of a claim of, 160–164
False advertising, remedies for, 165–167
False or deceptive advertising, 160–167
Federal Trademark Dilution Act treatment of domain names, 211–214
Federal Trademark Dilution Act, generally, 149–152
Federal Trademark Dilution Act, the, 9, 11, 151, 190, 209, 212, 274
Foreign marks, 66, 67
Functionality defense to infringement, 189
Functionality, 45, 47–55, 110, 111, 169, 189, 237, 272, 273

G

Generic terms, 13, 27, 29, 38, 90, 231
Genericism defense to infringement, 186–189
Genericism, 31, 32, 37, 38, 169, 186, 188, 273
Geographic indicators, 272
Goods, use of marks on, 68
Goodwill, changing the mark or the goods, 41–42
Goodwill, generally, 4, 10, 31–32
Goodwill, maintaining, 31–33, 43, 272
Goodwill, maintaining registration, 42
Goodwill, residual, 31, 43, 272

H

History of domain names, 209, 274
History of trademark law, 9, 37

I

Incontestability defenses, 113

Incontestability of registration, 112–113
Indirect infringement, 144
Infringement and likelihood of consumer confusion, 119–134
Infringement and respondeat superior, 146
Infringement, defense to, 48, 169–193
Infringement by dilution, 4, 149–157, 273
Infringement, indirect, 144–146
Inherently distinctive marks, 13, 21–23, 29, 70, 77, 78, 85
Injunctions, 10, 12, 197, 198–201, 207, 273
Intent-to-use applications, priority and, 82–83
Intent-to-use applications, priority based on registration and, 83
International law and criminal penalties, 266
International law and ownership and rights, 263
International law and process for enforcement, 264
International law and registration, 262
International law and remedies, 264–266
International law and trademark subject matter, 256–260
International law and treaties, 250, 251–255
International law and use and priority date, 262
International law and well-known marks, 66–67, 252, 256, 262–263
International law, 88, 249–266
International trademark law, the Madrid Protocol, 93, 95, 97, 117, 252–254, 311
Internet and linking, 243–245
Internet and phishing, 245
Internet and search engine liability, 225–239
Internet and virtual worlds and games, 245–247
Internet and website liability, 239–243

J

Junior user defenses to infringement, 79, 80, 172–173

K

Keyword advertising and search engine liability, 226–227, 229–233

L

Lanham Act, introduction, 4–5, 11
Likelihood of consumer confusion, 10, 11, 48, 99, 106, 119, 122–124, 127–129, 131–134, 137, 147, 150, 152, 156, 169, 172, 174, 175, 178, 180, 182, 184, 185, 192, 194, 198–200, 212, 220, 227, 230, 231, 233, 235, 236, 238, 244–247, 258, 260, 263, 269, 320, 321
Limited area defense, priority and, 84–85, 171–172
Limited area defense, priority based on registration and, 84–85
Limits on trademark registrations, 87, 97, 100, 272
Linking, Internet and, 243–245

M

Madrid Protocol, the, 87, 88, 93, 95, 117, 118, 272, 275, 311
Maintaining goodwill, 33, 272
Maintaining registration, 31, 42
Metatags, wallpaper and search engine liability, 236

N

Naked licensing, 31, 39

O

Obtaining rights through use, 14, 15, 21, 62–76, 88, 261–262
Olympic trademark, 57, 59
Opposition to application to register, 36, 75, 83, 106, 112, 99–100, 277–280, 282–285, 291, 293–295, 297–300, 303–306, 316–317, 319, 325
Ordinary course of business, use in the, 64
Ownership and rights, international law and, 263
Ownership, 9, 37, 61–63, 65, 67, 69, 71, 73, 75, 77, 79, 81–83, 85, 86, 88, 89, 93, 112, 113, 117, 120, 121, 146, 147, 151, 170, 171, 210, 230, 240, 249, 263, 272, 296, 309, 312, 335

P

Parody defense to infringement, 147, 151, 177–180, 183, 185–186
Patent law, relation to, and, 11, 27–28, 38, 48–51, 53–56, 110, 193, 237
Pending applications, priority between, 83
Phishing, Internet and, 245
Preexisting common law rights, priority and, 80
Preexisting common law rights, priority based on registration and, 80
Principal register, 80, 89, 90, 100, 117, 120, 121, 157, 187, 309, 313
Prior user rights against registered mark, 78, 83–84
Priority and constructive notice, 80–81, 173
Priority and constructive use, 15, 62, 80–85, 90
Priority and intent-to-use applications, 82–83
Priority and preexisting common law rights, 82–83
Priority and the Dawn Donut Rule, 83
Priority and the limited area defense, 84–85
Priority based on common law rights, 21, 69, 71, 77–82, 84, 170–172
Priority based on registration and constructive notice, 80
Priority based on registration and constructive use, 80–81
Priority based on registration and intent-to-use applications, 82
Priority based on registration and prior user rights against registered mark, 78, 83–84
Priority based on registration and the limited area defense, 84–85, 171–172

Priority based on registration and, preexisting common law rights, 80
Priority based on registration, 80–85
Priority between pending applications, 83
Procedures for Registration, 90–100, 315–322
Process for enforcement, international law and, 264

Q

Quality control provisions, 31, 40

R

Rectanus Doctrine, The. *See* junior user defenses to infringement
Registration and incontestability defenses, 113
Registration and incontestability, 112–113
Registration of trademarks, 15, 87–117, 261–262
Registration, cancellation of, 114, 116, 171, 307, 309, 313
Registration, international law and, 262
Registration, limits on, 87, 97, 100–112, 272
Registration, opposition to application, 36, 75, 83, 106, 112, 99–100, 277–280, 282–285, 291, 293–295, 297–300, 303–306, 316–317, 319, 325
Registration, principal register, 80–89
Registration, procedures for, 90–100, 315–322
Registration, supplemental register, 89–90
Remedies for false advertising, 165–167
Remedies, 7, 10, 12, 143, 157, 159, 165, 192, 197, 199, 201, 203–207, 249, 250, 264, 265, 267, 269, 273, 274
Remedies, barring importation, 89, 207
Remedies, damages, 143, 159, 164–166, 168, 172, 190, 192, 197, 199–201, 203–208, 265, 267, 269, 273, 274, 317, 320
Remedies, injunctions, 10, 12, 197, 198–201, 207, 273
Remedies, international law and, 264–266
Remedies, statutory damages, 206
Residual goodwill, 31, 43, 272
Respondeat superior, 119, 146, 148
Restatement (Third) of Unfair Competition, introduction, 5, 7, 53, 137
Rights. *See* obtaining rights.

S

Search engine liability, banner advertising or sponsored advertising and, 230, 233–235
Search engine liability, Internet and, 235–239
Search engine liability, keyword advertising and, 226–227, 229–233
Search engine liability, Metatags and wallpaper and, 236
Senior user defenses to infringement, 170–172

Service marks, 13, 17, 18, 29
Services, use of marks for, 69
Statutory damages, 197, 205–208, 265, 274
Statutory protections for certain words and phrases, 58–59
Supplemental register, 89, 90

T

Tarnishment, dilution by, 149, 152, 153, 156–158, 185, 224
Tea Rose-Rectanus Doctrine, The. *See* junior user defenses to infringement
Tertium quid, 47, 56
TMEP, 5–7, 16, 18, 23, 27, 90, 94, 98, 101, 103, 104, 108–111, 115, 116, 255, 316
Trade dress, distinctiveness of, 45, 46, 272
Trade dress, functionality and, 45, 47, 272
Trade dress, generally, 45–55
Trade dress, patent law, relation to, and, 54–55
Trade dress, tertium quid, 47, 56
Trade names, 17, 92
Trademark as source identifier, 15–17
Trademark Dilution Revision Act of 2006, generally, 11
Trademark Dilution Revision Act, 9, 11, 12, 151, 152, 185
Trademark dilution, 9, 11, 12, 120, 149–152, 154, 157, 185, 186, 190, 195, 209, 211, 212, 214, 222, 224, 244, 248, 262, 274
Trademark Manual of Examining Procedure, introduction, 5, 7
Trademark subject matter, international law and, 256–260
Trademark, type of mark, 17–18
Trademark, classification of marks, 17–20
Trademark, defined, 14–15
Trademark, distinguished from brand, 16–17
Trademark, distinguished from trade name, 17
Trademark, Lanham Act definition, 4–5, 11
Trademark, ownership, 62
Treaties, international law and, 250, 251–255

U

Uniform Domain Name Resolution Policy treatment of domain names, 217–221
Use and priority date, international law and, 262
Use in the ordinary course of business, 64
Use of marks for services, 69
Use of marks on goods, 68
Use, constitutional limitations, 65
Use, foreign marks, 66–67
Use, obtaining rights, 63–64

V

Virtual worlds and games, Internet and, 245–247

W

Website liability, Internet and, 239–243
Well-known marks, international law and, 262–263